And Gladly Wou

And Gladly Would He Teach and Learn

And Gladly Would He Teach and Learn

And Gladly Would He Teach and Learn

Bruce D. Johnson

And Gladly Would He Teach

Dedication

To my former students and colleagues
from the Osseo-Fairchild High School
and Badger High School
for calling out my best.

To my mentors
Miss Edythe Daniel, Miss Ruth Greene,
Miss Marjorie Hugunin, and Miss Thelma Rothe
for inspiring me when I was at my lowest.

To Diane, Debra, Dorian, David and Denise
and their families
with love and appreciation
for their love and support.

And especially to my late wife, Beverly Adkins Johnson ...

The major reason I could devote long hours to my work, hours far beyond
what was expected of me, was my wife Beverly. As one of her strongest
commitments in our marriage, she went to work to take some of the financial strain inherent in the teaching profession off me and free me during
summers. It was that way for our nearly sixty years of marriage.

Beverly was the handy person for our home on Madison Street in Lake
Geneva, WI. Anything that involved persistence, vocational skill, or ingenuity usually was done or at least initiated by Beverly.

With our five children, she took the lead on most matters. Her consistent, persistent, underlying dependability insured the maturing of our amazing children. The struggle to put four children through college, sustain the life of our youngest daughter born with cerebral palsy, and keep our professional lives going now seem like absurdly impossible tasks. But Beverly did the impossible.

For most of her twenty-five years in the classroom, Beverly taught mathematics to freshmen who found it difficult to learn. She was also co-creator of the special education program at Badger High School.

Throughout Beverly's retirement, she continued her life of giving to our children, grandchildren, great grandchildren, our church, her garden, but most of all to our youngest daughter Denise. The three of us traveled – four trips to the West Coast, twenty-two excursions to Texas, a three-week journey to Germany, and various other trips. Except for Germany, these travels were completed with a wheelchair in a van for our daughter.

Beverly, our children and our home were more human and enriching than I could have ever hoped. I have always marveled that two of us – such different individuals – could pull off our adventures in concert. But let it be known that the key to these adventures was Beverly. Hers was sacrifice, giving, forever giving.

Beverly got it right for her precious life and right out of the *Old Testament*:

The joy of the Lord is my strength. *Nehemiah 8:10*

Of all the duties which befall a high school English teacher, the most important, by far, is writing. In fact, if we could develop skills in expressing ourselves in our native tongue, we would be shocked by the power at our disposal. It is the skill vital to all other skills. It is true that it can be used for ill as well as good, but if the consideration of our nation's values can accompany the language-learning process, there is no telling what sort of great educated citizenry this democracy can produce.

Bruce D. Johnson

And Gladly Would He Teach and Learn

Chronology of Events

1927	Born in Fennimore, WI, the oldest of three children.
1945	Graduated from Fennimore High School, Fennimore, WI.
1945-46	Served in the US Navy, McAlester, OK,Naval Ammunition Depot.
1951	Graduated from the University of Wisconsin-Madison, Bachelor of Science Degree in the Dairy Industry. Married Beverly Adkins in Fennimore, WI.
1951-53	Served in the US Army (Korean Conflict) in Kobe, Japan, Food Inspection Detachment.
1952	Welcomed Diane Jean Johnson into our family.
1953-55	Owned and operated the Fenway Café, Fennimore, WI.
1954	Welcomed Debra Lynn Johnson into our family.
1956	Student-taught English at the Lab School, Wisconsin State College-Platteville. (Spring) Welcomed Dorian Kae Johnson into our family. Student-taught English at Platteville High School. (Fall)
1957	Graduated from WSC-Platteville (now UW-Platteville) with Bachelor of Science Degree in English and Education. Attended summer session at University of Minnesota. Welcomed David Bruce Johnson into our family.
1957-58	Taught English at Osseo-Fairchild High School, Osseo, WI.
1958-86	Taught English at Badger High School, Lake Geneva, WI.
1961-85	Produced the Graduation Projects for Badger High School.
1961-96	Compiled the Annual Scrapbooks for Badger High School.

1967-86	Taught journalism and advised school newspaper *Inquirer*.
1970	Welcomed Denise Marie Johnson into our family.
1986	Retired from teaching.
1988-2016	Wrote 1487 essays on my career, interests and family.
1994-2016	Wrote 250+ occasional columns for local papers.

CONTENTS

And Gladly Would He Learn

Preface

My years since I retired in 1986 have been productive: an ambitious reading effort and an energetic physical regimen. I re-energized my photography, attended class reunions and showed the graduation projects until 1995, and facilitated several family trips. Since 1988, I have written nearly fifteen hundred essays on my career, interdisciplinary interests, and family. Over 250 of the essays have appeared as columns in two local newspapers. The main thrust of my writing effort has been leading toward publishing this book.

When I left the classroom at age fifty-nine, I knew that writing would become an active vocation. I wasn't sure how or when that would happen. Almost two years later, I pulled a subject out of the blue – I don't even remember what it was – and started to longhand my way into what I was not sure. An hour and a half later, I was typing my draft on my used Smith-Corona Galaxie typewriter. That was April 1988. I used my Smith-Corona Galaxie typewriter to prepare all my essays.

Why did I want to write? Why did I want to write about being an English teacher? What makes me think I have something worth sharing with former students, colleagues, family, friends and the general population?

One impression that persisted throughout my teaching career was that the public generally does not take education seriously. I do not mean that most students are not serious about studies, or that parents are not serious about their children's academic progress, or that teachers are not serious about their missions. Instead, I mean citizens rarely discuss the purposes of education, the changing circumstances of youth, or the ways to make schools more relevant and effective.

High school students are busied with so much of what is new in their lives that time to persevere on their learning is rare. Often what alumni later remember about their high school years has less to do with the reasons public schools exist than with the social aspects of their experiences. Throughout their four years of social ferment, their classroom life is something to be endured from day to day, week to week, quarter to quarter, until four years have accumulated twenty or so credits. Learning in this regimented manner can become drudgery to be endured so "I can really live later." The arrival of 3 PM is the release and makes the day worthwhile. Somewhere in this adolescent excitement, learning and growing are reduced to a grind. During my thirty years in the classroom, I often thought how silly and counterproductive the grind is.

Very few teachers have attempted to write about their entire careers. Many who have were not writing about classroom experiences primarily. They had other motives, like their graduate degrees, their research, or their often humorous and anecdotal documentation of their first years of teaching. I have yet to encounter a volume which celebrated long-term classroom experience strictly for itself.

My motivation for writing is delight. As difficult and burdensome as some of my classroom experiences were, the central thrust of all thirty years was delight. I knew I had influence on high school seniors which affected them in profound ways. I understand that, but I cannot always say for sure how it came to be or why it is true.

All I know is that my influence is true. I hope to bring about a revelation about teaching, the English language, the classroom, the aspirations of students, the hopes of parents, and the delight and love of learning. All teachers have their own stories in their repository of classroom experiences. I am compelled to try to tell mine.

The substance behind teachers' participation in American secondary school education is worth telling. I hope my story has something of universal value to warrant public discussions.

I encourage other teachers to share their stories.

In closing, I wish to acknowledge some of the people who consistently and enthusiastically encouraged me to share my story. Janet Adkins called me often to inquire on the book's progress. Jan is a retired teacher, lives in Fennimore, WI, and is an Adkins family genealogist. Cathy

McCormick ('69) is a former student who visits me occasionally. Cathy lives in Granger, IN, and is an artist and an instructor of pastels. We share a love of Charles Schultz and his *Peanuts* gang. Gary Baughn ('69) is also a former student, a retired teacher of English, and a strong advocate for sharing my story. Bob Pavlik, a long-time colleague and friend, and I shared several visits and meals discussing the audiences and format of my books.

Bruce D. Johnson
Lake Geneva, WI
Winter of 2020

Introduction

Bruce Johnson and I have known each other since the fall of 1966 when I joined the faculty at Badger High School. We taught senior English courses for three years before I became the school's reading specialist for three years. Eventually, I became a professor of education.

From spring 1988 until summer 2016, Bruce wrote 1487 essays on his personal and professional life – mostly 2-3 pages in length. He often wondered what would become of his essays. Who would want to read the essays? Who could edit his essays? Who would publish the essays?

For years, Bruce and I discussed possible answers to those questions. He asked me several times to serve as his editor. While I was very interested in doing so, I declined because I had too many other projects to complete before and after I retired in 2012.

However, during the fall of 2017, I began to edit Bruce's essays, then a two-foot high pile. I read the essays several times and assigned them to various categories. A macro-structure emerged for three books:

> *And Gladly Would He Teach:*
> > *Becoming, Serving and Retiring as a Teacher of English*
> *And Gladly Would He Learn:*
> > *Exploring Diverse Interests*
> *Our Johnson-Adkins Families, Home and Travels*

Chaucer's description of the Clerk in the *Prologue to the Canterbury Tales* inspired the titles of the first two books.

And Gladly Would He Teach
From Bruce's 1487 essays, we chose 152 for *And Gladly Would He Teach*, focusing on his becoming, serving and retiring as a teacher of English.

After he was graduated from high school, Bruce worked his way through years of delays and frustrations to find a potential career as an English teacher. As you read *And Gladly Would He Teach,* you will discover Johnson's ultimate resolve, as his supervising teacher quoted him in her letter of recommendation: "If I'm not going to make a <u>good</u> teacher, I don't want to be one."

You will learn how he discerned the hopes and dynamics of his classes, motivated students, and developed what he calls the language integrity his students need to become contributing citizens.

And Gladly Would He Learn

We chose 92 essays for a second book entitled *And Gladly Would He Learn*, focusing on Bruce's diverse interests and avocations. During and since his teaching career, he read hundreds of nonfiction and fiction books about athletes, artists, movie stars, media critics, journalists, musicians, social researchers, presidents, singers, photographers, and others. In this book, Bruce uses his first avocation of writing to summarize what he learned from cultural icons about living creatively, productively and courageously in a democracy.

And Gladly Would He Teach and Learn

And Gladly Would He Teach and Learn combines the two books. Our first hope in combining both books is to show how teaching and learning interacted in Bruce's life. Usually, learning precedes teaching, teaching enriches learning, and eventually learning and teaching become integrated processes for careers. Such was the case in Bruce's career. The more he learned the knowledge and skills of the academic discipline of English before and during his career, the more he became inspired and confident to teach. The more he taught, the more he sought to grow in his interests and avocations. He used his avocations of writing, music, numbers and odds, photography, and sports to enrich his classroom instruction and conversations with his students. Eventually, Bruce integrated his learning and teaching to become a stellar teacher of high school seniors and an informed citizen.

Our second hope is to reveal his major goal for writing about his career and avocations: To encourage on-going discussions on the purposes, policies, and practices in our schools. Bruce encourages the general public to learn first-hand how society's changes are affecting schools, how language integrity is essential for our democracy, and how we can support our schools.

Our Johnson-Adkins Families, Home and Travels
The third book contains an even larger number of essays about the Johnson family history, the Adkins family history, Bruce's two tours of military service, life in Fennimore and Lake Geneva, and travels to family members in the United States, Germany, and Norway. Those essays have been photocopied for family and extended families.

Editorial Considerations
The 1487 essays constitute a treasure trove of information about Bruce Johnson's education, military service, restaurant owner, career, thinking, and interests during his lifetime. This book is perhaps the only one which documents a high school English teacher's entire career.

Given the especially large number of essays and given that Bruce wrote the essays randomly over thirty years and after his thirty-year career, we agreed on some guidelines for selecting and editing the essays.

First, our intended audiences for *And Gladly Would He Teach and Learn* are Bruce's pre-service, in-service, and retired teachers; former students and colleagues; family and relatives; and the general public.

Second, for the first book, most of the essays written should be considered as time capsules of developments from the mid-1950s to the mid-1980s. Factual information was verified, but developments since the mid-1980s were not updated.

Third, a separate book could be compiled easily for Bruce's essays on the over 100 students, colleagues and administrators. That would be too many to include in the first book. The selected essays represent individuals closely related to the topics of the chapters.

I am honored to have edited the essays of a man who taught and learned gladly, a man I deeply respect as a teacher, mentor, and friend. He inspired many of his students and student teachers to become literate citizens, teachers, journalists, and public servants. He inspired me as well.

I extend my deep gratitude to Diane Johnson Foster, Debra Johnson Ipsen, Dorian Johnson Boetcher, David Johnson, and Denise Johnson for their support in this work. Diane took charge of preparing the selected essays for publication through Kindle. Debra and David led the efforts to find photographs and select essays for their Dad's interest in music. Dorian facilitated the financial aspects of the pre-publishing process. David provided valuable feedback on the initial organization of the three books. Denise shared her joy whenever I updated her on the progress of the work.

Robert A. Pavlik
Glendale, WI
Winter 2020

Acknowledging My Most Influential Teachers

A teacher affects eternity;
he can never tell where his influence stops.
Henry Adams

For a long time, I tried to figure out what some teachers did that generated their impact on me. I concluded first that they were givers. They gave generously of time, attention, expertise and caring deeply about their students' future. My most influential teachers were not takers. They did not waste my time, ignore my interests, treat me like I had no background knowledge, or demand my respect more than earn my respect.

Second, my most influential teachers made understanding my future students and me integral to their teaching. What they were offering was what I needed. Despite their heavy class loads and despite everything that works against teachers and students connecting, these four teachers connected with me and helped make me the English teacher I became.

These four teachers, mentors by the highest standard, and I formed valuable relationships which I increasingly appreciated during and after my own teaching career. The first two teachers taught English and Latin at Fennimore High School. After I was graduated from the UW-Madison and completed two tours of military service, I met my second set of most influential teachers at the Wisconsin State College-Platteville – now the University of Wisconsin-Platteville.

CONTENTS

Miss Thelma Rothe
Miss Ruth Greene
Miss Marjorie Hugunin
Miss Edythe Daniel

Miss Thelma Rothe

Miss Thelma Rothe taught freshman English at Fennimore High School. She was physically fragile. Her health always seemed to be a concern. Beneath this misleading frailty was the directed, disciplined mind of a mentor who took each of her students seriously and expected more from each of them than they ever expected of themselves.

Miss Rothe was powerful in her influence on students. Forensics was her specialty, and she sent many graduates on their way with speaking skills and confidence that gave them a head start in basic training for any student's life, the English language.

Now I need to confess. I don't recall the details, but I was not one of Miss Rothe's prize English and forensics students. I did not understand the opportunities she was offering. I did not understand the faith she had in me. I must have blundered my way through freshman English. My interests and energies were elsewhere.

When I said my interests were elsewhere, I meant football. As a freshman in the 1940s, I made the varsity team. I don't regret the experience, but as we all know, athletics can consume academics, and I am sure that is what happened.

Demanding when it came to language basics, she must have sensed my reluctance. What happened was she met me half way. Miss Rothe was not going to let my grid-grandeur foil her professional mission. She must have engaged me in conversation about this love affair with the sport. If I loved football, then that was what she had to engage.

I told her of my interest in collegiate football teams. In fall, several national publications put out their All-America teams. I determined the consensus players, collected their statistics and pictures, and prepared a visual display. It must have been eight feet high and three feet wide.

Miss Rothe said she wanted me to bring the visual display and put it up at the front of the room. I remember it covered part of the blackboard and was near the door, so no one could miss it. It hung up for a quite a long time. I was very proud of it. From that time on, Miss Rothe was my consensus All-American teacher.

I'm sure she thought this project would generate my interest in language development. Maybe it did, but I don't remember it that way. So, my high regard for this teacher who took an interest in me was tempered by regret. I have no doubt that this mixture of contradictory elements played a more important role in my teaching experience than I will ever know. I'm sure Miss Rothe knew that a teacher's genius and burden are nccdcd to bc an influcncc on thc young.

Having been an English teacher, I know the nature of the struggle – the hard, never-ending battle, September to June. To learn what each student could do and then try to create the circumstances for each one to do it, is a hard, heady experience. Miss Rothe was as dedicated to this noble mission as anyone I have known.

When I was deep into my career, I must have thought of my attitude and lack of application for Miss Rothe when my own students did not respond. Her influence lives on. What she did has been multiplied by who knows how many others. I am proud to say that I am one of them.

Miss Ruth Greene

The second of my most influential teachers in high school was Miss Ruth Greene. A prim, proper and persistent soul, she was my Latin teacher during my freshman and sophomore years. Latin was difficult, but my recognition of its value as a major contributor to English vocabulary had inspired my interest. Yet something in her expectations kept me going.

Her influence came through as subtle but persistent encouragement. I have always thought of her as a model of academic discipline, though it was much later when I fully realized her influence.

When I became an English teacher fifteen years later, there was little doubt of the carry-over. Miss Greene's dedication and persistence became part of my teaching style, though I was never as organized or as efficient as this paragon of pedagogical thoroughness. She, however, was all business. I can't remember her in any other way.

Ms. Marjorie Hugunin

It would be another thirteen years before I encountered my second two most memorable teachers. I served in the United States Navy and United States Army near the end of World War II and beyond. After my second military service and a failed business venture, I enrolled at the Wisconsin State College-Plateville. No point denying it, I was at a disappointing low. I had no burning desire either to major in English or be a teacher.

Desperation will do that to people.

However, Miss Marjorie Hugunin's passion for teaching English literature, especially Shakespeare, captured my interest. She animated the contributions of English literature and the principles one must learn to teach Shakespeare and others. This buzz-saw deliverer of content and nonstop storyteller had me reading as I never read before. I have always been a plodding reader (and still am), but I was ready to put in the time.

Miss Hugunin's influence was forever, as I still catch myself phrasing and reinforcing my speech mechanics as she did. She required her students to learn the first eighteen lines of the *Prologue to the Canterbury Tales.* Yes, and we had to recite those lines in Middle English before the class and an ever-watchful mentor. I used that same assignment for twenty-eight years in my senior English classes at Badger High School, something for which I have a notorious reputation.

Miss Hugunin, who taught me for eighteen credits of literature, was more than affirming of my potential as a teacher. In a professional recommendation, she wrote, "He can analyze situations and come to excellent conclusions. He surely is not afraid to work. I like Mr. Johnson's good common sense, admire his abilities, and feel he will be a very successful teacher. I knew Mrs. Johnson and am sure she will be a great help to him in any position he may hold." Coming from such an energetic, inspired, and resolute practitioner of pedagogy, those were high compliments. And of course, she was right about Mrs. Johnson.

Miss Edythe Daniel

When someone asks who the strongest force was in my becoming a teacher, I say, without hesitation and with unconcealed verve, Miss Edythe Daniel. She supervised my student teaching at Wisconsin State College-Platteville. That was January to June 1956, before Sputnik, but after the Korean Conflict and the Senator Joseph McCarthy period. The Weavers had returned from blacklisting to Carnegie Hall, and the great protest period was only in its earliest stages.

When we first met, Miss Daniel immediately recognized where I was on life's motivation scale. Twenty-nine, a family and no career, I harbored serious doubts about whether I could be a teacher, especially an English teacher. Miss Daniel saw through to the heart of my dilemma and pressed the right buttons.

Miss Daniel was buoyant and all business. Slight of build, she was strong of mind, stout of heart, always stern about language practice, skillful, and spontaneous. Her dark, sparkling eyes emitted just a hint of mischief. When she looked at me with those business eyes, I felt the burden of my shortcomings. Here was someone who was interested in me. She had developed in me expectations about being the teacher she taught me to believe I could be.

I have known few others who pursued the complex language processes as assiduously as she did. I lived by her advice, awaited her critiques eagerly, and wanted to please her more than anything. For the first time in an academic setting, I achieved success.

In addition, I picked up on a principle I practiced for all thirty years of my teaching career. Miss Daniel promoted that most difficult of teaching objectives, that is, understanding as well as teaching students. That, and patience. Miss Daniel was teaching a universal principle: to understand, the better to serve. She was motivational miracle in my life and career.

One strategy I have tried in order to figure out how her magic elixir worked, was to compile a collection of things she wrote to me. Included are excerpts from critiques, notes, responses, Christmas cards, and such. Maybe they will help explain how her elixir worked on me:

- I want you to be dependable. Youth lose faith in a person who is not dependable. They expect you to be what you have promised.
- You compete with yourself, never against your associates. You are not infallible and will make mistakes. Teaching involves experimentation, and not all experiments work.
- Too many teachers lack 'salesmanship' and enthusiasm for their subject fields. Facts are regurgitated and quickly forgotten by students. How few teachers relate the importance of the subject to the past, present or future, or use the subject to 'get into' students. Unless this is accomplished, why spend time on the subject matter?
- Children are at the mercy of their teachers for many hours of each day during the most formative years of their lives. What

they learn they will learn from you. What you teach them is your privilege. What you do not teach is your failure.
- You are capable of doing professional work. I expect nothing less.

Can there be any doubt about the nature of Miss Daniel?

After I retired, I had an opportunity to see the personnel file Badger High School kept on me. I guess it had always been available to see, but I never did check it out. I asked the office secretary, with whom I was visiting on another matter, if I could see the record. What I wanted to see was the reference Miss Daniel wrote. I wish I had seen the reference before.

The first surprise was that she quoted me. Apparently when I filled out a form at the outset of my student teaching term with her, I wrote, "If I'm not going to make a <u>good</u> teacher, I don't want to be one." That does not surprise me. I was desperate to succeed at something. Then she goes on to write:

> And working with him this semester I knew he was sincere in that desire. Well, I have found him to be not just a good teacher, but an excellent one.
>
> He handles children well, requiring them to work hard at tasks he presents enthusiastically. His explanations are emphatic and clear. He is orderly in his thinking and organization. In addition, an adequate sense of humor relieves his drive toward accomplishment, providing a workable classroom rapport.
>
> He is neither shy nor aggressive: he willingly asks for help, graciously accepts it, and then proceeds with unusual initiative to carry through with suggestions.
>
> I have never had a student teacher who gave more of himself. He is a bit of a worrier and tends to minimize his own abilities, resources and results, contrasting them with others.

Yes, she was probably right. I am sure my progress may have been different had I the gutsy courage of my convictions. But having my own classroom as my major responsibility was a joy, and I have never thought my destiny lay elsewhere.

6

I was not the only student of Miss Daniel from our family. My wife, Beverly, completed student teaching under her as well. Both of us appreciate and respect this master teacher who represented the ideal of what American education should be.

Deciding to Become an English Teacher

My life was a colossal confusion when I was trying to decide whether I should become an English teacher. While I enjoyed English courses in high school and college, and while I was a good student, I had serious doubts about my own skills and knowledge for teaching English. I was immensely ignorant and naïve about the profession of teaching English.

My classes with Miss Thelma Rothe, Miss Ruth Greene, Miss Marjorie Hugunin, and Miss Edythe Daniel greatly influenced my decision to teach English. These master teachers were exemplars I could build upon for my teaching career. They modeled a deep passion for language, literature and writing, and they developed deep understanding of their students to discern ways to share their passions for language, literature and composition.

Somewhere along the line, I must have concluded to forget my doubts as well as my frustrations and distractions up to this point. Instead, going forward, I resolved to work very hard, remember the influence of my four mentors, and believe I could figure out what to do.

CONTENTS

Zigzagging to My Place in the Sun

Most people think of the 1950s as innocent, prosperous, uneventful times. For those of us who lived through that decade as adults, that is not a very accurate description. Deceptively inaccurate, in fact.

The Korean Conflict claimed over fifty-thousand American casualties. The debilitating hearings which Wisconsin's Senator Joseph McCarthy conducted on the supposed Communist infiltration, the introduction of amateurism and noise into popular music, and the ever-intensifying Cold War with the USSR changed our lives.

For me, the 1950s were a struggle, deviations and digressions, a zigzagging and twisting series of events which took me from university classes in 1950 to my own classroom in 1958.

Things started off with a bang. In June 1950, the Korean Conflict began and with it came my draft notice, even though I had an honorable discharge from the U.S. Navy and no service obligation. I received a deferment to finish my degree at the University of Wisconsin-Madison.

In 1951, I was graduated from UW-Madison, my wife-to-be Beverly Jean Adkins was graduated from Wisconsin State College-Platteville, and my brother Clyde was graduated from the University of Iowa, all these events on three successive weekends.

Less than a week later, Beverly and I married. For six weeks we lived here and there while I waited for my induction notice.

The notice came early in August, and the rest of the year was spent in my second basic training in Maryland, this time with the U.S. Army.

1952 took me to Kobe, Japan, where I was assigned early in April, just before the U.S. occupation officially ended. I served with the 519th Food Inspection Detachment (later the 67th) for close to seventeen months.

In 1953, I came home to meet my thirteen-month-old daughter Diane Jean for the first time. A child brings reality, and I wasn't sure what I wanted to do with my life.

After many weeks of fits and starts, we went into the restaurant business. Though we tried hard, we knew we were in the wrong work. If there is a tougher retail business, I don't know what it is. We survived through two years, living in an upstairs apartment, and then we had a second daughter, Debra Lynn.

By the summer of 1955, I knew something had to change. I was

9

generating an interest in writing and language. I decided to take my family to Platteville, major in English, and train at Wisconsin State College-Platteville to become a teacher. For two summer sessions and three semesters, I earned my second bachelor's degree and a teaching license. We also had a third daughter Dorian Kae.

However, my desire to succeed at something, my growing love of language, and my fascination with everything about adolescence captured my whole attention. Though I did my share of complaining, I was dominated by my new classroom adventure. At twenty-nine, I found my place in the sun. When the Russian Sputnik began beeping along in space in October 1957, I resolved to help my country regain its place in the sun.

Why did I become an English teacher? I do not recall that I consciously desired to become one. Desperation causes strange actions. I went back to college for studies in English. I began to edge toward a profession.

Before I knew it, I was an English teacher, married with three children, and I needed a job. I still had expectations, though when I consciously thought about them, I doubted teaching seriously, supposing something else would come along. Nothing else came along. What happened was a kind of gradual osmotic process in which I absorbed the fact of what I was about to become and began to attach all sorts of expectations, phantasies and metaphors to my future lot.

Teaching was ever serious for me, and when I began to understand what it was and who I was, my circuitous paths and uncertain factors began to dissolve and disappear. I am predisposed to think that teaching was a good career for me.

Misconceptions About Being a Teacher of English

When someone is asked who his/her favorite or most influential teacher was, often the answer is an English teacher. My four most influential teachers were English teachers. Being an influential teacher became one of my goals during this turbulent time for me.

At the same time, I was aware that misconceptions abound for who English teachers are and what they do. Truth be told, English teachers do not always agree on what they do. One reason is that language is very personal business. We are sensitive about our own use of language, and we don't like people criticizing it. Of course, if English teachers are worth their salt, that is exactly what they have to do. The secret is how to do it. I did not know the secret when I decided to teach English.

Another misconception was on my mind: English teachers are expected to be perfect in all of their linguistic activity. Not just competent, but perfect. Every time we opened our mouths, we demonstrated our language competence or incompetence. Every English teacher has to establish a reasonable language level, and then practice it. We also have to learn how to temper our expertise in relation to our students. I was not perfect in my language skills, and I did not want to be just another senior member of the language police when talking with students, reading their papers, or talking with their parents.

I was aware of some misconceptions about women and men as English teachers. Most English teachers were thought to be not only women, but unmarried women who had plenty of time to be real full-timers, and that is what the job takes. My memorable teachers were women, unmarried, committed and zealous about their missions. How could I be married, raise a family and be an influential English teacher?

I can recall being asked what my vocation was going to be. When I said English teacher, the reactions usually had startled elements in them. Real men don't eat quiche and don't teach English!

Should I Have Taught History?
I thought of teaching history. The process of civilization, the panorama of events, people and dates, of movements and their rises and falls have fascinated me.

At Wisconsin State College-Platteville, I took Dr. Edmondson's course in Russian History. I was captured by the scope, sweep and drama of Russia's history and by Dr. Edmondson's passionate teaching style.

But I was an English major in education, and I had already done enough shifting from here to there so that I could not afford that kind of slippery footing again. As my teaching career in English developed, I wondered how I would have fared if I had taught history. I always looked upon the idea with excitement. Not only was there the structure of history with civilizations, movements, people and dates, but there was also the opportunity to seek out information and details of a period of time, to try to piece it all together, and then attempt to bring history to life for students.

11

I did historical research when I taught English literature, but the history always had to serve the literature. I did notice that about the time things became historically interesting, we had to move on. On the other hand, was there ever a national leader who could not be enhanced and understood better by the study of *Julius Caesar, Hamlet,* or *Macbeth*?

Today, students have only the vaguest notion of historical chronology. I fear a generation is coming with no historical memory at all. How will we be able to understand and nurture our values and principles if we do not understand how we developed them. I sometimes believe yuppiedom energizes itself and gets its instant gratification in a vacuum.

A valid example of how we have changed in the course of my professional life is illustrated by attitudes toward President Abraham Lincoln and the part he played in American history. About the time of the centennial of the Civil War, Lincoln was thought of with a kind of awe, even homage. He was recognized as the means by which the Union survived its severest test and the initiator of emancipation which is still going on. There was reverence in reference to Lincoln. Today most references are superficial or trivial. He may as well have lived 300 years ago during England's most threatening civil war.

I wonder how today's post-World War II generation would answer the question: who was the most important person of the twentieth century? Could it be that those born after World War II would not understand how Gandhi, Churchill, FDR, and Hitler gave direction to this century? Now I am beginning to wonder whether I missed my calling.

Was I Serious About Coaching?
When I was a student in Fennimore High School, I played varsity football and baseball. If I had priorities, they were certainly athletically inclined. I acted as though I might want to be a coach someday. I organized sports for junior high boys in football, softball, and basketball. I kept records. I encouraged, nagged, and occasionally inspired young athletes to excel at sports. And I enjoyed it.

I think most people thought I would become a coach. But, as I said, I acted as though I might want to be a coach. I never committed myself to that end.

In my first year of teaching English in Osseo, I was required to be an assistant football coach. I could not afford to spend time studying the game, so I wasn't much of a coach. Long practices after long days of teaching was getting me nowhere. If I was to be any kind of a coach, I would have to spend time that the teaching of English demanded.

When we moved from Osseo to Lake Geneva, I was resolved that there would be no athletics in my future teaching career. And for the next twenty-eight years, I stayed out. Staying out of athletics was one thing. Steering clear of its influence was another.

"Waking Up" During My First Week of Student Teaching

I may have been a Don Quixote de la Mancha stumbling upon his mission:

> *Having thus lost his Understanding, he unluckily stumbled upon the oddest Fancy that ever enter'd into a Madman's Brain; for now he thought it convenient and necessary, as well for Increase of his own Honour, as the Service of the Publick, to turn Knight-Errant, and roam through the whole World arm'd cap-a-pee, and mounted on his Steed, it quest of whom he had read, and following their Course of Life, redressing all manner of Grievances, and exposing himself to Danger on all occasions, at last, after a happy Conclusion of his Enterprizes, he might purchase everlasting Honour and Renown.*

Well, why not? It may be that my calling came upon me in the guise of necessity before I understood its gravity. I was consumed by deep concerns for supporting my family, being late in finding my career, and being happy with my career. Before I knew what was happening, I was in a classroom, standing there before twenty-five students, at twenty-nine years of age, untried, innocent, ready for life's quest, its boons, and challenges.

The week of February 27 through March 2, 1956, was a breakthrough for finding my mission. The influence of Miss Edythe Daniel continued to work its magic on me during that week. Also, the birth of our third child took place on leap-year day.

CONTENTS

"Wake-Up Week" – Monday, February 27, 1956

Standing in front of twenty-three eighth graders on that first day, I had reason to be on edge. At age twenty-nine, I thought there would be never a moment when I would be in charge of a group of people. I learned almost immediately that no one can stare me down like a troop of curious and restless early teens.

No one else was in the room, only the twenty-four of us. In back were two large windows. Nothing could be seen through them, but it was a bit disconcerting to know that anyone on the other side had a splendid panoramic view. That knowledge was little extra reason for nerves.

How should I engage with people fifteen years my junior? All of sudden the lesson plan lying before me looked like distant, irrelevant pages of exertion. Forty-six eyes staring at me, and I couldn't remember names. The last thing on my mind was the seating chart. All the frustrations of my eleven post-high school years had crystallized.

Her name was Miss Edythe Daniel. The diminutive soul, my supervisor, was probably behind that glass in back concluding the worst about my uncertainties.

I plunged ahead. I could sense my voice trying to engage. I had introduced myself, then followed with a short biography. All those years of indirection and uncertainty were trying to take over again. Then, it hit me – this was an opportunity. It was not easy reviewing failings and defaults, but they did cross my mind. I resolved to forget the last decade of personal dramas and begin again. I could not call my new resolve to be a renewal – what was I renewing? I couldn't call it regeneration because that implied something to generate from.

Still student-teaching that first day was a golden opportunity. Peering into those fresh faces, I realized my advantage. Love of language. Maybe I was not an expert yet, but I was about to teach eighth graders about language. Not only teach them, but also try to convince them how essential this vehicle of communication is for their lives.

The reality took over. I had to figure out how to exercise this privilege. Before I knew what happened, the hour was over. I was on automatic pilot.

As I retreated from my first experience in charge of something, I found my first critique on a 4x6 card waiting for me, the exquisite hand-writing leaving no doubt about its source:

> Monday, First day. Bruce, these are your obvious teaching attributes: 1. fine appearance, 2. excellent voice, and 3. understanding of things which are important. I believe you'll be a good disciplinarian. When you say something, you say it as if you mean it.
> The weaknesses of your hour were that it moved a bit slowly and you directed an answer to one child instead of the group.
> Let's look real quick (quickly). Probley (probably). Becuz (because).   E.D.

Good grief, now I also had to worry about diction. There wasn't much doubt. Someone was paying attention. Someone was thinking with me, listening. Speaking of paying attention, someone at home needed attention. My wife Beverly was in her ninth month of pregnancy.

"Wake-Up Week" – Tuesday, February 28, 1956

The joy of satisfaction that overtook me lasted precisely twenty-three hours. I was so busy figuring ways to maintain momentum that when I noted (very quickly, by the way) that momentum will not survive twenty-three hours, I had to start over.

My concentration on the hour's work was so intense that the class seemed to start its own momentum, and my students were right with me.

A word about the subject matter. I was teaching a unit on spelling. The first day was to review rules of syllabification and drill. The second, the plural forms of nouns.

Miss Daniel required lesson plans be precisely delineated in the language I planned to use. In other words, write everything out. We fortunately did not have to work from such explicit scripts beyond the first week. I learned quickly that sticking doggedly to the words of a lesson plan was impractical and unrealistic. Interaction with students is bound to alter the precision of any preconceived plan. Having a concrete plan constitutes an effective cue, and it is not a bad compass either. I understood the requirement. When I had my own student teachers less than ten years later, I felt the necessity for the same requirement.

16

With so many matters to think about, I wondered how all details could be covered. Process was most important at this point. I was experiencing the first urgings of becoming a students' teacher. Nothing more, nothing less. I reveled in how this experience made me feel I was doing something worthwhile. Knowing my students were with me invigorated me.

This day I began to sense differences among my students. I had to learn names. The hour seemed to be running itself, but I never realized making nouns plural was such a remarkable chaos.

Miss Daniel's critique was as short as the hour seemed:

> Everything was nicely under control today and speed was better (you recognized that, too). Good work accomplished by both students and student teacher. E.D.

I did what came naturally. No gaps or dead spaces, no meandering minds which made me feel really good. We made progress. I even wondered whether I could address each student by name within one class hour.

Something else crossed my mind today. Teachers must learn to speak clearly, articulating every word and phrase. Tomorrow, leap-year day.

"Wake-Up Week" – Wednesday, February 29, 1956

Wednesday produced an entirely different tone. The Johnson family increased by twenty percent. More about that development later.

With my eighth graders, I learned to expect some unpredictability in my teaching. I sensed that I had to lighten up sometimes. I knew teaching wouldn't be easy all the time. Mixing humor and work is fine, assuming the latter dominates.

Hot off my lesson plan, here were the objectives for the day: "To learn to apply the rules governing the order of e and i; to learn when to double the final consonant; to drill on these rules."

Lest you think this lesson to be beneath the intelligence of eighth graders, here is the drill doctored a bit to preserve its integrity:

The for__gn th__f was br__f.
The cash__r rec__ved gr__f.
While this f__nd r__gned in misch__f,
His fr__nd brought rel__f.

My mid-week spelling drill was dictated. Then there was tomorrow's assignment about doubling final consonants.

It was a busy hour. Miss Daniel sat in on most of it. I found no added pressure. I even forgot she was there. Her critique, however, got my full attention:

> You and I both realized that the hour was crammed with too many things and too much of everything. Sometimes an hour necessitates it! The thing I like about your work to date is that you know your material so well that you can go beyond your lesson plan, in additional explanation or illustration.
>
> Your vocabulary is mature, and I think that's good, even with junior high youngsters. Occasionally you will want to qualify your difficult words with definitions or synonyms. (Today's work is not so comprehensive but will require initiative.) E.D.

Shortly after class, I received a note that wife Beverly wanted me to come home right away. She was carrying our third child, and the time for delivery was near. We drove the twenty-five miles to Fennimore, climbed the steps to Dr. Howell's second floor office, to learn that he thought she was not ready yet. We drove across town to see my parents. It was there her waters broke. After contacting Dr. Howell, we were off to Lancaster, twelve miles back down the road.

Not only was this the day I first felt full classroom involvement, it was the birth date of daughter Dorian Kae, February 29, 1956, at 3:20 PM. As fate would have it, Wednesday afternoon was Miss Daniel's weekly student-teacher conference, whose attendance was imperative, was already well established. The meeting was at 4 PM.

My bread-winning obligations just increased, and here I was in the midst of professional obligation. I couldn't leave Beverly immediately, and I had to introduce myself to our new daughter. The birth of child three was not like the births one or two, but the impact was the same.

My developing professional obligations were calling. Thankfully officers were not in evidence along State Highway 81 as I buzzed back to Platteville. Miss Daniel's weekly conference was in full swing. A few celebratory comments and I melded into the group's work.

"Wake-Up Week" – Thursday, March 1, 1956
After yesterday's events, it was a wonder I could even show up. Yet there I was, ready to go. My lesson plans were beginning to take short cuts, not always following Miss Daniel's paragraph plan. She advanced that criticism on my Thursday and Friday plans.

The major feature of an hour highlighting rules governing silent "e," turned into an active campaign to learn names. On this fourth day, it bothered me that I was not able to address students by their first names.

Now over fifty-five years later, I can see the patterns students use to choose where they sit in class. I learned later seating was an important facet of September organization. Generalizations: strong female students tend to sit front and center of the room.

Students who want to be near the action but not be in direct purview of the teacher sit near the front but in the side rows. Apparently, students did not think teachers utilized peripheral vision. Boys who thought they would be out of my direct line of fire, sat in back or behind taller people.

I doubt I recognized these subtleties during my first week of student teaching. Somewhere along the line in this first experience, I sensed the importance of beginnings. I later concluded that attention to such details in September established the pattern for how things would go all fall, winter and spring. I didn't do that to show I know the names of the months, but rather to emphasize how long the school year is.

These were things I learned later, but this class left its mark in my mind. I recall several students for a variety of reasons. Bright and studious Janet was the daughter of a local professor who was head of the department in which Beverly pursued one of her majors. Karen, intelligent, who did some babysitting for our family. Hope, the kind of socially aware person I associated with journalism and social causes. Dick, one of my back-benchers, whose grandfather was my father's partner in a hardware store.

I often wondered why Betts sat in the middle front row seat. Social awareness and peer recognition were probably the reasons. The longer I looked at that old seating chart the more I remembered. I realized I had to get to know students as individuals by becoming aware of what they say and do.

E.D.'s critique was short and sweet:

> Though I wasn't with you all hour, certainly the youngsters were working when I did come in. There was a sincere rapport evident.

I wondered whether my attention to faces and names had anything to do with the "sincere rapport."

"Wake-Up Week" – Friday, March 2, 1956

I can understand why Fridays turn out to be review-wrap-up-testing days. I often thought later that Fridays punctuated an unreasonable "period" on the week, making Mondays a lot tougher to engage. I agreed with breaks, but was it necessary to make a week seem like an isolated entity? I had to admit that at the end of my first week of teaching, I had reason to reflect.

In my first week as a student teacher, I needed to prove my capabilities to organize and execute. Writing out lesson plans was a good idea. How many supervising teachers require lesson plans, I do not know. There wasn't much doubt that writing lesson plans had extended effects on my work. I became aware that I had to work within a certain framework. Reflecting back, writing out lesson plans seemed a necessity. They were demanding, and they required thinking and organizing.

Being more adept at nuts and bolts work, I had to consistently keep an eye on matters of general organization. Even Miss Daniel appeared to have some suspicions on this fifth day of my first week. I would never have learned about those suspicions without jumping through the hoops of lesson planning in detail.

I was pleased with Miss Daniel's Friday critique:

> This ends your first week of teaching, and I have been completely satisfied. I hope that the nature of next week's work can be a <u>little</u> more relaxing. Also, I hope that the results of your test are good, as evidence of thorough presentation.   E.D.

Miss Daniel was saying she was impressed with my work . . . now relax and get back to work. I can look back on this week and say it was a turning point in my life.

Gaining a profession and a daughter in the same week were quite extraordinary events!

Moving to Lake Geneva, Wisconsin and its New High School

By 1958, I was considering a new job. Nothing wrong with our year and a half in Osseo, WI, but my wife Beverly and I felt strongly that we needed a more cosmopolitan atmosphere for raising our family.

English teachers were in short supply then. No sooner had my name been entered with the placement bureau at Wisconsin State College-Platteville than I received nine offers. During the first week of June, I signed a contract with the new Badger High School about to open in Lake Geneva. This relatively small town close to the metropolitan centers of Chicago and Milwaukee was interesting and diverse and beautiful. Geneva Lake was a bonus. Working in a new school was also a bonus. And speaking of bonuses, there were now six of us, three daughters and a one-year-old son David Bruce, who accompanied us to Lake Geneva in Walworth County.

CONTENTS

Coming to Live in Lake Geneva
Lake Geneva or Geneva Lake?
Twenty-five Board Members
To Consolidate or Not to Consolidate

Coming to Live in Lake Geneva

Beverly, our children and I had come from Osseo (near Eau Claire), a much smaller and thoroughly Norwegian community. I used to say upon leaving Osseo, what we needed was something more cosmopolitan. We certainly found it here with a mix of ethnic backgrounds. During the tour of Lake Geneva and the interview with Superintendent Vernon Pollock, I knew this lake city was influenced significantly by Chicago, and I remembered that Lake Geneva was being considered for the new U.S. Air Force Academy (1952). However, when the selection committee arrived, an organized protest met them. Further consideration stopped.

I took the teaching assignment at Badger High School in Lake Geneva in 1958. The major factor in accepting the position was Mr. Pollock. On the day his own twins were being graduated from the old Lake Geneva High School, Mr. Pollock spent two hours with Beverly and me. We got the tour of the city, the feature being a drive-by of the high school under construction, which left me wondering whether it would be ready by September. When Mr. Pollock interviewed me later in the day, I felt he had already checked my references and decided to hire me. We came here because Mr. Pollock deeply impressed Beverly and me. Also, Mr. Pollock and I both came from rural communities – he from Jefferson County, I from Grant County.

Coming to Lake Geneva and Badger High School in the late summer of 1958, I had no idea how profound and permanent the experience of the next sixty years would be. For twenty-eight of those sixty years, my classroom led to an understanding of high school seniors, which led to putting photography and music together to understand them further through their commencement.

Lake Geneva or Geneva Lake?

For over six decades, we lived on the north end of Madison Street over half a mile from the lake. On a sunny day, if anyone would stand out front in the middle of Madison Street, and if there is no traffic, a person can see the shimmering surface of the lake ten blocks away.

At an out-of-country family reunion a few years ago, someone asked if I lived near Lake Geneva. I said I lived in Lake Geneva. I was not sure whether my questioner meant the city of Lake Geneva or Geneva Lake.

Not being a native, though living here for sixty-plus years, I tend to be objective about local names and places. I cannot say that I grew up calling any local place this or that. It does seem logical to call the Geneva Lake simply as a matter of clarity since the city goes by Lake Geneva. But we know logic does not always rule in such matters.

I've lived with this name redundancy for these sixty-plus years. I've noticed that natives tend to prefer the city's namesake to maintain continuity, probably for fear of losing the Switzerland-Lake Geneva connection. Though I've never researched the subject, the idea that the Lake Geneva resembles the Lake Geneva in Switzerland always seemed to be a bit of a stretch.

I agree with area-native Jim Black that Lake Geneva is a state of mind, especially to people who do not live in the city. That is probably what my reunion questioner had in mind as he wondered how close we lived to the action. Well, there is plenty of it. When people come here, they are really coming to the city of Lake Geneva, since access to the lake is limited. Most of us do not use the lake at any time, except to look at.

The state-of-mind Lake Geneva is different from the town of the residents. The city is not a bad place to live, if you can breathe deeply when property tax time comes. The farther you live from the lake and downtown, the better. Except for the County H fliers and the crosstown raceway in season, this city is quite a quiet, peaceful place. Traffic is tolerable if you don't have to drive across town from Memorial Day through Labor Day

Then there are the growing settlements in the area, the burgeoning construction, the continuing development where once there were estates. Imagine, four hundred residences where Northwestern Military Academy used to be. Yes, it appears Lake Geneva is a state of mind and fast becoming a crowded urban city.

Twenty-five Board Members
In the area encompassed by Badger High School, there are twenty-five school board members. All twenty-five members did not serve on one board for the high school; only five serve what became known as Union District #1. The number twenty-five came from separate elementary districts and one high school district.

In an age when most state school districts were consolidated, a district with a union high school and separate elementary schools has been a rarity. Only a handful of over three-hundred state school districts survived, and all but one was in the southeast corner of the state.

Local control over education was highly prized especially in the local elementary districts. The problem, however, was that education has become a complex business. There was an urgent need for coordinated efforts. The elementary school districts were financially stressed to implement many of the state-mandated programs. Unless a district was rich, it was impossible.

Four of the five elementary districts that sent students to Badger High School were strong proponents of local school autonomy. They wanted their own elementary schools, and they were willing to pay for the state-mandated programs. The elementary school districts, at least three of them, were indeed well healed, and they paid their own way. They generally resisted full coordination of programs with Badger High School.

The Badger High School Board had no control over elementary and middle schools that sent students to its classrooms. Having been a teacher in this high school for twenty-eight years, I understand the value of local autonomy. I also understand the problems of numbers and the myriad of state-mandated programs school districts must fulfill. Let's face it, having five school boards with a total of twenty-five members does not guarantee a better education.

To Consolidate or Not to Consolidate
Badger High School is unusual. Since the badger is the state animal, and since the home university in Madison calls its teams Badgers, the name Badger High School could be almost anywhere in the state.

When two or more schools around the state consolidated, they had the problem of naming the new entity. Often, they did not abandon local loyalty: Sauk Prairie, Adams-Friendship, and Eleva-Strum, to name three unified districts. Iowa-Grant lies astride the border of two counties, drawing students from both. Delavan joined with a nearby village to form the Delavan-Darien School District. Geneva-Genoa was not considered.

Ever since the high school opened, there has been a degree of animosity on the part of both communities. It survives to this day because the two districts never did consolidate, but only share the high school with two other districts. Of the hundreds of Wisconsin school districts, less than a dozen never consolidated, and one has a high school named Badger, also known as Union District #1.

The school district paid $7000 for the forty acres, which originally was the northeast section of Big Foot State Park. Even in the middle 1950s, this cost was a gift at $175 an acre. Today, each acre would sell for at least $12,000 or $480,000.

On that land, a $3,800,000 referendum for a building was turned down twice. When the referendum was reduced to $1,800,000, it passed. No great imagination is needed to picture what happened to the resulting structure. The roof leaked almost from the beginning, winter winds made their way through the crevices and crannies as the years advanced, and a pared-down auditorium seating five hundred ninety-five could not seat all students at the beginning of the third year (1960-61).

Overcrowding was perennial, despite a four-classroom addition in 1963 and five classrooms, swimming pool, three shops, and two locker rooms in January 1966. Well over eight-hundred students started in the fall of 1966, and by the fall of 1974, over one thousand students enrolled.

Another unusual circumstance was socio-economic. Some of the highest valued land in the state was within the districts that fed students to Badger High School. The farmlands of Linn Township and the estates of the north and south shores of Geneva Lake were rich and conservative.

Families from all over the district moved in, moved out, and struggled. The transience factor extended to the City of Lake Geneva, since its major business was summer leisure. People arriving and leaving yielded economic instability.

When the Playboy Hotel opened in May 1968, local development has not stopped since. On the face of it, one would think Badger High School would reflect its rich and varied roots and have all the financial support needed to cope with its internal socio-economic inequities. But there has always been an atmosphere bordering urgency when it came to economic problems. There has never been the insistent spirit of a better education controlling affairs. Everything was always on economic terms.

Certainly, one reason for our economic challenges was the failure to consolidate. The State of Wisconsin has penalized districts which have not consolidated. But the desire for local autonomy among the elementary districts sending students to Badger High School keeps five separate school boards in existence. What this lack of consolidation does to curriculum and finances and harmony is easy to figure out. Our distinction is that our high school district has twenty-five school board members living in it.

On the other hand, some factors have made teaching at Badger High School a context for an enriching and satisfying teaching career. One of those was a cosmopolitan society amid a rural environment. Admittedly the influence of cities, particularly Chicago, was changing that, because development and population were increasing, and it was a lot less rural than it was in the 1960s. But there was no question Lake Geneva was an interesting place to work.

Another factor was a liberal philosophy of education, particularly with the administration. Experimentation, creativity, and a comfortable working atmosphere were taken for granted. Looking back over nearly thirty years of teaching at Badger High School, I see that the three or four innovations on which my approach to the classroom was based, would not have been possible in most other schools.

Teaching Language

How much knowledge of language structure do we need to express ourselves intelligently? Can we learn to read well and write well without understanding the way language works? How much of language use is habit, which once learned, need never concern us again?

Is using language like learning to walk, ride a bike, or type? A child's first words are more than memory or process. Something in our being is involved in language, right from the outset. Our lives are affected by it, from the beginning, and forever. Language is a large part of the way we live. Our language is us as individuals and groups.

CONTENTS

Exemplars of the English Language

It is easier to personalize the teaching of English than another subject. That's because we are language, and language is we. The most important impressions we convey are in our language. Our influence comes about primarily through language. What we say and how we say it tells others more about us than we can imagine. An English teacher becomes attuned to the way students manage their language, whether in speech or on paper.

Sometime early every year, I asked students to think of well-known persons whose command of the English language they admired – then we talked. I was not only interested in hearing the names, but also the reasons for their admiration.

Students chose names of actors, politicians and television personalities easily. However, they were not always precise about their reasons. Often, they selected people recognized for choosing words carefully and fashioning sentences clearly. They seemed to respect diction. The quality or distinctive nature of the voice was important, too. Sometimes they were forceful and commanding people.

I suggested that some of the most enduring communicators were poor speakers. I usually invoked the name of Sir Winston Churchill, who muttered and lisped his way through sentences, but the combination of his cause and his eloquent language far overcame the quality of his voice. I always strained to hear Churchill because I knew he had something to say.

By the time the discussion had run its course, students had some idea of the intangible, ambiguous power of language, that its mastery was worth pursuing, and that good thoughts do not come across without effective language.

Some of the names that crossed my mind when I tried to remember those discussions were Actor Tony Randall, News Reporter Robert MacNeil, Actor Charlton Heston, Congresswoman Barbara Jordan, President John F. Kennedy, Rev. Martin Luther King, Jr., and Actor Richard Burton. Such people impressed me because they spoke clearly and distinctly even as our nation was becoming a nation of mumblers.

We've made "going to" into "gonna" during everyday speaking. It's easier to say. Most of us say "gonna" most of the time. The dictionaries have not listed the word. That is surprising because lexicographers listed many nonstandard words which are far less common than "gonna."

However, the real lesson in muttering and mumbling is listening to popular music. Since the onset of rock n' roll with all of its constituent ingredients in the 1950s, a certain pride emerged for being unintelligible. Language is one of the main reasons that youth culture is essentially a separate culture. When adolescents reach their maturity, we see just how much influence pop culture has had on them. We also get a look at the degree of their education, especially their language.

On Semantics

Teaching English always demands being sensitive to words. Had I not been sensitive to words, I would have had trouble. As an English teacher, I became a symbol for accuracy and care in the use of language. So, I developed a modus operandi that kept errors under control and bestowed the power of concession and confession when I erred.

I developed a two-part system for responding to my own errors with words. First, admit them. Second, do some homework. Errors can happen in so many different ways that it is almost hopeless to cite only one or two examples.

Everyone brings different influences on the way he or she pronounces words, so that there is always someone to take exception. Fortunately, my problems were not severe, but one word in particular cropped up periodically. Apparently, my utterance turned the word to "warsh" with an R sound which is not there. Though "worsh" is listed as a variation in *Merriam-Webster's Tenth New Collegiate Dictionary* (MW10NCD), it is not common. Somehow, I picked up this aberration, and if I was not careful, I would say "warsh."

Not many students will take a teacher to task on a mispronunciation, knowing it leaves them open to the same form of criticism. However, when students figured out I did not "go after" those who did this, be sensitive or defensive, they were likely to chide me.

One year, the editor of our *Inquirer* newspaper seemed to take great satisfaction when I would utter "Warshington" or "warshing." Knowing what it took to become editor of the *Inquirer* tended to discourage me from reciprocating. However, if the bandwagon effect began to develop, I could step up the pressure.

30

I knew my diction always was a potential problem, so I wasn't going to be belligerent. But I did learn that students are more aware of a teacher's honesty and fair-dealing than they are with a few pronunciation problems. If I were trying to encourage accurate and articulate use of language, their first model was the teacher. I never was quite sure how positive an example I set.

The study of semantics can take many forms, though I preferred to treat it as a practical matter, keeping its definition and application simple. Semantics is the study of meanings. Application is a question of practical, interesting, bite-sized content. So, if we are to investigate meaning, we want to concentrate on words that really have meaning.

I taught that words came in two types: function words and value words. All words function in sentences, but not all bear real meaning.

The function words do only that – function. Their meanings are restricted to their jobs. The most common examples are those we use over and over again, words that give structure to language. Here are few: "the," "of," "and," "to," "an." Their meanings are narrow in specific, never changing. Here are a few more: "here," "are," "a," "few," "more."

Value words also function in sentences, but they bear meanings that rise far above their functions. I use the following sentence as a chalkboard example at the outset of my unit. The sentence below was from a student composition:

> The curtain was opening, the music was swelling, and then came
> that 'brave' smile, and I was on my way.

In those twenty words, only twelve function, seven carry meaning as well as function, and one word rises above the others and tells us something about the sentence's mission, which is essentially emotional. Seven are value words: "curtain," "opening," "music," "swelling," "came," "smile," "way." Each does something important in conveying meaning. Each could be replaced with a synonym. And of course, each word functions within the structure of the sentence.

This sentence transmits a series of actions:

1. opening of the curtain

2. swelling of the music
3. coming of a smile
4. moving onto the stage by the narrator, who clearly has a place in a musical show of some sort

Three of those actions are essentially mechanical parts of the starting of a show or a scene, but the coming of a smile is different.

Why would someone smile as she went onto a stage? The adjective "brave" at once answers the question. In fact, that word seems to reverse what the "coming of the smile" would otherwise mean. This young actress is, if not scared, anxious. The excitement is implicit.

The twenty words of that sentence operate at different levels. It is as though nineteen words working on two levels prepare the way for the one word that gives the statement its tone.

I wonder how the impact of that sentence in its context of other sentences would have been affected had the writer started looking for synonyms. What if the phrase read, "then came that courageous smile," or "then came that fearless smile," or "that bold smile" or "that valiant smile"?

"Brave" conveys simply the anxiety and suspense of a high school girl taking her first entry cue in an all-school musical. This one word, like a gemstone, is placed in a setting of the sentence's structure, movement and sound. It makes us focus on the subject of the action. "Brave" is a value word of some significance.

We can conclude that the narrator is going through some sort of emotional experience. The power to make words say beautiful things and convey forceful, incisive meanings is an important facility. That power is part syntactical skill, but it is also part language sense, word sense.

The processing of words we do all our lives is a matter of association. A new word that impedes the meaning of what we are either reading or hearing will be considered and rejected, considered and processed either by intelligent guessing or asking someone or consulting a dictionary, or ignored entirely. The habits that a child forms within the family will determine the quality of his or her processing.

My observations of students taught me that people tend to think in one of two ways. Something centripetally, inward as the movement into a whirlpool. Everything is taken in and processed with what is already there.

Others think centrifugally, outward as the waves caused by the casting of a stone into a quiet pond. Immediately, anything new is associated outwardly with other things.

After a while, one person develops a limited, basic, rather dull sense of what a word is or can be. The other finds that language is expansive, capable of wide variation, and relates in an enlivening way with language and its possibilities.

What a person really learns to do is train words. I learned to reject those that are not used and put the rest to work. Vocabulary building becomes a lifelong activity of relating unfamiliar words with familiar ones and seeing meaning as the right combination of words in a given situation.

Mark Twain's poem sets the tone for thinking about the power of words:

> I understand a fury in your words,
> But not the words.
> The important thing about any word is
> how you understand it.
> A blow with a word strikes deeper than
> a blow with sword.
> But my words like silent raindrops fell
> And echoed, in the wells of silence.
> The difference between the right word and
> the almost right word is the difference
> between lightning and a lightning bug.

What I was trying to convince students to do is develop their skills in training words. That's what we're up to, making words do what we want.

Writer Pat Gray, in his poem, *On Training a Word*, suggests the process:

> Until you're comfortable with it,
> it may fight you,
> refusing to roll off your tongue,
> threatening to slap you

with a mispronunciation suit
if you try it out too soon.
Parade it carefully,
call its name softly,
or it may turn sideways
to reveal itself
narrower than you thought,
or stand up
and dwarf you,
or lie down in snooze
when you want it
to perform.

The training of words is frustrating, rewarding, and a lot of fun. Words are fragile; a lot of faith is involved.

Language can then take us on journeys unimagined. Philosopher and language researcher Ludwig Wittgenstein caught the truth about language: "The limits of my language stand for the limits of my world."

What Was Going on in the Eleventh Century?

The first requirement of a prospering civilization is a flexible, comprehensive language. Considering when and how the English language developed, it is hard to imagine how our language became so flexible, comprehensive, resilient, extensive, with a vocabulary that far surpasses any other tongue. If we were to have a universal language, English would certainly meet the requirements.

At the onset of the second millennium, the English language was a collection of tribal tongues gradually being assimilated by languages of the most powerful tribes referred to as Anglo-Saxons. The Anglo-Saxon language was a loosely bound Germanic tongue with many dialects.

The Anglo-Saxon nation was ruled by a succession of kings, the most important of whom was Alfred the Great (871-901 A.D.). He was primarily responsible for what unification had taken place. However, trouble was ahead. The name of the Saxon king ruling in the year 1000 A.D. was a harbinger of things to come. He was called Aethelred the Unready.

Arguably the most important date in English history was 1066 A.D.,

34

the date for the Battle of Hastings, the Norman-French invasion. William, Duke of Normandy, laid claim to the throne of Anglo-Saxon England. Much of his argument is not fully understood but having the stronger army has shown that causes are not always the important considerations.

After his army landed on the Sussex coast in the fall of 1066 A.D., and with a series of fortunate circumstances most invading armies do not get, William defeated King Harold II near the village of Hastings on October 14th. In the 950+ years since, England has never been invaded.

Thus, William the Conqueror became King of England with absolute power. The French nobles who had supported him were given parcels of the conquered lands. And so, the feudal system formed in England.

While the ruling class used French, the common people spoke Anglo-Saxon. French never caught on. Anglo-Saxon became the basis of modern English. So, with this epic event occurring shortly after the beginning of the second millennium, its far-reaching effects can still be observed today.

David Howarth's book *1066: The Year of The Conquest* (1977) contains this description the famous engagement:

> Since gunpowder, deafening noise has been the essence of battle; it is hard to imagine now that the Battle of Hastings was comparatively silent, with only the evil thud of weapons, the sounds of the horses' hooves on the muddy ground, the snorts and neighs, the human cries of triumph and agony, and ordinary conversation. Nobody a mile way in English countryside would have heard the battle at all.

But a millennium later, we can still feel the explosive effects of that event, including the dramatic expansion of the English language.

Growth of the English Language

Why does the English language have over a million words? No other language has anything close to that amount. Why does English have the reputation as the world's most flexible language? Other cultures have readily influenced English. We borrow shamelessly from other languages.

German practices economy in the size of its vocabulary. Italian and Spanish have a singing quality. French is almost the opposite of English. France actually has laws about compromising that purity of their language.

35

The French are particularly combative when it comes to borrowing from English.

A second reason for the language's flexibility and extensive vocabulary has to do with the tricks of history. English is an Anglo-Saxon tongue. It was the language of the Germanic tribes that invaded, then settled Britain late in the first millennium. Around 1000 A.D., unifying forces tended to combine a single tongue we now call Anglo-Saxon. It had an efficient grammar, and its words were basic, reflecting a hard-agrarian life. That language is the structural basis for modern English. The grammar of today's English is fundamentally the same as the Anglo-Saxon spoken at the end of the first millennium.

In 1066 A.D. came the Norman-French invasion. William the Conqueror was a grim task master, and his nobles became Britain's ruling class. Their language, customs in laws? Why, French, of course. French became the official language of England. Relatively few people spoke it, but they were important people.

Another major language influence came from the medieval church. In their monasteries, monks carried on the business of teaching, translating, and record-keeping in Latin. It is no exaggeration to suggest that seventy to eighty percent of English words originated in Latin. So, within the English culture after 1066 A.D., French, Latin and Anglo-Saxon interacted to guarantee English would have the world's richest vocabulary.

A third reason is the influence of Great Britain upon the rest of the world. The British were interacting with most other cultures. The main advantage of a language of a million words is not the volume as much as the variety in the flexibility that results. Anglo-Saxon, French, and Latin are not only the major sources of English words but also the providers of three distinctly different cultural flavors.

Anglo-Saxon was the people's language. Its words were simple in general in meaning. Saxon words, since they were Germanic, have lots of consonants. Their meanings generally focus on personal responsibility.

French was the language of the ruling class. Its words are literary, more sophisticated, carrying deeper meanings. French words were longer and had to do with governing responsibility.

Latin was the learned language, the voice of the church – highly organized, with lots of prefixes, roots and suffixes with which to form new words. Latin represents a limitless resource for new vocabulary.

A good way to examine these linguistic flavors is to compare words which have the same general meeting:

The sun will <u>rise</u> every day.
The night <u>mounts</u> his horse to go into battle.
The Lord <u>ascended</u> to heaven on Easter Sunday.

All three verbs have the same general meaning, but in the context of the three cultures suggest different shades of meaning. "Rise" is general and direct. Everyone watches the sun rise. "Mounts" carries a subtler meaning. How the knight gets on his horse is as important as the action itself. "Ascends" has a religious connotation, an unearthly tone in this action.

Based on these examples, we should be able to tell the source of each of these three words: "shield," "fortify," "protect." The peasant took up his sword and shield. The army fortified the town against the invading force. The common, one-syllable "shield" with its four consonants is a typical Anglo-Saxon word. "Fortify" bears a broader meaning. One person does not fortify; a community or nation does that. This word has a governing responsibility. "Protect" is an example of a Latin prefix and root at work.

Why do so many words have nearly the same meaning? For example, "wish" and "desire." "Wish" is simple; "desire" is more complex. Or "buy" and "purchase." "Buy" is a common action; "purchase" means to suggest more. What is the difference between a "home" and a "residence"? "Home" is personal; "residence" sounds official.

Does "assist" mean exactly the same as "help"? For some reason, "help" seems simple, more basic. "Assist" has some sort of responsibility beyond what "help" suggests. Is "work" the same as "labor"? There is something more complicated and organized about "labor."

"Town" means home and community. "Municipality" means organization and government. "Tell" is simple, like a story. "Announce" means formality, something more organized.

As a generalization, the simpler, more basic word is Anglo-Saxon. The more organized, complex ones are French. Here are more examples:

luck, fortune	frugal, thrifty	beginner, novice
antique, old	foe, adversary	potent, mighty
scatter, disperse	conversation, talk	anger, irate

But our language has exceptions. One interesting case the word "people," which came from the Old French word "peuple." The Anglo-Saxon word "leod" had disappeared. It appears to have been a useful change.

It should also be pointed out that French is a Romance language. That means French grew out of Latin, one of five European languages to do so. That means most French words can be traced to Latin. "Peuple," which became our word "people" derived from the Latin word "populus."

This Latin-French connection has caused some unusual things to happen. Latin, for instance, had a word "fragilis" meaning "easy to break." In French, "fragilis" turned into "frele," which the English borrowed and turned into "frail." Later on, seeing "fragilis" in the dictionaries, writers decided to use it, and it became "fragile." Both "frail" and "fragile" still mean "easy to break," but consider the differences between them. One refers to people who are in less than robust health. The other, according to the MW10NCD, "implies extreme delicacy of material or construction and need for careful handling (a fragile "antique" chair)." One refers to people; the other refers to things.

Latin, as a source for new words, cannot be understated. Words are like people; they have families. The Latin verb "specere," meaning "to look at," has sired a family of words that seem endless. All of the following words can be traced back to this Latin verb. Some connections are closer than others. Also note the important parts prefixes and suffixes play:

speculate	retrospect	spectrum	introspective	spectacular	aspect
prospectus	specimen	specify	despicable	perspective	species
conspicuous	circumspect	respite			

So, Latin was the learned-church language of limitless resources. French, the sophisticated, literary language, gave us word of deeper meanings and of governing responsibility. But Anglo-Saxon, the mother tongue, the language of Germanic tribes, gave us most of the words we use every day as our simple, popular vocabulary.

Every word of the following little story is of Anglo-Saxon origin:

At the stroke of five each morning Mother and Father leapt out of bed. Then they began to do many chores about the house. Before the sun rose Mother took water from the well while Father went out into the fields to feed the cows and look after the horses. In summer or in winter, in good weather or bad, everything had to be cared for.

As a small child I often thought how much they must have hated that daily work. They never showed anything but love and hope in our home. They bore hardship without one word of sorrow, and even found time to teach us children how to swim and ride horseback.

To continue the story ...

In the evening, at dusk, they also taught us the Gospel in little songs about the goodness of God in the wonderful gift of life. They were so thankful that they could give us food to eat and milk to drink as we grew up. They were kind and lovable indeed! To my brother and sister and me they were not only kinfolk but true friends.

The common, everyday things of life have Saxon names. And you could not tell such a story without the basic grammatical words, which are also Anglo-Saxon.

The modern English language is a delightful, delectable diversity of over a million words. English may not be as efficient as German, as lyrical as Italian and Spanish, or as uncompromising as French, but a richer, more flexible language cannot be found.

How could I impress students with the degree to which English has borrowed words from other languages? The major thrust of our discussions to that point had been that Anglo Saxon, French and Latin were the major players in the evolution of the English language. I did not want them to think that was all there was to it.

So here I was, trying to figure out how to demonstrate this fact. I don't recall where I got the idea, but I know I wondered if I could find words beginning with every letter of the alphabet, each from a different country or culture. To my surprise I found hundreds, and I suspect thousands exist. So, it didn't take long to find twenty-six words from twenty-six different cultures.

By this time, my students were well versed on chasing down the histories of words, so my assignment was routine and simple. I gave a word to each student, the assignment being to find out where the word came from. If anyone had any doubt about its meaning, they were prepared to supply a definition.

The following day each student gave his or her finding orally. Here is that list, each word followed by its language of origin:

algebra	Arabic	naïve	French
barbecue	Haitian	orangutan	Malay
commando	Afrikaans	panda	Tibetan
granite	Italian	taboo	Polynesian
immune	Latin	verandah	Persian
kayak	Eskimo	xylophone	Greek
llama	Peruvian	yodel	German
moccasin	Am. Indian	zombie	African
furlough	Danish	ski	Norwegian
geyser	Icelandic	tycoon	Japanese
hominy	Am. Indian	umbrella	Italian
igloo	Eskimo	voodoo	African
motif	French	zinc	German

Using so many words from different countries can make us feel like citizens of the world. Every one of these words is now part of the English language. This assignment worked so well that I made it an annual activity in every class.

This list could go on indefinitely. No, I would probably run out of "x" words. For some reason, they are all Greek.

So, is English equipped to be a universal language? I think it already is.

Borrowed Words and Phrases from Latin

I wonder what people who have not studied Latin think about those hundreds of phrases which the English language borrowed from classical Latin, the language of the Roman Empire. Some are so common that everyone knows their meanings.

"Ad lib," for example. It is an abbreviation of "ad libitum," meaning "at pleasure." We use it also to mean "to speak offhand, without notes." Or "status quo," which refers to "the existing situation or state of affairs."

English borrowed many words and phrases and anglicized them, made them to look English in form and function. But many Latin phrases came to English in Latin form and have stayed that way. "Ad infinitum" is a Latin phrase whose form has never changed. It still means "endlessly, to infinity." "He played the same tune, 'ad infinitum.'"

An example of a Latin phrase which made the trip to English in its original form and altered forms is "vox populi." It means "voice of the people" and is used in the context of popular opinion. Both "vox" and "populi" have come to English as different words in different forms. The words "vocal," "voice," and "vocation" derived from "vox." "Population" from "popular," and "populist" from "populi."

I studied Latin as a freshman and sophomore in high school, so most of my life I've been aware of the extent of the influence of Latin.

Some linguistic experts place the percentage of Latin derived words in English as high as seventy-five percent. We have borrowed heavily from French and less so from Spanish and Italian. These tongues, in addition to Portuguese and Romanian, are called romance languages, meaning they derived from Latin, which in turn means that most French words we borrowed have Latin roots. The percentage may even be higher.

But what about all those folks who have never had the opportunity or the inclination to study Latin? They are at a real disadvantage.

Take the word "intramural," for example. Most of us recognize that the word is often used in connection with school athletics. What is meant by the phrase "intramural sports"? Those familiar with Latin instantly recognize "intra" as meaning "within," and "mural" as deriving from "murus," meaning "wall." The *Merriam-Webster's Tenth New Collegiate*

Dictionary says the word "intramural" means "being or occurring within the limits of a community, organization, or institution." Thus, "intramural" sports are "competed only within the student body," or within the walls of the institution.

Thousands of English words are put together in this way with Latin components. Latin is one of the reasons the language of law seems foreign. It is replete with Latin words and phrases. One well-known Latin legal phrase is "habeas corpus," which literally means "you may have the body." In English law, the phrase refers to "a writ requiring that a person be freed from detainment and formally charged." That idea is at the heart of English jurisprudence.

Latin is essential to English. And in many ways, Latin is English. It is more than a connection between the Roman Empire in our democratic republic. It is the major source of our adjectives, nouns, and verbs, the stuff that makes English the richest in meaning of any modern languages.

I have always considered Latin one of the most valuable courses I ever took. Maybe that says something about its importance. Or the people in the class. Or the teacher. Or my none-too thorough language training up to that point, which was ninth grade.

I don't recall doubting Latin's value, even though I was thoroughly aware it was a dead language. Unless I were a Roman Catholic, I would have had no occasion to speak (or sing) Latin. I was a lukewarm Lutheran, so I had no need for Latin in my speech. Latin had other value. Many Latin words not only looked like English words, but they bore direct relationships. I remember thinking the similarities made it easier, except when the English word in the Latin word did not have the same meaning.

The Latin word for "king" is "rex." Obviously, we didn't inherit our word "king" from Latin. Not being intellectually curious enough, I did not follow through. "Rex" was only the nominative singular form of the word. Nine other noun forms, both singular and plural, all begin with "reg-."

Our words "regal," "regale," "regalia," "reign" and "regnum" all come from the Latin word for "king." Furthermore, the Latin verbs "regere" meaning "to rule" and "regnare" meaning "to reign" – eventually came to English in the following forms: "regicide," "regimen," "regime," "regiment," "region," "regent," and "regency." "Monarch" came into Latin during the late Roman empire from Greek. "Monarchy" entered

English during the Middle Ages from French.

The Romans had no word for "king" in the sense that the Anglo-Saxon language did. We didn't borrow the Latin word "rex," but rather words relating to power and royalty of ruling. The words "royal" and "rule" are French, but go back to Latin, the important fact being the French gave the words their meanings.

The word we use first when we think of all these words is "king." It is the basic word and a true English word, Anglo Saxon to the core. Generalizing about English words is easy, depending on which language they came from. "King" is the general word, and quite naturally it is the native English word. When we think of the power of the king, French words like "monarchy," "royal" and "rule" come to mind. When we think of the religious and ceremonial aspects of kingship, Latin words like "regal," "regalia," "regent" and "regimen" are handy.

The three cultures had a lot to do with the nature of the words which came to English. After the Norman-French conquered England in 1066 A.D., their power held sway for centuries. French culture affected the English monarchy. The Church dominated England of the Middle Ages, and Latin was its language. The great borrowing from Latin began during the Middle Ages and accelerated during the English Renaissance.

The English language, however, was a Germanic tongue. Anglo-Saxon words provided the structure of the language. The influence of the ruling French or the tidal wave of Latin words later did not change that. The basic functioning words and the general names for things are mostly native Saxon words. Even though the native Saxon words represent only about twenty-five percent of modern English, they are fundamental, essential. The language could not function without them.

So, what is the influence of Latin words which constitute upwards of sixty percent of our words, directly, or indirectly? Richness, depth, variety, endless choices. The languages of Anglo-Saxon, French, and Latin – representing three cultures and languages – brought rich diversity.

Though I did not catch on to that knowledge during my two years in Miss Greene's Latin class, the groundwork was laid, and when I became an English teacher, it was like stumbling backwards into a gold mine.

The Bounty of the Bard

It seems remarkable that one person out of the hundreds of millions who have spoken and written English during the second millennium, could have had such influence in giving the language its character and color. As a teacher, I impressed on students the bounty bestowed by the Bard of Avon. The problem is we take this instrument of cultural sustenance, yea, of our very existence, for granted.

"It's high time" you heard "the naked truth" about Shakespeare. He was not "a man of few words." He did "yeoman's service," giving the "working day world" hundreds of words and expressions.

"The short and long of it" is he did not "hold his tongue." "By word of mouth" through the centuries, his language has "led a charmed life."

If you've ever said, "not in my book," "love is blind," "what's in a name?" or "not so hot" ... then credit Shakespeare.

If you've used expressions like "cold comfort," "grim necessity," "the crack of doom," or "pomp and circumstance" ... then credit Shakespeare for "method in his madness."

Where did the expressions "elbow room," "strange bedfellows," "fool's paradise," or "brave new world" came from? "As luck would have it," they came from Shakespeare, who "made a virtue of necessity," turning "all the world (into) a stage." He also created these expressions: "the game is up," there's "something in the wind," or "too much of a good thing."

Or suppose you "hold your tongue," "show your heels," "lie low," or "kill with looks." You are using Shakespeare, and it is "as easy as lying."

"Be that as it may," you're reciting Shakespeare when you say, "good riddance," "short shrift," "foregone conclusion," or "out of the question."

If you've ever been called "a laughing stock," "a blinking idiot," "a sorry sight," or "a rotten apple," you have Shakespeare to thank.

Do you use expressions like "a horse of a different color," "every dog has his day," "love at first sight," "no stomach for a fight," "truth will come to light," and "what's done is done"?

Have you ever said, "It's Greek to me" or "It's a mad world" or "... is as white as the driven snow" or "Brevity is the soul of wit"?

44

Which reminds me, these expressions could go on "forever and a day." But this is "the beginning of the end." "The wheel has come full circle." Since "discretion is the better part of valor," I'll "not stand on ceremony," but "vanish into thin air."

"All's well that ends well."

English: A Changing Language in Unpredictable Ways

Bill Bryson, author of *The Mother Tongue: English And How It Got That Way* (1990), discusses the ways in which English evolved. What becomes clear is that change is the dominating factor. One can hardly think of any aspect of language without considering change. In fact, I don't think I would get much argument if I said language is change.

How can a teacher ever settle on a set of dependable rules for the classroom? On one side is this body of students looking to learn how to use the language at an age when they desperately need things to depend on. On the other side is this amorphous mass of symbols on which survival depends, but which ceaselessly alters in some unpredictable, decisive way. That's the way it is with language.

I always found it hard to mount a usage campaign to which students would respond, if I wasn't sure myself of the language premise on which the campaign was to be based. One thing an English teacher cannot allow is wavering or hesitation in the administration of language rules he expects students to master. Right in that sentence is an example of what I mean. The principle is called agreement. We have pronouns to eliminate the necessity of having to use nouns over and over again, when shorter, more direct words may stand in for them.

Here we are, delivering a thought. We use a noun, and then later in the sentence we want to use it again. But that would be redundant, so we call upon a pronoun. If the noun is singular, of course, the pronoun must also be singular. If plural, the pronoun should be plural.

In the sentence above, the noun was "teacher," and fourteen words later comes the pronoun. The noun is singular, so the pronoun must be also. It takes a nimble mind to hold attention on the idea while at the same time thinking about rules of language which have to be applied constantly.

When I began teaching, I found I was not as sure of the principles governing the agreement of nouns and pronouns, and nouns and verbs, as I

45

thought I was. I used great care and was more deliberate in speech, as well as in my writing. I felt strongly about the teaching of rules without being able to apply them myself. I got so I could apply most of them consistently, and that generated my competence to stop students when they ran afoul of a rule.

Back to the sentence. We have a singular noun, so all we need is the singular pronoun. But wait! Late in the sixties and early seventies, the women's rights movement brought on another problem. Note I chose the pronoun "his." Why not "her"?

The custom over the years has been to use the masculine "he," "his," or "him," when the noun or indefinite pronoun to which the personal pronoun refers is either masculine or feminine. A universal pronoun is needed.

Various methods have been tried in recent years to solve the problem. One is to avoid the problem in the first place. That can be done, but in many cases, the alternative is less efficient, less direct, and often more ambiguous, even awkward.

Another is to invent a pronoun. The only one that is anything close to common is the "his/her" combination. That certainly does not encourage fluency. Also, the next problem would be which pronoun will come first, "his/her" or "her/his"? Some have even suggested that a new word be coined: "hisser." Another alternative is to disregard the agreement rule entirely and use the plural form of the pronoun, of which there is only one – "they, their, them."

None of these alternatives seems reasonable. Thus, I reverted to the original rule. I'll take my chances on being labeled sexist over a mechanical hang up in the language. I worked up my stock response in case a student called me on it. It seemed that when push came to shove, I used the masculine pronoun, while trying to find alternate methods.

Change is constant. a certain logic dictates that in order for language to work, some semblance of order must exist. People must agree on certain rules. Most language problems can be solved by applying the rules that work. The exceptions, like the feminine-masculine aspect of the universal pronoun, can be managed against the backdrop of the teacher's consistency in applying the other ninety-nine percent of the rules.

A teacher must have mastered the language, its problems and quirks, to a reasonable extent before he can expect to gain the confidence of that group of students who need things to depend on. See? I used "he" to refer to a "teacher" without a second thought. A "teacher" needs to be confident about his or her language which alters in unpredictable but decisive ways.

Parts of Speech: Nouns

Nouns are a special problem. For several reasons. One is their numbers. Our language has more nouns than all the other functions put together. That's because we have to have names. As the old definition expressed it, we have to have names for persons, places, and things (abstractions). We are also notorious borrowers from other languages, and those borrowings usually stay in the forms of the languages from which they came. We can imagine what that does to our noun forms and their rules.

Actually, the English language has few hard and fast rules for noun forms. That could be part of the problem. Some of the difficulties have to do with singular and plural forms, possessives, and the ever increasing bugaboo of telling nouns from verbs.

Why do pun possibilities seem so common in English? Part of the answer is that nouns pronounced the same and even those spelled the same sometimes have different meanings. Even nouns that sound almost the same cause trouble, but punsters love them. Example, this sign at a reducing salon: "Stop! Look! Lessen!" Or this one in a bakery: "Keep your wait under control. Take a number!"

Another problem is that we use nouns as adjectives as well as verbs. Their forms don't change. We just drop a noun in front of another noun, and we get an adjective modifying a noun. We can appreciate what habits like that can lead to and why anyone learning English as a second language has more than little trouble.

In 1970, the *Chicago Tribune* ran an essay about "modifier noun proliferation." It was an effective parody. Here is a good example:

Have you noticed the new look in the English language? Everybody's using nouns as adjectives. Or to put that in the current argot, there's a modifier noun proliferation. More exactly, since the matter is getting out of hand, a modifier noun proliferation increase. In fact, every time I open a magazine these days or listen to the radio, I am struck by the

47

modifier noun proliferation increase phenomenon. So, I decided to write – you guessed it – a modifier noun proliferation increase phenomenon article.

When Bruce Price, the essay's author, got to the end, he had used a nineteen-noun modifier noun proliferation. Though exaggerated, it is not far from actual practice. With the hazards of using nouns, is it any wonder learning to use English effectively is rather trying? We would think that making nouns plural would be easy to do. Just add "s," right? Wrong!

Nouns ending in "sh," "ch," "s," "x," or "z," require "es." How about nouns ending in "y" with a preceding consonant? Change "y" to "i" and add "es." Then we have nouns ending in "f" (half, leaf), which require changing the "f" to "v" and adding "es." Some nouns ending in "o" (echo, tomato) also take "es."

How about those whose plurals are the same as the singular (sheep, elk)? Or those most common of the common nouns that form plurals without any "s" at all (man, woman, child)? Remember that proper nouns do not follow these rules, just the basic "s" and "es" endings are needed.

These examples suggest the snarling we have in English. Maybe this bit of doggerel will be a reminder of our affair with nouns: If more than one mouse is mice, then more than one spouse is spice. Fortunately, not many nouns exhibit these problems. The trouble is that those we do have are basic, common nouns like "foot" (feet) and "tooth (teeth).

Here is additional proof about the seriousness of word forms and pronunciation, here is a verse printed some years ago in the *Foreign Language News Bulletin*, State Department of Education, New Mexico:

Who said English is confusing?
Beware of heard, a dreadful word
That looks like beard and sounds like bird.
And dead; it's said like bed, not bead;
For goodness sake, don't call it deed;
Watch out for meet and great and threat,
(that rhyme with suite and straight and debt).
A moth is not a moth in mother.

Nor both in bother, and broth and brother.

If we can scan this headline and pick up its meaning, we are indeed sharp:

Golf courses weather effects of slow start.

Five of the seven words can be verbs. The same five can be nouns. Three could be adjectives. So, where do we start?

Reading English sentences is almost wholly dependent on word order: subject-verb-object, and the variants we learned early in life.

Once we become practiced at our language integrity, we might wonder what was so hard about doing so. Many of us need patience to follow through, even if it takes but a couple seconds. We have too much reading to do to labor through sentences, whether they are in headlines or buried within long paragraphs. What could possibly suffer but meaning?

This dilemma might be compared to travel on the interstate. If potholes and other encumbrances dot the otherwise smooth surfaces, you're bound to have to slow down, take corrective action, while trying to keep your mind on the traffic.

I don't know whether you are now more noun-conscious or not. Reading one English teacher's experience on the subject will achieve little. Only practice and perseverance produce results, and like driving the highways, we cannot take our minds off the task.

Parts of Speech: Verbs

The verb powers the language engine. Although its importance may be likened to a necessary power source, it is more than power. Verbs establish the meanings of sentences. They set the tone of meaning, too.

If in speaking we could direct our attention to choices of verbs, not only would general meaning improve, but also such matters as intention and attitude also would be clarified. If in developing our vocabularies we concentrated on verbs, the rate of language facility would improve more quickly. Verbs give color and texture to language which affect consistency, literacy, and articulation.

One assignment I gave in the fall grammar unit was to write a paragraph at least five sentences long, but no more than ten, in which verbs outnumber adjectives two to one. It is difficult to do and of course not necessary, but dramatic in effect. The only writers who can apparently do that are poets, and the only one who did so consistently was Shakespeare. The effect is to enhance the animation and meaning of sentences (poets do write in sentences).

Here is one of those assignments:

I sat on the hard ground and listened to subtle whispering of the trees. Wind ran past my face, swooped down and chased dry leaves. Chipmunks chattered. Squirrels gathered nuts. Birds packed up belongings and began to leave. Wind changed to snow. Brown became white. The earth slept.

As this paragraph moves from longer to shorter sentences, the verbs remain consistent. They give muscle and depth to the expression. That is why we call them action verbs. All of these verbs – sat, listened, ran, swooped, chased, chattered, gathered, packed (up), began, leave, changed, became and slept – are little engines that give movement and meaning to nouns. The writer was forcing nouns to action, was forcing herself to make judgments and decisions about nouns. That is how meaning is advanced.

The reason for pitting verbs against adjectives is that people tend to overuse adjectives, creating cumbersome, top-heavy phrases.

In writing references for students, I tended to begin by describing students with a lineup of adjectives, such as, "He is a dedicated, dependable, incisive person." If I could verbalize those descriptive words, meanings could be extended, and I could say something concrete:

I can depend on him to turn in assignments by deadlines.
He dedicates himself to the activities in which he participates.
Like a surgeon he incises the toughest of academic problems.

Out of context like that, those sentences may seem somewhat unrealistic, but in context they give muscle and depth to expression about the subject.

I am not trying to discourage the use of adjectives, but simply to show how verbs make things go. Adjectives are static, sitting as they do in front of nouns. Nouns without verbs are also static, ponderous, and by themselves do not convey meaning; nouns can only move when they become subjects of verbs or they themselves are verb forms.

Verbs move meaning. If nouns and their adjectives are to take part in intelligent communication, they must be impelled. Think verbs! See what verbs do to nouns. The example assignment has twelve verbs. Two words are verb forms which have the effect of verbs – "whispering" and "leave."

There are only three descriptive adjectives: "hard," "subtle" and "dry." Each was well chosen, enhancing meaning the same way verbs do.

No language on earth has the power to describe actions the way English does. Our language includes many colorful verbs, which represent a wide variety of actions. The sounds of many verbs even suggest what they mean. According to the MW10NCD, they are onomatopoetic which means:

1. Naming of a thing or action by a vocal imitation of the sound associated with it (as buzz, hiss);
2. Using words whose sounds suggest the sense.

I sometimes gave this assignment when I was trying to get students to think verbals: Find as many verbs as you can which indicate motion of some kind. This investigation usually turned into a useful little game that went far beyond participles, gerunds, and infinitives. We use verbs in various ways. As the year progressed, I saw some students making conscious efforts to apply their new power. One game required finding verbs to describe how certain animals move. One student wrote:

| zebra gallops | flies whiz | puppies scurry | cows hobble |
| antelopes leap | rabbits hop | hippopotamuses wallow | skunks stroll |

Skunks apparently gain a certain amount of respect from man, which allows them to "stroll."

Games then can lead beyond games. They have to if students are to apply what grammar has to teach. Anyway, through all of this activity, the nature of English verbs begins to emerge. Those that describe motion best are one- or-two-syllable Anglo-Saxon verbs, hard and physical in sound, basic and elemental in meaning. These begin with the letters "sl." For optimal effect, say them aloud:

slink, slam, slide, slosh, slice, slog, slug, slop

The sound of words is important. If I think of the meaning of "slink" as I say it, I can picture certain actions with meanings to match. For instance, note this sentence: An animal slinks along a fence. That seems to suggest stealth because of fear or shame. A woman slinks along the street. This time I sense a provocative manner. The word is derived from an Old English word meaning creep, related to another meaning to worm or twist.

Speaking of "twist," see how these words draw some fine lines on the idea of movement: twist, turn, tumble, twirl, twitch. Then I asked students to take several of their verbs and use the participle form, preferably "ing," to finish out phrases by adding four to ten words. Our t-words might be carried out as follows:

twisting in the howling gale
turning the last of the pages
tumbling down the hill with Jack and Jill
twirling her pigtail over her head
twitching nervously before the alarm went off.

Students develop a stronger sense about what verbals are and how they are used, encouraging a sense of the wealth of basic, elemental words which can color and enliven language. These one-syllable Anglo-Saxon verbs of movement provide some daring and defying verbal opportunities: smack, clout, roar, swoop, throb, clip. Imagine how these verbs came into being.

Parts of Speech: Adjectives

Write a paragraph without using adjectives. Doing so is the best way to learn what an adjective is and is not. We're talking about the muscular kind of adjectives that change or modify their nouns. A year later, I received this anonymous paragraph:

> I sat wondering if I would ever write that paragraph. I tried not to use adjectives, but my life and feelings were full of them. I babbled on with no end. Then I let slip an adjective. What a crazy paragraph it was.

What a nice try! My student was never at a loss for nice tries. As usual she had done something which exhibited thinking, application, a nice try. She succeeded in the sense that the only real descriptive adjective is the word "crazy" in the last sentence, put there as a kind of dramatic punctuation, showing that she really understands adjectives better by using them than by not using them.

The seven others are less conspicuous, either because of their nature or because of the manner in which they are used. Two are articles (a form of adjective indicating a noun is coming): "an" in sentence four and "a" in sentence five.

Like the adverb "not," the adjective "no" in sentence three reverses the meaning of the noun it modifies. But that is as far as its modifying goes. "My" in sentence two modifies or alters the word "life" in the sense that it limits it. It's not "your" life, but "my" life.

The word "that" in sentence one is similar in the sense that it points out. It is "that" paragraph, not "this" paragraph.

"Full" is a "full-fledged" adjective. What makes it different is that instead of preceding the noun it modifies, it follows it, or "them" (a pronoun) in this case. It is really my "full" life and "full" feelings.

The final adjective is the least conspicuous of all but may well be the strongest in the paragraph. Since the adjective is a verb form, it carries the power of a verb with it. But its position and use are such that it modifies and does not "assert" as a verb does. The word is "wondering," and it describes the pronoun "I" in sentence one. I am a "wondering I." This kind of verb form is a participle.

So, we have eight adjectives modifying nouns and pronouns despite the effort to curtail them. They are ubiquitous, and that is part of the trouble. We tend to overuse them, and they are easy to use.

The American poet and critic John Ciardi maintained that the poet should strive to use only one adjective for every two verbs. That is a rough assignment, try it. Somewhere I read that the most successful achiever of that two-to-one ratio was Shakespeare in some of his dramatic blank verse. That says something about adjectives, but it says more about verbs.

Parts of Speech: Adverbs

It is easier to intelligently use adverbs than adjectives, but it is easier to use adjectives. So that is what we do: use adjectives badly and adverbs not enough. Since a significant percentage of the populace doesn't know the difference, perhaps a little grammar lesson is in order.

Grammar comes down to managing nouns and verbs, and then knowing how and when to qualify or modify each with adjectives and adverbs. Adjectives perform this function on nouns, and adverbs on verbs.

It is easier to use adverbs well than it is to use adjectives. With adjectives we tend to overuse. We also use them injudiciously, at the wrong times and in the wrong ways. But the main problem is overuse.

With adverbs, the problem is different. We could use them better, but we need to use them more. People do not use them because they do not know how. We come to understand, however, that it is possible to overuse adverbs, too. Some fiction writers tend to modify verbs with adverbs too often. When we overuse constructions in the English language, someone will eventually make a game of it.

Early in the twentieth century, a series of books about the adventures of Tom Swift was the rage with children. They were part of what was called pulp fiction, that is, formula writing. We have it today – just look on the fiction bestseller list.

Back to Tom Swift. His exploits are long forgotten, but the way he said things was memorable. He never simply said anything. Verbs that indicated speech seemed never to be without an attendant adverb. Tom Swift said things thoughtfully, excitedly, or slowly. We developed a word game based on this quirky adverbial habit. The object was "to create an adverbial link between what is said and how it is said, with puns at a premium." It's time for some examples:

'Enough of your fairy tales,' Tom replied grimly.
'You have the charm of Venus,' Tom murmured disarmingly.
'What I like to do on a camping trip is sleep,' said Tom intently.
'What our ball club needs is a man who can hit sixty homers a
     season,' said Tom ruthlessly.

Locating adverbs is easy. Using them wisely is hard. One of the problems is that adverbs are not always single words. They can come in phrases and clauses:

'Quick, Watson, the needle," Tom said in a serious vein.

The idea here is that the word function might well be used more often.
     Making a game of these patterns could lighten up the whole process. Playing the game was the only device that worked fairly consistently.

'OK, I'll have another martini,' said Tom drily.
'The horse won't stop,' said Tom woefully.
'Get to the back of the boat,' said Tom sternly.
'I just lost at Russian roulette,' said Tom absentmindedly.

Parts of Speech: Conjunctions
Lessons in conjunctions are not so uninteresting that they can easily be reduced to a few lines at the end of the discussion of word functions.

Nothing can derail a sentence's meaning faster than misusing a conjunction. Consider, for example, what would happen if the two conjunctions in this sentence simply disappeared.

Ah, ha! You don't know where the two conjunctions are, do you? But forgive me. We need to begin at the beginning.

What is a conjunction? The word itself contains its own definition. That's a good sign that it is a Latin word, which breaks down as follows: con-junc-tion. The process of "-tion" joining "junc" together with "con-."

Conjunctions connect words, phrases and clauses.

There are three kinds. Two are strictly conjunctions; the third is an adverb with a connecting function. The most basic is the coordinating conjunction. It connects equal elements. The subordinating conjunction connects only clauses, one independent and the other subordinate.

It is important in writing to make sure coordinating conjunctions connect equal elements, that is, nouns and nouns, verbs and verbs, etc.

Here's what happens when a writer ignores connectors:

I thought about him and the past two weeks all the way home and all summer.

Things get spread out and awkward. Look closely, and you'll see the culprits are the two conjunctions. Nothing really grammatically wrong exists here; we're just stretching the conjunction function a bit too far.

Three of the seven coordinating conjunctions are common. I asked my students to think of the seven coordinating conjunctions as forming a goal post:

```
and      so
or   nor for
but      yet
```

The left leg contains the most common ones. The right leg contains the least common. And the ones that rhyme constitute the crossbar. To encourage the memory aspect of conjunctions, I suggested that the lighter ones were at the top ("and" and "so"), and the heavier ones were at the bottom ("but" and "yet").

The goal here is to make sure that these short, basic one-syllable words are not taken lightly, that they were right at the tips of tongues. Coordinating conjunctions are the stuff of sentence construction, the mortar linking larger functioning units.

Subordinating conjunctions require a different approach. Although they connect, their real function is to show relationships between major elements of sentences. They connect clauses as they show the relationship between the clauses.

Each of the two preceding sentences has a subordinating conjunction. "Although" in the first, and "as" in the second. These words qualify. The clauses they introduce qualify and or modify the other clause.

Yes, these qualifying clauses are really adverbs, and naturally we call them adverb clauses. Many subordinating conjunctions are needed to introduce them. About thirty-five. They are either adverbs, or they make you think of what adverbs do.

The more common ones are as follows: "because," "unless," "until," "if." "Before" and "after" are also subordinating conjunctions, but they are also prepositions. "When," "where," "whether," and "while" are also subordinating conjunctions.

Conjunctions are not as simple as they first appear. Then there are those conjunctive adverbs referred to earlier. They perform connective functions. There are about twenty-five. Some common conjunctive adverbs are as follows: "therefore," "moreover," "however," "nevertheless," "otherwise," and "consequently." Others are phrases such as "on the other hand," "for example," "for instance."

That in brief is the conjunction chronicle. Those little words are low-level functionaries which can cause mayhem as in this sentence:

In Russia the symphony is told what music they can and can't perform, and then only on certain occasions.

The trouble starts with "and." Someone was not thinking of the fundamentals of one of the most common words in the English language. The reader is hard pressed to tell what the second "and" is connecting in that sentence. Of course, it is also not a good idea to have two "ands" in the same sentence connecting separate sets of words or phrases.

The coordinating conjunction must connect words, phrases, or clauses of equal function. In that sentence it is almost impossible to tell what is to be connected. The important factor is that two or three meanings are now possible. That's the real problem.

Just think about the well-worn phrase, "no ifs, ands, or buts," and you will get a pretty good idea of the importance of conjunctions.

Parts of Speech: Prepositions

> *The grammar has a rule absurd*
> *Which I would call an outworn myth:*
> *A preposition is a word*
> *You mustn't end a sentence with!*
> Berton Braley, *No Rule to Be Afraid Of*

Not a very exciting proposition is the preposition. Teaching it as one-of-the-seven word functions has its hazards. Prepositions do not do the big jobs of language, as nouns, verbs, and adjectives do.

Rather, prepositions are connectors; they relate words to each other. I employed the following job description in my classes: the preposition shows a relationship between its object and another word in the sentence.

The word "preposition" itself can be traced to the Latin verb "praeponere" which means "to put in front." The preposition precedes its object. We call what results a prepositional phrase. Some examples: "from the beginning," "in trouble," "upon your honor," and "despite the storm."

The pattern is always the same: "within earshot," "by me," or "above the fray." First comes the preposition, then its object, with modifiers in between: "Beyond all comprehension," or "across the sparkling lagoon." A kind of rhythm attends prepositional phrases: "down the road," "near the lake," "like a scholar," and "to the end." My students placed parentheses around prepositional phrases when asked to identify them. Like these: "through the morning" or "on the roof."

A preposition is the word to which its phrase relates. Prepositional phrases modify these words. They are really adjectives and adverbs modifying nouns and verbs. Examples: "go (during the break)," "the fence (along the road)," "the view (outside my window)," "ride" (past the first gate).

The first and last are adverb phrases. They modify verbs "go" and "ride." The two in between are adjective phrases modifying the nouns "fence" and "view."

Something to remember is that the preposition provides the glue that

58

connects and relates other words: "the shelf (beneath the sink)," "tell (about your experience)." "Beneath the sink" identifies "shelf." "About your experience" modifies the verb "tell."

The most important consideration is choosing the right preposition. Each one expresses a certain relationship, but it is easy to choose wrong relationships and hence wrong prepositions.

Some critics say that it is impossible to consistently choose prepositions accurately. Language guru, Sydney J. Harris, said that prepositions are "utterly capricious, peculiar, and arbitrary." He cited some examples. "In England people get 'in' and 'out' of a train. In America we get 'on' and 'off' it."

"And," continued Harris, "who knows why we tamper 'with,' but tinker 'at;' why we find a fault 'in' a person but find fault 'with' him." Usually if you think about it and perform a little research, you will find the preposition that clearly represents the relationship you want to show.

A student wrote, "As a young man he became skeptical 'toward' the church." I ran a red line out to the margin and wrote the preposition "of."

Another time I encountered, "Conrad had much time to contemplate 'about' life and men." On another line to the margin I put "not necessary."

But what preposition is used may be important because accuracy may be involved. A common problem involves "between" and "among." These prepositions separate things. "Between" separates two, "among" distinguishes among three or more. Here are two sentences which can easily remind one of the differences:

He distinguished 'between' the two objects.
She must share that 'among' five persons.

There are exceptions to this rule. "Apart from discussions 'among' Washington, Paris, and London on the prospective conference..." Clearly 'between' would be preferable, despite the rule. But this is an exception.

Without subjects and verbs and their various forms, writing sentences is impossible. When you look at a list of prepositions and compound prepositions, you might conclude that even though you cannot write sentences, you can string together meaning with only prepositional phrases, limitations notwithstanding. I challenged students to write something using only prepositional phrases. Only the title "First Date" in the following student poem is not a prepositional phrase:

In his best suit	up the walk	for her	among friends
at his home	with doubt	in a box	on the dance
amid confusion	at the door	of flowers	floor
out the door	across the room	out the door	at midnight
to his car	to the porch	to the car	to her home
down the street	in her best dress	up the street	up the walk
at her house		to the dance	without doubt.

Parts of Speech: Pronouns

Pronouns may be the easiest of the seven word functions to master. They are short words. There aren't very many of them. They seem easy to grasp because they serve such a direct and useful function, i.e., giving us substitutes for nouns especially proper nouns. Piece of cake, right?

Wrong! Pronouns are pesky and painful. Because they are only substitutes, we take liberties with them, expect them to carry their "direct and useful function" no matter how we apply them.

Do we really know the difference between "I" and "me"? "He" and "him"? "We" and "us"? "She" and "her"? "They" and "them"? "Who" and "whom"? "Its" and "it's"?

When someone says, "They say it will be cold," who is "they"?

We invent nouns by tens of thousands, but why can't we find a pronoun that stands for a person, a citizen, a human being, to replace the age-old but misplaced usage of masculine pronouns standing for all people, both male and female.

And the use of the noun "thing" to stand for everything or nothing in particular. "I have to do my thing" can mean anything or just something. What we are doing is using "thing" as a pronoun, and as we know, pronouns can substitute for just about anything. Not very good for accuracy and precision of expression.

What is the antecedent of "thing"? Every pronoun must have an antecedent, the noun to which the pronoun refers. Ambiguity has its place in language, but not laziness. As a practiced teacher, I learned that pronouns provide the most rapid access to students' understanding of, and ability to apply the rules of, language. Pronouns are a problem because their misuse causes awkwardness, misunderstanding, and inaccuracy.

Check these differences: "A clever dog knows (its, it's) master." In the first case, the dog understands its (who the master is) master. In the second, the dog knows that it is (it's) the master. Quite a difference. Or try this one. "My brother likes golf better than (I, me)." In the first, my brother likes golf better than "I" like golf. In the second, my brother likes golf better than he likes "me." The difference could cause hard feelings.

As for high school seniors, I discovered in a hurry whether they knew about pronouns. I gave short tests like the following. Quick fifty-fifty type choices. A practiced, nominally-educated American should be able to buzz through it in thirty seconds, forty-five at most. If it takes more than one minute, chances are the person is wasting time in their use of language mechanics.

Here is the exercise. Each entry is a complete sentence:

1. (You're, Your) now going to practice.
2. Just between you and (I, me), who did it?
3. (Who's, Whose) idea is this?
4. (Their, They're, There) worth the effort.
5. (Its, It's) an interesting study.
6. The only one at home was (I, me).
7. (I, me) was the only one at home.
8. (Its, It's) problems are many.
9. (Who, Whom) do you want?
10. (Their, There) are many picky people in the world.

We can scarcely utter a sentence without a pronoun. We cannot write very long without them. We read only so far before we are keeping people, things, and ideas straight with pronouns. When writers do not keep their pronouns, antecedents, and verbs consistent, misunderstandings can occur as in this student sentence:

The ear has three main parts of which extends deep in the skull.

Like all pronouns, "which" must have an antecedent. "Which" refers to "parts," which is plural. Therefore, the verb "extends" needs to agree with its subject, which is "which." The verb should actually be "extend."

My students used to ask, "What's the difference? You understand what I mean." The phrase "which extends" gives the impression that this is a single thing extending in (into) the skull. But it isn't. It is three main things (or parts). Accuracy certainly is involved here.

Then there is the problem of case. Some pronouns have different forms, which are used in the different functions. For example, "they" is used as a subject in sentences; "them" functions as direct object or object of preposition. A student wrote in a narrative:

> She let out a scream and then immediately told my brother and I to get into the house.

'I' is the subject form; 'me' is the object form. This is an object function.

In this sentence, the reverse occurred: "Music is something that I think us humans just couldn't get along without." "Us" is a pronoun giving emphasis to "humans," and since "humans" is used as a subject, the pronoun form should be "we." There probably will not be a misunderstanding, but the constructions are awkward. A sure sign of something short a nominal language education. Try this sentence:

> By the time a student begins their junior year in high school, they probably are thinking about what they will do after they graduate.

This student writer used the plural form "they" three times and "their" once. The antecedent for all four pronouns is "student," which is singular. The chief alternatives are "his" or "her."

Until about twenty-five years ago, the standard practice was to use the masculine form to cover both genders. It certainly is handy. "Her" works fine, too, but since it is relatively unfamiliar in this role, many shy away from it. So, the equal rights movement has caused quite a problem, as anyone who reads and writes very much will testify.

One alternative is the catch-all and rather awkward form "his/her." In speech particularly, many are using "their" to avoid the problem. But to the practiced eye and ear, this usage is more awkward than "his/her." And it definitely is inaccurate. Another alternative is to change "student" to "students" (change "begins" to "begin"), and poof! The problem is solved. But it doesn't always work that easily.

Another test. No fifty-fifty choices this time:

1. But everyone's perception of things is different.
2. Just between you and I, case is important.
3. Some parents feel embarrassed talking to their children about sex.
4. Each pronoun should agree with their antecedent.
5. Her and her classmates are thinking about graduation.

It should be quite clear from this pronoun essay that there is an immense difference between learning rules and passing tests, and mastering those same rules in practice, in everyday speech and writing. Though it is the individual student's responsibility to learn and apply, the teacher can provide opportunities, persistence, and the support necessary to encourage the process.

Pronouns are handy, short words in short supply. Their function is direct and useful. They are a measure of language mastery.

Parts of Speech: Indefinite Pronouns
Believe it or not, I've wanted to write about indefinite pronouns for quite some time. Don't ask me why. I guess I feel it's part of my professional responsibility to elaborate on my work, even though one may ask who wants to hear about pronouns, especially indefinite ones. Aren't there enough things indefinite about English already?

My work remains the English language. Of all its phases, the one least adored is structure, or function, or mechanics. You know what I'm getting at – grammar.

Of all the elements of English grammar, the one with the most elusive set of rules is the pronoun. There are six or seven kinds of pronouns, depending on how you view them. And the most elusive of all are the indefinite pronouns. Mostly because of what they are – indefinite.

Why do we want indefinite pronouns when what we need to be is definite? As authorities are supposed to respond – good question!

In using language, there comes the time when we must be indefinite. We have thirty-two of these slippery noun substitutes. Well, that is what pronouns are – substitutes. Substitutes for nouns.

Pronouns are the means by which we can write about a person and not have to repeat the person's name every time it is used. But, as you already know, if you are required to use standard English in anything you do, pronouns can quickly get out of hand.

Four of thirty-two indefinite pronouns end in "thing." You know them. You use them all the time. "Anything," "everything," "something," and "nothing." It doesn't take a degree to figure out that originally these four were eight words: "any," "thing," "every," "thing," "some," "thing," and "no," "thing." Yes, "no thing" is how we got "nothing."

Maybe you never thought of it that way. Users of English have been combining words to make new words for centuries. We still do it regularly.

The word "thing" is a noun. But it is a kind of pronoun-noun, because a "thing" has to be "something," "anything," even "everything" or "nothing."

So, what does the noun thing refer to? When someone says, "I have to do my thing," what precisely does "thing" mean? The noun "thing" has a crutch word. All accurate pronouns do, they have antecedents, that is, the nouns to which they refer. Ambiguity has its place in writing, but imprecise pronouns are not ambiguity, but laziness. We would rather not search for precise words. It's too much trouble.

Understanding that some knowledge and care are necessary, let's look at these pronouns called indefinite. Sometimes it is handy to have words that allow us to be accurate in a general way. For example, how many is "few," or "some," or "several," or "many." We cannot be exact always.

If someone asks you whether you would like some peanuts, it is easier to say, "I'll have a few," than to say ten, twenty, or twenty-three. Indefinite pronouns are handy. Pronouns like "all," "none," "each," "every," "most," and "more" allow dealing with numbers in reasonably accurate ways.

Did you know about little families of indefinite pronouns? The pronoun "any" led to "anyone," "anything," and "anybody." "Every" did the same thing: "everyone," "everything," "everybody." The same with "some": "someone," "something," "somebody."

It worked a little differently with "none," but the idea is the same: "no one," "nothing," "nobody."

Most of the rest of the indefinite pronouns deal with numbers. I guess all indefinite pronouns do to some degree. But these definitely do: "one," "both," "either," "neither," "other," "others," and "another."

For accuracy, "much" and "such" may also be indefinite pronouns.

Although the thirty-two indefinites have paraded before you, you are not guaranteed appropriate use of them for the rest of your life. But in the name of language integrity, I thought it could do no harm.

Back in the first paragraph, I wrote a sentence which required the use of an indefinite pronoun. I'm having second thoughts about whether I was fair in choosing the one I did. Here is the sentence with the pronoun duly noted: "I guess I feel it's part of my professional responsibility to elaborate on my work, even though 'no one' wants to hear about it."

The only pronouns that will fit are "many," "most," "nobody," and "few." Logic eliminates "many" and "most." "Nobody" has the same effect as "no one." It appears "few" will work, and I'd like to think it is more accurate than "no one."

Please indulge me in this exercise of indefinite pronouns. No matter how you or I feel about it, mastering their use is important. They say you'll be in perpetual trouble if you don't.

Now, I've committed a pronoun sin. "They say…." Who is "they"? But that is another pronoun problem, and I think we've had enough just to get us this far.

Changing Forms and Functions of Words

A major change in English grammar has been the altering of the relationship between forms and functions of words. Form has become less important; function is as important as always. More important are the reasons that form has become less dependable in determining function.

Words must function if they are to be useful, even though their forms have changed in the name of simplification. It hasn't made grammar any easier to understand and to use, and especially to teach. Try an example: English has a number of simple one-syllable words that are forced to do many jobs (functions), but never change form. Let's look at "like."

Of the seven functions words can perform, "like" is capable of five of them. It can be a noun: "I never saw the 'like' before." It can be a verb: "I like you." "Like" can modify, as an adjective: "They have like characteristics." It functions as a preposition: "She performed like a true champion." This is probably the world's most important function.

It would be better if the fifth function did not exist, but it does. That is, "like" as a conjunction: "I love to feel grown up, 'like' when my parents go out of town." This awkwardness is caused by ignorance of "like's" functions. However, the usage is not going away. We must face facts, "like" is widely used as a conjunction. Language has no other word which can conduct direct comparisons as efficiently as "like" can.

"Sparkle 'like' the dew." In this case, "like" is a preposition, whose job is to relate its object to another word in the sentence. It is reassuring to find when reading the two elements of a comparison easily and quickly. Using the word "like" to "connect" rather than "relate," clouds its usage.

The ever-dependable *Elements of Style* does not mince words:

'Like' is not to be used for 'as.'
'Like' governs nouns and pronouns; before phrases and clauses
    this equivalent word is 'as.'

That is why I have always liked this "little book." That is why for many years I supplied my students with copies, not to be checked out and then checked back in, but kept, and used. Like most other disciplines, language needs rules and someone with authority to set down those rules clearly, directly. Believe it or not, students like rules, especially dependable rules.

Listen to Strunk and White lay it on the line: "The use of 'like' for 'as' has its defenders; they argue that any usage that achieves currency becomes valid automatically. This, they say, is the way language is formed: It is and it isn't."

An expression sometimes merely enjoys a vogue, much as an article of apparel does. "Like" has long been widely misused by the illiterate; lately it has been taken up by the knowing and the well informed, who find it catchy, or liberating, and who use it as though they were slumming.

If every word or device that achieved currency were immediately authenticated, simply on the ground of popularity, the language would be as chaotic as a ball game with no foul lines. For the student, perhaps the most useful thing to know about "like" is that most carefully edited publications regard its use before phrases and clauses as simple error.

Earning a reasonable mastery of language has always been considered part of an education. I was not reticent in taking up its cause in my classroom. One of my formidable adversaries was television. Since most people do not know the difference between "like" and "as," and relish using slang and nonstandard English, advertisers figured to sell more cigarettes and hamburgers if a little grammatical mischief was performed. Quite a few years ago, it was, "Winston tastes good – like a cigarette should." Some years later, "Nobody can do it 'like' McDonald's can!" In each case, "like" is connecting two clauses.

Clauses are groups of words containing subjects and verbs. Some are independent and can be sentences all by themselves. Some are dependent, or subordinate; i.e., when they are connected to independent clauses, they show a relationship between the two clauses. But subordinate clauses cannot be sentences by themselves. They function within independent clauses but are not independent.

The magic word that makes a clause dependent and not independent is the word which introduces the subordinate clause, the subordinating conjunction. In McDonald's magic ad line, "like" is functioning as a subordinating conjunction, which is the means by which the relating of the two clauses takes place.

But "like" is a comparing word, not a relating word. "Sparkle 'like' the dew." "Dew" is being compared to whatever it is that "sparkles." No such comparing is going on in "Nobody can do it 'like' McDonald's can." It is a relating, that is, "as McDonald's can" or "as well as McDonald's can." Comparing is relating, but not all relating is comparing. Clear comparisons are hard enough to come by without bastardizing the one word in the language which can compare directly and clearly.

As with most fads the use of "like" is carried to extremes. In the late-1960s and early-1970s, adolescents used "like" to start almost any verbal utterance. The usage went from a stay against not having anything to say, to a cool social nicety.

One of my editors of the student newspaper came into the habit. Like many of her classmates, she often began many of her spoken sentences with "like." It was especially noticeable in her because she was intelligent and otherwise quite articulate.

During a talk we were having in private, I told her firmly what she was doing. I also told her she didn't do it in her writing. I said, as a student leader, she could really have influence over such matters.

I never heard her use the word incorrectly again. That is a hard habit to break, because it becomes almost a reflex. She must have performed amazing mental gymnastics to rid herself of that habit so quickly.

So, among other functions, "like" is a preposition, which relates its object to another word in a sentence, and thereby carries out a comparison. The English language is full of long-established, colorful phrases, which describe in their comparing. Here are a few: like a breath of spring, like a bump on a log, like a ton of bricks, like an open book, like clockwork, like the wind. Those are clear and direct comparisons, so much so, in fact, that one need not bother to include the rest of the comparisons.

When "like" relates phrases and clauses, however, all sorts of problems develop. I listed examples of the misuse of "like" found in student writing. The ten examples that follow all involve the misuse of "like" except one. Also, one of the examples is not a sentence. Note how the function of "like" is not nearly as clear as in the direct comparisons:

- No matter what I wrote, it didn't come across on paper, like it had in my mind.
- Like I said before I do enjoy being around people.
- He apologized like the good sport he is.
- I hope he doesn't act like he did yesterday.
- Just like no two snowflakes are the same, no two people are the same.
- Critiques talked of the movie like it was 'Gone with the Wind.'
- It's like he has to gasp for air for each breath he takes.
- But with the demand and efficiency increasing, computer prices are dropping like calculators did.
- Just like we've always been doing it.
- I feel somehow rested, like I am at peace with myself.

A mature observation can be cut short by an immature use of "like": It's like Mother Nature is giving a last farewell before she closes the door on summer.

To most Americans, the previous examples are acceptable. They transmit their meanings. What more can one ask? Indeed, what can one ask? It is an example of what misuse can lead to. In the following three sentences, it seems the problem with "like" is leading to other difficulties:

1. I like the idea of hunting game like primitive people.
2. This is because they are supposed to be very temperamental like women are, and just as unpredictable.
3. Each type of wine has its own special glass, just like bottles.

In sentence 1, the writer expects "like" to act as a subordinating conjunction, and then fails to provide the subordinate clause with a verb. In sentence 2, the looseness of the construction seems to allow for "unpredictable" to modify "they" or "women," which are clearly not the same things. In sentence 3, the implication is that "bottles" are like "glass." The writer failed to produce a verb for the subordinate clause.

It becomes clear that as important as a functional word as "like" is it needs a clear path to the recognition of its function. The word can have five functions, but never changes form. Users of English must develop a precise sense for what the word does. I found the following sentence on a paper written by a senior:

It's like your all by yourself in a place no one ever goes.

How do I ever begin to counsel a student who will let such a sentence get through? And no word processor can detect any of the problems. No words misspelled: yet on the face of it, the grammar is chaotic. The student told me, "But you understand what I mean." This vehicle of your thoughts has several mechanical failures, and I don't think I will ride along with you. We are sure to have a breakdown.

"Like" is the only word with multiple functions. Here is another, the word "back." Five functions, five examples:

I can strain my back.   I can back a team.
I can try the back door.   I can come right back.

And with a little help from a fellow word, I can stay back of the fence.

"-ize" Verbs?

I remember students wondering aloud, "What's wrong with '-ize' verbs?" Nothing, but like most useful patterns in English, it can be "extremized."

It takes little effort to think of a noun, and then think of it as a process, as action. No doubt that is how the useful "-ize" verbs got their start. "Summarize," "materialize," "harmonize," "scenarioize" are "abominations," as *Elements of Style*, Strunk & White's famous little book of usage, calls such verbs.

The suffix "-ize" means to "submit to the action indicated by the root of the word as in "burglarize" and "hospitalize" or to make like the thing indicated in the root as in "sterilize" and "slenderize." The problem is keeping the use of "-ize" within reason. The following verbs are standard, useful, specific in meaning: "organize," "harmonize," "jeopardize," "criticize." We would never question their value. Their use is established, integrated to the language. They have been employed by writers for centuries. It is easy to set an eye on their meanings.

According to MW10NCD, "Thomas Nashe (1567-1601) claimed credit for introducing it to remedy the surplus of monosyllabic words." Most were not necessary and caused awkward formations. One scholar said he "folderizes" his ideas until he is ready to use them. Once I heard a news radio announcer say, we will have "to 'detailize' future snow removal operation" (1979). One of my students turned in a vocabulary card in 1983 with his illustrative sentence: "I want to be aware of what others expect but not 'despotized' by it" (*Notes to Myself*, Hugh Prather). "It was a Mendelssohn's 'recitalizing' which resulted in the popularity of (the music)" came from a classical radio station (1988). The malady even spreads to other countries.

In a student's paper one time, I saw "agatizing." This use appears to be typical student carelessness or frustration at the maze of hopeless language usage problems. I have been told it also was an attempt to coin a new word from "agitate" and "advertise," which, thankfully, did not take hold. The question in deciding such matters: is the word necessary? If a reasonably educated populace can run that test, most such coinages will disappear.

But Mr. and Ms. Careful Writer, why is it that when an English teacher attempts to put the hex on such habits, students show little curiosity? They do not seem to be interested in reasoning with the problem. They do not place high enough value on the skill of language.

Usage Rules and Language Integrity

Teachers have no foolproof method of checking out students on usage rules. In this age of visuals, however, the sets of simple, widely used, one-syllable forms seemed to tell me a lot about students. The forms "its-it's," the three forms "too-to-two" and the three forms "there-their-they're" are real tests of usage rules.

If students have developed a fairly strong integrity of language, then they seldom misuse or misspell these eight forms. It is easy to misuse one inadvertently. However, I seldom saw such misuses or misspellings since my students were responsible for catching such errors.

When students misspelled or misused any of these forms, I considered them spelling errors. Then, in spelling tests, composed entirely of words students misspelled in compositions, I dictated short sentences using the form I wanted spelled. Here is an example using "there-their-they're":

_____ coming back.
_____ will be tests.
Will they get _____ act together?

Students were forced to think of the forms in the context of sentence. No other certain way exists to distinguish among the forms. In the first example, the "-ing" form of the verb requires a helper, and the sentence needs a subject. So, "they're" or "they are" must be the form. Only the expletive "there" will fill the bill in the second sentence. The third example needs an adjective. The possessive form "their" points out whose act it is.

Whenever possible on the tests, I used the same sentence in which the student misspelled or misused the form. The point being that students sensed a new dimension of language integrity. I tried to come across in a manner that suggested I was trying to help them. Students either knew

71

these forms or they didn't. If they did, they were able to choose the appropriate form with ease. If they did not, I quickly conveyed the idea that I was willing to help them in their campaigns. I called this language integrity, and it was serious business.

In the famous "little book" called *The Elements of Style* (1999), the most useful short volume on English matters, William Strunk resolved "it's" and "its" problem with this example, "It's a wise dog that scratches its own fleas."

The only comment accompanying the example was: "A common error is to write 'it's' for 'its,' or vice versa. The first is a contraction, meaning it is. The second is a possessive."

How could anything be simpler, clearer? But students did not think and apply. They often assumed there must be some rote method of applying rules. Their assumption was faulty.

Do Usage Rules Matter?

Some time ago, the popular game show *Wheel of Fortune* used a phrase in a puzzle which involved the word choice "further-farther." Practically every word was filled out with letters, but attention ran to the first vowel of a word which still had not been found. One contestant guessed the answer to be "Couldn't be further from the truth," and he was declared incorrect. Naturally the next contestant was correct with "farther."

This case was one of hundreds in which fine distinctions could be made, and accuracy was served in the process. After all, we wanted accuracy and fine tuning in language and in the meanings which result.

I consistently called students on usage errors in class. However, gradually I found myself modifying my strictness. What was happening was compromise. Students each year became less and less attuned to careful language use, and I was seeing the limits beyond which any good would come. The result was a subjective standoff. I would quickly judge whether the infraction was worth stopping for, interrupting a train of thought which might not regenerate later.

Someone has to be a language arbiter. Not many of us are left. Parents are in a position to be the most effective ones, but how many can or are willing? We put a lot on the line when we get the reputation for calling other people for their language errors.

The problem of the usage expert was being consistent without being a bore. Many teachers just won't try anymore. Some teachers still call students on errors. Language discipline requires at least strong encouraging from others.

Only three of my colleagues stopped poor student usages in class. Each of them was serious about correcting usage errors; each was respected fully as a professional. As one fellow-teacher of mine used to say, "I'm not here to make friends." That response can have different meanings, but clear accurate language is always about as potent a skill as an individual can take into adult life.

But where do we adults start? I remember thinking, who am I to be calling a student for violation of a rule I myself violate? Does it really make a difference whether it is "further" or "farther," "like" or "as," or whatever? If I don't have that strip of chrome replaced along the right rear fender of my car, will it really make any difference? It has no effect on the vehicle's operation. The car would look better with the strip back on, but it lies in the trunk. The residue of the plastic backing on the fender is peeling and rust is beginning to corrode the exposed areas. It doesn't affect the operation of the car, and it probably never will, but there it is.

We have hundreds of language distinctions and rules that are part of the fabric of our language, the language, which, in turn, is part of our beings. What we say and how we say it will always have an effect on how meaning is perceived and received.

If I had written, always have an "affect" instead of "effect" in the last sentence, would anyone have noticed? Would it have made any difference in meaning? Maybe, because most people who are in a position to act upon what a writer is writing, will recognize the error. They might ask, "If I do not care any more about the vehicle that conveys my thought than that, what will be the value of my thought?" At least, an error is a distraction from the more important matter of trying to follow thought. I'm always afraid that the thoughtful person in the best position to use the ideas I am writing about is probably going to note imprecise language. I found this group of words on a student's paper:

I do know that the most important thing that I want in my life is happiness.

It's one of those temptations that comes to English teachers occasionally. It seems to be the perfect straight line, but I restrained myself and wrote in the margin: "You must love words to take 16 to say that."

One reason this sentence strayed so far beyond its writer's intentions is that he wasn't sure what he wanted to say, but felt he had to say something. Another reason is the inexperienced writer will qualify as he goes, not paying much attention to what modifier goes here and what clauses go there.

But the most serious problem is that the student did not check over what he had written. Most practiced people – and we're all daily practitioners of language, are we not? – could look this sentence over and see there are not sixteen words-worth-of-meaning.

This same message might be sent by the headline writer, "Student Wants Happiness." A telegram might say: "Important – Send Happiness." In a straightforward declarative sentence, it might be "My greatest desire is to achieve happiness."

Student writing will tend to be wordy and clumsy if someone does not offer guidance. That's the teacher's job. Not just English teachers. But how can students master usage rules without understanding the structure of English sentences? Yes, the g-word, "grammar." Students are asked to learn usage rules without understanding the basis for them. No one has patience with rules which cannot be traced to substantial reasons. Those reasons are becoming more and more inconsistent as we bend and break rules which were consistent and basic.

I found many students did not relate the fundamentals of English grammar to the practice of English usage. That without doubt is the major difficulty in teaching about the English language.

As an example, let's consider a serious and widespread anomaly. That is the matter of nouns and verbs taking exactly the same forms. For example, let's use a word which has uplifting connotations. The word is "smile."

The smile is the most enduring and endearing feature of the human countenance. Women can be overwhelmed by a man's smile. Men can dissolve into dazes by a woman's smile. And a child's smile carries the magic of all humanity. When someone smiles at me, I am touched or moved, which makes me wonder why I do not smile more. All endearing and enduring characteristics of humankind seem to be inherent in a smile.

Like so many human actions, the English word expressing the act of smiling is the same as the word expressing the action. According to the MW10NCD, a "smile" is "a change of facial expression in which the eyes brighten and the corners of the mouth curve slightly upward and which expresses especially amusement, pleasure, approval, or sometimes scorn." The same source says "smile," the verb, means "to have, produce, or exhibit a smile."

Since the word "smile" can be both a noun and a verb, I thought you might give it a go (See, I'm just like the rest of us. I used "go" as a noun when "try" or "attempt" would have worked as well, though both can be verbs, too).

Each sentence below contains he word "smile" or one of its forms. If "smile" is a noun, underline once; if verb, underline twice.

1. Smile, you're on candid camera.
2. Try smiling once in a while.
3. Can certain people's smiles upset metabolism?
4. The eyes are what really smile.
5. With a smile like that, who needs laughter?
6. Smile when you say that.
7. Alright, don't smile.
8. If you try to smile at him, he looks away.
9. But I will continue to smile at him.
10. Smiling Lou Jacobs' clown face was the emblem of circus pleasure for over 60 years.
11. Will you smile at me again?
12. Corey smiling sets soul a singing.
13. Her smile melts metal.
14. I will never forget that smile.
15. I'll bet you're not smiling now.

Of these fifteen uses of the word "smile," four are nouns, six are verbs, and five are combinations of functions because they are verbals.

If you have had enough, you may go your way, though you will not find out "farther" was the wrong answer to the *Wheel of Fortune* puzzle.

If not, check the definitions: a noun names, a verb asserts. A verbal is a verb form which retains the characteristics of a verb though it has other functions, one of which is a noun. Which two forms of "smile" are adjectives, which modify or alter nouns and pronouns? We unconsciously learn these functions of words as children. We learn them by use. We mimic them in others. We learn to speak by the rules of grammar, and to one degree or another, master them.

As we mature, the problems of usage arise in inverse proportion to the degree we did this unconscious mastering. The students I remember as having the most developed writing skill were those who seemed to understand language structure best. They may not have been proficient in the formal study of grammar, but they were able to make grammar work for them. That, of course, is the important thing.

Now how about those who have not absorbed these principles along the way? Somehow English teachers have to be able to communicate with those students about the language and its structure.

Grammar is unavoidable. But we make it a cold, hard, unappetizing venue of language study in the classroom. We have not wedded it to language use. Until we manage that, the problem will continue, causing us to move further and further from being articulate as a society.

Oh, yes, about "farther" and "further." William Strunk, Jr. and E.B. White's useful little book on English usage discusses the matter thus:

> The two words are commonly interchanged, but the distinction is worth observing: 'farther serves best as a distance word, 'further' as a time or quantity word. You chase a ball 'farther' than the other fellow; you pursue a subject 'further.'

And on the game show, you "couldn't be 'further' from the truth."

Dictionaries in the Classroom

The dictionary is changing. It has become less the expert, the court of resolution, than the reporter, the recorder of usage. We all know that is not raising the standards of language. People who do not use dictionaries tend to think they are the last word in settling language disputes. That is not true, if it ever was. It reports usage, and if a word is used long enough it will be recorded in *Merriam-Webster's Tenth New Collegiate Dictionary*.

I suppose that is a fair role for lexicographers: they record usage, and what they found is the dictionary. They are not proclaiming what is acceptable and standard and what is unacceptable and nonstandard. Lexicographers record the facts, and people decide how to use words.

We do not have many places to go to find the arbiters of language. If the dictionaries are not one of those, then the field of experts is narrowed to individuals whose experiences and position put them in a mode to be expert, e.g., William Safire of the *New York Times*. Very few people want to accept the mantle of expert on words. My experience tells me we need someone or something to decide certain things about language use. Not dictate, but advise and suggest, something for parents and English teachers to pick up on. It is reasonable to expect the general citizen's education will include instruction and experience in the debate of word use. Unless we have some experience in common with words and their use, how can an intelligent linguistic citizenry develop?

It was an editor of *Merriam-Webster* who said the dictionary "represents a reflection of society." If we do not like what we see, we can make it part of education to see that it is discussed, debated, and reported.

Me: I told you, it's under your desk.

Student: Why is it there?

Me: To make it easier to use when you need it.

How many times I have said *that* is impossible to calculate. Habits are hard to change. When I began keeping dictionaries under student desks, I was trying to encourage better language habits.

After all, when the need to search out a word arises, it is easy to talk your way out, or rising and walking to the shelves where dictionaries are and carrying on a search in front of peers. Most students will think, I'll do it later, or I'll let someone else do it, or I don't want to interrupt. Rationalizations all. They won't do it later. Someone else may not do it. They know that interrupting to look up a word is not interrupting at all.

So, before the first day in the fall term, I placed one MW10NCD under each student desk. Students put a lot of things under desks. They had their own books, notebooks, purses, and anything else they needed to carry for other classes. Also, to be found were gum wrappers, candy wrappers, lunches, morsels from lunches, scrap paper, coins, notes, crumbs, and plain old dirt. Occasionally an errant crib note turned up.

If that shelf was not cleaned out regularly, the accumulation was startling. Janitors made it a practice to tip the desks so that whatever was underneath would slide out into the aisle for an easy sweep-by with a push broom. However, when all the other stuff slid out, the dictionaries were going to slide out, too. No self-respecting custodian was going to lean over twenty-five times to put dictionaries back under their seats.

I tried a number of strategies. One was having the various classes tip up the desks and carry out the cleanup periodically. The trick was to remember to do it. Another was to campaign students to take care of their own desks. This strategy required even more discipline on my part. The third and least desirable method was to clean them up myself. Somehow, I managed to keep a dictionary within reach of each student.

The secret to language discipline is good habits. With words, it is that automatic reflex that goes with translating a word problem into the reach for the dictionary. I think students saw that I was doing something concrete to encourage their developing these positive language habits. No miracles performed, but I can remember as word problems arose in class, students automatically reached under the seat and pulled out the MW10NCD. No miracles you understand, but it did happen, and what is most important, often without prompting.

I remember one volume lost a battle with a wad of freshly chewed bubble gum. The gum got caught between the dictionary and a shelf. The gum stuck to the back of that MW10NCD for at least a year and a half. And all of this in the name of good language habits.

Me: The dictionary is under the desk.

Student: I know, I know.

The Right Word

A student told me he was going to do an in-depth study of economics for his project. That is a difficult enough subject for trained economists. He needed to do some focusing and limiting of his subject. But what I wanted to know was what he meant by an "in-depth."

As that compound word has developed into an adjective and now treated as a single word. I wondered why this prepositional phrase has been counterfeited to an adjective, albeit in steps: from "study in depth," to "in depth study," to "in-depth study."

It is a 1960s-coinage typical of what has been going on since World War II, when "in" was used as a noun to mean "advantage" or as an adjective meaning "currently acceptable; popular."

Next came the "in thing." Prepositions can be used as adverbs and are widely used to make new verbs and adjectives. Adjectives like "in-house" and "in-service" were common. Other common prepositional-phrase adjectives are "in-print" (in-print volume), "in-flight" (an in-flight procedure), and "in-residence" (in-residence doctor). All are post-WWII coinages except the last one from 1845.

There certainly is nothing wrong with adapting words in this manner. At first, they seem awkward because of their limited use. As a teacher, my main objection to coinages like this is that people use them because they cannot or will not look for better, more precise words. For quite a long time, I noted various uses of "in-depth" and listed other adjectives which would have been as, or more, accurate.

When people say "in-depth" study, they could mean "careful," "exhaustive," "comprehensive," "deep," "penetrating," "thorough," "painstaking," "complete," and even "profound" and "absolute."

No two of those adjectives mean exactly the same thing. One could say a considerable range of meaning exists among them. When employers, editors, and teachers talk about precision in writing, they often mean accuracy in choices of words. A significant difference exists between a careful study and an exhaustive study, between a comprehensive study and a thorough study, between a penetrating study and a painstaking one.

Getting students to find "the right words" when they are searching for meaning is difficult. Developing the desire to demand precision in one's expression must begin early and grow gradually into a top priority. The problem is that we have no quick and easy formulas.

My advice is regular and diverse reading. Watching writers express themselves regularly will encourage the process and broaden experience.

When I noted that students were uneasy about being called "average," I began a search for an alternative. "Normal" was not a good word. Certainly "mediocre" was not. Finally, I began to use "typical." It kept the integrity of being in the center of things without the connotations of dull middle, inferiority, or abnormality which the other words transmitted.

Where we use words is as important as how. When I make a judgment about experience, I may decide it was unique, i.e., one of a kind. If I talk to someone else about it, I may decide to be more conservative, to describe it as "different." Then if that person and I observe someone else and his experience, we may decide to call it "strange."

Each word has a common meaning. Each denotes deviating from a norm, or as the middle meaning has it, "different." "Unique" stresses the original, unusual, novel aspects of the experience. "Strange" stresses the unfamiliar, unusual, peculiar aspects.

The meanings the words have in common are their denotational or dictionary meanings. The meanings which separate them are called connotational, i.e., their figurative sense. The definition I used was "the suggested significance of a word."

Applying an idea socially, i.e., outside one's own mind, is different from doing it privately. Language is a tool which can be worked to suit our own purposes, and not always with accuracy and integrity in mind.

I tried to convince students to determine the general meaning they wanted before settling on a word. Most often we use the first word that comes to mind, especially in speech. But even in writing, we are not selective enough.

One student wrote the following in a character sketch:

It had to be done and he was the only one who had the guts to do it.

What did the writer mean to convey through the word "guts"?

S.I. Hayakawa, the noted semanticist and U.S. senator, published a volume called *Modern Guide to Synonyms and Related Words*. The book is a useful compilation of words with general meanings, each followed by a list of related words. Each word is discussed and explained in terms of the general meaning. For example, one of the entries is the word "pleasing." Following are "agreeable," "attractive," "engaging," "enjoyable," "gratifying," "nice," and "pleasant." Each word is discussed in terms of general meaning, which "pleasing" represents.

Back to "guts." What did my student mean by "guts"? Could we figure out the general meaning into which this word fits? So, I checked Hayakawa's index for "guts." There it was. I was referred to the general category, "stomach," where I found the word, along with "abdomen" and "belly."

Unlike "stomach," "belly," or "abdomen," "guts" applies almost exclusively to the internal organs of the pelvic cavity. In plural, it is a synonym for "entrails" or "intestines" and in the singular, for the entire digestive system, especially that of an animal.

"Guts" emphasizes the earthlier, revolting aspects of the intestines when they are not functioning properly or have suffered injury: the beggar's "guts" growling with hunger; a horse with its "guts" hanging out. "Guts" has the slang, figurative meaning of courage or effrontery: to have "guts" to cross a field under gunfire.

I told my well-meaning student that the slang word "guts" was not the most precise word he could choose. The hallmark of slang expressions is imprecise. Slang marks language as non-standard. Although Americans generally seem addicted to slang, that is no reason to sacrifice accuracy. The hearers of your speech and the readers of your writing, however, expect accuracy.

It is clear from the Hayakawa entry and the context of the sentence that "courage" is the meaning intended. OK, let's see whether "courage" is one of the general categories. It was, with the following synonyms listed: "backbone," "fortitude," "grit," "guts," "nerve," "pluck," and "resolution." I don't remember the precise context of the student's sentence, but he was trying to establish his subject's personal strength and influence. We energetically discussed how a single word can carry characterization.

Teaching vocabulary is a hopeless task unless students are enthusiastically involved. Once students see the value of precision in word choice, they need little urging. I found all I could do was to keep the devices, temptations, and other lures constantly before them. I tried 3x5 cards, implementation of words which turn up in units, testing, all sorts of reinforcements. I tried to make sure words, once they were introduced, reappeared in class use, even if I had to do it myself. You would be surprised how things like that catch on. The best device of all is the dictionary. Keep them handy, within reach if possible. Then maximize the opportunity to use them.

My enthusiasm for language must have had a great deal to do with my teaching. What it comes down to is a respect, a reverence for language; for it is language that makes us what we are. I cannot explain my deep respect and love of language. I don't know why I paid little attention until a lot later in my life. I do know that I did figure it all out by myself. And thirty years of teaching and over thirty years of reading and writing later, I can confirm I have learned a lot. But above all I know the power of words.

Now if I could only figure out a way to convince my countrymen that we hold all the power we ever need, latent though it is, within our facility with language. I don't know whether my student learned anything from our conferring over the word in his sentence, but there is always a chance that he did and that he may have generated the same respect and love of language that I did. Would it not be marvelous if all of this caught on?

Points of View Game
Here is a game which will generate thinking about the diverse and profound capacities of words. It demonstrates a number of aspects of word use. One is the range of connotations that words of the same dictionary meanings can have. Others are the importance of attitude in word choice and, of course, the importance of point of view.

The game or exercise apparently originated with Bertrand Russell. The idea is to find three words or phrases which represent three points of view. The first is what I privately believe. For example, "I compromised." The second is what I will reveal to another person about that person: "You appeased." The third is what that person and I will conclude about a third person: "He sold out."

82

I am wary; you are cagey; he is mistrustful.
I am forceful; you are a trifle pushy; he is domineering.
I made a technical error; you goofed; he made an inexcusable blunder.
I have principles; you have ideology; he has dogmas.

Character is a description of ourselves as we want others to see us.
Language is a tool which can be worked to suit our own selfish purposes.

I am a gourmet; you are a big eater; he is a glutton.
I am sparkling; you are unusually talkative; he is drunk.

This game demonstrates some powerful truths about language use and the
humanity it represents.

Spelling is Not Important?

How important is spelling? Spelling is to writing what pronunciation is to
speaking, and you cannot let the latter get too far out of hand if you want
to be understood or taken seriously. When you stop to think about it, most
misspelled words do not impede the flow of otherwise clear sentences.
They do distract, the way a threatening sound under the hood of your automobile distracts. Somehow misspelled words are associated with the mind
that is composing the sentences. The medium conveys that the ideas must
be amiss.

Idea and language must function as one. If the idea works, it is because the language is working. If the language is working, the idea should
come through. But if the language is not working, the idea is dead even if
it is otherwise valid. Language is the vehicle of meaning. Spelling of
words is a signature of language precision, just as diction is to precision in
speech.

In practice, spelling becomes a serious matter only if it is not corrected along with all the other problems that collect in drafting. Teachers
tend to seize on spelling because it is relatively easy to isolate as a problem. However, it is minor, important only as it affects readers' recognition
of words.

Too many teachers of English think that teaching spelling and grammar is teaching composition. It is not, any more than a skilled mechanic can drive successfully the race car he or she has maintained. In writing, one must be both driver and mechanic because language is personal. Only I can control both and keep them reasonable in perspective. So, I must master reasonable control of word forms as well as develop ideas into clear sentences and paragraphs.

I have heard students say they will always have secretaries or assistants to take care of these details. That is not developing an independence of mind or controlling one's destiny in matters of the intellect. The habits that control these skills should be developed and practiced through all of one's schools. In most cases they are not.

Unfortunately, this job falls almost entirely to the English teacher. These language skills which are almost universal in their application are considered the special territory of the English teacher. I doubt that students can be successfully trained unless these skills are expected in every classroom.

One important reason they are not is that teachers are not trained in them. Therefore, they cannot demand them from students. Many students told me in one way or another that English class is the only place where such matters are discussed, and only a few English teachers required the discipline of these skills.

As a tenderfoot teacher, I was shocked that teachers generally did not enforce language requirements in their classrooms. We were, and are, all language apprentices, but that does not mean ignoring the skills that lead to mastery. Language is difficult, its disciplines hard to master. But I'm afraid that today we are producing perpetual neophytes in our schools.

Practicing spelling evermore will not help much, but I finally figured out a way to use spelling and its idiosyncrasies to get student's attention.

Eats, Shoots and Leaves

> *Punctuation is a courtesy designed to help readers*
> *to understand a story without stumbling.*
> Lynne Truss

I just finished a little book about punctuation. Don't laugh. It was number one on the *New York Times* bestseller list, and it does two things very well. It entertains, while teaching "the traffic signals of language." As anyone in serious linguistic pursuits can tell you, we need that.

I wasn't sure I understood this bestseller phenomenon, until I read *Eats, Shoots & Leaves: The Zero Tolerance Approach to Punctuation* (2003). You're right, some explanation is in order.

First about that title. It's the comma. Consider how the phrase changes meaning when the comma is removed. There's a story here, about the eating habits of the panda. The book's dust jacket explains that a panda walks into a restaurant, ordering a sandwich, eating it, and then drawing a gun and firing two shots into the air.

The dumbfounded waiter asks "Why?" as the panda heads for the exit. Upon producing a "badly punctuated wildlife manual" and tossing it toward the waiter, the panda says, "Look it up."

The waiter finds the explanation. "Panda. Large black and white bear-like animal, native to China. Eats, shoots and leaves." That led to a man-goes-into-a-bar joke, or the panda-goes-into-a-bar joke.

That's a complicated way to achieve a title for such a small volume. It is a dramatic example of how a comma can radically alter meaning.

The author, English journalist Lynne Truss, became so frustrated with the way people ignore the rules that she had to do something about this "world of plummeting punctuation standards." With considerable intelligence, major practical experience, and an affable sense of humor, she thrusts these resources into a major defense of punctuation.

She admits she is a "stickler." We don't hear that word much now, but I can remember my mother using it often decades ago. MW10NCD says a stickler is "one who insists on exactness or completeness in the observance of something."

Truss is definitely a stickler about reasonable language rules and particularly punctuation, whose marks, she says, are "the traffic signals of language: they tell us to slow down, notice this, take a detour, and stop." Note how meaning would change if that last comma were removed.

Her battle cry is "Sticklers unite!" Those of us who practice the rules of punctuation have plenty of reason to insist that others do. It is trying to convince most students to accept the importance of something that less than a decade later they will wish they had learned and practiced. We need to be sticklers. Truss's most revealing statement is one I wish I'd seen when I started teaching:

> The reason to stand up for punctuation is that without it there is no reliable way of communicating meaning. Punctuation herds words together, keeps others apart. Punctuation directs you how to read, in the way musical notation directs a musician how to play.

Why have we so blatantly ignored these road signs of language? How can we bypass a system so useful in preventing traffic tie-ups in sentences?

One of the most dramatic aspects of Truss's work is her use of examples to emphasize points. Some of them look pretty permanent. Carved in stone in a Florida shopping mall one may see the splendidly apt quotation from Euripides, "Judge a tree from it's fruit: not the leaves."
Stickler Truss explains,

> Confusion of the possessive 'its' (no apostrophe) with the contractive 'it's' (with apostrophe) is an unequivocal signal of illiteracy and sets off a Pavlovian 'kill' response in the average stickler.

She points out that the difference is "extremely easy to grasp." "It's" stands for "it is" or "it has." If the word does not stand for "it is" or "it has," then what you require is "its." How could anything be clearer? The apostrophe, which has been referred to as "one of them floating comma things," has an interesting, if checkered, history which Truss summarizes. We can't live with the apostrophe, but we certainly couldn't live without it.

She says imagine the confusion and frustration this headline causes: "DEAD SONS PHOTOS MAY BE RELEASED." Three possibilities: son's, sons', or sons. The first is singular possessive, one son. The second is plural possessive, more than one son. The third, the one in the headline, makes no sense, or at least strains ambiguity beyond tolerance. The headline, Truss said, was intended to be the plural possessive sons.

Then there are commas. The author shares this verse:

A cat has claws at the ends of its paws.
A comma's a pause at the end of a clause.

"More than any other mark," Truss writes, "the comma requires the writer to use intelligent discretion and to be simply alert to potential ambiguity."

It's amazing what we can make words do by manipulating commas. Check out these identically worded sentences:

A woman, without her man, is nothing.
A woman: without her, man is nothing.

Try this one: "The driver managed to escape from the vehicle before it sank and swam to the river-bank." The vehicle did not swim to the bank. A comma clarifies. The following sentence makes sense but is all wrong.

The convict said the judge is mad.

The sentence is in dire need of commas: "The convict," said the judge, "is mad."

Truss examines other punctuation marks like the hyphen, that little horizontal line which marks the mid-point to a phrase's becoming a compound word. We are making far too many of them.

Anyone who knows German understands the frustration compound words can cause. My best example was: "eisenbahnknontenpunkt," a railroad station, literally meaning "iron-road stopping point."

English is proliferating compound words. As Truss asks, "Where should hyphens still go, before we sink into a depressing world that writes:

Hellohowareyouwhatisthisspacebarthingforanyidea

Hyphens alter meaning, too. Example: "A re-formed rock band is quite different from a reformed one."

To us sticklers "… it is a matter of despair to see punctuation chucked out as worthless by people who don't know the difference between 'who's' and 'whose,' and whose bloody automatic 'grammar checker' can't tell the difference either."

Speaking of computers, why can't someone develop a virus that can stop bad grammar. Most viruses are bad – here's one that might be very good. Truss talks about the Strunkenwhite Virus (after *The Elements of Style* by William Strunk and E.B. White) whose function is "refusing to deliver e-mails containing grammatical mistakes."

Would that this practice could happen. This was an idea initiated by Bob Hirschfeld (*Washington Post*, 1999) "for the delight of readers simply to satirize the public's appetite for improbable virus scare stories."

The problems of language mastery run far beyond the rules of punctuation. Even as I was writing this essay, frustration took over and for a while dominated my perspective.

Lynne Truss generates encouragement about writing dilemmas. And it is reassuring to know that others endure the same struggles with language. As she says:

> We may curse our bad luck that 'it's' sounds like 'its;' 'who's'
> sounds like 'whose;' 'they're' sounds like 'their' and 'there;'
> 'there's' sounds like 'theirs;' and 'you're' sounds like 'your.' But if
we
> are grown-ups who have been through full-time education, we have
> no excuse for muddling up.

It's syntactical justice to close with the period. "The full stop is surely the simplest mark to understand so long as everyone continues to have some idea what a sentence is, which is a condition that can't be guaranteed."

Hyphens, Dashes and Other Breaks in the Action

I wish the publishing world would get its act together on hyphens, dashes, and other little straight lines of varying lengths which pass for hyphens and dashes.

All those silent little dots, curves and straight lines we call punctuation should be standard and universal in their silence. Those which are easily recognized are hard enough to use with reasonable mastery as it is.

Dots are dots, and it is difficult to mistake a period. The danger is in overlooking it. The comma is likewise easy to recognize, though I have seen computer printouts which seem to defy standardization. For example, the square period or the comma that does not curve.

On the whole, however, the various combinations of marks, periods, commas, colons, semi-colons, quotation marks, apostrophes, the ellipsis, are readily recognized. Even the question mark and exclamation point, which involve a curve and a straight line along with the dot, are easily recognized.

The hyphen and the dash would be easily recognized, too, if we could decide on what lengths they should be and then stick to them.

A hyphen divides words or makes compound words, word elements, or numbers. The word "hyphen" is Greek meaning "under one." Hyphens are used within words. It is a horizontal line no longer than the space a letter takes.

A dash works, not within a word, but between sets of words. It is a punctuation mark used to indicate a break in the thought or structure of a sentence. It is used to emphasize or bring dramatic impact to what follows. The dash is a horizontal line which should cover the space of two letters. I remember I put down two hyphen marks, then dutifully backspaced and filled in the space between the two hyphens – just like that!

The English teacher cannot depend on publishers to serve up clearly distinguished marks so students can reinforce rules learned by examples of others. Our local newspaper, for instance, never used a full dash, but two hyphens without filling in the space. In other words, two hyphens. In the short columns into which newspaper copy is typed, requiring considerable dividing of words at the ends of lines, we can imagine the confusion that ensued.

With an ever-increasing use of compound words, we have all the more need for hyphens. Try teaching high school students the rules and expect them to apply them accurately. But it can be quite easy:

The hyphen is short,
The dash is long,
Keep the first within,
The other without – and strong.

The problem is we let the middle ground become muddy.

You Say Clichés Are Old Hat?

"Parenthood is the cliché that follows rash improvisation." That is not exactly the definition of the word "cliché," but it certainly conveys its meaning in terms most people will understand.

Our lives are filled to the brim with clichés. Be that as it may, before we get down to brass tacks, we need to get a handle on the word itself. First things first. We have to fill the bill with a definition. The fact of the matter is there are three of them.

Merriam-Webster's Tenth New Collegiate Dictionary says a "cliché" is a "trite phrase or expression … something that has become overly familiar or commonplace." Also, a hackneyed expression, as in the preceding paragraph, contains seven of them.

Most clichés start as fresh, catchy phrases, which become popular, like the "rash improvisations." But as it is the wont of human nature, we tend to overuse them. If they persist, they become part of the language.

Run through the following phrases, each of which employs a color to enhance its meaning: black sheep, true blue, pickled pink, ivory tower, red-carpet treatment, purple prose, green-eyed monster.

These are really metaphors, phrases that describe one thing in terms of another. A black sheep, for example, is a deviant or an eccentric, the least admirable of a group. Black sheep were once considered less valuable than white ones because their wool could not be easily dyed. People recognize the phrase as useful, so for close to two centuries it has been a regular part of the English vocabulary. Until someone comes up with a newer, catchy phrase to describe the family eccentric, black sheep will stay with us.

When phrases become clichés, we soon tire of them. We're all tiring of "no problem" or "have a nice day." Most clichés simply disappear because "the handwriting is on the wall," which dates back to the *Book of Daniel* in the *Hebrew Testament*. In Christine Ammer's book, curiously called *Have a Nice Day – No Problem: A Dictionary of Clichés*, the phrase is explained:

During a great feast by King Belshazzar, a mysterious hand appears and writes some words on the wall. Daniel is to interpret this message and tells the king it is a sign of his coming downfall. Later that night,

Belshazzar is killed and Darius of Persia takes over his kingdom.

The cliché will live as long as the language itself.

Weather is an enduring topic, too. It is one of the first concerns of the day, and one of the most common daily topics. Also, nothing that distinguishes optimists from pessimists faster than the weather. Here are some optimists' clichés: breath of fresh air, making hay while the sun shines, chasing rainbows, clearing the air, and a place in the sun. Sorry, but here are the pessimists' weather clichés: come hell or high water, slower than molasses in January, tempest in a teapot, snowball's chance in hell, or hot air.

But if you want mystery in your weather, try wind clichés: there's nothing in the wind, getting wind out of something, it will soon blow over, take the wind out of someone's sails, straws in the wind, and knowing which way the wind blows.

It goes without saying, clichés are everywhere, right under our noses. Right out of the blue they come, rain or shine. The sky's the limit. Don't save them for a rainy day but use them as the fair-weather friends they are.

Enough is enough. Things are out of hand, but I'm glad you're along for the ride, even though my gift of gab has run its course. If I'm not careful, they'll be calling me long-winded as the writer and persistent as the demands of parenthood.

What animal is the most valuable in the lives of humans? Nominees might include the dog, cat, horse, cow, hog, bird.

While researching clichés and other familiar expressions, I found almost two hundred which used animals as their basis. Three particular animals turned up often. We have a dozen expressions for dogs and birds. But the hands-down winner was the horse. Over two dozen horse expressions and phrases wound up on my lists, and one suspects many more exist.

Although the horse's utility has lessened as the twentieth century proceeded, the noble animal is still common. Clichés and other expressions involving horses are also common. Wild horses couldn't drag them out of me. But hold your horses, and I'll stop horsing around. Anyway, I guess I have the cart before the horse. Here are some clichés about Equus caballus, straight from the horse's mouth.

Horses are considered intelligent animals. One way to tell is by the amount of advice you can find referring to them. The one about locking the barn door after the horse is stolen or changing horses in midstream. And you know what they say, you can lead a horse to water, but you can't make him drink.

Did you ever notice that people who hang around horses seem calm and confident? But that's a horse of a different color. There is horse sense, the horse opera, a dark horse, horsepower and horseradish.

When you get serious, you horse trade. When you want to calm, you steer for the horse latitudes. If you appreciate history, the horse and buggy may be for you. More likely you'll opt for the horseless carriage. I believe we have as many as there are expressions about them.

I don't know what the horse population of Walworth County is, but I'll wager it's in the many hundreds. You would have no trouble finding a horse to ride. If you take the bit between your teeth, and you don't get on your high horse, you can be in the saddle in no time. No horseplay! I'm not kidding. And speaking of riding, you can ride hell bent for leather, and you can ride for a fall. Or maybe you'd rather I ride off into the sunset.

Using the Mighty Metaphor

> *Words are, of course, the most powerful drug used by mankind.*
> Rudyard Kipling

All hail the mighty metaphor! What would happen if we could not use one thing to describe another?

When high school seniors get into their last spring together accompanied by the likes of *Macbeth*, they become pensive and philosophical about the changes they themselves are about to undergo. One of Shakespeare's most powerful figures (of speech and a character) is Macbeth's final airing of his lot in life:

> *Life's but a walking shadow, a poor player*
> *That struts and frets his hour upon the stage ...*

The Bard invokes his vocation to illustrate the tragedy of Macbeth's life. What makes us more nervous than an actor, comedian, or singer who can't

92

remember his lines, yet has to sustain his thespian stance? More than one actor has struggled before an audience of parents and peers. The Bard calls upon that inner uneasiness to illustrate a fool's emptiness.

Yes, the mighty metaphor. When we compare one thing to another, we're setting loose possible connections and complications.

High school seniors set me about trying to describe their condition. I tried to figure out adolescents. When I encountered Arthur Koestler's observation, it seemed so simple, "Adolescence is a kind of emotional seasickness."

Using metaphor is trying to understand something by relating it to something else. As an example, let's use the concept of love. That's about as universal a consideration as is possible. Marty Grothe is a metaphor collector who published some of his results in *I Never Metaphor I Didn't Like*. Here are some examples:

> *Love is a fan club with only two fans.*
> Anatole Brovard
> *Love is the only disease that makes you feel better.*
> Sam Shepard

Metaphor make us feel one thing (love) through elaboration of another (nature):

> *Love comforteth like sunshine after rain.*
> William Shakespeare

At other times, the comparison sends a spray of impressions out in many directions, forces thought beyond the base of the metaphor:

> *To say that you can love on*
> *All your life is like saying that*
> *One candle will continue to burn*
> *As long as you live.*
> Leo Tolstoy

A real provocation of thought, don't you think?

93

Metaphor can shake things up. James Geary in his book, *I Is an Other: The Secret Life of Metaphor and How It Shapes the Way We See the World,* says that metaphor is so common that you "find yourself in the middle of a metaphorical blizzard." He uses an Elvis Presley tune to illustrate:

> *She touched my hand, what a chill I got*
> *Her lips are like a volcano that's hot*
> *I'm proud to say that she's my buttercup.*
> *I'm in love; I'm all shook up.*

Geary points out that "whenever we describe anything abstract – ideas, feelings, thoughts, emotions, concepts – we instinctively resort to metaphor." Just look at those lines. A touch is not a touch – it's a chill. Lips are (like) a volcano. And she is not she, she is a buttercup. "And love is not love, but the state or condition of being all shook up."

Metaphor is how we extend meaning, cause a blizzard, shake things up. Metaphor provides brain food, and the nutrition makes us who we are. Yes, all hail the mighty metaphor. It is a great humanizing element of our thought and our language. Einstein balances our science selves and our literary selves:

> *We should take care*
> *Not to make the intellect our gods;*
> *It has, of course, powerful muscles,*
> *But no personality.*

Euphemisms

I have always been fascinated by euphemisms, i.e., words and phrases in which we "substitute an agreeable or inoffensive expression for one that may offend or suggest something unpleasant" (MW10NCD).

That use seems like a good idea. There is nothing wrong with being agreeable or inoffensive, but the realities of life suggest otherwise. What is gained when an airline refers to missing luggage as "mishandled," when in fact it was "lost"? If it is your luggage that is missing, what is the effect of airline officialdom calling it "mishandled"? Substituting a pleasant term

94

for a blunt one may seem like useful strategy. But is it, really?

I would consider it at best an irritation, at worst, an insult. Comedian George Carlin performed with euphemisms years ago. One time he described a soldier affected mentally by warfare. In World War I, his problem would have been called "shell shock." During World War II, it was "battle fatigue." In the Korean Conflict, the euphemism was "operational exhaustion." Vietnam produced "post-traumatic stress disorder." It is natural to treat with compassion the afflictions resulting from war. But there is another side to the euphemism aberration.

The National Council of Teachers of English publication, *The Quarterly Review of Doublespeak,* describes a euphemism as "an informed and entertaining presentation of current instances of inflated, over complex and often deliberately ambiguous language." Here is an example: "Companies don't want to admit to layoffs these days. Instead, layoffs are termed "schedule adjustments," "a career-change opportunity," "reducing head count."

This softening of language has been going on for a long time. In 1969, *Time* magazine ran an essay: "The Euphemism: Telling It Like It Isn't." In it was the following: "Almost any way of earning a salary above the level of ditchdigging is known as a profession rather than a job. 'Janitors' for several years have been elevated by image-conscious unions to the status of 'custodians' or 'maintenance engineers.' So, a rock guitarist playing three chords can class himself with Horowitz as a 'recording artist.'"

Cadillac dealers refer to autos as "pre-owned" rather than "secondhand." Government researchers concerned with old people call them "senior citizens." Ads for bank credit cards and department stores refer to "convenient terms" – meaning "eighteen percent annual interest rates payable at the convenience of the creditor."

These uses are attempts to bring color and comfort to an otherwise dry and dull language. But the intent is often to deceive. No one in his/her right mind would consider the terms of credit referred to above as convenient. The phrase "senior citizen" glosses over the main fact of life for those folks, that of age. The term "pre-owned" ignores the fact of use, the wear and tear of a period of ownership. And "janitorial" duties suggest the drudgery that "custodial" does not.

Language integrity cannot be well served by semantic deceit.

Accuracy in use of words means care in choice. We have many ways to face facts of life without inaccurate and sometimes offensive euphemisms.

A *Time* essay got at a more profound factor:

> A persistent source of modern euphemisms is the feeling, inspired by the prestige of science, that certain words contain implicit subjective judgments, and thus ought to be replaced with more 'objective' terms. To speak of 'morals' sounds both superior and arbitrary, as though the speaker were indirectly questioning those of the listener. By substituting 'values,' the concept is miraculously turned into a condition, like humidity or mass, that can be safely measured from a distance. To call someone 'poor,' in the modern way of thinking, is to speak pejoratively of his condition, while the substitution of 'disadvantaged,' or 'underprivileged,' indicates that poverty wasn't his fault.

Linguist Mario Pei writes that by using "underprivileged," we are "made to feel that it is our fault." As *Time* points out, this "modern reluctance to judge makes it more offensive than ever before to call a man a liar; thus, we have a 'credibility gap' instead."

No teacher today will call a student "stupid" or a "bad student." The student who is not producing results is rather called an "under achiever" or a "slow learner."

My experiences suggest that the spirit of the euphemism is a positive force. When deceit is the driving force behind its use, there is trouble.

The more euphemistic we become, the greater the chance we will become extreme in its use. Calling a "used car salesman," for example, a "transportation consultant" seems silly. Or maybe you have heard that "fat" is an "alternative body image." Or that "being drunk" is being "sobriety deprived." Maybe the dubious word "manhole" can be replaced by "personnel access structure."

A final note: "death" will mean "being terminally inconvenienced."

Teaching Literature

Even before I became interested in teaching, I recognized the value of literature, but I felt I could not master reading as an art. That, obviously, is no way to approach literature.

After studying to be an English teacher, I attacked literature with an intensity I had not before. As a reader, I was a plodder; and though much has changed over the years, I worried constantly about being a slow reader. During my career, I developed a passion and confidence for teaching English literature. My goal was to awaken in eighteen-year-olds the insights, wisdom, humor and courage needed for their lives.

CONTENTS

On Literature and Me

I have always had the uneasy feeling that I am outside the land of literature, that since my reading ability and appreciation developed slowly, I could not feel comfortable within the lands and kingdoms which the giants of literature created.

Even before I became interested in teaching, I recognized the value of literature, but I felt I could not master reading as an art. Therefore, I must be uncomfortable with it. That's no way to approach literature.

After studying to be an English teacher, I attacked literature with an intensity I had not before. As reader I was a plodder. I worried constantly about being a slow reader. Even today I cannot fly through narrative. I always find something to blame for my slow rate: small print, archaic style, academic difficulty, punctuation, and syntactical problems from different times and styles and writers.

Don Quixote has these problems. Thus, it is a challenge, a kind of mental boon granted by some far-off kindred spirit. What makes me attack it at a time when counterattacks of all sorts are about me, I do not know.

It must be an accumulation of influences and forces, but the one which persists when I think about the problem is Miss Marjorie Hugunin. She did two things for me as I studied English literature at WSC-Platteville and as I served as a teacher of Shakespeare at Badger High School. She created active interest where there was only passive interest before. Then she moved forward onto the next writer, the next movement, the next period, the next play or novel or poem.

This momentum of literature study overwhelmed me, but I wanted to keep up. I skipped little, I needed to penetrate what I had to leave behind, and in the process, I became a better reader. I can't remember dead spots or lazy time in any of her class hours. I often thought that I should not blink my eyes or I'll miss something.

With twelve semester hours in her courses, my interest overcame my discomfort and the literary matter overcame my uncertainty. I grew my own kind of persistence. I was still a laboring reader lacking significant confidence, but I got a peek at literary land and the process was begun.

When I began student teaching, my first teaching assignment was *David Copperfield*. About all I can remember is that it proceeded routinely, and I was left with a spot in my literary heart for Charles Dickens' autobiographical novel.

But I can't remember much else. I can't find or didn't save the notes I used. In thirty years of teaching, I tried to interest students in it, but I have difficulty getting a handle on salient parts, characters, plot lines, effective episodes. Someday I will "attack" *David Copperfield* the way I am doing *Don Quixote*.

Where the problem developed was in all the other classical and contemporary literature, in which I was supposed to be expert enough to inspire eighteen-year-olds to want to read. When students asked questions I could not answer, I would scramble before the next day to find enough information and offer something approaching intelligent advice.

I tried to fit extracurricular reading into my schedule, but that was difficult because reading papers and keeping up on the literature I was teaching consumed considerable reading time also. The realities of being an English teacher of high school seniors were quickly taking their toll, making me adjust, yet awaking me to the possibilities of influencing my students.

My uneasiness in literary land never went away. It couldn't. It was endless. I woke up some mornings to find it shocking me, forcing a kind of honesty that admits I can't know it all, but I can find out enough to make a pitch to students who are curious and energetic enough to want to know.

All the problems of my life of teaching literature descended on me as I plodded (let's make that persevered) through *Don Quixote*.

The factor that makes a man a man is the brain. The brain will not work well unless trained. Part of that training is understanding our culture and how it came to be what it is. Not superficially, but profoundly. It is mental work, anguish, persistence. It requires an active interest.

What Did My Students Read in High School?

What did students read in my senior English classes? What works do teachers assign? Are they the same books that another generation read a few decades ago? The *New York Times* ran the results of two surveys reporting the percentage of public high schools assigning various literary works to students. The first was conducted among two hundred twenty-two public high schools in 1963. The second, among 322 public high schools in 1988. Each reported the ten most frequently assigned works.

The work assigned most in each year was *Macbeth* in 1963 and *Romeo and Juliet* in 1988. Each was assigned in ninety percent of schools surveyed. The work ranking second in 1963, *Julius Caesar,* was assigned in seventy-seven percent of high schools, and in 1988 (*Macbeth*) in eighty-one percent of schools. All three are Shakespeare plays.

Of those works commonly taught in 1963, six are no longer among the most assigned ten. They are *Silas Marner, Our Town, Great Expectations, Hamlet, The Red Badge of Courage,* and *A Tale of Two Cities.* Of those commonly assigned in 1988, six were not among the leading ten in 1963. They are *Romeo and Juliet, To Kill a Mockingbird, The Pearl, Of Mice and Men, Lord of the Flies,* and *The Diary of a Young Girl.* Only four of the ten most commonly assigned works in 1963 were still among the top ten in 1988.

Six of the ten most commonly assigned works in 1963 were written by English authors. In 1988, only four were. None of titles written by Dickens appeared in 1988, but twice in 1963: *Great Expectations* and *A Tale of Two Cities.*

Works of American authors increase from four in the 1963 survey to five in 1988. Steinbeck's works did not appear at all in 1963, but there were two in 1988: *The Pearl* and *Of Mice and Men.*

The two American works that increased in use over the twenty-five-year-period are *Huckleberry Finn,* from twenty-seven percent to seventy-eight percent, and *The Scarlet Letter,* from twenty-seven to sixty-two percent. *Huckleberry Finn* was the only American work that was assigned in as many as seventy-eight percent of public high schools.

The only American writer to appear twice was John Steinbeck: *The Pearl* and *Of Mice and Men.* The famous work *Grapes of Wrath* was not assigned in most American high schools.

It was of interest that Shakespeare was the only author on either list, except one, who wrote plays. The exception was Thornton Wilder's *Our Town.* Shakespeare was the only one of eleven writers represented whose works are in poetic form.

Ten works assigned most in 1988 appeared in an average of sixty-nine percent of schools, while among those listed in 1963, the top ten were assigned in an average of forty-nine percent of schools. A couple of generalizations developed about these results. Consideration of the subject matter of these works indicates that major shifts have taken place in recent decades. Also, there seems to be a shift from institutional values in the 1963 works, to personal values in the 1988 list.

Teachers choose the books student read, but they are certainly sensitive to students' interests. It is not surprising that more books and more subjects are not tried in classrooms. Nuclear war, racism, a love story, and social injustice are not surprising subjects. The fact that a wider variety and more complex subjects are turning up is to be expected.

Now we need a way to measure how intent and persistent students are about the literature assigned to them. I would guess a lot of reading expectations are lost in the flood of activities which provide more rapid and tangible satisfaction.

Introduction to England

Warming high school seniors to sorting out the names and relationships of English royalty was a difficult procedure. When we came upon Henry VIII and his complex relationships, however, the pace quickened.

Adolescents are always curious about his six wives and how each came to his threatening throne. But most of all they were interested in the fates of his six spouses. One year a student gave me a bit of doggerel verse which helped solve the problem of names and ends:

Henry the 8th to six wives wedded;
One died, one survived, two divorced, and two beheaded.

Another curiosity was six wives, but only three children. Considerable interest was generating.

Then those British rock groups continually invaded our shores with their strange but successful songs. In 1965, on the coattails of the Beatles, came a group of five English boys called Herman's Hermits. They used an authentic music-hall song written in 1911 to create, if that is the word, "I'm Henry VIII, I am." That echoed for years after, when we talked about the eighth Henry.

Another question that usually grew out of this talk was why British rock groups came to dominate pop music in America. By now, interest was pretty hot.

On the first day of our studies about England, I wrote a collection of quotations about the English people on the chalkboard. Sometimes class starts with its discussion, or I ignore it entirely. Chances are, however, it will arise during the hour because the aim for the first day is to try to characterize the English.

What inspires the choice of the quotation may be some indication of character in a particular group of students, an impulse of my own, or simply the use of one I've not employed for a while. All five of these quotations work:

- Mad dogs and Englishmen go out in the midday sun. (Noel Coward)
- The English take their pleasures sadly, after the fashion of their country. (Duc De Sully)
- Of all the nations in the world, at present the English are the stupidest in speech, the wisest in action. (Thomas Carlyle)
- Not only England, but every Englishman is an island. (Novalis, pseudonym for Friedrich von Hardenberg)
- They are like their own beer: froth on top, dregs at the bottom, the middle excellent. (Voltaire)

The reason they work is that each conveys a national characteristic veiled in an allusion of some sort. It is surprising how aware some American students are about the influence of the English, or put another way, how essentially overstated American students may recognize the characteristic understatement of their English counterparts. When examples of this quality cannot be extracted from a class, I choose from one of the following two examples, which I found in journalism of the 1960s.

The first was a short news item distributed by United Press International. The Earl of Arran, reflecting British anger at President Charles DeGaulle of France, called DeGaulle a 'bottle-nosed old giraffe' yesterday and proposed a boycott of French wines and women. The Earl wrote a column for the *Evening News* of London.

He (DeGaulle) isn't just a head of state but a common or garden variety dictator. And no, he didn't save France. Britain did. They've never forgiven us for it.

Don't buy anything French: wines, women, food, scent, clothes, books or stationery. Don't go to France. Unless you're very rich, you won't be able to afford it anyway, and you'll be rooked for a certainty. If you have any French friends, write and tell them of their tin pot dictator.

I know this sounds very petty, but I feel petty. France and the French have let us down. And incidentally, I am more certain than ever that Joan of Arc WAS a witch.

My students usually identified with that piece, noting the reasoned and civilized tone of the English, their humor, and always the understatement.

In the 1960s, unrest on college campuses led to many crass, downright embarrassing scenes. The following editorial appeared in the *Milwaukee Journal* on October 14, 1969, and represented a different approach to campus trouble:

The warden (superintendent) and fellows of Wadham College, Oxford, recently received a list of 'nonnegotiable' demands from a group of students. The warden sent back this letter: "Dear Gentlemen: We note your threat to take what you call <u>direct</u> <u>action</u> unless your demands are immediately met. We feel that it is only sporting to let you know that our governing body includes three experts in chemical warfare, two ex-commandos skilled with dynamite and torturing prisoners, four qualified marksmen in both small arms and rifles, two ex-artillerymen, one holder of the Victorian Cross, four karate experts and a chaplain. The governing body has authorized me to tell you that we look forward with confidence to what you call a 'confrontation,' and I may say even with anticipation." The students at last report were considering new strategy.

I have no way of knowing how that approach entered into the experience of less sophisticated and less restrained Americans, but students certainly understood the humor, if not by definition, by effect.

Occasionally I assigned the following question: "What is England's place in the world?" I asked for the response during the last fifteen minutes of the class period. The date was October 23, 1969. Here is one of the responses:

England's place in the world is the same as a grandmother's place in a family. She has patience and wisdom which only comes with age. She presides over family (the free world) not as a military or forceful power, but as a persuasive power.

And another:

I have always admired England. She is the fashion setter. Her clothes are copied. Her government procedures are set up as models, and her speech mimic(k)ed. Deep within her bosom, the spine-chilling mysteries of her misty moors are born. Her literature is held up as examples of great work. She stands deep in tradition, and her mind is bordered by ancient castles and cathedrals. In the world, she is the aging yet beautiful mistress of the seas who has fallen in love with peace in the autumn of her years. Her step is light and bouncy but taught by experience to be cautious. In a world of impetuous, immature grapes, England is the dark, sweet wine of patience and knowledge.

The boy who wrote the first reflected the hardy life of his farm background, and he left to work on a college degree. The girl who wrote the second displayed a talent for her native tongue, and I have no idea what happened to her. Each understood something of his or her cultural heritage.

The idea of the first day is to provide expectations before going back to the beginning. The English fascinate and influence us today as they always have. Dickens, Churchill, the Beatles, all have something to tell us.

There are many ways of introducing the English to American students. One is relating the English to other Europeans. Another is the great unwritten alliance between our two countries. Others are fashion, music, and travel in England. Coats of arms are fascinating; some students pursued their family backgrounds in coats of arms. The decline of the empire and the persistence of English influence also generated interest.

I used Henry Steele Commager's *There WILL Always Be an England*, which originally appeared in the *New York Times Magazine* (1961) and was condensed in the *Reader's Digest*.

Still another way to generate interest is to compare England to the state of Wisconsin in size, shorelines, and population. A prosaic presentation of facts, until we get to population. England (minus Scotland and Wales) has 50,327 square miles compared to Wisconsin's 56,154 square miles. England coastline runs about 2000 miles while Wisconsin's is 673 miles.

Then when we try to imagine a state which has a population of over four million to have 50,000,000 instead, the eyes open and the jaws drop, and it isn't long before someone wonders how they feed themselves. Where does the food come from and how do they pay for it?

Then I introduced a companion question. What other nation in the world has parallel circumstances? An island lying off continental landmass. One which depends on imports, so must export. Japan is soon identified, in the comparison turned into a contrast.

What was supposed to be an approach to English literature could turn into twentieth-century social history, economics, political science, any number of subjects. I can remember turning off some promising discussions for the demands of time and the lesson plans. But I figure students now know more about the nature of the English and England, and if they want to pursue these other matters, they can do it on their own. Isn't that what education is supposed to do?

In a column headed "Europe According to *Peanuts*," humorist Art Buchwald assigned Charles Schulz's *Peanuts* characters to European countries. It is important to note that by the late-1960s France withdrew from NATO, that England had not been allowed to enter the common market, and that the U.S. was as usual caught in the middle.

I asked students to suggest which character is which country. Sometimes the challenge took hold and the speculation was brisk. Other times the results were less energetic, even passive. The important thing is that looking at countries as having character works.

Which of the three major *Peanuts* characters is England? Charlie Brown, Linus, or Lucy? Which characters are the United States?

When we open the English literature anthology and journey back to Anglo-Saxon times, students seem to recognize that at least our institutions have roots in the English-past, a millennium ago. They seem to understand that what we are today came from somewhere, sometime, somehow, and that it is a good idea to examine this legacy of language, literature and law which the English bequeathed to us.

Some of the Contradictions of *Beowulf*
Back in 1965, when I was just getting the hang of teaching *Beowulf*, controversy arose in the *London Times* about whether teaching *Beowulf* is necessary. A majority thought it was, but the reasons were interesting.

Beowulf is suitable for teaching in English schools because it is one hundred percent pure. Not once in the 30,182 lines does this Anglo-Saxon classic use four-letter words, which remains the most durable Saxon contribution to the English language.

It is those words one hears almost universally. They have survived, but not as the ideals the society holds dear. These words survived even though they were seldom printed and not rarely condoned for public use. One of them seems to be the easiest combination of sounds to utter. A one-syllable four-letter word which slips from the tongue as hammer smashes finger, toe trips table, or idea runs awry. It isn't taking the Lord's name in vain, but its reference is fundamental to our animal existence.

Those ideals of conduct which governed Saxon society were of a high sort. They had to do with loyalty, glory, and fate. They were the essence of Beowulf, the hero. They are the foundation of English character. And maybe the Saxons did well to keep their baser selves below the surface.

Chaucer and 'tis the Season
The end of November and into December in my classroom is Chaucer's age. Though the setting was April and the time for pilgrimages, somehow warmth of hearth and home, or in this case the Tabard Inn and folks preparing to travel together, was enough to span the seasons.

It is time to discover that traveling back in time, talking to people six hundred years away, is not all that much different from social energy of the classroom and its talk and its reading. Chaucer's famous *Prologue of The Canterbury Tales* helps fortify that bond.

Student: But Mr. Johnson, it doesn't sound like English.

Me: Of course not. The Saxon tongue was still rather primitive, and the French were giving it broader meaning and sophistication. Modern English will grow out of that.

Student: Mr. Johnson, I can hardly pronounce those words.

Me: You'll learn how. There aren't many differences.

Student: You aren't gonna make us read this the way it was six hundred years ago, are you?

Another student: I heard he makes us memorize it, too.

Still another student: You're kidding!

Me: The 'a' is the same as in 'bah.'

Student: That's what I say, too.

Me: Or the 'a' in 'rah' or 'hurrah.'

Student: How about 'faux pas'?

Chaucer is using French to give a more cosmopolitan bearing to the sound. The "a" is like the "a" in "father."
I began to recite:

Whan that Aprille with his shoures soote,
The droghte of Marche hath perced to the roote,
And bathed every veyne in swich licour,
Of which vertu engendred is the flour...

By now students are all looking at me hard, panic dissolving into wonder.

107

Whan Zephirus eek with his sweete breeth
Inspired hath in every holt and heeth
The tendre croppes, and the yonge soone
Hath in the Ram his halfe cours y-ronne...

Now I am feeling my power, and I am tempted to do other than recite it straight. But I know better. I recite it straight:

And smale foweles maken melodye,
That slepen al the nyght with open ye,
(So priketh hem Nature in hir corages)
Thanne longen folk to goon on pilgrammages...

Probably the most famous line in English before Shakespeare. Again, I want to stop and relish. But again, I recite it straight:

And palmeres for to seken straunge strondes
To ferne halwes, kowthe in sondry londes;
And specially, from every shires ende
Of Engelond, to Caunterbury they wende ...

They are really listening hard. They are with me. Every teacher's dream. How can I sustain? I continued:

The hooly blisful martir for the seke
That hem hath holpen, whan that they were seke.

Silence.
They are impressed. They are in awe. The "a" is like the "a" in "awe." The "a" in "father." They do not really want to do this academic exercise, and some fear they cannot do it. But it doesn't matter. This is the time of year we can do such things. And more.

Culture and Chaucer Continuity

Times never seem to change, do they? We talk about the revolutionary of our age, but some things never change.

Sunday, which was September 24, 1995, the *Milwaukee Journal-Sentinel* ran an Associated Press story which was introduced by the headline: "Shelving Chaucer: High School to bar 'Canterbury Tales' over sexual content."

On November 16, 1961, the local *Lake Geneva Regional News* ran a story on page one, which was introduced, "Chaucer Gets Heave-ho on Parents' Complaint." I remember the headline, the incident, the jarring effect such things have on schools.

The grand old man of English literature has survived it all. And why? Like all enduring works of literature, his contain universal qualities and quandaries expressed in language that gives their subjects universal appeal. Common subjects, but uncommon language. If there had been journalists in Chaucer's time, his social commentary would have made it to print. He understood human nature.

Above all, he was a poet. In fact, in his time and for hundreds of years before and after, no other poet had endured as he has, with the possible exception of Shakespeare, who lived a hundred years later. Chaucer's was an expression that would stand time's most ruthless scrutiny, six hundred years to be precise.

But these are not the real reasons Chaucer survives. He was an observer of human nature. In the late fourteenth century when authors were writing about tales of chivalry, knights and heroism, and about things that could never have happened, Chaucer was writing about people he knew or at least had met. *The Canterbury Tales* is a story with stories.

The general frame of the work involves a religious pilgrimage. One of the popular pastimes of Chaucer's era was to make journeys to the famous Canterbury Cathedral to pay respects to the martyr Thomas á Becket, the archbishop who was murdered in his church by hirelings of the English King Henry II over two hundred years earlier. It was common for people to travel together because the dangers of attacks and robberies were real.

One of the most popular inns was The Tabard, where people stayed before embarking on the long journey. It was one of these pilgrimages that served as the backdrop for Chaucer's famous work. About thirty folks, including Chaucer, agreed to travel together. Although most artists portrayed Chaucer's pilgrims on horseback, most walked, and it was over fifty miles from London to Canterbury. They told stories induced by an offer from the owner of the Tabard, one Harry Bailey, who offered free lodging on the return trip to the teller of the best tale.

The Canterbury Tales is Chaucer's telling of the stories and reporting the social interaction among the pilgrims, who were a cross-section of English society. Nobility, the church, and commoners were all represented. Peasants, guildsman, and professional people. The educated and the uneducated. People from the upper and lower echelons of society.

The church had its representatives: a nun, a monk, a friar, a country parson, and the infamous pardoner. The nobility was represented by a knight, his son, and a yeoman who served the knight.

Just as people today when they travel in groups, they sought out those with common interests, those who spoke the same level of language. Among the pilgrims were several who must have been accustomed to telling off-color stories because that is what they did. Chaucer placed each person in character and set them among their fellow travelers, letting nature take its course. Coarseness soon set in as these loose-tongued pilgrims told a story at the expense of another.

What is so unusual about that? If you've ever worked on a construction crew or any service job that required a number of people working together, you know the level of language and storytelling is inelegant. Four of Chaucer's characters were in this pattern and made fools of themselves by showing off their stations in life. Chaucer elevated the language, but the stories remained coarse. Let's face it, a dirty story is a dirty story, even in iambic pentameter with rhyming couplets.

Most high school anthologies carry the *Prologue* and one or two of the stories. None of the questionable tales is printed in texts. However, paperbacks of the complete work are available, and many of them are prose versions of the original or later modern English poetic versions. These readily available prose-story editions naturally read differently. The poetry is gone, and Chaucer, whose poetry was his hallmark, is little better than hack writers today.

The *Prologue* contains description of the characters, which transmit a pretty good idea of what to expect when storytelling comes. I restricted my classwork on Chaucer to the *Prologue* and a couple of the tales.

Curious readers asked me about which of the other stories they should read. I would make individual recommendations privately, based on the students, their interests, and their literary leanings. Most years I taught *The Pardoner's Tale* or *The Nun's Priest's Tale.* The former has been described as the first real short story in the language. Irony is what gives the story a punch. It is an exemplar on the nature of irony on many levels.

The Nun's Priest's Tale is a barnyard story about the Chanticleer, the ruling rooster, and his hens, and the fox. Its subject is pride and vanity, and although it is about animals; it is really about people. It is allegory, a story with a moral.

Teachers who have trouble with their communities over content usually bring it on themselves. A 1961 colleague broadcast the content of some tales. Naturally adolescents are impelled to seek out no-noes, the first things they seek out.

Chaucer used subtlety. Effective teachers do, too. Taking the poetry out of Chaucer, teaching Chaucer as bare, bawdy stories is pointless. He was trying to appeal to a broader audience than the nobility, which is what most writers of the time did. General audiences require a more common, earthier touch. They like gossip, slapstick, graphic stuff.

But Chaucer was not going to sacrifice his art for the nature of his characters and their conduct. Rather, he placed his pilgrims and their proclivities on an elevated language platform. Their mundane, superficial lives took on a different perspective. They seemed much more than they were. As Chaucer knew, these never change, not their nature, not their appeal. Below are two quotes from newspaper readers:

> An old English classic, 'Canterbury Tales,' denuded of its dignity as a study of prose by lusty English translation, came under fire by a group of parents at the Badger school board meeting Monday night.
>
> *Beloit Daily News*, November 15, 1961

> I think it would be tragedy if Chaucer were not included in an advanced English college prep class. There are certainly far more

graphic, far worse images on prime-time television every week.
Milwaukee Journal-Sentinel, September 24, 1995

Choosing Between a Class in Psychology or Shakespeare

I'd take a pass on modern psychology in exchange for the understanding and insights of poet and playwright William Shakespeare, born 455 years ago.

Exactly what day is still open to discussion. It does seem strange that the man who brought human nature into sharper focus than any other mortal should not himself be better understood. Four and a half centuries have not diminished the Bard of Avon's influence. Indeed, grew stronger.

Although many ingredients are responsible for the power of his plays, what matters most are the characters emerging from the fabric of his narratives. The Bard created believable people who represented humanity in all its goodness and glory, its deviltry and destructiveness.

One of the most absorbing facets of life is the human personality, its appeal, its depth, its beauty. Twenty-eight years of working with high school seniors demonstrated those facets convincingly. Allowing for the dramatic enhancements that stagecraft demands, Shakespeare's characters are to be found all around us, everywhere. All we have to do is look closely. This requires time and patience.

Within each person lies the essence, the stuff that makes each of us different from all others. Take time to smell the roses. Shakespeare did, and in the process, created timeless and universal characters. We relate to them because they are us.

For example, there is an ambitious person who will do almost anything to get ahead. Someone who seemed rather common in accomplishment could create insights that ran far beyond his or her station in life.

Have you felt the pangs of love so strongly you could hardly think of anything else? Or, can you think of someone whose promise was so great that subsequent failure seemed not only unlikely but impossible?

All these describe Shakespearean characters, part of his universal stage. All of us know people who demonstrate, to one degree or another, these traits.

Does the following describe anyone you know? "He's like all the rest of us, really; he's just a stupid _ _ _ _. He's got a frightful temper. He's

112

completely selfish and utterly inconsiderate. He does not for a moment think of consequences of what he has said. He is simply bad-tempered arrogance with a crown perched on top. He obviously wasn't spanked by his mother often enough."

That quotation was noted actor Laurence Olivier describing one of Shakespeare's most profound characters. It is King Lear, from the play of the same name. Lear's problem, and he had quite a few, stemmed from something within, causing an acting-out of personal motives and impulses without consideration of consequences. You can get away with that sort of behavior if you're a king. At least for a while.

Rational people fight these inner tendencies and defeat them. Lear's actions gradually accumulated, until finally everything came down on him at once. He suffered from a backlog of wrongs, most of which he brought on himself.

Shakespeare probably wrote *King Lear* after Queen Elizabeth died and James I became king. The nation was confused and uncertain about where England was headed. Having a Scottish king rule England was not fully appreciated. Elizabeth left no immediate heir, so this son of a cousin was next in line. It didn't help that the cousin was Mary, Queen of Scots.

Lear seems an unusual character to introduce in a society inflamed by civil and religious strife and ruled by a king about whom the people were uneasy. James, however, promoted the arts and never objected to the play, which could have been interpreted as questioning his right to rule.

What it did question is much broader. Seeking peace in his old age, this mythical king of Britain made foolish mistakes, leading to terrifying results. His living out the results forced audiences to consider the process of governing. It is well to note that Lear advances lessons that would not be lost centuries later.

On another level, Shakespeare seemed to relish creating characters who were poor, uneducated, undistinguished, but unable to keep to themselves. What's more, many had redeeming qualities, the cardinal example being Falstaff. Sir John Falstaff, the monumentally self-indulgent braggart, who, in addition to nurturing a plentiful girth, lies without scruple. The man's knavery, however, is so engaging and his lust for life so intense that he became one of the favorite characters in all of literature.

What about Falstaff appeals so strongly? What is redeeming about this bar clown? Orson Welles, who played the part several times, claimed Falstaff had a serious, even tragic side. He is "a wit rather than a clown."

Falstaff himself boasted that he is not only witty in himself but causes wit in others. He has since his first appearance on the Elizabethan stage, turned up in songs, paintings, operas, and beer. He's the only character to appear in four Shakespearean plays. His name has been transformed into an adjective, "Falstaffian," defined by the *Oxford English Dictionary* as "characteristic of or resembling Falstaff, a fat jovial humorous knight."

Eighteenth-century scholar and the first lexicographer, Samuel Johnson, described Sir John as "Thou compound of sense and vice, of sense which may be admired, but not esteemed, of vice which may be despised, but hardly detested." In other words, a contradiction. A puzzle. An enigma. A rascal philosopher. And maybe as representative of humanity as one could ever hope to find.

Then there is youth. Did Shakespeare write about "flaming youth," as Hamlet describes that phase of life? He wrote a lot of interesting things about "salad days/When I was green in judgement" *Antony and Cleopatra*. In *Hamlet* it was "in the morn and liquid dew of youth." Also, in *Antony and Cleopatra*: "He wears the rose/Of youth upon him."

The young played important roles in Shakespeare's panoply of players. He also seemed to encourage the energy of adolescence.

In *The Merchant of Venice* – "Why should a man, whose blood is warm within, /Sit like his grandsire cut in alabaster" (a reference to an alabaster effigy on a tomb). Shakespeare also recognized that "Youth's a stuff will not endure" (*Twelfth Night*). Having passed through that phase, we all might breathe easier.

Proof of the Bard's skill with the young is convincingly portrayed in *Romeo and Juliet*, the tale of idyllic love set within feuding families. It was his only romantic tragedy. We are challenged how to explain how this mischance of young love works upon our psyches, and how it still plays out in life today.

Norrie Epstein in her *The Friendly Shakespeare* sets the scene:

It is summer in Verona, the air shimmers with heat. The tension is palpable, with street brawls, family feuds, and ancient animosities. Welcome to the hothouse atmosphere of *Romeo and Juliet* where everything happens quickly: Romeo and Juliet meet, grow up, and die in less than five days.

The play is usually performed by actors whose adolescence is a distant memory. Shakespearean actress Dame Ellen Terry said when a woman is old enough to understand Juliet, she's too old to play her. However, in Franco's Zeffirelli's 1968 *Romeo and Juliet*, the most successful Shakespearean movie ever made, its actors were adolescents: Leonard Whiting (17) and Olivia Hussey (15).

First love's exhilaration is spontaneous and thrilling. Yet its emotional thrust can contain the seeds of tragedy. Romeo was a Montague; Juliet, a Capulet. These warring families, in a time when parents chose mates for their children, could never consent to a marriage with the other family. The contradictions of idyllic and illicit love serve as the play's emotional substance, its driving force.

Romeo and Juliet have little chance to grow as individuals. They are swept up by love's passion, then trapped by circumstances. We see them as a product of their tragedy. They are really one character, standing forever as a symbol of ideal love made dramatic by their circumstances.

When I began teaching (1957), *Romeo and Juliet* was rare in high schools. It was *Julius Caesar* for sophomores and *Macbeth* in the senior year. Occasionally *Hamlet* was studied in classrooms of active minds.

The 1968 Zeffirelli movie was no doubt a motivation for teaching the play to freshmen. The play is complex. Its poetry is rich and deep and sometimes slips by even mature readers. Understanding Elizabethan England and the English renaissance is also important. That means some history. Footnotes and glossaries are a must. There is so much to understand in order to understand.

Yet, the play is about adolescents caught in the surge of first love. Who is better to understand, at least on earthier levels, than high school students?

Shakespeare is still speaking to us; his characters tell us about us. The lessons of the elder Lear warn about our lives and times. Falstaff, despite his contradictions, peers inside us, producing thought while making us laugh. Romeo and Juliet test our hearts and cause us to sympathize with the young and, therefore, the future.

All these souls of the stage seem to understand truth, even though they do not always act upon it. Yet they are able to deliver its substance. That is quite a trick.

Shakespeare: The Renewing Force
Spring brings with it many statements of renewal. One of the most power-ful is Shakespeare. None of his plays could be called spring plays, but sev-eral of them have the capacity for, and the spirit of, renewal, of renais-sance. Indeed, Shakespeare and his times were English Renaissance.

All three of the dramas I worked with were true Renaissance works. *Julius Caesar*, *Macbeth*, and *Hamlet* are plays of human spirit and re-newal. All three tragedies by type lift the human spirit. Though seeming paradoxical, we find cause for hope through human error and tragic out-comes. *Julius Caesar* focuses on citizenship and social responsibility. I cannot observe that play except from the viewpoint of the conspirators. Their cause, though noble, ran to excess with chaotic results.

Marcus Brutus is tragic hero whose fortunes must be viewed through society's eyes. We knew when he joined the conspiracy, something was wrong besides the conspiracy itself. It is no wonder man was superstitious. Reason will not lead to clear solutions, so we look elsewhere. In *Julius Caesar,* we suffer our way through the conspirators' obtuse trains of thought, all because no one can tell for sure whether Julius Caesar's inten-tions are more than the good of Rome. The Ides of March became a sym-bol for uncertainty, tragedy, and eruptions of nature.

But *Macbeth* and *Hamlet*, though carrying many of the same themes and ideas, are more personal plays. Each tragic figure penetrates our sense of personal strengths and weaknesses. Macbeth, a Scottish general, is the chief means by which the king's throne is saved. He is, however, endowed with several circumstances that make the reader suspicious right from the beginning. His "vaulting ambition" has no durable, long-range objectives. He has only this itch which becomes witch-inspired.

His conscience was consumed in less than two hours by his wife, who saw no reason for hesitating when kingship (and queenship) was within grasp. From the moment Macbeth agrees to murder the king, his life is sleepless, his mind "full of scorpions," ever in turmoil. We suffer the en-tire tormenting course of his demise.

We know exactly what is going to happen because the universality of the story cannot let us forget and because every fragment of detail points the way. Something of humanity in the struggle continues to hold our attention.

For a while we think he might turn back or give up or repent, but that possibility slides to oblivion with everything else about Macbeth. It is as remote as bringing King Duncan back to life. No, we struggle through more murders, the ghost of one of his victims, the imagery of practically every objectionable force in nature, and the inevitable revolt against him.

Upon receiving the bothersome news of his wife's death, he is inspired to utter what appear to be thoughts of despair about the nature of man. They make us feel that despite the needless deaths, the long suffering, something in man renews hope, even if that man is Macbeth.

The very name seems tinged with evil. Maybe it is the jolting contradiction that these lines come from Macbeth himself and not from someone else. I want to feel sorry for him because he is a fellow human with worthy qualities. It appears that one sudden but deliberate act changed everything. His society cannot see what we see and know the degree to which he suffered.

Why did he commit these acts? Because self-preservation was a stronger force? He was a professional soldier and defending himself was a reflex. When he needed to cover up, which was immediately, he found that acting quickly became easier and easier. The little messages of his guilt went abroad until general suspicions grew to open hostility. The futility of his position made acting and reacting diffuse. He took actions which led to a reign of terror. He was reduced to animal instincts.

Amid the terror of events sweeping in upon him and the hopelessness of his moral position, he uttered with balance and beauty these words:

Tomorrow and tomorrow and tomorrow,
Creeps in this petty pace from day to day
To the last syllable of recorded time,
And all our yesterdays have lighted fools
The way to dusty death. Out, out, brief candle!
Life's but a walking shadow, a poor player
That struts and frets his hour upon the stage

And then is heard no more. It is a tale
Told by an idiot, full of sound and fury,
Signifying nothing.

These words are a means of focusing attention on man, earth, life. Is this all that life is, a sequence of trivial, trifling episodes with no meaning? Is life not only fragile, but fleeting? Are we but cosmic accidents? No, I think not. That we can perceive Macbeth's tragedy, that we can think of the play as our tragedy, and that we have found out something about life suggests otherwise. I know that this play, indeed all of history, has been full of such deeds. It is all worth thinking about.

One of my favorite cartoons shows a middle-aged couple emerging from under a theater marquee. Above them, huge letters spelled out M-A-C-B-E-T-H. The wife, looking over at her husband, says: "And you thought you had troubles!" I put this cartoon up every spring during the unit on Elizabethan literature.

Eighteen-year-olds about to graduate are especially subject to the questions posed by *Macbeth*. I could not teach Shakespeare without being aware of the great questions of the world and how they apply to maturing in the twentieth century. As with most everything else about the public schools, the numbers and the time restrictions allow for little more than cursory treatment, but the renaissance and renewal that are spring somehow evoke thoughtful talk and meditation.

The idea is to get students to relate to the tragic hero in the same way as they wish they could relate to their own circumstances. Students could not understand why Macbeth did not reject temptation and why Hamlet cannot act. It is now easy to ask, do I find it easy to reject temptation? Do I always find it easy to act?

Renewal in Shakespeare is asking these questions over and over again, then listening carefully, and promoting the discourse of spring. It is sort of aiding the process of maturity.

I once thought adolescents could take their time to think about what was happening to them. But they are forced to grow up so fast that they don't have time, and what is worse they don't realize they don't have time. In my later teaching years, I found it impossible to expect my students to think and hold discourse on such matters as Shakespeare brings to life.

Hamlet was forced to mature too rapidly. American eighteen-year-olds, at least the thirty-five hundred or so I met, were also forced to mature too rapidly. When I first taught *Hamlet*, students of the 1960s and 1970s thought Hamlet's circumstances were strange and unusual. The children of those students, when they studied *Hamlet*, didn't think them strange at all.

Circumstances for growing up have changed. The constants of family structure have been altered, forcing children to take on the world long before they are ready. They don't have time for scholarship, and those that do come from families in which the major objective is raising and educating children.

Part of being educated is learning about ourselves so that we can determine what sort of person we want to be. One way to do that is to have heroes, others who stand for things we want to achieve. As we all know, this is not an age of heroes. In order to have heroes, we need causes.

Adolescents are made to think only of themselves. If the 1970s and 1980s are known for anything, it is liberation, freeing one's self socially and sexually. The crowning achievement of the age of liberation is the divorce. We test each other physically even before we know each other, much less before we marry.

Many of today's eighteen-year-olds can relate to Hamlet's circumstances. They have just come home from college to discover strange things have happened while they were away. Their father who is king, has died. Their mother has married their uncle, and he has become king. Their father's ghost appears and says he was killed by their uncle, telling them to avenge the murder. They suspect two of their best friends are now working for their uncle, helping to plot their death. They love a girl whose father takes sides with the king against them. They are sensitive, uncertain, perplexed by life, ready to laugh, quick to anger. They are wrenched and tugged by their emotions.

Why should an early seventeenth-century fictional character interest late-twentieth-century students? Actor Richard Chamberlain, who has played Hamlet, once answered that question this way:

Hamlet is like a lot of young people today. He is clever and bright and, in a way, feels himself betrayed by a corrupt power group. But that's not the important reason Hamlet can be played in this age. The real thing is that the fascination of his character passes all time barriers. There is something mysterious about Hamlet, something that makes an actor want to play the role and solve the mystery for himself. Hamlet is a many-sided person. And since human nature doesn't change, he can seem as much alive to us as he did to Shakespeare's audience.

Hamlet's dilemma represents the human dilemma, posing universal questions. It provokes such complex matters as perfection in man, justifying revenge, responsibility of intellect, necessity of violence, nature of inner conflict, responsibility for one's own actions. Maybe the message is as simple as "To thine own self be true."

Teaching and studying *Hamlet* can generate endless questions. The variables are the group of individuals making up a class, the community's social tone and circumstances at the time, and the many options the teacher can exercise in teaching the play.

But Hamlet the man intrigues us. Mark Van Doren in his collection of essays entitled *Shakespeare* opens his piece *Hamlet* in this way:

It has been said of Hamlet that something in his genius renders him superior to decision and incapable of act, and it has been pointed out that he dominates the busiest of all known plays. Both views are right. His antic disposition has been analyzed as a symptom of abnormality and as a device for seeming mad. Neither theory is without support. He has been called the best of men and the worse of men. One judgment is as just as the other. Opinions have differed as to whether his deepest attention is engaged by the murder of his father, the marriage of his mother, the villainy of his uncle the King, the senility of Polonius, the apparent perfidy of Ophelia, the reliability of Horatio, the meddling of Rosencrantz and Guildenstern, or the manliness of Fortinbras. Any of them will do. Scarcely anything can be said that will be untrue of this brilliant and abounding young man the first crisis in whose life is also, to our loss, the last.

Hamlet is left in our experience as a short, bright life engaged in impenetrable manifold difficulties. A student said to me once, "I wish I could stop my life and examine where I've been and where I'm going."

Hamlet provides something as close to that as we have come. The most common reaction to Hamlet by students is frustration over his inability to make up his mind, to act. Yet isn't that the most difficult thing anyone has to do in life, making decisions, deciding what to do?

Laurence Olivier, whose own *Hamlet* is probably the best known today, states, "I prefer to think of Hamlet as a nearly great man – damned by lack of resolution, as all but one in a hundred are."

At age eighteen, Americans are faced with choices, dilemmas, decisions, as never before. *Hamlet* is an environment for the airing of the ambiguities of life and investigating life's great questions. Spring is one of the reasons *Hamlet* works. As personal and thoughtful literature for the young, there is nothing quite like it.

I used to wonder why Shakespeare titled many of his works in such nominal ways. His one hundred fifty-four sonnets are either numbered or known by their first lines. All of his tragedies are one-word titles using the names of the protagonists. The exceptions are cases in which there are two protagonists: Romeo and Juliet, Troilus and Cressida, and Antony and Cleopatra; and cases in which there is another name of identification: Titus Andronicus, Julius Caesar, and Timon of Athens. He understood the impact of a play's value lay in the person around which action turned and that the sooner the audience or reader understood that, the sooner we get to the heart of matters. Simple and direct.

Young people like that.

Why Don't We Have Shakespeares Today?

> *It is a sad fact about our culture that*
> *a poet can earn much more money writing or*
> *talking about his art than he can by practicing it.*
> W.H. Auden

> *The play was a great success,*
> *but the audience was a disaster.*
> Oscar Wilde

A perennial question arising each spring in my classroom was, why don't we have Shakespeare's today? Discussing that question might easily comprise a substantial volume. Since I didn't document those annual discussions, we'll have to settle for recollection, research, and reflection.

My personal history with drama does not predict compatibility with Shakespeare. My early attempts at reading drama were usually failures. I don't recall how old I was when I first saw a real stage play.

Movies were of a different order, but it happened to be a film that first stimulated my thinking about drama. Laurence Olivier's production of *Hamlet* (1948) caused an inner response which led to concluding there must be something to this business.

Another experience which had an opposite effect occurred in my first year as a teacher in 1958. Part of the deal in my first contract was to direct a senior class play. We won't talk about it. Let's just say it didn't take the form of encouragement.

The Bard's influence is omnipresent in our culture. When you teach high school seniors, you cannot ignore Shakespeare; you must teach him. At the time I entered the fray, *Macbeth* was the standard fare. So was *Julius Caesar*. If you were courageous and had good minds in front of you, it was *Hamlet*.

As I gained experience, I came to understand we have no giants like Shakespeare around today. Why aren't there writers who can command a national audience? Of course, that's the key: national audience.

Shakespeare and other playwrights and poets claimed broad audiences in their time. Why? Simple. The queen of England. Elizabeth I promoted the pursuit of dynamic language, encouraging poetry and the theater. It is no accident that the results were powerfully poetic.

Elizabethans exuded a pride of language. They loved to play with words, make words dance, and fill heads with dizzying impressions. To relish the turn of a penetrating phrase, or to make metaphor the broadening device of experience were some of the requirements. Elizabeth was queen, but imagination was king.

We have people with these talents today, but they are a tiny minority, which, of course, they were in Shakespeare's time also. What they had were great audiences. In order to have the genius of great language expression, there must be demand. People must want poetry, great theater, serious character delineation.

This phenomenon occurred in England in the late sixteenth century. The English navy had just defeated the Spanish Armada and thus England became the world's leading power. This caused a release of national energy that in the next twenty years produced the King James *Bible*, world exploration and early colonization, and voluminous translations of Roman and Greek classics.

But the crowning achievements of the English renaissance were the poets and playwrights, a literary output not since equaled. The greatest of these was the Bard of Avon, William Shakespeare. The result was the Elizabethan theater and its universal audiences.

Another hinderance to a broadly appealing art is diversions. We have too many technological amenities, too many escape routes from the disciplines that develop skills in the language arts. We engage too little in time for reflection. I recall students who gazed off into space and seemed not to be in the mainstream of things, but that did not mean something important was not taking place. Because someone separates himself from the group and seems to be lost in thought, it could be exactly that.

A liberal education is important because of the perspective it encourages, and no reasons exist for why people cannot achieve it on their own. Elizabethan audiences loved Shakespeare, not only because of the action and suspense of his plays, but also for the awareness of human foibles and the dilemmas they provoked. Apparently, the English of Shakespeare's time were feeling some responsibility for being the world's most powerful nation.

We have plenty of artistic successes today, but relatively few people to appreciate them. It all comes down to how much we are willing to expend on such activities. As one of America's premier poets, Walt Whitman, reminded us over a hundred years ago, "To have great poets, there must be great audiences."

This process starts with parents and the values they develop in their children. Our schools could use more students who are ready to learn, who are prepared and in a frame of mind to learn.

I used to tell students that if Shakespeare were alive today, he would be writing and producing TV commercials for Madison Avenue. That is where our priorities are, where the money is. In order to produce third-rate drama, we must have first-rate commercials. Irony of ironies.

Today we do not want to engage the real literary folk who are trying to get through to us. The act of reading runs to brevity, short and easy because attention spans have shriveled. They are shorted because we are reacting to many more social forces. It is easy to be dominated by the marvelous conveniences of the age, the technological achievements that make life easier and comfortable. Look at them: the ubiquitous, ever-consuming television; the restless, easy appeal of the highway. Movies, computers, CD's, cell phones, and radios are everywhere.

We have the ever-present means of communication. You'd think these amenities would help us achieve the kind of culture that produces great art. But they do not. They make only speed. Do more, faster, ever faster. This busy-ness is not necessarily useful or productive. Henry David Thoreau's reaction to the news that because of the telegraph we could now talk to Texas, still goes: but do we have anything to say to Texas?

Why are there no Shakespeares today? Popular culture is under no illusions about producing quality, only quantity and the profits which that produces. All these splendid devices make life easier and quicker. Yes, and making us as a nation feel superior. Mohandas Gandhi, who came from that part of the world for which we have, all of a sudden, generated intense interest, said, "There is more to life than increasing its speed."

Actor Richard Ganoung (Class of '76)

> *The real actor – like any real artist –*
> *has a direct line to the collective heart.*
> Bette Davis

Some say teachers are actors. Generally, that may be true, but teachers are not conveying another's character, another's emotion. They bring their own personalities and experiences to bear. I cannot convincingly convey another's emotion to an audience; I have trouble enough transmitting my own.

As a teacher of high school seniors, I've had my share of experience with intrepid theater types. But against this backdrop, my admiration of them is abundant. And when one comes along with whom I can

124

communicate, I quickly take advantage. Richard Ganoung was one such. This tall, intense, and sympathetic soul seemed to be on track with my teaching strategies right from the start. I didn't realize it at the time, but while he was inspiring me with his unflagging interest and artistic talent, I was inspiring him as well.

Richard played the Stage Manager in Thornton Wilder's *Our Town*, the senior play for the Class of 1976. He sat at the side of a bare stage and narrated the story of Grover's Corners. In the spring of the bicentennial year, this play not only was appropriate but thrived because of its capable, articulate Stage Manager.

Richard takes his power to communicate very seriously. A friend of his and mine took me to see Richard in Shakespeare's *Measure for Measure* at the Off-Broadway Theatre on Water Street in Milwaukee.

Something you have to understand about this play. In addition to being one of the Bard's lesser-known works, it resists classification as tragedy or comedy. It has strong elements of both. Its low humor is omnipresent. Richard's character, Angelo, is not the kind of person to whom one is easily drawn. In that sense he is similar to Macbeth. The part requires treading a fine line between the character's tragic nature and the potential melodrama in the play's scheme of things.

As the plot progresses, Angelo comes into his own. Contradictions within him seem almost unsolvable. As the *Milwaukee Journal-Sentinel's* review put it, "Richard Ganoung's Angelo is intense enough to be scary and conflicted enough to be affecting." Richard pulled it off. He brought a sharp focus to the play's tragic theme. Angelo's redeeming qualities took on some heroic dimensions.

As the play's director wrote, this is "a subtle, well measured story of people somewhat adrift in a corrupt universe, who find redemption in the sacred power of forgiveness, and joy in the tempering power of love." Who says Shakespeare is out of date?

Richard said I was responsible for introducing him to Shakespeare. Richard, you've made me feel like a successful investor who has hit it big. For a teacher that means students who achieve, who have learned the "direct line to the collective heart." I don't know whether you remember or not, but the words you wrote for your school annual seem particularly appropriate now: "I am made whole through the people I love, and I am only half the person I can be in their absence."

We're both teachers. We're both in the arts, where we cannot always appreciate substance. I am inclined to believe prolific writer and American literary guru Christopher Morley when he writes, "Things of the spirit differ from things material in that the more you give the more you have."

Exploring Our Own Amazement

I love poetry. I try to get close to it, but often conclude that I just don't get it. I was able to teach poetry that I understood thoroughly. But I have a hard time paraphrasing poetic lines. Despite these troubles, I usually understand enough of poets' intentions to feel fulfilled.

Poetry is for the expression of ideas, experiences and feelings which have significance and for which we have a strong attraction. Poetry moves us as close to understanding and appreciating important things as any form of expression. But I am not an exponent.

Why do we try to fashion our thoughts in the fine apparel of poetics? Some things should be expressed in the most beautiful, effective manner language can provide. The problem in writing verse is that the major ingredients of language have to be in sync. In prose one can get by with aesthetic homicide, which in poetry would be suicide. Here is a paraphrase of a famous short poem:

> *At seven o'clock on a spring morning,*
> *a hillside covered with dew, a flying lark,*
> *and a snail on the thorn show the divine order of things.*
> *They assure us that the world is OK.*

There is little of the poetic about that. It is prose, a simple statement. The words convey only a set of facts, a set of fragments. Nothing much ruminates among the phrases. So, nothing much rises above the literal meanings of the statements.

Now the famous poem that used these ideas:

> *The year's at the spring*
> *And day's at the morn;*
> *Morning's at seven;*

126

The hillside's dew-pearled;
The lark's on the wing;
The snail's on the thorn;
God's in His heaven –
All's right with the world!

The poet worked these details until words, phrases, indeed the whole sentence, blended into a rhythmic little gem of meaning. Everything works as though it were ordained to do so.

The poem is from *Pippa Passes* by English poet Robert Browning. It is one of four songs of Pippa, a young factory worker. She spends her one holiday of the year walking through her town singing. Unknown to her, the four songs – at morning, noon, evening, and night help four important people of her city through a crisis in each of their lives.

Christopher Fry's words demonstrate how I feel about poetry: "Poetry is the language in which man explores his own amazement."

From Drowsing to Devouring Spenser

As a student, I used to drowse through literature classes. Poetry, since it is elevated and often seemed distant, induced dozing. Words that encourage yawning and snoozing have their place, I thought, but in class where slumber was discouraged, I had to struggle with Morpheus.

But then who was to know that later I would be sitting in Miss Marjorie Hugunin's English literature class reading poetry that ten years earlier had only encouraged somnolence. For reasons I do not fully understand, I was now devouring English poets: Chaucer, Byron, Milton, Pope, Wordsworth, Auden. They focused on such subjects as freedom, idealism, realism, love, immortality.

One poet who awoke in me a love of words and their magic was Edmund Spenser, an Elizabethan. He is remembered for his influence on later literature. For example, he introduced pastoral poetry to England. The habit of simple and beautiful picturing of country life has been popular ever since in English poetry.

In the *Faerie Queene*, the longest poem in the language, he used a stanza of his own invention, which became known as the Spenserian stanza. Each has nine lines of iambic pentameter, but the ninth had two

127

added syllables (making it iambic hexameter). The first and third lines
rhyme; as do the second, fourth, fifth, and seventh; and the sixth, eighth,
and ninth (ababboboo).

One stanza used widely in high-school anthologies, caught my eye. In
its ninety-two syllables, Spenser described the House of Morpheus, who is
the god of dreams, the son of the god of sleep, in Ovid's *Metamorphoses*.
The Greek word "morphe" means shape, form, i.e., the images called up in
dreams. When we say "in the arms of Morpheus," we mean someone's
asleep. As you read these seventy-one words, look for soft sounds, the
kind that lullabies and love lyrics have, with plenty of S's, Z's, N's, L's,
W's, and M's. Also try to stay awake.

> *And more, to lulle him in his slumber soft,*
> *A trickling streame from high rock tumbling downe,*
> *And ever-drizzling raine upon the loft.*
> *Mixt with murmuring winde, much like the sowne;*
> *Of swarming bees, did cast him in a swowne;*
> *No other noyse, nor peoples troublous cryes,*
> *As still are wont t'annoy the walled towne,*
> *Might there be heard: but careless Quiet lyes,*
> *Wrapt in eternall silence farre from enemyes.*

The combination of sounds suggests somnolence: Mixt with murmuring
winde. I love his use of alliterations when like consonant sounds are re-
peated:

> *No other noyse, nor peoples troublous cryes.*

Listen to the effect the six "o" sounds have on those seven words. That is
called assonance, internal or vowel sounds repeating.

When it comes to words, I no longer doze or drowse. I have been having a dazzling love affair with words ever since.

Dickinson: Divine Disclosures

Some combinations of words stick with us. Something in the meanings they produce penetrates the senses and accumulates more meaning. Sometimes it is certain individual words that perform this magic. Sometimes it is the sum of the words. More often it is a product, something much more than the sum.

One particular set of words (twelve of them) has stuck with me since I first encountered them. They lead to a revelation – every time I read them, they perform the same revealing little miracle. Poet Emily Dickinson wrote this poem:

That it will never come again
Is what makes life so sweet.

What a divine disclosure. Almost Delphic in its implications. When life leaves us, our experience, our knowledge, our expectations, our consciousness, our beings, end. What made us living creatures, the chemistry that formed and energized our lives, is no more. Nothing of this earth can again make us what we were. The atoms, the molecules, the protoplasm, the chemistry of our conscious lives, have dispersed, to be chemistry in other forms.

Life is indeed magic. It is precious by all measure. How can something of such splendid worth change, end, and turn back into the common chemistry of the earth? How can this "quintessence of dust," as Hamlet described it, lose such marvelous form and power and being?

With the magic comes fragility. We humans are the flower of the earth. We germinate, grow, blossom, then die. This may be why we love flowers. In a miniature we see our own lives, which only seem longer.

But the stuff of which we are made alters, transforms into new forms. We believe we beings, built from the chemistry of the earth, are more than the sum of our parts, that something transcends our functioning earth bodies. If that is so, we are ill-equipped to understand it. We seem to be vehicles passing through and playing parts, destined to be, without understanding the precious consciousness with which we are endowed. I wonder if understanding is enough consolation for not enjoying it.

Golden Ragwort on Lake Geneva Walkway

Oriole among cattails on Lake Como

David Copperfield

David Copperfield is autobiographical for certain. I have encountered overt evidence. When Copperfield writes about his writing, he is brusquely Dickensian. His references are peripheral. The intertwining of plots and subjects is quite complex. It isn't Russian in the sense that it becomes nearly impossible to follow them, but the dilemma is that no apparent direction or relationship develops among them. There probably will be no swift, dramatic pulling together of plots. This book is autobiographical, though not strictly.

Dickens' fiction is so convincing that truth seems to manifest untouched. The main reason seems to be his ability to create characters whose lives, and therefore their natures, are so embedded in the plot that they are hard to extract.

Writers today seem to have private agendas, all of which involve bank accounts. They write what will sell. I won't bother to list those subjects, but this so isolates fiction in corners and crevices, and in other private, personal places, that its reality is restricted to its own characters and episodes. Who would think of remembering most fictional characters today as memorable, as having something important, even universal, to say to us?

That is what is so disarmingly different about Dickens. Though created over one hundred years ago, the characters are as valid today as then. We may chuckle and poke fun at Victorian habit and delusions, but we cannot fault the treachery of Uriah Heep, the bumbling heroism of Wilkins Micawber, and the difficult childhood and steady maturity of David Copperfield. That is heady stuff that can be enjoyed while teaching something of the vagaries of human nature. And what is amazing is that Dickens' work was published serially in the current press of the day. Yes, Dickens wrote for money, too. However, if ever a writer precipitated truth, it was Dickens. As one of his *Copperfield* characters declared, "It was as true… as taxes is. And nothing's truer than them."

On Books Not Read

It is easier to discuss movies one hasn't seen than it is discussing books one hasn't read. If we think about that, it could well lead to considerable differences between motion pictures and books. But the motive of this writing is to encourage the idea that books and movies are useful ways for advancing the human condition.

Involvement with books can be intense and memorable. Reading allows one to stop, reflect, reread, think toward the larger picture, check context, even make notes. Reading can often become very personal.

Since reading is a soundless process, the mind and all its resources can be employed over and over again. The reader must be active, the movie viewer can be passive. We feel a kinship, with authors. With movies made from books, that connection seems to evaporate in the mechanics of production with its time constraints and finances.

Books allow quick reference. To get back to review a movie, whether in a theater or through a DVD, requires time. One pass through a two-bar movie seems more time than one should spend sitting in one place and not necessarily allowing the mind to play a part.

Most people will say movies are strictly for entertainment, yet entertainment without substance is not all that much better than nothing. Maybe that pattern has something to do with why people have more books they have not read than books they have read. Now people also have more movies than they will view again.

Discussing the content of movies should be a natural byproduct of viewing them. Otherwise it seems their value is questionable.

I don't watch many movies. Exceptions are rare, but as a teacher I understood that many adolescents spent considerable time parked in front of the big theater or home TV screens. Not making use of the cinema in classes seemed opportunity lost. So, a strategy evolved.

The object was to learn as much about a motion picture as I could. I had many ways to wax wise about current movies. The chief one is reading at least two reviews. Another is to gather impressions by consulting colleagues and friends. In other words, considering the current chatter among fellow adults.

If a movie is based on a book, I pay special attention. Try to find writing that gets at the motives behind making the movie in the first place.

Often it is money.

Survey techniques like this place a teacher in a better position to lead discussions. The best way to describe my method: keep eyes and ears open for anything on the subject movie and especially listen to students talk.

Then subtly but openly make it known you had not seen the flick in question. Whatever the nature of the discussion, if interjecting movie talk might help the process, let it happen. After all, motion pictures are part of adolescent life and how can you relate to them, and them to you, without a connection common to both you and them?

I never consciously made plans to use movies in my classes. My students initiated the discussions of movies connected to our studies. Movies are an effective classroom tool – and I don't ever have to show one.

One of the scary side effects of teaching English is the fear that someone will ask about a book I have not read. It turned out that was not as much of a problem as I thought it would be.

Some of my catchup readings included *Walden, Catcher in the Rye, Don Quixote, Return of the Native, Our Town,* and *David Copperfield.* I know, how could I call myself a useful, functioning English teacher without those classics? Can anyone know how unreasonable it is to expect English teachers to have read all the volumes necessary to avoid embarrassing in-class moments? Well, I know. Not long ago, I read a book called *How to Talk about Books You Haven't Read* by a French professor of literature named Pierre Bayard (translated by Jeffrey Wehlman, 2007).

He laid out a convincing case that one cannot possibly read all there is of value to be read and maintain a reasonable perspective. "… even a prodigious reader never has access to more than an infinitesimal fraction of the books that exist." And what is more, he writes, you don't have to try. I wish this fellow had been around when I began teaching, when I was most painfully aware of my reading deficit.

Teaching Writing

The more I taught, the more I believed that my most persistent and enduring influence has been the teaching of writing. The most difficult and time-consuming of human tasks, writing is important because it provokes and structures thinking. Developing the individual's thinking capacities is the central task of any school. It is also the most difficult and cannot be done directly. A teacher cannot say, "Today we learn how to think." The process involves getting the mind to do what we want it to do. Only the individual can control this mental discipline. The teacher's function becomes one of inspiring and inducing the desire to "work the brain."

CONTENTS

Writing at the Heart of Education and Democracy

To be thought of as an educated people, Americans should have broad knowledge and be able to express themselves on a variety of subjects. Most of the time, these expressions will pertain to one's profession, avocation, or a personal subject and how it relates to others. Understanding how one's function in society relates to the world's realities is important in a democracy. It's called liberal education.

Relatively few Americans can verbalize a logical sequence of thought in their speech. Even fewer can do so in their writing.

Writing is the product of thought, and we do not insist that it be practiced at home or in schools. Expressing one's self is at the heart of education. The surefire test of a subject's mastery is being able to think and write about it. Apply. Of what value is education if we do not use it?

To test mastery of subject matter, students must be able to express themselves, not simply parroting back information, but applying it in response to questions and problems developed in the classroom. In other words, writing essays.

The first words in the dictionary definition of the word "essay" are TRIAL and TEST followed by EFFORT and ATTEMPT (yes, in capitals). The idea of the essay is to apply knowledge and to elaborate on what has been mastered. Could there be more convincing proof of learning?

The ability to write an essay, on the spot, in response to questions asked about subjects studied, is the only real test of education. But this test is not easy for the student or the teacher.

Imagine reading essays for over one hundred students every time you give a test. Whoever decided that someone teaching the most fundamental of all skills must have five classes a day with twenty, twenty-five, or thirty students in each of them?

On the other hand, what are we expecting of our schools? The fundamental processes of reading, mastering, and writing are not widely practiced. One reason is that teachers are not trained to do it. Also, this deficit is not something that can be corrected in a summer course or two.

If we were to look into the backgrounds of teachers who can apply subject matter and these processes, we would find in most cases it began in their early upbringing. They were reading regularly from the start.

That leads to the second reason why our society is failing students in the development of their literacy processes. Parents are not requiring development of self-discipline in their children. Reading is a fading skill. We read in shorter and shorter spurts and call it education. The trivia-type mastery encouraged on TV game shows is an example of the product of shorter attention spans. Instant recall leads to instant gratification.

Mastery of details for mastery's sake is not real education. Today's schools are playing to these short attention spans. If students don't put subject matter to work constructively, they haven't mastered it. We as teachers haven't tested it.

Quick solutions to this problem do not exist. It can only begin with a generation of children who come to understand they have been shortchanged and resolve to control their own training. Then when those children become parents, they will by habit provide their children with the encouragement and necessary skills. Out of that new generation, then, should come a generation of teachers who can energize and inspire on a level that produces the well-educated citizenry we desperately need.

Current children and adolescents are often called the millennial generation. Their older members are now beginning to be graduated from college and are at the leading edge of the next civic or heroic generation.

Our democracy needs an educated citizenry that can intelligently participate in a globalized society, able to think and express themselves on a variety of subjects. Well-educated citizens will become the fundamental rule of survival.

One prerequisite for personal success is the generating of self-confidence. Learning to use what one has learned requires meeting and interacting with people. I recall many students who had a wealth of potential, whose minds were ripe for great missions, but who lacked confidence. Come to find out, they did not trust their facility with language. They had been left behind in the learning of skills that make practicing a profession possible.

One year we had a foreign exchange student from New Zealand whose mastery of English was extraordinary, at least by American standards. I can recall my students wishing out loud that their language was as articulate and polished as hers.

Inevitably, I would ask them how they thought she had achieved this competence. We decided it was due to many factors: hearing language used well, reading language well, then emulating what was heard and read. Practicing receiving and using language well are not easy unless we have a lot of both going on around us. What level of language do we hear in our families, our schools, on television, at work, or our reading?

If we are going to be articulate, we need to practice. It begins, develops, and pays off with language – the reading, speaking and writing of language.

Achieving status as a literate citizen is a long process. Becoming an experienced and trustworthy driver does not take place overnight. And of course, one academic school year would be equivalent to overnight.

But once realizing that we are becoming good at using one's language skills, confidence follows. We appreciate the power language can bestow, and we use them more. There is less hesitation. We become more positive. We become articulate spokespersons for our professions, for anything we stand for, and more important, for ourselves.

People who master language are often interesting. They are so involved in what they are doing that it seldom occurs to them how it all works. Their work is part of them and they part of it.

One day they will realize they are performing one of humanity's miracles, the mastery of language. Then they are likely to know the confidence of their convictions, to be purveyors of intelligent opinion. I don't mean to disappoint, but this mastery can only be relative. It doesn't matter because competent language is now part of how they live.

Unfortunately, it is not cool to be thoughtful and articulate. This attitude is an American shortcoming. One day it could do us in. As corny as it sounds, masters of articulate English are often not American heroes.

Writing, the Most Neglected Discipline

For sure, writing is the most demanding of the academic disciplines. Why I was ever attracted to its awesome demands, I'll never know. I guess I didn't know about the awesome demands. My desire to write dates from university days when I was transferring from one major to another.

I concluded that my resolution at UW-Madison was not very strong. I had no plans, little determination. The only exception (and strangely enough not in my major) was two radio writing courses which showed me to have little talent. At the time, I could not write a coherent paragraph. I feared writing assignments right into a summer school at the University of Minnesota at the end of my first semester of teaching (1957).

But at UW-Wisconsin, I took a radio production course that required writing scripts. Though the emphasis was on production, I had some choices. I chose writing, as opposed to production assignments, which required no writing. The reason was music, particularly jazz.

I wrote one script that involved the use of recorded music "with voice over" as production people say. The year was 1950 when recording equipment was in its infancy. I had a tape recorder, a Sound Mirror. On the day of my presentation, I carried it from Camp Randall all the way up to Bascom Hall, which was about a half mile with quite a steep climb at the end. The recorder was suitcase size and heavy. It was quite a chore, but my presentation worked. My classmates and teacher were impressed.

I stood there reading my script with the music synchronized to my words, or vice versa. One of the reasons it worked was my love of music and the strong feelings I was developing about expressing it. I felt so strongly, in fact, that I don't remember writing as a chore at all.

Everything else I can remember about writing assignments at the University was loaded with negative baggage. Who would have ever thought in 1950 that eight years later I would be teaching? And teaching English? And to high school seniors?

I was not teaching English because of my writing ability. Rather, I had a desire to write, and when I went back to college to train for teaching, I chose English because I perceived it as a training ground for me as well as for my students. From this experience, I learned the primary ingredient for successful writing. Hands down, it is the most important constituent in the process. Desire ... the will to do it.

Most teachers of English and most students do not bring vigor to the task. Most English instruction is of a nominal nature. Cold, dull, academic. What good will teaching be, what will students gain, in such environment?

What has caused this sudden outburst of professional zeal? I will tell you. I read a story in today's newspaper topped by the headline: "Students need to spend more time on writing, U.S. report says." The U.S. Education Department's National Assessment of Educational Progress issued its 1992 *Writing Report Card*. Writing samples from thirty thousand children in grade four, eight, and twelfth were required in informative, persuasive, and narrative writing.

NAEP reported that schools seem to be putting more emphasis on writing instruction. Compared to its 1988 writing assessment, "students are being asked to write somewhat more frequently, at greater length, and in assignments requiring more analysis and interpretation."

The report said, however, that testing found deficiencies at all three levels, particularly in the ability to write persuasively: "To become good writers, students need expert instruction, frequent practice, constructive feedback." Yes, we need skilled, vigorous, dedicated teachers.

The *Writing Report Card* blamed poor study habits for much of the problem. For example, eighth graders spend only two hours a week on writing, including time in the classroom. Those same students spend fourteen hours a week watching television. Not surprisingly, I observed a correlation between poor writing skills and frequency of TV viewing.

Education Secretary Richard Riley said, "Writing needs to be an integral part of every academic subject, and more time needs to be devoted to teaching children this basic and very important skill." He also said, "All the reforms and laws that we pass in Washington will not matter a great deal unless parents are parents and give their children a love of learning." Parents need to be parents.

Training students in ways that they generate desire to express themselves is the key. If they want to express themselves, they will work at writing. My experience is that when students figure out what a powerful tool writing is, their demeanor regarding academics alters dramatically. They develop confidence. They feel a power that begins to assert itself in other phases of their lives.

I am a case in point. My interest in music was growing. I saw writing as a tool for my expression of that interest. I forgot that writing assignments were negative baggage.

Within a period of eight years, I not only cleared the fear and developed an ambition, but I became an English teacher. I went a circuitous route to my classrooms, but once there I settled in. I knew my services were valuable. I put up with the close-to-intolerable class loads, the busyness of bureaucracy, and the ever-mounting social problems that took their toll of student learning.

I found outlets for student writing – journalism and the graduation project. I cultured the art of the critique. I came to know my students. I developed curiosity about them and the learning process.

When I retired, this facility did not leave me. Neither did the writing. In fact, I can say now that they are stronger than ever. Though my relationships with students were over, the writing has continued to develop.

My beliefs regarding writing and its discipline are very strong. I trust that is obvious. I also trust it is obvious that our schools are working very well because we do not insist that they do. Our indifference has produced undirected youth, 8 A.M. to 4 P.M. union teachers, and a useless bureaucracy. Families no longer set the patterns of education. Social problems determine the priorities. Schools are really social and counseling centers. Talk about a cry in the wilderness.

Importance of Language in the Classroom
Writing is at the heart of language skills. If English classes are supposed to train students in the use of language, can there be a more effective means than writing?

In driver education, students reach the point where classroom training demonstrates its limitations. Until they get behind the wheel of a real automobile, the whole business is academic.

Why should it be any different with language? Literature, vocabulary, semantics, grammar – how can these be anything but preparation? To read, speak, and write – that is the name of the game. Since Badger High School reserved the sophomore year for speech (no English classes), I felt all the more strongly that writing must be the focus in my classes. To learn to express one's self in the native tongue – it's as simple as that. Until a student can state and develop an idea on paper in his/her own words, English class is something short of the real thing.

From the beginning of my life as an English teacher, I knew these beliefs to be true. Practicing it, however, was another matter. I doubt most people understand what being an English teacher in the public high school really means.

First off, we English teachers need to have a reasonable mastery of the language. We also need to have a reasonable mastery of ourselves. We can't just know language; we must be able to convey our understanding. And we cannot get away with bad personal language habits and expect students to follow the rules. If we think that, we had better back off and dream again.

We cannot fool high school seniors. They may allow us to think we are getting away with something, but that would only be in the name of making things easier for themselves.

One of the easiest jobs for the English teacher is assigning a composition. Nothing can manifest the authority of a teacher faster than laying on the line the rules for a composition assignment. It makes us sound authoritative – telling students what to do. Then they do all the work. We set a deadline, and poof! That is all there is to it. That is the easy part.

The day that the "in" basket fills up with 120 compositions begins the hard part. Reading 120 three-to-five-page papers is one thing. Doing something with them is quite another. How long will it take to read 120 papers averaging, let us say, five hundred words. That is sixty thousand words. If you read 200 words per minute, and you read straight through, you can do it in five hours.

But that is not the way students' papers are read. We must do more than read them. We must decide what is good and what needs help. We should praise what is done well and decide how to advise about the problems. We cannot praise everything that is good, and we cannot nitpick every little problem.

Each paper is different. Each student deserves individual treatment of what he or she has written. Clearly, reading each paper is only the beginning. The written critique and notations which follow will, on the average, take twice as long as reading the paper.

As an English teacher for nearly thirty years, the only serious complaint I had was the number of students in relation to the scope of the task. Since retiring from teaching, I have given considerable thought to the matter: class load is a direct cause of the teacher's dilemma.

In the early years when I was learning to make reading student papers a reasonably efficient task, I assumed that when I gained more experience, the process would settle into a reasonable regimen. That never happened, because as I became more skilled in the task, the more I found I could do with individual students and their writing talents and problems. I became energized by the powers of my experience. The problem was – time. As my career progressed, I was amazed by what could be done, so I worked hard on the control of my class load.

One of the reasons I sustained journalism was that it changed the emphasis of part of my reading load. I took on the task of editor of a school district newsletter for several years. In that, I admit my chief impulse was load control.

Most English teachers can avoid real engagement with student writing. For most of my years as an English teacher, I was the only member of my department whose major stress was on composition. It was far short of what high school seniors needed to improve their language skills. It's all a matter of load.

How could teachers possibly have their students writing a paper a week and not be taking shortcuts? Teachers have many ways to shortcut the reading and evaluating processes. They can decide which papers will get only a cursory treatment with only a grade and a phrase or two of comment. No matter what the rationale, that cursory treatment shortchanges students the time and energy they invested in their writing. Or teachers can decide that one paper per year will not be read at all. But what if a student is on the brink of a breakthrough and they chose to disregard this important one?

Learning to write well is, along with reading itself, the central tool of education. It is not treated that way in American high schools. We are expecting too much of teachers whose classes involve over a hundred students every day. It is impossible to perform the teaching function with that many students.

English teachers are not trained to teach about the elements of composition. I was not. I learned it as I went. Not everyone can be expected to do that, nor should they have to. If we recognized that language skill is important, we would make sure English teachers were of the highest order, we would give them reasonable class loads, and we would recognize that with experience the English teacher can be a valuable aid in teaching other teachers. If only we realized the importance of these beliefs enough to act on it.

Language, Thinking and Learning

*There is nothing either good
or bad but thinking makes it so.*
William Shakespeare

Language is the vehicle that manifests thinking and learning. The abilities to develop an intelligent opinion and support it with rational thinking and orderly documentation require guidance over the formal learning years.

The elements involved in effective written expression are so many, varied, and complex that no one single formula could possibly work all of the time. Constant writing practice, which stresses the most important of these diverse elements, is the best bet.

Apart from curiosity, desire and time, the process involves a subject, a tentative thesis or controlling idea, and the many varied and complex possibilities and problems. Simplified, it means reading, thinking, writing.

Since words stand for thoughts and since communication depends on words, the nature of words, their meanings, and possible uses, are the fundamental heart of mature language study.

We must have judgements, questioning, and study. Critical thinking is the term given to this process, which has central importance in a responsible life. I contend that reading, thinking, speaking, and writing are not being done thoughtfully, thoroughly, or critically in the public schools.

Students can easily locate a relevant fact, copy it from a source onto paper, and call it his own. Teachers can easily pass on a set of facts as a set of facts. However, is it the primary task of teachers to transmit facts? It is the student's job to absorb them. Not entirely. Rather, understanding those facts, their importance in a context, and their application within a perspective are important.

Understanding is the objective, understanding of principles through their use – reading, thinking, writing about them. No fact or set of facts can be justified by themselves. Only when applied, made personal by application to one's own contexts, can subject matter be mastered. That is learning.

Tough Business of Teaching Writing

One does not teach writing; rather, one teaches about it. That idea grew gradually.

I can remember the thrill of autumn, knowing it was a time to search out talent. Long before the last leaves had fallen, I knew that the thrill was gone, not because the talent was not there, but because so many other activities were masking and deluding students about what is important.

The spearhead of academic training is reading and writing. Since the brain trains slowly, the attack must be carried on regularly over a long period of time. In fact, its rigors are such that if we do not love its processes, it is doubtful we will succeed.

What these comments all add up to is the premise that teacher and student must have a reasonable degree of desire to succeed at what they are doing for teaching writing and the learning to write well to take place.

Teaching writing takes a high degree of faith. Learning to write well takes desire, persistence and energy. The student's part is most difficult. The relationship would make no sense if that were not true.

The teacher's role takes the form of reading, evaluating, careful critiquing, and the consuming of time. The teacher's problem involves the number of students in which he or she must exercise faith, the numbers of papers to read, evaluate, and critique. Record keeping and a good memory are essential. As student papers are read, critiqued, and returned, it is important to assess the way the student is developing. Is the student advancing in his or her use of language skills? Is his or her approach to subject matter and the revision process realistic? Constantly, teachers make judgments. It is challenging, engaging, rewarding work. My love for it grew consistently over the years.

The National Council of Teachers of English has for decades recommended that no English teacher meet more than one-hundred students per day. When considering the nature of the process and what it takes to successfully engage students in it, eighty students is too many.

One way to appreciate the time problem is to consider the routine. I assigned a paper in English classes, that meant, let's say, eighty papers to read, evaluate, and keep within the frame-work of needs of each student, or rather eighty students. I have never kept record of the time it took to read and critique papers.

144

The most difficult part of the process was trying to decide what to praise and what to criticize. It is generally good advice to begin with a statement of praise dealing with the general approach to subject matter and then go from there. Generalizing must be done constantly while providing the student access to the specifics of problems. The general tone must be positive, but the real problems must be addressed vigorously.

With a 300-500-word paper, can these processes be done realistically in less that fifteen minutes? Knowing what I want to say is one thing and writing it in so many words is another. But even if an idealistic average of fifteen minutes per paper could be sustained, that is twenty hours of work.

This kind of work must be sustained only so long at a time. It requires concentration, a minimum of interruptions. The class day is not good for this kind of work. Interruptions are common during non-class hours.

I have had colleagues tell me that once they got the hang of a student's approach, subsequent papers were easier. That sounds like a cop-out to me. When one "gets the hang" of a student's approach, it is time to exert effort toward change and improvement, not to routinely accept students' habits. After all, isn't that the idea, to encourage students to advance themselves in this skill? It is the kiss of death to let any part of this process become routine.

What I am asking students to do is not routine. Why should any part of it, especially my effort, be reduced to routine? It is the student who accepts the routine, and the results are only too clear in papers. Students will take routes that demand less. They will do that because their interests are elsewhere:

> I am into athletics. It is exciting. I see progress. I am reported in the press. It is recognition. Or I am in a play. I learn my lines. I will play before an audience. People depend upon me. The results are concrete.

But in the future, what will matter most? Is this business with language really a skill of survival? Yes, it is. Ask employers anywhere. But our twenty-first-century world has provided a thousand easy reasons for believing otherwise.

145

Write to Mine Your Mind

I cannot tell you what to write. You must decide that. But remember, if you are not part of what you write, it cannot represent you. You cannot marshal all your resources. How will you be able to mine the minerals of your mind?

Maybe if you just start, something will lead somewhere. It depends on how engaged you are. It's all in the mind.

Tell a story. Any story. Just tell one thing after another. And think as you tell. Is what the telling reveals more than a sequence of events and observations? Is something else growing out of your storytelling? Unless you let it out, it will stay within. Then what good is it?

Solve a problem. Something in our lives needs explaining. Something we can't figure out. Write around, over, under, and through it. The solution will probably pop into our heads because we let something out which we did not count on, or know, or understand. It's all in the mind.

Describe someone who is mysterious. Characterize the mind, the actions, and the physical presence of your subject. Something will occur to you as you consider the potpourri that is pouring out of your mind, a person fashioned right out of your mind.

Whatever you do, keeping going once started. Don't stop for anything. Not to consider a thought already down about which you are having second thoughts. Not to find a better word. Not to check a spelling. Don't stop for anything.

In fact, fight to keep going. Not until you finish do you stop. Sentences, words, and spellings can be attended to later, but not always the content pouring from the mind. That flow can stop in a moment of hesitation.

What a satisfying feeling it is to know what you think is now what you have written. Thoughts, nebulous thoughts, now concrete stuff right there on the paper. You, in person, for you to see. What could possibly reveal more than something you fashioned into a form which anyone can understand? I can't tell you what to write, but I can share the plum, the prize of your mind's effort. I can hardly wait.

Tell me why writing is so important. I can tell you. It lays the mind out where you can see it and how it works. And you don't have to go public until it is the way you want it. But rough or smooth, it is your mind, as close as we can get to it.

Writing through something does satisfy. Writing seems to make the brain manifest, gives the mind the knowledge that there is some understanding. Perhaps it's explaining how an auto can perform certain maneuvers and attain certain speeds. The effort is pointless until the vehicle attains and performs what its creators tried to build into it.

The activity brings satisfaction, then, without having been read by anyone else. But someone else reading and understanding is the ultimate test. It is satisfying to articulate an idea, but not like being able to make someone else understand. What I learned about the state of education as a teacher is reason enough to try what I am trying.

I like this little poem which appeared in the *Christian Science Monitor* many moons ago. I didn't record the date, but the poet is Bonnie May Malody, whoever she may be. But the important thing is her poem:

> Write a love letter
> To someone
> Every day.
> Even if you have
> Nowhere to send it,
> Even if you have
> No one,
> Write.
> To the day,
> To a rainbow,
> To a blossom,
> To yourself,
> To God.

What persists about this poem is its hope, its every-urgent message that writing is important, especially when it is positive, when it is about important things.

Inciting to Write

I used to try to find interesting writing subjects that could provoke students' interest. During the middle of the second semester, I wanted students to write short, thoughtful pieces that could be written within the class hour.

These impromptu pieces served many purposes. It was a way of varying writing practice. I could present a variety of subject choices quickly, hoping one would inspire students who had not yet been motivated. I could also get an idea how students' impromptu writing differed from their take-home assignments, which were subject to other influences. I occasionally stumbled into dramatic differences in style, which usually meant overzealous home help.

These subjects seemed destined to appeal to students, often yielding quite a distance between initial excitement and substantial follow-through. I reworked the topics and their wording. Each of the topics was designed as a 20-minute, in-class writing assignment:

- What you would teach if you could take over one of your classes?
- Effects upon you of a decision someone else has made recently.
- A description of what you would put in a ten-by-ten-foot room if you were confined there for one month (no people allowed).
- A comic strip that presented your philosophy of life.
- What would you do with $_____?
- The one thing you must do by the time you are ___.
- A description of yourself as your parents see you.
- Most important thing you have learned about yourself this year.

These subjects placed the student in the middle of things. I wanted their experience and judgement to be foremost. The subject most commonly chosen was the ten-by-ten room.

I always considered the class in choosing the assignments. I never offered more than three choices at a time. I tried to include appealing subjects which I hoped would produce thoughtful responses. The goal was to increase the possibilities of students generating mental energy. I used a photograph to prompt students' writing, so I tried it myself. Here it is:

The waters are Geneva Lake.
Why not Geneva, Switzerland?
Why a western sky?
Why no eastern?
Why sun setting?
Why not rising?
It is a golden sky,
and Sol is settling into the horizon,
taking the day with him.
The scene is about clouds,
long, horizontal, wispy,
thinning toward a line of hills.
They are gold.
The sky is gold.
Even water is reflecting gold.
Perhaps this is what is to be,
a photograph of tomorrow –
in the west, golden,
with gossamer dreams,
somewhere.

I finally found the Margery Allingham words about her process of writing:

I write every paragraph four times:
once to get my meaning down,
once to put in everything I left out,
once to take out everything that sees unnecessary,
and once to make the whole thing sound as if I had only just
thought of it.

I kept that on the bulletin board near my desk in room 207 for many years.
Oh, that it could be that orderly a process.

Knowing Your Reader

One matter a writer must deal with right from the beginning is the relationship between oneself and the reader.

We have all been readers from as long ago as we can remember. We probably never give much thought to writers and their producing of what we read. In fact, we may be naïve about the writer and his function. It is easy to take printed matter for hard, naked truth. Would that it was so.

When I read, I give myself over to the writer and what he or she is trying to do. I must go a certain distance to allow the writer to establish a basis, background of facts, and context.

It is very easy to trust writers. Those who are skillful in establishing their contexts always sound authoritative. They are believable. Most readers probably are secretly in awe of writers. No wonder we tend to believe what we read.

Writers learn that they must establish themselves with readers. One of their functions is to sound convincing. When my students got around to that point in the year when their own writing began to take on the problems of believability and integrity, I read them a piece I called *The Problem of the Reader*.

In doing so, I wanted students to think about reading and writing together. They had been readers for as long as they could remember. But writing, that skill which must be mastered before anyone can read, seemed to be something new to them. This insight was worth considering as they took on writing assignments which gave them options and choices. Here is *The Problem of the Reader*:

We become so involved in what it is we want to say and how we express it that we forget that at least fifty percent of any communication is the audience. The job is to reach the reader and do all we can to make him understand what we must say. That doesn't mean we have to sweet talk him or accommodate him, but we cannot be so naïve that we forget he has a point of view, prejudices, and experiences that make it impossible to see things exactly the way we do.

The reader doesn't know all; he doesn't understand the facts and circumstances underlying your subject. The idea is to build those as part of your writing. In short, you cannot assume that he understands the context of the subject matter as well as you do.

For example, if you are trying to relay an experience to him, you must fill in appropriate background and "set the scene" so to speak. You cannot simply jump into the middle of your subject matter without remembering to fill in details, which you know very well, but he cannot possibly appreciate, unless they are spelled out.

The most common example of this problem is the newspaper reporter and his readers. He may decide he is going to start writing with an interesting excerpt or experience from the details of his subject. This done, he jumps right into the story without identifying his subject, or setting the scene, or pinning down the time and place factors, or including important background material.

The result will be that the reader cannot follow the important thread of meaning. He may appreciate the experience, but he will not have a frame of reference against which he can set that experience. Instead of following the train of thought, the reader will be worrying about details which the writer understands, but which are now becoming a kind of guessing game with the reader. In short, he is not with you.

I'm sure you have had several personal experiences in which a person has told of something that happened and has failed to tell you important background information. In conversation one can rectify the situation by asking to clarify, but in reading that is impossible because the writer is not present – all the reader has left is a set of black symbols on white paper. Anything he has failed to supply is left to guesswork.

As writers, we must allow for the framework, the context. It is easy to see that simply writing a piece is not enough. The writer must re-examine his or her work, revising or supplementing with secondary material. I don't know how much good that did, but it was one way of keeping the reader-writer equation balanced. Too many writers think as givers, and too many readers act only as receivers.

As a writing practitioner in my own English classes, I found an opportunity to practice both, and see both for what they were: the original survival skills, each dependent on the other. The nature of the interdependence is complex, but that is the heart of academic education.

Sentences and the Feel for Writing

What is a sentence? Probably we think no more about what a sentence is than when we think about an automobile once we've learned how to drive one. The comparison may be good up to a point. We take each for granted until something goes wrong with one.

When the car breaks down, it is only the cost of what it will take for someone else to fix it that concerns us. For the most part, the episode is between each of us, the car, and the checkbook. We may take some ribbing about that lemon, or some such, from a few close friends, but the problem is in someone else's hands once the someone is convinced that he will get his money.

With sentences, it is different. If something we write down fails, the problem is immediately personal. Something within failed. Something of our beings is hurt. And once away from the classroom, it is difficult to find someone to whom we can take the problems. It becomes a matter of pride.

I can reason, that here I am, educated, or so I thought. But I didn't learn where and how to solve my own language problems. Pride is involved in taking a language problem to friends, parents, and especially former teachers. I also didn't learn how it feels to sustain the writing process from my writing purpose to a completed and confidence-building manuscript. I do not have that confidence.

Of course, the basic unit of this problem is the sentence, the ability to write a sentence that transmits what I want to say the way I want to say it.

One of the first lessons that writing practice teaches is that the first draft of a sentence is just that, the first. As I write, I learn a touch, a feel, that tells me when a sentence is right. This touch comes from practice, conscious, regular practice.

At this point, the mind and the discipline come in. I doubt there is, or ever was, a writer who does not have to depend on such resources as the dictionary, old usage handbook or text, research sources, favorite copy reader, pride and patience. The business of writing is stringing together sentences so they add up to what we wanted to say in the first place.

I found that students do not become serious about sentences until they have tried to make several of them add up to something worthwhile. Until then, we must muddle along, single out the most serious writing problems, and practice until the light comes on that turns us serious. Then we will make sentences work because we want to make them work.

When the power of language hits us as writers, when the process is wed to the purpose, then we may be able to consider what a sentence is. It is time that sentences (or most sentences) are groups of words that convey content and have at least one subject and one verb each.

But now we know how important the sentences around any single sentence are. An idea is transmitted through a sequence of sentences, each relating to the others. In the end, a consistent sequence of ideas must parade through these sentences. We know that any one sentence is simply part of a tightly integrated set of sentences.

It is at this point, with the impact of all the other sentences of the draft ringing in our ears that we can consider one sentence, and again ask, what is a sentence?

Penmanship

> *Handwriting is an art, like gardening, open to*
> *any amateur, for the delight he gets from it*
> *himself and the further pleasure he gives to others.*
> Lewis Mumford

To a teacher, penmanship is important. The rest of the world seems to have rejected the idea, but a teacher cannot avoid it, especially an English teacher.

It's chalkboard, critiques, comments on tests, writing passes. It is also student penmanship. Much of what students do is in long-hand, and if they produce that way (as most of mine did), the teacher is in for a range of writing woes and calligraphic calamities.

Completing the trifecta of penmanship dilemmas is the occasion when the teacher has personal problems with hand-writing.

I had it all. I used the chalkboard daily; I wrote critiques on compositions. My students chose to turn in compositions in long-hand, and I saw a range of penmanship you would not believe. But the real burden in my teaching was my own penmanship. Thus, my attitude toward the poor handwriting habits of many students was tempered by my own, which bordered on the desperate. As a child, I must not have realized the advantages of good penmanship. In those days, it was practiced daily in elementary schools. I received a grade for penmanship. It was on my report card, right along with reading, arithmetic, and all the rest. There was no way to ignore it.

That didn't mean I improved; it simply meant the problem was right up front all the time. I did not improve, and there must have been a reason. Whatever happened, I took this baggage into the classroom as a teacher twenty years later. If you think I took criticism for my hieroglyphic scribbling in the age of the typewriter, you can imagine what happened with the coming of the computer and the word processor.

Right from the beginning, I faced the problem head on. Teachers should be honest with teenagers. I did not make excuses. I plowed ahead, trying to keep longhand in a straight line, carefully dotting i's and crossing t's. I figured if I was readable that students would be tolerant. Standing at a chalkboard in front of twenty-five high school seniors, trying to write a sentence in a straight line, was always an act of faith with me.

I gradually became comfortable sharing my innermost calligraphic dilemmas. And the students seemed to understand. Though I would have trouble proving it, I think my attitude and approach made students more conscious of their own penmanship. Especially in compositions was this notable. Of course, that is where I wanted to see self-improvement because my job depended on it. Their self-improvement as well as mine.

Reading typewritten pages was much easier, and I promoted the idea of typing compositions. But I was not overzealous in this promotion because I could not always tell who was doing the typing, while there was no doubt with longhand. I was a proponent of the students being entirely in charge of their own writing efforts, right down to producing their own manuscripts.

Handwriting is a worthwhile art. I envy people who do it well. That is no doubt because I do not do it well. My sister Carol used to address her letters with great style and flourish. As the example shows, she could have her wildly artistic flourishes and the post office still managed to get them to our house. I put examples of her writing on my bulletin board, and students marveled at this example.

Whether these efforts had any effect on students, I cannot know. But I always had the feeling of a mutual acknowledgement that we would all exert a little more effort to make our scribbles at least tolerable. However, the real problem was that my students had only to master my penmanship, albeit a problem. I, on the other hand, faced one hundred different writing styles. Some years my penmanship presented monumental problems for my students, which gradually worsened over my teaching career.

Generally, we are not conscious of our penmanship when writing papers. We are occupied with delivering our messages, so we concentrate on that. Some character traits filter through our handwriting, so a trained observer detects all sorts of things.

I learned to be trained observer. I learned the difference between poor penmanship and carelessness. Both in the same student are deadly.

I saw handwriting that was exquisite and perfect. It made me and my penmanship look insignificant. Some papers took hours to write out.

I observed the delicate art of interchanging "i's" and "e's" so I couldn't tell one from the other. Students who did not know the "i"-before-"e" rule practiced this skill often. These practitioners swore they could tell their "i's" from their "e's." Some students put loops in letters that were not supposed to have them and forgot them where they were supposed to do so.

Once students became enthused with what they were writing, their penmanship usually showed signs of improving, which leads me to believe they were about manipulating their graphological skills to vent their displeasure about having to write. All in all, however, I found students conscientiously worked to improve their writing.

Most students are probably stuck with their penmanship. They learned habits in childhood, which, once established, could not so easily be changed. Like me, most students did not realize its importance as they were learning it. They did not realize how important it was to become.

Then there were hands that seemed so firm and practiced that their styles seemed absolutely mastered. It is one of these I use as an example. Despite its style and discipline, it was mind-wrenching to read. It is easy to see the difficulty reading the example on page 157. Everything slants to the right about forty-five degrees. You would think since the slant moves in the direction of reading, it would enhance the process. It may for some people, but I had difficulty.

I tried everything I could think of. I held the page away from me, thinking I could catch phrases and lines better. I tried to hold it closer, reasoning that the general sweep of the slant could be minimized. I even used paper to mask all the page except the line I was reading. Nothing seemed to work. I still become dizzy trying to concentrate on the page.

I even did some research on the behavior. What does it mean when writing slants to the right? Handwriting experts abound. One claimed that this trait indicates friendliness and affection in the writer. Another suggests it is someone who responds with more emotion, the farther to the right the more the emotion. And another says it indicates attitudes about the future.

I tried to turn the page so that the slant was straight up and down. It worked but trying to sustain reading uphill was a challenge. The problem of penmanship when you have to read assignments, essay tests, and over one thousand compositions a year, is indeed substantial. It is well to remember what one of the experts in my research said about penmanship. "It is the mind that inspires the hand to do the writing." As with most everything else academic, penmanship is really an act of the mind in which the subconscious is sometimes revealed.

Patty Hearst is now on trial for the Hibernia Bank robbery. Federal Judge Oliver J. Carter and a jury of five men and seven women must decide whether she is the "lonely child" born to fortune and now innocent victim of vicious political kidnapping, or the vengeful revolutionary who would rob a bank at gunpoint. Patty has been on the stand in her trial and through fearful and weak tears and a body shaking with emotion she has told of her terror and abuse while in captivity.

I wondered what possessed one student to make little circles instead of dots for "i's" and periods. Or smiley faces inside "o's." Indeed, handwriting is an art, but like painting it helps to know what the writer had in mind, what meaning he or she is trying to transmit. If I cannot read it, what good is it, no matter how fancy?

Research and Senioritis
The research dilemma. A teacher responsible for language training of seventeen and eighteen-year-olds planning to attend college must make certain that skills necessary to do research are practiced.

In an accelerated class, I would conduct a long unit culminating in a research paper or as I preferred to call them, research essays. No matter what I called them, it was something short of a full-fledged research project. The idea was to give the opportunity for practice in overall skills.

In the other so-called honors classes where students ranged from the energetic but less practiced, to the lazy but good-intentioned, the formal research unit was not a good idea. Shorter assignments, short papers utilizing as many research skills as possible, were appropriate.

It was difficult to put high school seniors on their own for very long in the name of research. They found more ways to put off the inevitable, to squeeze a six-week research unit into two nights. Even when I made them adhere strictly to as many as seven deadlines in the course of the work, they managed to find ways around them.

The great single advantage of the five or six-week research unit was that there was never any doubt about assessing the intensity and persistence of students' efforts. That was the easy part. Then it became a series of devices, conferences, and other strategies to encourage them.

What was very important to remember was that seniors were enduring the winter of their last year in high school. They grew listless, lackadaisical, and irresolute. They knew and felt their last semester. They had been through this stage four times, and now it was all but over. Their college applications were long ago submitted, and a few of the acceptances were arriving.

Winter, dreary jobs, the endless routine of assignments, or tiring peer relationships produced senioritis. This malady was a state of mind, a realization which produced persons of idle, indolent or inert bent who sustained themselves lethargically through the long break-less weeks of winter. Maybe an occasional snow day or conference championship broke the spell, but it could only be temporary. Excuses were so common.

So, research was an exercise in futility with many, but not all. In fact, a few students always came into their own during this period. Who knows why? As my reading of papers continued, I returned one occasionally which inspired a student. I either said the right thing or, more likely, the student had done the right thing. As I conferred with those who needed help, we sometimes hit the right combination of advice and response, and they were off on an ambitious jog.

Out of all these interactions, one development was apparent. Students appreciated the fact that I gave them the time to proceed on their own. Whether they took advantage of it or not, watching the ones who did was worth all the rest. And the rest knew what to expect. Third quarter grades were by far the easiest to calculate. By that time, students had been isolated by their habits and achievement, or lack of achievement. The fundamental nature of the first semester, in addition to telling me who had what skills, made clear what needed to be done. That was the constant.

The variables were the students' desire and application. I played observer, assessor, advisor. No matter what approach the class took to research, the important factor was attitude.

Were the students cut out for the future they thought they wanted to pursue? Were they active about their plans? Or were they headed in no direction with no end in mind? I let drifters know how I felt about their plans or lack of plans. I especially pointed out contradictions in what they wanted to become in terms of their preparation, their skills.

The senioritis smoke screen may have been the game they were playing so they would have to do as little as possible until June. Who knows when a student will do an about face and catch the brass ring? The third quarter and research were the turning or testing points of the year.

After that, only the inertia produced earlier and Shakespeare could save the weary senior. They were weary in the sense that they knew it was time for a change and that there was not too much they could do to change what the first seven-eighths of their high school careers had produced. American students generally are not in the habit of academic scholarship, and a teacher's expectations must be reasonable, optimistic, but firm.

Reading All Those Papers

"Mr. Johnson, don't you get bored reading all those papers?" No, I don't. If a rare student doesn't stimulate my mind with his or hers, then I pass the time documenting spelling errors and wondering why thoughts could not follow in some order. I try to figure out ways to convince students they should work at writing (that's mind-training).

Sometimes I got so worked up that I made critiques crackle with a hard sell that softened even the most resistant minds to criticism. At other times, I got so worked up I couldn't wait to get to class so I could give my animated board drill of anonymous adolescent sentences.

It's not boring at all – it's tantalizing, heart-stirring. Reading papers was prologue, then epilogue, but in between the great whirl of mind-stirring goes on. Just enough students pick up the challenge to make it work and allow me to implement it. If all students took me seriously, the whole thing would have been impossible. I sometimes had "boring" times, but don't call reading students' papers one of them.

Writing Critiques

Responding to student writing was generally stimulating and satisfying. But it was also scary and difficult. Telling writers that they are unclear and incorrect while trying to write clearly and correctly myself was the ultimate balancing act. After all, a critique was a first draft.

I can recall writing some critiques out on a scratch paper first, and in some cases, it was well I did. But how laborious and time-consuming that was. I always had more papers to read, think about, and respond to. Most of the time, it was one blood-red shot. One chance to get it right, or at least be responsible.

Playing critic is never a pleasant task. The premise of the job was negative. After all, I was trying to encourage improvement in a highly subjective business. I was looking for everything from syntactical blunders, usage lapses, inadvertent mental slips, to fact faults and real mental mistakes and spelling errors.

But the first rule of critique writing is to say something positive, and say it first, even if there is little to warrant it. In this job, I could afford to have a reputation for being negative, even though the meaty heart of critiquing pursues mostly problems. If students knew I would praise when there was something to praise, they were most likely to work at it. Some moved heaven and earth to gain my praise. The trick was to be positive and fair.

It is important not to unload on every error, every mistake, every blunder. Concentrate on recurrent, serious problems. Keep a balance in mind between the subject and the language. There is no point in detailing mechanical, syntactical problems when the content is flawed. In the end, the student's development was the most important matter.

Another worrisome matter was following reasonable language rules myself. I must admit my major problem was penmanship. By the time we were seriously into critiques, I had openly dealt with the joke that was my penmanship. That took place early in the year, in class, on the board, with the whole class as witnesses.

Another critique problem was vocabulary. Certain words were overused. On the positive side, it was tiring to use the word "clear" again and again in describing the way students developed ideas. On the negative side, I tended to overuse the word "vague" when in most cases a more specific word could be found. I cannot believe, for example, that years ago I had trouble keeping a clear distinction between "vague" and "ambiguous."

I began to compose lists of synonyms and kept them handy on 3x5 cards for instant reference. I was amazed at the nuances of meaning among words that at first seemed synonymous. Here are some that are in the same league with "clear:" "lucid," "definite," "graphic," "explicit," "clear-cut," "express." And if I wanted to send someone on a dictionary run, I tried "perspicuous" or "trenchant." My favorite, however, was (and still is) "incisive." I used that for those special cases in which a student had penetrated an idea and found just the right word or words to express it.

On the other side of the critiquing coin, someone who is "vague" may be "obscure," "equivocal," "cryptic," or "unintelligible." "Ambiguity" is not always negative. I can remember only once I went so far as to use the word "abstruse."

When I wanted to praise a student for choice of words, I tried "selective" or "discriminating." Sometimes students were sentimental. I had this list to choose from: "effusive," "gushing," "maudlin," "mushy," "romantic," or "slushy."

The act of writing involves so many elements that care must be used not to overkill. One moment I may be investigating a student's organization. Another, trying to check why his point of view is not consistent. Then there is the matter of being concise. How about sentence structure? And usage and mechanics? Is he or she an accurate reporter? Or maybe the student is not keeping his or her audience in mind.

Indeed, writing critiques was a balancing act, a civil exercise to bring students to the recognition that writing should be the precipitation of thought to be shared.

I Need Quiet to Read Papers

I needed quiet, privacy for reading papers. How could I sustain this complex balancing act when distractions abound?

I never could read papers during the school day in free hours. Interruptions were always likely. My mind was on other things because classes preceding or classes following clamored for attention. Something from that last hour needed attention. I needed to make sure things were ready for next hour. I needed to go to the office. I could hear through the walls to the next-door class. Someone bounded through the music department door across the hall with some noisy distraction. A student came in. The board needed erasing. If that bulletin board was going to be of any value, I had to get it up.

At the end the day, my mental activity was not dependable. Late afternoons and evenings were out, too. My mental discipline was unlikely as my napping was likely. My time to read papers was early in the morning.

Routines for My Teaching Career

Something about routine fascinates me. Sometimes within seconds of the fascination, routine becomes revolting. Routine is the means by which things get done. Routine also repels ambition and makes me want to do anything to change it. But most of the time, I am aware of the rewards and thus follow routine.

Those who know much about me probably think I am a slave to routine, and I know lots of people who allow routine to rule their lives because they do nothing, or seem to do nothing, to change it. The more a person uses the mind in daily regimen, the more likely the chance to find routine-breakers within routine.

When I realized how time-consuming the reading and evaluating of student papers was, I began to control as many of the variables as I could. Never a rapid reader, I found that to work through a hundred student papers in reasonable time and be helpful and fair in the process, I had to change some habits. I found my efficiency was best when three requirements were met: when I was mentally alert, was alone, and had as little else on my mind as possible.

For years I was a late-night person and still tend to be on Friday and Saturday nights. The only one of the three requirements which was working, was being alone. But even that was not truly working. With radio, record player, TV, and domestic traffic of various sorts, I was hardly alone, at least mentally, where it was most important.

How could I be alert after a long class day? That's why we sleep, to encourage being alert. And of course, that time of day was when one had the most on his mind. Any problem magnifies. All the worst of everything tends to emerge at 11 P.M. We all tend to be mental midgets by midnight.

162

When I began teaching, I did not realize that such factors existed. My thought was I cannot go to bed without some of this or that work done. So, I sloughed through the work, inefficient, tired, all the while any problem which arose looked larger than it really was.

Of course, another reason I worked at night was smoking. I let the concentration at my desk at home and cigarettes become part of the same process. Smoking did relieve tension. A long lungful of a cigarette seemed to make the problems easier to take. I even thought they were eased a bit. They weren't. It was my brain and nervous system being numbed. It wasn't long before I figured out that the numbing might be permanent.

Finally, after a number of false alerts, on December 2, 1962, at 12:30 A.M., I tossed my last cigarette out the back door and listened to it sizzle as it hit the snow. I promised myself that was it. And as it turned out, it was.

This significant event took place five years into my teaching career, and I was beginning to control many of the toughest parts of the job. The processes of reading and evaluating papers were progressing well. And along came this self-inflicted stopper to my paperwork. I was no longer able to concentrate, especially in the evenings. I was nervous. I couldn't sit still. I started going to bed early.

Then I began to rise early in the morning to work. I do not recall the steps I took to change my behavior, but I resolved to start doing my reading and evaluating at a time when I did not smoke, and that was morning hours, particularly early morning hours. Talk about being hooked on a drug.

Several encouraging events occurred in the months following the tossing of that last cigarette. One was the new classroom. In March 1963, I moved into my newly constructed classroom, room 207, which was larger than room 112, and it was all mine. A renaissance of organization took place. Planning, teaching, and even reading and evaluating papers became easier. I was in that room for just over twenty-five years, and I was gaining control of my sources, my physical surroundings, and my own organization. What a blessing is a routine.

Later, in 1975, when I started walking the two and half miles to work. I was able to have about two hours alone – from 5:30 to 7:30 A.M.– before anyone arrived at school. Until a person actually does it, one cannot know how alert and ready the mind can be early in the morning.

As far as stuff on my mind was concerned, problems just looked less ominous in the morning. Most problems were solved early in the day and never got to the classroom. Problems I used to fret myself silly about at 11 P.M., somehow looked reasonable at 6 A.M. Besides, typically adolescents who cause a problem one day will forget whatever happened the next.

I don't mean to make this regimen out to be a panacea. If I had not set my mind on having dependable routine, it never would have happened. It isn't the routine itself that fascinates me; it is what the routine can lead to. I don't know how I could have taught as I did without a strict and dependable routine. So many worthwhile responsibilities depend on the will, the will to get results.

On Teacher-Student Conferences

I read somewhere in my quest to become a teacher: Don't schedule conferences; they will happen automatically if you're doing your job.

I don't think I consciously decided not to make conferences part of my regular classroom routine. I certainly had plenty of them. And I am convinced they were of a higher quality because students initiated them.

It is possible some reluctant souls were left out in the process, but that has never bothered me. The reason is that students usually did one of three things. They made sure they initiated the conferences. Two, they accomplished the equivalent. Or three, they adjusted their academic habits so that conferences were not necessary.

Some of my students would not do anything to achieve private talks with me. They of course were often the same students who were not going to do much anyway. Reluctance to confer was simply another way of my determining who was hanging back.

Students had hundreds of ways of indicating that private talks were necessary. Here are some icebreakers I remember:

- Can I come in and talk during 5th period?
- Do you think I should transfer to a different class?
- I thought I understood what a participle is.

164

- I agree with the grade you gave me, but could you explain some things?
- Why am I having so much trouble with my writing?
- I did not understand some things you said in class.
- Do you think I could be a teacher?

I was usually precise about pinning down the purposes of conferences. With over a hundred students submitting compositions with regularity, some controls were necessary. If the reasons were clear and sincere, conferences could turn into detailed discussions. One of my shortcomings in one-on-one talks was knowing when and how to terminate it.

The heart of a teacher-student relationship is communication, with the understanding and trust that entails. Building these qualities takes time. I loved talking with students face-to-face. It probably was a good thing more students did not take part in this kind of opportunity.

You can almost sense from those icebreakers what students' motives were. Most conferences were successful because my system for judging seriousness of purpose worked most of the time. "It's time we talk, Mr. Johnson." That approach sounded intimidating.

Some icebreakers were self-serving. One fellow started, "I just have to have an academy appointment. Will you write a reference for me?" I answered, "Sure, but first I want you to be sure *you* understand that your effort and attitude in class are the most important considerations." He never mentioned the subject again. I don't even know whether he succeeded in gaining acceptance to an academy.

How about this one? "Am I really a troublemaker?" Students who begin that way have answered their own question. The point is that since conferences take time and there would have been no way to have held a hundred or more of them, I wanted to make sure the motive and attitude were in sync with my objectives.

On the other hand, a student who begins with "Will you help me decide?" is going to get a hearing on the spot or in a conference later.

Content-Mechanics Controversy
One of the troublesome contradictions in teaching about writing was the disparity between content and mechanics. At what price would I, teacher,

accept writing from students? Would I read for ideas and content, heedless of the forms that mechanics take? Even if I can buzz right through the prose, should I ignore the way words and sentences work? Would I run the risk of discouraging worthy content by pointing out syntactical problems and word-form blunders?

For the first seven or eight years of teaching, I did not know what to do. I tried various approaches. I could not in good conscience settle on one method that would lead just to consistency, but I could not accept papers that carelessly violated language rules. The purpose of language instruction would be defeated if I did not give prominence to otherwise well thought through subject matter.

One Friday afternoon in April, at a faculty in-service session, Nellie Thomas from Rockford, Illinois, talked about reading and writing. I don't remember a lot of detail, mainly that she was determined and dynamic. What I remember best from that session was an idea Nellie Thomas presented for gaining students' attention and respect in matters of language: Don't accept a student composition which has spelling errors and comma splice errors.

At first that idea sounded unreasonable. However, I got to thinking about the implications for my classes as I went home that evening. It was nothing I could rush into practice the following Monday, but from then on, I thought of it regularly as the school year continued.

Unless I could get students serious about language, I could not energetically and conscientiously teach English, especially writing. Two rules eventually turned out to be a means to a student wakeup call: compositions would not be accepted unless they eliminated spelling errors and comma splice errors.

But let's have a look at the way these rules worked when I made the first writing assignment in September:

Me: Comp. #1 is due Friday, and there are a couple of things I'd like to have you keep in mind. We discussed manuscript procedures yesterday, and I showed you how I want papers folded and where to put identifying information. Oh yes, there is something else. I need to have a way to make sure you are paying attention to your language. You know, mechanics. I want you to pay special attention to spelling and comma splice errors. Every word spelled right, right?

This dialog took place in early September when students were listening. They were cooperative, fresh, and ready to go. But they also recognized old English-teacher devices. I glanced at my new class list.

Me: Your name is Brad, right?

Brad: Right.

Me: Well, Brad, you are correct. You need to make sure words are spelled correctly.

Steve: And what are common splicing errors?

Me: It's comma splice error. It refers to the kind of punctuation to use where two independent clauses come together.

I sensed uneasiness.

Trying to concentrate on the idea that these high school seniors were beginning their thirteen years of formal education, I turned to the board and said, "There are three ways to punctuate between independent clauses. One is a comma and a coordinating conjunction like 'and.'" I dutifully place a comma followed by the word "and."

Me: And a semi-colon.

I popped a period on the board, under which I jotted a comma.

Me: A period is followed by a capital letter on the next word.

Now as I turned back toward my mute scholars, I could see expressions ranging from the curious, intent on understanding; to the smug, who were sure they knew what I was talking about; to the would-be scholars, who would like to be sure they knew what I was talking about; and to the nonscholars, who were sighing about losing their hopes of an easy senior year.

> Me: I think you understand this better than you think you do. I just want to test a fundamental rule of punctuation, which most of you have been practicing all along. When I put it to you like this, the impulse is to panic.

Some semblance of life returned to the assembled faces.

> Me: Now spelling. That you can do something about.

This new rule was not going over in a big way. A girl raised her hand.

> Me: Let's see, are you Patty?

> Patty: Yes, I am. I don't think I could do a paper and not have spelling errors.

> Me: Oh, yes, you can. Make it part of your language scheme of things. I don't think anyone has made you think about spelling this way before.

I saw that I had a little more compliance now.

> Me: What good is spelling unless you practice it? Get this rule under control on your writing, and we'll have no spelling tests.

That clearly struck home.

> Me: And I think we have to be reasonable about this. No more than four spelling and comma splice errors on a composition, and you're home free.

I was trying to be reasonable and fair while still insisting on the rule. I wasn't laying down an ultimatum or expecting an impossible goal. Most students are reasonable and are going to give a fair trial to anything that strikes them as equitable. The important factor here was the students' desire to pursue writing aggressively and energetically. For any chance of success, students must accept the fact that reasonable mastery of language was requisite to successful writing.

I found that a consistent and serious pursuit of these two rules opened the door to the general problem of grammar and usage. After all, why should I read what students write if the medium through which we mutually communicate was not mutually respected?

The idea of consultant Nellie Thomas for capturing students' attention and respect for language worked. Brad and Patty never had a paper turned back for want of spelling mastery. Steve worked at it some, but he had to bring himself to exert the effort. After all, whose education was this?

Class Loads for Teaching Writing

I thought that meeting five high school classes every day was a reasonable design, if the numbers in those classes were reasonable. Of course, they were not, for me or others in the required, crowded academic courses.

In a typing course where the content does not become any more personal than the energy and discipline applied to striking keys in a regular and ever quicker and more accurate sequence, a teacher can manage a group of twenty-five as a group of twenty-five. The need to know something of each student's academic characteristics is minimal. The teacher can deal with the group, as a group.

I have observed teachers in social science attempting to handle classes in the same way. In these courses where content is essentially a mass of information or knowledge to be mastered, teachers commonly resort to objective tests to check mastery. This quantifying of students as groups does not seem fair, even in the classes where these tactics seem justified.

But it is common, and I cannot defend teachers who do it. Some teachers are driven to it; others simply do not want to teach. Forever, the nature of the work requires learning to know individual students as well as possible.

Mastering the native language is not only a matter of mastering a body of information; in fact, it is hardly that at all. It is, rather, mastering a structure which has options in its use. Judging the facility with which a student has learned to write cannot be reduced to (a) good, (b) better, (c) best, or (d) all of the above. I have never encountered a more subjective exercise than writing composition.

Teaching writing requires much of the teacher. He or she must have a degree of mastery of the language which provides a useful judgmental scale for others and the ability to be neutral when making judgements. It is not easy. When students, for example, put on pressure about the importance of the grade, the college they are about to enter, and the job that takes twenty hours of their week (which doesn't leave much time for English composition or anything else), it was difficult to remain neutral through the process of evaluating a paper they have done with superficial effort, sometimes with contempt.

I learned how to get to know twenty-five students in all five classes. Having learned that writing is the most effective language practice, I required as much of it as possible, knowing all the while that when I had a hundred students, each writing assignment means a hundred papers, not only to read, but to evaluate. In short order, I learned short cuts.

However, certain things must always be done. I noted and learned personal traits. I found out what students' academic characteristics were. Is reading a chore or a joy for each of them? Has each learned the structure of the English language in a functional way? Is writing generally fluent and intelligent? Is the vocabulary base broad and building? Do the students love learning? Do they take care of usage problems without rancor? Do the students let go and allow teachers to help language experience grow?

An English teacher must gain insight to these matters early in the school year so that instruction can be developed intelligently. I need to know my students if I was going to help them improve their language skills. I assumed that from the beginning. I did not begrudge the time it took because I assumed all teachers did it, and because it worked. An understanding of the nature and habits of each student seemed essential. I always worked at that.

I found that most teachers paid little attention to personal traits and academic characteristics. Some did not know how to do it. Others saw that the numbers offered a permanent rationalization out of the responsibility. Others thought of teaching as an eight-to-four job. But most were teaching subject matter, and it was the students' responsibility to learn it.

170

By the time I had figured out the variance in teaching goals, I could not teach any other way, and, of course, it was a good thing. Making connections with many of my students during the school year was satisfaction of the highest order, and if I had control of the essentials, I was satisfied.

At one point, the administration and faculty at Badger High School debated about the "sixth" class. Many teachers already had six classes, and it was a common load in other schools. I could not help wondering how we came to move toward more and bigger classes. Anyone who can remember their high school years understands that the significant influence of a given teacher was due to his or her care in understanding and serving personally as many students as possible. Many adults are what they are because of outstanding teachers in their formative years.

I know the taxes are tough. I pay them, too. But we get what we pay for, and time is the key to the enterprise of education. I know inefficient, ineffective eight-to-four teachers are being paid as much as the effective teachers. But how long will they last once taxpayer parents see the bargain that their sons and their daughters could get? I also know there is a terrible misunderstanding of what teaching is. When I think of all the ways I used to soften the crunch of class load, I wonder who won in the end.

Directives for Teaching Writing

One of the salient symbols of military life was the directive. The art of military prose informed the way things got done in the service. It was an example of direct communication. No argument was considered. Officers told subordinates what they wanted done, how and when.

The problem with military directives was that they do not allow for the human factor. The necessities of military life dictated that speech and action be direct. The human factor was a secondary consideration.

A good example turned up on the front page of the *Lake Geneva Regional News* toward the end of my teaching career. A story reported on a directive from the superintendent to the staffs of the two school districts he heads. The directive stated, "Writing will be done in every curriculum area and graded on a minimum of at least every five sessions, or a once a week basis, but more frequently in academic subjects." In addition, it ordered measures for teacher accountability. "All teachers are required to submit detailed lesson plans on a weekly basis. These lesson plans will include

171

evidence that the writing directive is being met."

The headline over the story left no doubt about what is to be done: Administration Orders More Student Writing.

Teachers cannot order students to write, any more than administrators can expect teachers who have little writing experience to teach the skill. Teachers can make assignments, but they cannot ensure that students will write, or that what they turn in is really theirs.

Writing is an intensely personal activity. Unless teachers develop a trusting rapport with students, the dialogue necessary to develop an atmosphere, in which thinking and writing can thrive, will not occur. Teachers and students will merely go through the motions.

Our society does not demand a high level of language competence. For proof, all we need to do is read what is printed today – newspapers, commercial appeals through the mail, personal letters, intra-house communications, TV commercials, books.

Who's to blame? Family, schools, the media? If my parents did not successfully encourage a high level of language use, then I had to learn its importance and apply myself in school or in my profession. The best chance to learn is at home during childhood. The culture, with these factors at work, determines the language level. It takes expertise to deduce where that level is in our society. It also takes experience to know it cannot be ordered done.

If I would ever meet the superintendent, I would ask these questions:

- How would you get ready for students who say they want to learn to write, but have no idea of the discipline required?
- When you make your writing assignments, how will you insure the optimum opportunity for original work?
- How will you make certain students write on subjects important to them?
- What language requirements will you hold them to?
- How can you ensure that the papers will be treated in a fair and equitable way, even though each student's language experience is different?

Teaching writing is more complex than teaching most every other subject. The idea is for teachers to be objective in their approach to students, while writing is about as subjective as a skill can become. This does not mean it cannot be done; it means it must be done carefully, exhaustively, and with some attention to the characteristics of each student. It means careful observation and implementation. We not only have to learn about our students as individuals, but also their experience with language.

When I began, I could not. It took me years to learn what I would later wonder was not taught in college or student teaching. With me it was strictly a matter of teaching myself first.

I met only a handful of teachers who could teach writing effectively. In your directive ordering all teachers K-12 to teach writing, you are asking something that is highly unlikely. Not only must you have teachers who can do it, you must have students receptive to the tough demands.

Teachers Who Write Continue to Learn
A longtime colleague and I recently discussed the following two statements about writing and learning:

- The teacher who writes teaches differently than the teacher who does not write.
- The teacher who continues to learn teaches differently than the teacher who doesn't continue to learn.

Though both statements are structurally parallel, the content seems to proclaim some fundamental, diverse stuff about teachers and teaching. We're into the matter of attitude here. I remember I became so uneasy teaching writing that I wondered when my inadequacies would expose me. I was not too many notches above minimal reader status. My education was a collection of credits gathered along the way as I veered from one major to another.

Desire comes differently to different people. My parents placed a clarinet in brother Clyde's hands when he was in the fifth grade. I stepped into my first classroom at age twenty-nine. My brother pursued music as a career from age ten. He pursued nothing else.

But I am beginning to wonder whether I wasn't pursuing teaching a whole lot longer than I think I was. I turned to it after failing in business. I was not worked up over teaching until I met a teacher who was inspired. That happened in early 1956 when I was twenty-eight.

What happened when I saw what teaching is was a kind of consolidating of experience. I saw that despite my weaknesses I could grow and thrive while doing something about the problems (they were not really weaknesses, but problems to be solved.) Thus, a lack of reading background could be remedied. Grammar, syntax, semantics could be mastered at the same time my students learned them.

And the toughest problem of all, writing, could be solved over the years, methodically and gradually. Care, time, common sense, and application turned me into something of an expert, though not always an efficient critique writer. I found that student responses, their confidence, and most important, their application, were prospering. This growth was so because I was demonstrating an interest in them as individuals. I was disappointed that this professionalism was not a common characteristic among teachers.

After about ten years, I figured all this out, and I began to see how powerful a tool teaching writing was. My resolve may have awakened in 1956, but in the mid-1960s this awareness took hold.

Writing and continued learning made my teaching work. It was a matter of attitude. When my only goal was teaching English, everything else related to it. Important matters in students' lives became part of their language training and experience. When learning to master the English language is central in a student's life, then language and culture begin to assume the importance they deserve.

Diverse Proverbs

It seems we are forever examining the differences between the world's cultures. I suppose that is partly because of our national diversity. We live literally among the people of the world whose cultures differ from ours.

I was looking for a quotation the other day, and I noticed the variety of proverbs from different cultures. So, when I encountered a quotation-marked proverb, I copied it down and noted from whence it came.

I found thirty proverbs from sixteen different cultures. I began wondering whether characteristics of a culture could be determined through their proverbs. Now this research was a rather random act. I was looking for a quotation, and those subject areas were where I checked for proverbs. While my research would not pass any test for objectivity, perhaps it could generate a little interest.

What is a proverb? MW10NCD defines it as "a brief popular epigram or maxim. An epigram is a "a terse, sage, or witty and often paradoxical saying." A maxim is "a general truth, fundamental principle, or rule of conduct." A proverb is a popular and brief saying, expressing a principle or rule of conduct. Here are several proverbs from different cultures:

- No one is rich enough to do without a neighbor. (Danish)
- He understands badly who listens badly. (Welsh)
- One man may teach another to speak, but none can teach another to hold his peace. (Polish)
- It is stupidity to suppress what comes into one's mind. (Hindu)
- Even the best needles are not sharp at both ends. (Chinese)
- There are no faults in a thing we want badly. (Arab)
- When we are merriest, it is best to leave and drive home. (Czech)
- Might never prays. (Bulgarian)
- Heroism consists in hanging on one minute longer.
- God made time, but man made haste (Norwegian)
- It is in its own interest that the cat purrs.
- Who brings a tale takes two away. (Irish)
- When one is helping another, both are strong.
- Jealousy does more harm than witchcraft.
- Whoever cares to learn will always find a teacher. (German)
- Bad habits are easier to abandon today than tomorrow.
- Better ask ten times than go astray once.
- Small children disturb your sleep, big children your life. (Yiddish)
- Tomorrow is often the busiest day of the week.
- How beautiful it is to do nothing, and then to rest afterward.
- If three people say you are an ass, put on a bridle. (Spanish)

- By asking for the impossible we obtain the best possible.
- Love is a thing that sharpens all our wits. (Italian)

It is tempting to comment on these intriguing maxims, these national nuggets. But each reader will be informed, entertained, or turned off as he or she is inclined.

Wisdom on Writing from Writers

For a long time, I wished to compose an essay using quotations as the major content. I used quotes because they are in words that I could never assemble myself. That is why I use them – someone has said something better than I could have said it.

I collected quotations and started a folder labeled "Important Statements." Recently I took out the folder, emptying its contents on my desk, and began reading, assessing and classifying. These sentences played an important part in my pedagogical past. I used them in classes, kept them handy as reminders, or employed them as reassurance in a rough world.

Since quotations are made up of words, I thought it fitting to start with the five sentences I put on the board when I wanted students to ponder seriously the importance of words. This activity sometimes was at the beginning of my poetry unit. Other times it was at the commencement of a semantics unit used in different ways with different classes.

Upon reading these five sentences, note that words go beyond their sounds and literal meanings. Two of the five are from poems:

- I understand a fury in your words, But not the words.
  Othello, Shakespeare

- The important thing about any word is how you understand it.
  Maxims, Publilius Syrus

- A blow with a word strikes deeper than a blow with a sword.
  Richard Burton
- But my words like silent raindrops fell
  And echoed, in the wells of silence.
  Paul Simon

176

- The difference between the right word and the almost right word is the difference between lightning and the lightning bug.

  Mark Twain

Putting words in an order that allows meaning to survive was not an easy task:

- A sentence should read as if its author, had he held a plough instead of a pen, could have drawn a furrow deep and straight to the end.

  Henry David Thoreau
- Drudgery is a necessary to call out the treasures of the mind as harrowing and planting those of the earth.

  Margaret Fuller

Dangers are at every turn. We research too little and conclude too fast.

- A generalization is a plateau where the tired mind rests.

  Unknown
- No generalization is wholly true, including this one.

  Benjamin Disraeli
- Education should bring students to questioning,
     to disciplining, to dedicating.

  Unknown
- I respect faith, but doubt it is what gets you an education.

  Yours truly
- Perhaps the most valuable result of all education is the ability to make yourself do the thing you should do, and when it ought to be done, whether you like it or not.

  Thomas Huxley
- An interview is concerned with information; a conversation is concerned with character.

  Bill Moyers

- It is easier for a man to be loyal to his club than his planet; the bylaws are shorter, and he is personally acquainted with the other members.

E.B. White

- Flattery is the art of telling another person exactly what he thinks of himself.

Anonymous

Muse for My Writing

One of my students asked me whether I had a muse. I was surprised by the question and did a double take. Upon recovering, I told my questioner …

Me: Why, yes, of course I have a muse.

Student: How do you know?

Me: Because of inspiration, I become inspired, and I know some force is causing me to exert in ways I wouldn't ordinarily.

Student: OK, I looked up the word, and it said there are nine goddesses in Greek mythology. They inspire people.

Me: Right. Depending on what your skill is, you have a muse to match. I teach English which includes literature and writing. When I write, I depend on my language muse to guide me.

Student: Your muse gives you inspiration.

Me: Quite often. Sometimes I think my muse forgets about me, and then I have trouble. But most of the time, my muse makes sure I keep going.

Student: Is your muse part of you, Mr. Johnson?

Me: I think so, but I am sure there is some outside help. I think we all have some higher guidance.

Student: You mean God?

Me: Maybe. I suppose it depends on how you think of it. Someday I want to write about my life in teaching. I want to figure out how and why teaching worked for me. I'll need all the language powers I can muster.

Student: You mean you don't just sit down and write?

Me: No, no! When I give you a writing assignment, do you just sit down and write, as you say?

Student: No way. I go through a lot of pain before I write.

Me: Why?

Student: I never know what to write about. I know you tell us to think first, but I find writing hard.

Me: You wouldn't be the first. It's always been hard for me. I think it's hard for anyone.

Student: Then how do you do it?

Me: I have to have something to say. Something in my mind begins to want out. I must find the words to make thoughts into sentences that take me someplace. Then I need a plan. Then I just write, think, and make ideas come out. I swallow hard a couple of times. If I'm thinking about my subject, and I keep going, soon my muse kicks in, and the stuff just tumbles out. This is when you should forget everything else and write, write, write. Forget sentence structure, forget spelling, forget everything but what your mind and your muse are feeding you. Write, write, write.

Student: Like you tell us, worry about grammar, spelling, and other stuff later.

Me: That's right.

Student: But you still haven't told me what your muse is.

Me: Or who?

Student: You mean someone else can be my muse?

Me: Why not? How often do other people inspire you?

Student: A lot. Now that you say that, I know who my muse is.

Me: Tell me about it.

Student: Well, when I run cross country, I think of Roger Bannister. He was the first to run a four-minute mile. I try to imagine how he did it. I also think he must have worked up to it. When I think of him, it makes me work harder. I seem to have a reason to push myself. Something sort of takes over.

Me: You know who inspires me?

Student: Knowing you, Mr. Johnson, I'd say it's your students.

Me: You're right. It is. The whole idea of learning and teaching energizes me. I look forward to every class. I know that sounds corny, but it's true. It's my muse, my inspiration.

Student: Thanks for telling me about your muse, Mr. Johnson.

Teaching Journalism and Advising the *Inquirer*

Starting in 1967, I took on teaching journalism and advising our school newspaper. Then the Wisconsin Department of Public Instruction insisted on at least a minor in order to teach journalism. They would not grandfather my dozen years of experience, so Principal Karl Reinke changed the name of the course. We called it "Publications" and, of course, enrollments dropped. I was as capable as most other advisors and teachers, or at least that is what I have been regularly told by the only people who really knew, my students.

CONTENTS

Importance of Journalism Classes

It is hard to imagine an American high school with a thousand students not having a student newspaper. As a local community newspaper reported not long ago, three of the eleven high schools in Racine, Kenosha and Walworth counties had no school newspapers. One of them is the school for which I was journalism teacher for eighteen years and student newspaper advisor for twenty-eight years.

Teaching journalism is never easy, just as practicing journalism is not easy. Journalists, particularly reporters, have schedules which never allow quite enough time to research thoroughly, check sources sufficiently, or revise sufficiently. The patience and discipline journalists must exercise are often in conflict with deadlines. These problems can never be eliminated. They go with the territory.

Then we have adolescence, those optimum years for learning the skills, developing self-discipline, and considering vocations. But these are also years of maturing. They're the years of spontaneous ambitions and passionate causes. It's when emotions and verve can power constructive application one minute, then do an about-face, and head in the opposite direction the next.

What journalism requires is a steady, even handed practice of language skills and a curious, ever-alert mind about facts. Showing a student-journalist the difference between facts and opinion is fairly easy. Getting them to demonstrate the difference in real reporting is quite another. Impetuous eagerness is every bit as difficult to direct as spelling, agreement, and syntax ever were.

It is easy to understand reluctance to teach such language basics to unpredictable teenagers. Yet there is really nothing as consistently invigorating and rewarding either. All of these challenges have something to do with how I got into journalism in the first place.

Something I learned early on was that English teachers can easily operate in isolation. Very few other disciplines have much time for what English teachers do. Try teaching physics without a mastery of the English language. When it comes to language competence, we could all use editors.

Next, English teachers who take their missions seriously, learn to make writing the center of their responsibilities. Making writing assignments effective requires a great deal of work. I won't go into detail, but English teachers will do almost anything to avoid the disciplines of writing. The adage "it's five percent inspiration and ninety-five percent perspiration" fits perfectly. Once we find the payoff to be worthwhile, the drudgery almost becomes palatable. I seldom considered it drudgery. Composition should clearly be the center of life in the English classroom.

Writing requires an outlet. We can't simply talk about writing. The quickest route to a writing outlet in the public schools is journalism. Relatively few students can participate on a newspaper staff, but the major impact is that when students knew that I was the teacher who advised the newspaper, they tended to look at the writing discipline differently. Most were not going to reform and apply themselves immediately, if ever. It's the idea that the journalism advisor is associated with an outlet for student expression that is not only attractive but reassuring. Expression is something adolescents have little opportunity to pursue.

Since schools are places where students are supposed to learn the skills and values associated with being citizens in a democracy, we need to provide opportunities for them to do so. It is hard to believe a high school has no student newspaper.

Advising the *Inquirer*

Being an advisor of a school newspaper was a precarious mission. I stood between zealous, well-meaning students and the ever-vigilant student body, teachers, administration and community. At times, I received letters or phone calls and even visits from irate readers stating that I should exercise more control over the content of what student journalists write.

Giving relatively inexperienced students opportunities to handle assignments was a risk. It involved too many complications. But as an advisor colleague of mine used to say, "We'll never know until we give them a chance."

The extremes of a professional activity were readily apparent to journalism students. While it is great to have an audience and become a celebrity of sorts, the pressures can be devastating. Inexperience in any activity brought mistakes and the inevitable criticisms. Teenagers in their exuberance became intensely competitive. Their zeal often produced conflict. Sometimes their ability to accept criticism was impaired. The success of the activity suffered.

The task of advisor is taxing and ever the balancing act. The editor must be given the authority to do the job. Since inexperience is the crucial ingredient in this mix, an advisor must learn to understand his or her students well enough to predict how they will perform in different roles of leadership. Once committed to editors for a school year, advisors have to learn to live with the results. Advisors do what advisors do; they advise. I have coaxed, criticized, cautioned, and consoled. I don't regret any of my appointments. That's because I worked too hard at making them work.

Being an advisor allowed me opportunities to know my students in a different dimension. I could see my students taking on responsibilities assumed in their roles. Also, my colleagues and fellow community members could observe my students in action. I enjoyed having helped a group of students produce the *Inquirer* a few times each year.

The Editor's Game

I've never been an editor. I was a journalism teacher and advisor for close to twenty years. From what I know of professional newspaper editors, it is one tough job. I've not had those kinds of responsibilities.

However, I appointed editors to school's newspaper for two decades. It was difficult to learn what being an editor involves unless we've been one, and a high school newspaper editor has some restrictions which make the job almost impossible and certainly not realistic.

A school is a highly controlled institution which allows degrees of freedom, but not the kind that allows an editor to be a real editor. After all, student journalists are inexperienced and prone to making sudden, sometimes unthinking decisions. It is a learning process.

Being an editor of a school newspaper involves a special set of circumstances. The school administration often frets about what will come out in the next publication. Some administrations have been known to censor student papers. Some fellow student-journalists may not understand the powers an editor is supposed to have. Then, some readers, fellow students, peers, and teachers are quick to criticize and apply pressures of various kinds.

A student editor is supposed to organize and execute the publishing of an intelligent newspaper. The second level of editors – news, feature, sports – are peers who tend to compete. They are not being paid, so editors must make things work with the power of their minds, wits, and patience.

Adolescence is the age of rapid change and growth. We never know what the course of any student journalist's career will be. It is important to carefully observe students all the way along their first year in journalism. Appointment of editors for the second year was never as hard as I feared. Working hard to make success possible is what is important.

Of all the complaints I've heard from student editors over the years, the most common came in the form of the question: Why don't we get letters to the editor? We did get them, but not very many. Show me an editor in professional journalism who doesn't wish he or she knew more about what readers thought. Letters are the chief means of response and probably the only reasonable way to determine what readers think.

Most letters react to some issue or opinion expressed therein. Readers love to point out errors, too. Finding out what the readership thinks about a newspaper is close to impossible.

When I think of the letters we received, I recall we thought them of higher value than they really were. We valued them mainly because someone took the time to write. The point is that journalists often don't have time to think about what readers think. We put one issue in the hands of the readers, and it is time to start work on the next one.

Reporter Terry "Ted" Dunn (Class of '69)

Ted was the kid who dreamed dreams and nourished ambitions. He had a feeling for underdogs. He may even have thought of himself as one.

Though I think he'd like to have been an athlete, his size and those physical traits that competition forces, were not in his favor. Ted was a sports fan instead, and he was a reporter on the *Inquirer*, the school newspaper, his senior year.

As a reporter, he was a winner. He gravitated to feature stories, having the ability to penetrate the heart of subjects quickly. The story that brought him notoriety and honors was a piece about underdogs. Ted found his element; sports and underdogs. The subject was Badger High School's varsity basketball team.

Ted concentrated on three senior players who saw limited playing time in games but were the fodder that made practice scrimmages possible. He built the story around these – but let his story's lead tell it:

> They call 'em sparring partners in boxing, but in basketball
> there's no word that shows any compassion or grants mercy. They're
> only benchwarmers. These were behind-the-scenes athletes that
> every team has.

Ted's story won district competition in the annual Associated Press writing contest and took third in state. But even prize winners are doomed. When the story was originally set up in three columns, the second and third were reversed. The error was discovered too late. How embarrassing!

Nonetheless, the respect that accompanies such work manifested itself quickly. One morning, the chair at the end of the staff table facing the door had a sheet of typing paper fastened to it. On it was the proud affirmation: "Mr. Dunn."

Ted, the fellow of many names and many dreams, and a fighter for underdogs, had made his mark. By the way, next to his picture in the school annual is the following: "Whenever I get to feeling indispensable, I take another look at the old saddle hanging in the garage."

Journalist Marybeth Jacobson (Class of '69)

Marybeth Jacobson visited at my home recently. For almost three hours, we talked about those years at Badger High School, journalism, the people we knew, and the writing I am doing. Immediately the nature of this interesting person returned.

My memories of everything from her razor-sharp intelligence to her guarded little chuckle, which is Marybeth's social signature, returned. Her penetrating mind will understand most everything. Those deep-blue eyes see through everything.

We talked about how such a sensitive person could face the realities of journalism, but we've done that before. As always, my respect for Marybeth is of one tender-tough person for the *Milwaukee Journal*. She isn't really a cynic: she simply does not have patience with people whose foibles she herself has overcome long ago. But through it all shines realistic, honest Marybeth.

Marybeth attempted to change some intolerable circumstances with the *Lake Geneva Regional News*. It was also Marybeth who convinced me that changing the name of the course from Journalism to Publications was not going to be the end of journalism at Badger High School.

Office Manager Tammy Anderson (Class of '83)
Some people simply come to mind when I think of our school newspaper. Tammy Anderson is one of these students. She took journalism as a junior and then again as a senior while being a member of one of my senior English classes.

She assumed the function of office manager for the *Inquirer* and made it an important function to reporters' work. She was truly a manager. Most staff members would say Tammy was quiet but dependable. Her agenda was service to Badger High School's newspaper.

I agreed with her classmates; she was dependable. But she was also loyal. She seemed to be thinking of what was best both for newspaper staff and English class. She had a protective, motherly instinct. Her reliability became a kind of trust. I came to think that no matter where she went and what she did, peers would be supportive, uplifted by her presence. If ever an image were in clear focus, it is the mind of Tammy. Her influence will grow from her tacit and dependable nature, strong and sure. Maybe that is why she keeps reappearing in my mind's eye.

Letter to the Editor of *The Week*: Student Newspaper is Vital
Dear Editor,

It is with no small touch of sadness that I read Bruce Johnson's recent column about the demise of the student newspaper at Badger and other high schools in southeast Wisconsin.

As a Badger graduate, I was not privileged to have "Mr. Johnson" as a journalism teacher, because he had not yet begun that assignment. But I had him for senior English and can attest he was an excellent teacher of both literature and writing. His enthusiasm for our reading of great authors, and encouragement to hone our writing, were among the causes for my choosing an English major in college and eventual career as a newspaper reporter, editor and publisher.

My regrets about the cessation of journalism classes at Badger and many other schools are as follows:

1.   The skills learned in J-class and in producing a student newspaper are directly related to real life. The disciple of research, sorting of information, time management, working under deadline stress, development of language skills as well as practice of writing, are excellent preparation for both the rigors of academic study in college and a variety of careers afterward.

2.   An understanding of the need for and difficulty of gathering facts on all sides of an issue, deciding on their relevance and relating them accurately without bias is an excellent prelude to adult lives as news consumers. Our democratic society depends on the public schools to provide us with graduates who understand the imperative of news media free to investigate and report about the government and other things relevant to readers and writers.

3.   Students without a school newspaper are deprived of an opportunity to build the lifelong habit of reading news that is relevant to them. And, they are short-changed of a source of useful and interesting information and views, produced by their peers who are uniquely capable of understanding critical and often stressful times in their lives.

4.   Parents and taxpayers are deprived of another view, besides the official view of the boards and superintendent and principals, of what's going on in the school they support and what's important in the lives of their teenagers. No other curriculum imparts those benefits to the degree and intensity of the school journalism experience.

Regrettably, school administrators regard journalism classes as suspect – more job training than academic. But the reality is that only a tiny minority of high school journalists will ever practice the craft professionally. But all will practice for a lifetime the critical-thinking skills polished in journalism classes and service on school newspapers. Also, regrettably, many administrators find students exercising their right of free inquiry and expression a threat, or at best, a nuisance that might bring up topics or issues relevant to students but embarrassing to adults.

In either case, tight school budgets are frequently an excuse to reassign the journalism teacher and shut down school papers.

Economic necessities must be dealt with, but no one should suppose that a death of a student newspaper is without severe cost, much less a victory.

Emmett Smelser
President and Publisher
The Star Press
Muncie, Indiana

Producing the Graduation Projects
and Annual Scrapbooks

The graduation projects distinguished the commencement ceremonies at Badger High School for twenty-five years (1961-1985). The essays below contain descriptions of the origin, purposes, processes and challenges for producing the graduation projects. The last three essays present the purposes, history, and maintenance of the school's annual scrapbooks.

CONTENTS

Significance of High School Commencement

Graduation, especially high school graduation, is an imposing, inspiring event. It makes a distinct turning point in the lives of the graduates. No matter how accomplished the students, it is a break with the past. In fact, it marks the end of a stage of life whether the student is ready or not. Rarely do students who have not graduated return to finish with their own classmates gone.

The ceremony itself is geared to symbolize changes. The relationship between the past and the future is celebrated. The salutatorian welcomes his or her classmates and talks about the past, especially their last four years. The valedictory is a goodbye with a look to the future. Commencement is the point at which the great hope of youth is expressed and done so publicly.

The most common expression of the moment is the hiring of an accomplished outsider to make a speech. His or her expertise, the theory runs, is called to appeal to all graduates. It's a success story which is supposed to inspire the eighteen-year-olds for the future. Rarely can such a speaker command the confidence of graduates. They may respect the speaker's accomplishments, but they find it difficult to translate them into their circumstances. He probably knows little about the community or the school. She may not know any individuals there, except the individual who was responsible for her invitation, and that would not ever have had to involve personal contact.

This high point of the commencement ritual may tell us something about the way we go about much of the business of the institution. The speaker has come to deliver inspiration without a stake in the graduates and their learning. If he or she has something to offer them, it is delivered without an emotional link. Her life and the students' lives do not interact, except in the minutes during which she speaks to them.

A teacher may have students for one-hundred-eighty days of the school year and never have any more genuine interaction than during graduation. So why should graduation be any different? That sounds cynical, but it is very near the truth in many cases.

What an opportunity commencement is to represent what high school is or should be. It should be an expression of the hope and optimism of youth. Sometime during students' four years, they need a public recognition of their achievements and an expression of their hopes.

If we could only develop some sort of method to express this important turning point. We would think that with all the great technology and the ease with which communication is possible, that public high schools could find ways to involve their students in the process, to make graduation mean something significant for them, and them primarily. Graduation should not just be another formality to suffer through. It ought to be uplifting, positive. It should carry over into lives in some ways. It should be memorable. It should involve everyone who is experiencing it.

Is such an experience possible? What commencement needs is the infusion of community, communal spirit, and something that tells us that we did this together. After tonight, we may never see each other again. Of necessity something is ending, beginning, and binding.

At a reunion, the graduates may come back to relish their experiences again in the faces, voices, and community sharing. They may be proud of their experiences, or they may feel uneasy. Or they may want nothing to do with their memories. But reunions are times to renew the stories of themselves and their community, the continuing occasion of their growing from adolescence to whatever it is they are becoming.

No matter what we do to change graduation, to eliminate it, or to reduce it to the bare minimum of a hot June night, commencement signifies the opportunities of the next American generation, and we need to celebrate its success.

Origins of the Graduation Projects

Badger High School replaced the commencement speaker with a medium using 35mm color slides accompanied with a taped narrative and music. These elements were tightly coordinated, attempting to achieve something approaching an artistic whole. Its major objective: visually representing each of the graduates in comfortable, candid and typical settings.

This medium did not appear by magic. It developed during my student teaching under Miss Edythe Daniel at Wisconsin State College-Platteville. Early on in the spring semester of my student teaching, Miss Daniel said that her eighth-grade students would write and perform a play in the "Little Theater" during the graduation ceremony.

Somehow, she found out that I practiced photography and thought aloud how great it would be to record our eighth graders' in-school and out-of-school activities on slides and make it part of the play they were to do. I was far from certain how this project would be done, especially the showing of slides within the context of an on-stage play. In the end, Miss Daniel not only provided the idea, but also managed to execute it in such a way that it appeared to be my idea.

It was not my idea! The stage problem was solved quite efficiently. The setting was the living room of a home in which two children were graduating, a boy and a girl. The major feature of the set was an exaggerated television placed upstage center in an opening created by the curtain. Then backstage a projector directed its images onto frosted glass which was the TV screen. The slides were projected backwards so they would appear normal to the audience. The eighth graders provided the script, and the script within the script was cued so the slides carried out a visual portrayal of the eighth-grade experience.

It was a hit. I remember thinking that device might have some future use. Less than five years later, Badger High School abandoned the traditional commencement speaker in order that the graduating class could be center stage at their own commencement. Let me repeat that – so the graduates could be center stage. This pre-digital project was commencement feature from 1961-1985.

What drove this demanding, time-consuming activity was my evolving desire to understand and interpret the American high school.

My love of teaching and that temporary status called high school senior have etched a permanent mark in my experience. It really changed everything. Now I eagerly anticipate the encounters, visits, sometimes almost scripted approaches former students make with their mentor.

"Mentor" has such a broad expanse of meaning that I am not sure how I am using it. Like teaching, learning and influence generally, it is impossible to know how one came across in the unique relationship between teacher and student.

Yet I think about it. Then one of those former participants shows up and the whole matter is up for grabs again. But it always has to do with being a senior, that last stop on the way to one's destiny. Commencements can catch the spirit and essence of this transition.

The Real Reasons for the Graduation Projects

How else could I know enough about a senior class unless I knew their context, their community, unless I worked directly, daily, with a goodly percentage of them. That was probably the key to project-making.

It meant sometimes sacrificing good ideas, possible implementation, satisfactory photo coverage. But, for the most part, it worked. A lot of endurance and disappointment was involved. That is also why I tell people the graduation project was an extension of my classroom, an application of the skills practiced there. The two were integrated.

Work on the project started when classes were running reasonably well. And even after it began, work came to a halt many times, for many reasons. Three of the twenty-five projects were actually incomplete when all of the gear had to be hauled off to the gymnasium to make the deadline. About the same number allowed decent time for practice and polish.

Reasonably, one can ask, is it really worthwhile? Is this kind of time necessary to ensure seniors are pictured on a 10 x 15-foot screen for all to see on the night they are graduated? Is it necessary to develop narrative and fit music for an occasion which will no doubt be lost on most? Will anyone ever see a project in a context which will allow them to absorb what was built into them? Is this simply Mickey Mouse? Isn't there something more substantial than fleeting images, generalized ideas, and music which probably was shooting too high?

I have always thought the answers to all of those questions were positive.

Isn't it commendable for seniors to participate in their own commencement? Speeches by a valedictorian and salutatorian hardly pass for participation. Singing goodbyes is a limited sort of participation. I am talking about seniors expressing themselves about their experiences. Do students really understand the process in which they have taken part? Do they see most of their classmates as anything but contemporary blur? Most seniors could legitimately ask, am I a part of something larger? Or is it me against the system? Anyone who has honestly worked his or her way through high school knows better.

The situation is more complex. While in the buzz saw of adolescence, how can anyone really understand the institutional function of a public school? Does the occasion ever arise for a visual (and auditory) testimony of what a high school is and how it functions? Can we ever see into every classroom, laboratory, shop, office, meeting room, when the institution is running? Can we ever, in the course of thirty minutes or less, see the current senior class individually, each in a context of his own, without leaving one's seat?

One of the reasons we do not appreciate the public high school is that we do not realize its scope, what it tries to do. Students cannot. Teachers do not. Few administrators will try. I wouldn't, if I had not done twenty-five graduation projects. So, these commencement retrospectives allowed thoughtful expression, expressive music, and the panorama of two hundred seniors within the context of their high school. Anytime we do these things, of course, a range of responses can be expected, from Mickey Mouse to "my most moving high school experience."

Project '61 – "Like Young" by Andre Previn and David Rose

One of the satisfying finds at the ALS Music Mart this year was the Andre Previn-David Rose song, "Like Young." It is one of twelve tunes under the title *Secret Songs for Young Lovers*, an MGM LP which dates back over fifty years.

"Like Young" was used in Project '61, the very first commencement project. I've been trying to locate the recording for years. The 45rpm disc was long worn, gone, given away, or whatever happened to it.

As the title suggests, it seeks to portray the youth of 1961. It would not pass the test in 1994. But it did then. It was straight adult music since youth music as such was not a well-established genre. David Rose's was a studio band with its big string section and all, and a young and talented piano man, Andre Previn, who wrote the song.

The tune's major thrust was lyrical and optimistic, though it had a hint of uneasiness and uncertainty, which made it speak for the early-1960s.

I remember the slides that we used over "Like Young." They were closeup head shots of seniors against a bright and deep blue sky. The subjects were the recipients of top votes in a class election for certain character traits. The best way to understand how it worked would be to hear the Rose studio band and the Previn touch. Since we can't do that in this essay, I thought sharing the script that ran over the music might help.

As the tune commenced, the narrative began:

> Now what about the class personality? It has been classified as happy and serious, ambitious and lazy. Not much help, is it? A look at individual seniors may furnish an answer.
>
> Youth must have rhythm, movement, change. New things, experiments, curiosity, elbow room, freedom – these are the characteristics of youth.
>
> The music of youth is revealing; it is free, loud, intense, and much of the time immature. Their music speaks. Let's see what it has to say about our seniors.

At this point, the narrator elaborated the characteristics as their images were projected onto a 10x15-foot image screen. I can still hear the resounding voice of colleague Mr. William Hintz, paced to allow a few seconds for each face:

Friendly	Happiest	Prettiest	Wittiest
Talkative	Cheerful	Well-liked	The Artist
The Singer	The Dancer	The Actor	Talented
Most Bashful	Sincere	Regular Joe	Peppiest
The Athlete	Sweetest	Hardest Worker	Philosopher
Most Charming	Most Winning	Personal Touch	Most Ideas
Best Dressed	Good Looking	Brainiest	
Most Interesting	Ambitious	Best Smile	
Most Likely to Succeed			

In 1961, the idea of using slides and a taped narrative to replace a commencement speaker seemed incongruous, to say the least. The mechanics of such an endeavor at the time seemed insurmountable. Today that first graduation project seems primitive, archaic.

Students are now used to all sorts of sophisticated media presentations. Project '61 was indeed not that. But as I listened to "Like Young," I recognized the spirit in all twenty-five of those projects. They clearly demonstrated that catching the nature of each senior class was a worth-while endeavor. All seniors could be part of their own passage.

As the medium became more sophisticated and capable, different ways of doing it evolved. But somehow Andre Previn's "Like Young" caught in a poignant manner the realities of being young and graduating in 1961.

First Week of June: Graduation and Project '68

The assassination of Attorney General Robert Kennedy took place fifty-five years ago while Project '68 was in its final stages of preparation.

In addition, Project '68 was a first to have student participation from the beginning. Two not necessarily compatible souls grew to understand that their cooperation and compromising were absolutely necessary.

Terry Moorhouse was the non-graduating member, who wrote three of the four narrative sections. Deanna (DeeDee) Deignan was a senior whose emotional involvement naturally governed her participation and who wrote the last section. The three of us understood that it was the junior Terry whose creative efforts were the underpinning, and it was DeeDee whose loyalty and involvement with her class that was giving the final edge and polish to the effort.

The morning after the assassination was a sad time. Much of our work session was spent in silence. Other society-shaking events had already occurred, and we felt that somethings were happening which were bigger than what we were doing and yet that being a high school senior was more serious than before. But that seemed to make our mission all the more important. In two days, we were going public with Project '68. In the end, the angst of social unrest of 1968 along with Kennedy's courageous spirit for social justice were part of Project '68.

On graduation day, when polishing was the order of the day, we spent a couple of prime hours reducing the number of times DeeDee appeared in project slides. That was important to her; hence, it was important to all three of us. DeeDee, active and popular senior that she was, naturally turned up often. In the seventeen projects which followed, I always made it a point to work both ends – get all graduates in the presentation and keep the number of appearances per graduate within reason.

When Superintendent Pollock showed up for lunch and his sneak

197

preview, we confessed we had work to do and we told him why. Not only were we making an effort to see all seniors are pictured, but we were trying to control the frequency with which seniors are shown.

The first week in June involved long hours, weariness, tension, sacrifices. At the same time, it was fulfillment at the highest level. I knew we were doing something unique. True, this medium had its technical flaws and time limitations, but it also had its heart and spirit. I will always think of the first week of June as the opportunity of a lifetime, because it did something special for our graduates.

We do care about our youth and seeing to it that they are sent into the world with the community's blessing and support. We need to make direct, realistic, compassionate statements to them.

Earth Day and Graduation Project '70

Earth Day. Hard to think of the green movement without recalling Wisconsin's own Gaylord Nelson. The environment and its care are Senator Nelson's legacy. In 1970, his movement started as a manifestation of Earth's problems.

Badger High School's 1970 graduation project tried to recognize the movement. Many students were interested, and some were active. People have pointed out the historical value of the projects. Events bearing on national life always seemed to make their way into the content. And why not? Anything that affected student life during the school year had a place in the projects.

It was a challenge doing the project each year so that I never thought much about broader implications. Now as we transfer the projects to another medium, I think about their influence frequently.

Even transferring projects to DVD, which is how we do it now, I am not as aggressive as I once was. Thus, there is some irony in sending Project '70 recognizing the important mission of taking care of Earth.

Another factor in making sure this project is taken care of is that two 1970 graduates are especially important. One is Ed Kist, without whom this transfer business would probably not happen. The other is my eldest daughter Diane who helped organize the reunion for the Class of '70.

Project '76 – The Ploch Experience Invigorates Writing Life
Each Friday evening, I get around to scribbling to see whether my writing still had signs of life. Lord knows enough has happened recently to provide the impetus, though not the time.

When we go out of our way to reach students, the results aren't always apparent. I suppose I influenced high school seniors and never realized it. Somehow, we know a connection has been made – it's just that it never seems to manifest itself. That may even be a factor in teachers leaving the profession so soon. Are we really aware that we have an effect on the hundreds of young minds we engage? I do know we are expected to do too much with too many, so how can we expect to have all that much influence on any particular individual?

I am doing some rethinking of my influence after Geri Ploch Altshire set me straight. She is one of the seven children of Dick and Janice Ploch graduating Badger High School between 1975 and 1983. Five of the seven were students of mine. Geri was not. A senior in the 1976-77 school year, she took part in the mid-term early graduation program at the school. That meant she could not complete full-year courses her senior year. My senior English class was one of those. So, Geri did not sign up.

Over the twenty-five years of Badger's graduation projects, I learned the importance of picturing every senior. So, mid-term graduates were gone when the bulk of my photography was done. I made sure I knew those graduates and tried to make sure I had them in my slides collection. Somehow, I missed Geri Ploch. But I'll let her tell what happened:

> When I returned to partake in the June graduation ceremony, you sought me out of a crowd of hundreds of students to tell me I wouldn't see myself on the screen. That somehow, I'd managed to dodge the camera, your camera, and you felt dreadful. It is sometimes little things that make big differences.

I have difficulty remembering the exchange, but it doesn't surprise me. I did that sort of thing more than once. What really got to me was what Geri wrote next:

After all these years, I'm blessed with the opportunity to tell you how much that meant to me. One, that you noticed, and two, that you took the time to tell me in person.

She went on to say things that make me believe there is a reward for teaching. We may never find it out, but it's there, and often in surprising places. What caused all of this feedback was a photo I took of the seven Ploch children after father Dick Ploch died. It was the marvelous sense generated seeing several children from the same family, each of whom I had shepherded through one hundred eighty days of senior English.

When I went to the post-funeral luncheon, the youngest of the clan, Steve, came up to me and began to recite the first eighteen lines of the *Prologue to the Canterbury Tales* which was one of the requirements of my course. Suddenly, several Plochs were joining in. I was a little embarrassed but quite honored.

Soon someone mentioned photography, and it wasn't long before I said I'd cross town to get my camera if all would bear with me. Out of this came an image, which led to 5x7 prints, which led to framing, and, well, Father is not going to be around this Christmas, but his progeny will be. And they needed a little reminder of who they are.

I want to close out this bit of meandering with a sentiment Geri also wrote: "Individually we are a product of our genetic makeup. Collectively we became a spirit of all those who have influenced us in our lifetime. Thank you for your influence, for although brief, it has been lasting."

I suppose it is a bit ironic that the Ploch who got through to me was never my student. I doubt that matters. This was a family affair. As Mother Ploch wrote about the photo, "It is a wonderful, wonderful treasure I will cherish forever." Now tell me, is this business of classroom teacher important or what?

Project Photographer Tim Schinke (Class of '67)
Tim was a good student. He sent his considerable intelligence off in other directions, and all those directions wound up in the same place. It's called photography.

He saw my photography on graduation nights as he came up through the years. He saw something in my work that made him attack

200

photography. That is the only way to describe it. He was aggressive, blunt, single-minded, when it came to photography. He was all business.

During high school, the darkroom was his. He simply took it over, accepted its responsibilities, and no one complained, because the service he rendered was too valuable. He was a diligent student. He was not going to let his mentor down. And he never did.

He put his money where his interest was. He owned three or four Nikon camera bodies and a collection of lenses before he left high school. His work rose in demand. He did an enormous amount of photography for the graduation project during his junior and senior years. Then, while a student at UW-Whitewater, he continued to cover night photography for me – athletic events and dances. And when he quit, I noticed.

Fifteen years after he left Badger High School, when the school reached the state basketball tournament, he spent the first day in Madison recording the event when I could not attend. He told me he was still repaying a debt. Tim is made of solid, marvelous stuff. All business. Determined.

The Scrapbooks – A Sort of History of Badger High School
Scrapbooks and projects! To someone unfamiliar with my work and experience at Badger High School, those two words mean little. They were so broad and unenlightening that observers would pass them up.

Those eighty-plus, two-inch loose-leaf folders filled with the media stuff which was the prime informer of what has gone on at the school since it opened, remain completely unknown to the citizens of the district.

Those twenty-five commencement programs consisting of 35mm slides cued to a tape narrative and music, were but fleeting memories to those who saw them, and an unknown entity to those who didn't.

The scrapbooks kept a record of the ways Badger High School has grown as well as the activities and events which took place in the name of the school. The graduation projects showed on the average of two hundred graduates for twenty-five years doing what students do in high school.

Both historical accounts indicate a continuity which every institution develops, but few people record and remember.

From my experience at Badger High School, I concluded that remembering anything beyond the current academic years was simply not part of the process. Yet how can a public institution grow and thrive unless it has a sense of itself, its history, and the people who made it happen? That would be its students and teachers, its continuity.

School loyalty, students and teachers alike, has become a much different matter than it was in the late fifties and early sixties. I am not at all certain about the mechanics of the changes, but I doubt anyone could find many people who would say the changes are for the better. High school is a much different experience than it was just a few decades ago.

If I were going into a new community and wanted to measure civic loyalty, I'd head for the public high school. Adolescents are the most honest and significant indicators of community values. It isn't that adolescents reflect values. The reason is they have attitudes about them. They look at community matters with fresh, unjaundiced eyes. Inexperienced to be sure, but the schools are in the business of making students aware of what the community, state, and nation are, so that they can become productive, worthwhile citizens.

It takes a special kind of teacher and intelligent, community-conscious parents to cultivate the values necessary to achieve those ends. The school is the community, and the community is the school. Or at least that is the way it should be. Everyone teaches and learns. We do both all lifelong. We do not need to isolate schools and make them something we cannot afford and cannot use.

I think scrapbooks and graduation projects have something to do with the school, its history, its current practices, and its future. I like the sentence Neil Postman writes in the preface of his book *The End of Education* (1995):

> The faith is that despite some of the more debilitating teachings of culture itself, something can be done in school that will alter the lenses through which one sees the world; which is to say, that nontrivial schooling can provide a point of view from which what is can be seen clearly, what 'was' as a living present, and what 'will be' as filled with possibility.

As Postman says, worthwhile education "can be about how to make a life, which is quite different from how to make a living." I was in education too

202

long not to be affected by the fact that we do not have priorities, much less our efforts, straight about public education.

Scrapbooks and projects are not the whole answer, but they certainly reflect what has guided education at Badger High School in the past, what is currently happening, and could allow thoughtful citizens and planners some decent perspective for the future.

Ms. Esther Soderberg's first clippings and informal loose-leaf notebook contained highlights of Badger history running back two years before the new high school opened in 1958. In fact, the first clipping is a piece about a special course for students with reading problems. Times have not changed, have they? That entry was dated September 20, 1956.

Mr. Phil Gates inherited Esther's efforts for part of his two years at Badger High School.

Keeping a record of the school I considered a worthwhile activity. Thereafter, I sustained the gathering, organizing and pasting of clippings for the scrapbooks from 1961 to 1996. Since the journalism advisor's job also entailed handling information about the school for the local newspapers, I saw the scrapbook as a necessary record of how the newspapers were handling the information I was supplying.

Three papers were interested in Badger High School at the time: the local weekly, the *Lake Geneva Regional News*; the dailies, *Janesville Gazette* and *Beloit Daily News*. The three had a friendly competition which kept me alert. The two daily correspondents were local ladies, both efficient and competitive.

Any number of adversarial elements made life interesting. The weekly *Regional News* carried a Thursday dateline, but the paper was on the streets Wednesday afternoons. The two daily correspondents complained when I did not distribute releases to them so they could make publication on Wednesday afternoons when the *Regional News* was distributed to local newsstands and store. I was always under pressure to supply them liberally and equally with stories.

My problems came down to the fact that a full teaching schedule limited these community reporting activities. I always felt I was under some pressure to do more. Superintendent Pollock assured me I was doing fine. All he wanted was someone responsible for getting out highlight releases and maintain some equity among the three publications.

Then in the fall of 1967, when I commenced a journalism course and resumed advisor role of the school paper, the scrapbooks assumed another function. They became a source for my student reporters, and although they were not utilized to the extent I hoped, they were the backgrounding for many a story.

The scrapbooks received another boost when my student newspaper staff produced the *Regional News* for one issue in each of three consecutive years, 1970, 1971, and 1972. This one-week project, which was conducted during the second week of March, took student staffers off their scholastic schedules, and we spent the week working for the *Regional News* at the Regional News offices. Though these projects were not easy, they intensified the journalism program and made the scrapbooks an even more valuable asset.

The clipping, filling, organizing and pasting up of items which related to Badger High School were difficult to sustain. Usually I did the work in the summer, but at one point in the late-1970s and early-1980s, I got several years behind. Two of my student editors were instrumental in saving this project.

Ellen Dare Burling (Class of '82) and Amy Schroeder Kalaigian (Class of '83), in addition to being dedicated student journalists, worked on their own time during and after they left Badger to help me catch up on this work. I am sure I would have abandoned these scrapbooks had I not received their help.

Once this work was caught up, I knew I could never let it lapse again. After I retired in 1986, I continued the work for ten years, funding the work myself. It costs $150-$200 a year for materials plus my labor which is difficult to assess. However, I never thought to drop the work because of costs, but I did think of dropping it because of the time it took.

But I found no better way to get the feel of a school year than to clip, organize and paste up what the public sees of their community high school. I have always been a student of public schools and in particular the high school district I worked for. There is no question I have learned a great deal from this work.

Though the school probably should have been the recipient of this collection of over eighty loose-leaf notebooks, I had no qualms about keeping them. The only times they were ever pressed into service beyond my classroom were for display purposes during the 1975 North Central Association evaluation of Badger High School and in my annual trek to the central office to let Superintendent Karl Reinke have a look at the current books.

The single most important thrust of encouragement occurred during one of those visits to Superintendent Reinke's office. When he became superintendent in 1972, he hired a budget director by the name of Mr. Jess Laundrie who was struck immediately by the scrapbook project. At that time, I was putting the pages into loose-leaf notebooks which were inexpensive, less sturdy than was desirable. Their capacity was also limited.

Mr. Laundrie determined that we were going to get sturdy, fancy, vinyl-covered Wilson-Jones two-inch loose-leaf binders with fancier acetate covers for the pages. A few weeks later, two large cartons arrived with the notebooks.

It is doubtful that anyone will sustain the scrapbooks in the manner I have. Chris Jacobson Brookes (Class of '67) has shown more than passing interest. She worked for over a year to update the scrapbooks.

During the mid-1990s, I met with Principal Mark Pienkos to discuss the possibility of housing the scrapbooks in the high school library. He graciously made the arrangements, and the scrapbooks are housed there to this day.

Memories and Continuity: BHS Announcement Board

Sometimes I wonder just how valuable memories are. They don't seem to produce tangible things or results one can use "right now." We can't live on memories.

Not so fast. Aren't memories part of the mental device that allows us to comprehend continuity, to string events together in order to make sense of them, a continuum, a narrative, a meaning to life?

One morning recently a friend, who is a local businessman and former student, called to ask what happened to the announcement board which for twenty-eight years had greeted people as they turn from County Highway H onto South Street on their way to Badger High.

He said his wife drove by the school and thought she remembered it but was not certain. "Of course, it's there," he said. "Not anymore," she replied.

He thought of calling me. I told him as far as I knew the board was still there. "Not anymore," he said. I told him I would check into it.

This phone call happened during one of those weeks when pressing and pulling are the rule, allowing not a whit of leeway. So, it was three days before I could go out to see for myself. Ironically, it was at the hour of the groundbreaking for the $18,000,000 addition and renovation, being held on Walter Jonas Field.

The announcement board was not there. A bulldozer took it down. In its place was a temporary sign with a Bucky Badger and the school's name.

My first thought was to call Mr. Herb Erikson, retired social science teacher, who, with members of the Class of '70, built the board.

Herb was a mason before he became a teacher. Political science was his specialty, both in his community of Williams Bay and his classroom. When the Class of '70 raised just enough money to buy the materials, it was master mason Erikson who was drafted for the job. He and several members of the class built the sturdy structure whose base contained three yards of concrete and whose brick matched the Badger building.

The member of the Class of 1970 I called was my eldest daughter Diane. I can't repeat her first words, but it was clear she was annoyed. She wanted to know why someone from the class had not been notified, why a notice had not appeared in the *Regional News*. If the board was in need of repair," she said, "I am sure we would have raised the money."

As it turned out, the Class of '97 had raised money to purchase a new announcement board, this time an electronic message board which can be controlled from inside the building. Then the decision was made to raze the old board – at the expense of continuity and allegiance from a community whose support the school badly needs.

Schools need communities. Just because most citizens graduate from high school does not guarantee lifetime endorsement. Just because most of us have or will have children who attended or will attend high school, does not mean we understand schools.

Links need to be made and sustained between school and community. We need to understand what made Badger High School what it is. It has been over sixty years since the institution opened its doors. Over ten thousand students have made the four-year trek. Five superintendents, five principals, hundreds of teachers, and countless deeds and interactions, have made the tradition that is Badger High School.

The Class of '70 was reaching across the decades and generations when they bequeathed their announcement board to Badger High School. They even buried a time capsule in the foundation. This generous class endeavor was forging a link between the past and the future.

Only a prudent measure of maintenance was necessary to sustain its life, and the solid piece of masonry could have easily been adapted to accept the marvels of the electronic age. Then the two classes, a generation apart, would have aided the sustaining of continuity.

Memories are our link to our institutions and to the past. This history is the stuff of the future. We are all part of a continuity, and community would be served if we understood that.

Badger's Story

The annual scrapbooks and the graduation projects were extensions of my classroom. They fed my interest in understanding high school students. The scrapbooks served as a journal, a means by which to keep a handle on the school as a whole and how it looked to the community.

The graduation projects allowed me to see high school seniors as a cross section of American society and to interpret them in terms of their experiences.

I gained great satisfaction from taking the pulse of both the school and its seniors every year. Now that over thirty years have passed since I left Badger High School, I want to make sure the school receives the products of these activities.

Eighty-five, two-inch scrapbooks, two for each year running back to 1956 when ground was broken for the building were made through 1996. They represent a history of Badger High School for its first decades of operation.

I want the school to have this collection, but there are a couple of problems. One is their upkeep. Clipping regularly, organizing, and pasting up the material all must be done on a regular basis. If a week were missed, the whole collection would lose its currency. The continuity would be lost.

The graduation projects can all be assembled and presented, since the slides and tapes are in good order. Several years ago, Ed Kist (Class of

'70) and I began to put the projects on videotapes and DVDs so that they might be preserved.

As wise as making videotapes and DVDs of the projects sound, doing so is not a perfect solution to preservation. The most serious problem is the fact that slides are both vertical and horizontal, and the television screen is horizontal. Obviously, something must be sacrificed. Also, DVDs are fast becoming the medium of choice over videotapes.

There must be some value in these slides and scrapbooks. They represent a continuity of this community's high school: the scrapbooks for all the years of the school's existence, the projects for the first twenty-five of those years.

I think it would be appropriate if I had the opportunity to demonstrate and explain these two activities to the school board and any other interested parties. That would mean more than simply trying to explain.

One observation I've made over the years is that the school has shown little interest in encouraging and developing relations with the past and the continuity which each new school year represents. No contact is kept with graduates. The school has nothing to do with class reunions. Graduating classes are not encouraged to take part in maintaining continuity and tradition. No attempt has been made recently to engage the community in encouraging an active tradition at Badger High School.

I do not know whether these artifacts would be of value along those lines, but it seems to me they would. We cannot forget our pasts. That is how we got to the present and very well might be the key to the future.

These scrapbooks and graduation projects document the story that is Badger High School. It is an interesting story, but we do not seem to care about such things. Maybe it is a community characteristic which can never be changed. Maybe all it needs is some heart-felt, responsible leadership. I have always felt that adolescents need a demonstration that the community really cares about what goes on at Badger High School at other times than commencements and property tax time.

Interacting with Students

Good teaching results when teacher and students reach a level of mutual respect and motivation. The chemistry is different with every teacher, student, and class.

So, the best any one teacher can say involves what has worked for him or her. For example, known only to myself, in each class, I identified one or more "class barometers" who seemed to always know what was going on and who could gauge the temper and tone of his or her classmates. I remember several students on whom I could depend for representing how their classmates felt, whether this or that question was fair or clear, and whether this or that activity was working or not. I learned to do this assessment by reading eyes, observing gestures and body language. None of the "class barometers" ever knew who they were. At least I don't think they did. Below are accounts and beliefs for my ways of interacting with my students.

CONTENTS

Engaging with Students

When high school seniors entered my classroom in September, they probably had already had thirty-five or more teachers in their twelve previous years of formal education. They certainly learned something about the range of humanity and the kinds of methods that teachers use.

If we don't use a civil reasonable approach, we can count on students' efforts being at a bare, just-get-by minimum. It's no fun trying to teach people who do not respect us and who give us nothing but their grudging attendance every day.

My rationale was, what would happen if students had a choice of whether to come to my class or not. How many would show up? Well, all I can say is I quickly learned how to read expressions and body language and how to test motives. If I was convinced my students looked forward to my classes, I went about my job with more vigor. It made me work harder and expect more. I'm sure all that translated back to the students. The entire process fed on itself.

It is then that I have the luxury of separating those students who want to learn from those who do not want to learn. Different tactics for different problems. It is at that point the teaching mission becomes self-fulfilling adventure. The only obstacle of real importance is the number of students. If that number is too high, teaching fairly and fully becomes very difficult. Then I have to start such cutbacks as increasing general techniques and reducing individual attention.

It is possible to treat adolescents as equals and still maintain the authority necessary to administer a classroom. Two-way communication is much more comfortable and mutually rewarding than one-way streets.

I never considered the relationship between teacher and student a one-way street. More than knowledge flowed between my students and me. I worked hard to develop a significant reciprocity. I doubt I'd have stayed in teaching if it was only a one-way relationship and simply receiving a salary.

To explain. I always became excited for September when my new students arrived. They would be seniors embarking on their final year. Behind each one of those faces was someone worth getting to know.

When teachers meet over a hundred students a day, engaging every student is difficult; let's face it, it is impossible. Yet that was always the objective: get to know each student.

Teachers have a number of ways to do so. Even though teachers may face twenty-five or more students in each class, it is surprising what making eye contact, observing without judgement, and encouraging general interaction can do to enhance understanding and respect for our students.

Students respond to teacher stimuli in many ways. Between students who can't wait to express themselves and students who will bend heaven and earth to avoid any teacher contact, there were all matter of in-between students. When teachers become aware of their students as individuals, even as they conduct daily-class business, students will respond.

Keeping students' attention is not always automatic. Teachers must be aware of class chemistry. My students had been together for at least their high school years and some since kindergarten. Though they didn't know it, I had in-class operatives on whom I could depend to know the condition of intra-group relations. I thought of them as "class barometers." If something was going awry, but I couldn't put a finger on it, a glance at one of any barometers often directed me to the problem.

Barometers were students who always were on task, who were aware of any activity or deviation from class protocol. They never knew who they were. In later years, when I had occasion to inform some of these folks that they were indeed one of my barometers, they were often shocked.

All of these practices were designed to enhance communication and understanding. Nothing gets students' attention faster than knowing that the teacher is aware of and interested in them. Teaching would have been an empty, uninteresting profession if I couldn't have engaged students as individuals.

After my retirement, several students established a scholarship in my name, and although its funding allowed it to exist for only two years, I became more aware of my influence as a teacher and mentor. During that period, I was inspired to go back through my twenty-nine years of student records and list the names of students who somehow registered more than attendance and grades in my classes.

Of nearly three thousand students, this list produced 385. Imagine: 385 individuals whom I thought to have understood beyond the typical teacher-student relationship. There is something a bit intimidating about that. Yet I have a profound desire to speak with each of these individuals.

Thoughts I Never Said
I wanted my students to see how important developing their minds and learning their language were for their lives. Hopefully, my day-to-day actions spoke these thoughts which I never said:

- I always see the best in you even when you don't think I can see it.
- I expect more of you than I will ever get back.
- I wonder what you will do with my expectations of you.
- I believe in you but, like you, I need to be shown once in a while.
- I know how self-discipline works. It never will work, unless you act on the T-R-Y factor.
- Someday you will think back to this year of third hour classes and wonder why you didn't seize the opportunities.
- Tomorrow you will drag yourself through that door and not realize why you cannot understand.
- I hear you. There are too many more important things. If you don't hold that job, you won't be able to go to college. If you don't hold onto this job, they won't let you into college.
- The trick is to be able to think of other things while conveying the impression you are alert and with me. That won't work either.
- I wonder if anyone knows you as well as I do. You keep showing me what you're made of and how you play only for today.
- Next week is too late. The agenda will be different then.
- You can be as difficult, different, and diffident as you will, but I am playing a limited engagement.
- Did you know that this is your last year with a free education?
- This is a required course, and you expect to graduate.
- If I didn't give tests, could you prove you had learned something?
- Do you comprehend how the factors of your education work?
- I don't make students do anything. I lay out the course and its possibilities and make an offer to help.
- Yes, I always see the best in you, even when you don't think I do.

Spending Classroom Time Wisely

"Don't you take attendance anymore, Mr. Johnson?" Mike should be commended for his powers of observation. I assumed the hand was quicker than the eye in such daily drudgeries.

By November, I could take roll without saying a word or conveying signs that I was conducting the chore. I couldn't blame Mike. He got used to my making a big deal of it back in September when I was learning names and figuring out what kinds of minds I would have for nine months.

But as autumn deepened, I completed this task in a few seconds, and no one but Mike and I knew it was even going on. Yes, I made a point of talking to him at the end of the hour. All he said was that most of his teachers labored the activity which, I added, takes time, and it isn't something that deserves a lot of time. Then I recalled something somebody said one time, "He saves time who spends it wisely." I think it may have been my mother.

Few people in education think much about efficient use of time. I know most students didn't think about it. Unless teachers give a charge to a 50-minute hour, nothing much will happen. Teachers have to be self-starting generators every day. We cannot depend on students, for example, to remember where the class was at the end of the previous hour. Those who do recall, will not let on. Peer pressure is a factor among adolescents.

When I suggest teachers have to be self-starting generators, I mean it literally. Even when taking roll, we learn how to generate surreptitiously. One example is to start by asking a provoking question that seemingly has nothing to do with yesterday's (and today's) work. We need to plan ahead how to make the discussion from that question lead quickly back to business. I looked forward to "self-generating."

Asking an apparently unrelated question helps us find out in a hurry who does remember where we were at the end of the hour the day before.

Students didn't recognize the method in my madness. By the time the hour's work generates, it didn't matter. My impression was that students thought fifty-minute classes were too long. That's why when the buzzer or bell ended the hour, somebody wondered out loud where the time went.

Asking Questions

> *There is no such thing as a worthless*
> *conversation, providing you know what*
> *to listen for. And questions are the*
> *breath of life for a conversation.*
> James Nathan Miller

Asking and answering questions constitutes a major part of a teacher's work and is fundamental in a student's learning.

Every time I asked a question, knowing only one student could speak at a time, it was important to understand that other students were going through the mental process and were coming up with their own ideas to share or questions to raise. And if the answer a student gave left something undone, then others could expand on that answer or verbalize their own thinking. This interactive process is the heart of education in classrooms.

The challenge is that teacher-student interaction is often a one-way street. Many teachers ask all the questions, and probably in too many cases also answer them. The key to classroom effectiveness, it seems to me, is a kind of balance between teacher and students, involving an exchange which respects the participation of both parties.

Think of what effective teacher-student interaction means. Not lecturing for long periods. Spending a lot of time getting to know students – observing, interacting, sharing the stage, so to speak. It means serving as advisor, guide, implementer. These roles not only encourage balanced participation, but they build trust among all the participants. Trust is what makes the classroom not only tolerable but important, interesting, and invigoration, and even compelling. Tolerable is not the right word since it suggests a kind of grudging acquiescence. We don't want that.

Every once in a while, our students will affirm the importance of our work together. I was hurrying from the main office to my room between classes. The halls were crowded. I came up behind two students engaged in conversation. One of them was headed for the same class I was. As I darted unseen around them, I heard my student say, "I have to hurry, I don't want to miss English. I don't even want to be late." Assuming a majority of each class feels that way, we're going to find classes invigorating, and even compelling.

Questions and the answers that follow are the engines of classroom life. Students used my questions as indicators of where we were heading. I used their questions to make the same assessments. Student questions also provided insight into their thinking processes.

Not all adolescents understand that the shift to more freedom in their lives requires a similar shift to more responsibility. Their questions belie their motives. For example, even high school seniors in the middle of interesting, intelligent discussions will ask, "Is this gonna be on the test?"

Some will even interrupt to ask, "What do I need to get an A?" or "Does this count for a grade?" We can see where some students' priorities lie. Just about the time I was sure class rapport had developed fully, someone will ask, "What's your first name?" or "How old are you?" We have to wonder whether they are interested in job one. I mean really interested. After weeks of established rules and routine, it was discouraging at test time to get questions like "Does this have to be in pen?" or "Is this an open-book test?"

Why don't I get questions like "Why aren't there more great teachers like you?" Even if that were possible, we must face reality.

Asking and answering questions provides the substance of education, leading to mutual understanding and a lot of learning. The whole idea is to have them thinking the community of learning, instead of just personal motives for at least one hour of the day.

Groucho, one of the famous Marx Brothers, who knew something about conducting conversations, uttered the following on the human urge for one-upmanship. "Years ago, I tried to top everybody, but I don't anymore. I realized it was killing conversation. When we're always trying for a topper, you aren't really listening. It ruins communication."

There you have it. Intelligent questions and deep listening to answers.

Class Rapport

Merriam-Webster's Tenth New Collegiate Dictionary says "rapport" is "a relation marked by harmony, conformity, accord, or affinity." Achieving classroom rapport involves all of those, but the desired end is feeling that we understand each other well enough to get things done. It's the mutual nature of the classroom and all that entails.

To say the teacher is entirely responsible for rapport would not be true, but without the teacher we have no leadership, no direction, no coverage, and therefore no mastery. The teacher's job is to awaken students, encourage, and create the conditions for learning. But first, build class rapport.

I developed the ability to look at one student and see others. I consciously practiced this skill. Peripheral vision is a handy tool. I always thought that students didn't get away with very much in my classes. They often thought they did. However, as my confidence about what control means grew, I observed many things going on, ignored some, or rather, stored them away. Students thought I was not observing their activities. When the distractions grew, I chose an opportune moment, and then confronted them with the proof, usually several examples and usually visual documentation.

Standing while teaching was the price I paid for being aware of all students at once. I heard about that omnipresent and overwhelming bearing I was supposed to have had, but I figured as long as I kept these potential disadvantages in mind and worked on them, it was a small price to pay for a panoramic aerial view.

My demeanor did not have to produce an overbearing tone simply because I spent my time looking down at students. It was how we talked with each other that mattered. It was the nature of the relationship, not whether I was looking down at them and they up at me. That was only a physical manifestation. A respectful and understanding relationship was what counted.

I have sat on the circumference of a circle of chairs and tried to carry on learning through this orb of equality. Discussion is the substance of communication with students, but leadership, direction, and coverage are also objectives of the fifty-minute class hour. Undisciplined conversation, chat, and gossip are natural adolescent tendencies when students are given what appears to be equal opportunity. In a circle everyone becomes a miniature stage from which can emanate surges of adolescent nonsense.

I would rather physically oversee the entire class and bring about the communication that the ideal circle seems to promise. Individual responsibility and class rapport are essential for useful classroom teaching and

216

learning. I believe my classroom was a comfortable place to be, if my students could reasonably be expected to want to learn and respect language.

Never-Failing Classroom Phenomena

There's nothing wrong with teenagers
that reasoning with them won't aggravate.
Anonymous

They were the never-failing phenomena of my classroom experience. I recall thinking of these free-spirited adolescents alternately as con-artists, the something-for-nothing crowd, and sometimes the distracted folk of room 207. These students followed along with their classmates all year long but produced no effort. They became mental no-shows, hangers on.

On the first day of class appeared this eager-looking beaver who sat ramrod-straight in his seat hanging on everything I said. Nodding assent to stuff that required no response, it quickly became clear that this student was going to be one of my prize students.

I was taken in for a while by some of these sneaky clean masters of first impressions: "When do we start, Mr. Johnson? Can I get my first writing assignment today? Do you give extra-credit work?"

Here we are, the first day, and I guess he doesn't recognize starting when he sees it. Don't worry, the first writing assignment will come soon enough. And extra-credit comes after credit, which comes after work.

I could spot these people almost instantly. They somehow did not think teachers could see through their adolescent ploys. For the first few weeks of the year, one fellow would hang on my every word, ask questions, take part in discussions, and seemed aware of the structure and direction of the course. But he never brought a pencil, a pen, textbook, notebook –nothing. Class to him was arriving, sitting, impressing, and leaving – period!

Some students pursued their sit-ins all year long, managing just enough effort to garner D-minuses. Some actually changed their ways. I was responsible for some of these problems, but more often it was the pressure of peers, parents, and the value of the course work. After all, language is a survival skill.

Some transferred to other English classes or tried to. Some dropped out of school. The senior year is a big dropout period, especially the first month and the beginning of the second semester. Somehow it becomes unalterably clear that over their four years they have not accumulated sufficient credits, and out they go. It's a tough decision because peers, with whom they have been classmates for nearly thirteen years, are now going to be graduated, and they are not.

Some vulnerable students will stick it out to the end. One eighth-semester boy showed up for class, burped a bunch of beer all over his desk, and left. Later he apologized and promised to have his late assignments in over the weekend.

I remember early in my career when book reports were part of my assignments. I received a disturbing array of adolescent fakery. Good intentions and naivete marked the attitudes and efforts of many high school seniors. These were con-artists and distracted folks and the something-for-nothing crowd.

One of the survival techniques was to learn what they could get by with, then mete out the minimum. Ninety-nine times out of a hundred they received their diplomas. They would not be earning an education, but whose loss is that? This prosperous society with its distractions and lack of national purpose is not the adolescent's best friend.

It becomes a life of excuses. Where's my compass? Wait 'til my ship comes in. Where have you been? I'm spread too thin. Fools rush in. How've you been?

Keeping Track of Students' Minds

Is it possible to tell whether students' thinking is with us or not? Can we be absolutely certain? Of course not.

But I was interested in reasonable certainty and the clues that point in that direction. The students' minds can engage in many activities while still pursuing the context and movement of a class of which they are a part.

It is not good to break continuity for wandering minds, except when there is good reason. The students are not impeding the class activity. All I knew was that they were or were not "with us." I would rather mentally note what I observe. If the mental meandering happens with frequency, I

218

can debate tactical options. If it doesn't happen with frequency, it's no big deal. Putting students on the spot for reason of what may be a rare mental lapse affecting no one would be silliness.

Students participate in a kind of mental vagary. Blooming adolescents, boys particularly, love to show off their mental powers at the expense of the hour's substance. One person can crush the concentration and follow-through of a class hour by one moment's nonsense. Better to ignore it or try to turn it back into the work of the hour.

One thing about adolescents is that they quickly forget grievances. In twenty-three hours, it's as though nothing had happened.

Who knows whether a student is thinking about the class discussion, calmly considering how fragments fit a whole, or simply daydreaming? By November, I will have caught up with most of these habits, so that starting in December I could freshly approach the same students with new understanding, new tactics.

Peppermint Patty is about as loose and predictable as students come. When her teacher accuses her of daydreaming, she is mildly dumbfounded. "Daydreaming? No, Ma'am, I wasn't daydreaming. I was just conceptualizing!"

Can't you just see the euphemistically-slick students trying to pull the wool over the eyes of naïve, unhip pedagogues who have not attuned themselves to sweeping social changes?

Teachers as Advisors and Counselors

One aspect of teaching often overlooked is advising, counseling. The obvious occasion arises when students ask for advice. I thought about what it meant to dispense counsel to adolescents. It seems safe to assume that students asked for advice because they thought I could tell them something they might use. They trust and respect experience.

When teachers do not accept the seriousness and responsibility of that phase of teaching, students lose faith in them as guides and mentors. Teachers then take on reputations of being overbearing, superior, or even impenetrable. They show the hard edge of discipline, ignore clues students send out that invited dialogue, or set up an outward aspect which shuts out a great deal of what education should be.

I assumed that learning meant involvement. As a student myself, I looked forward to it – inspired when I got it, disappointed when I did not.

When I began teaching, I assumed cooperation between teacher and students was essential. I needed to be involved in teaching my subject, and they needed to participate in their learning. We have to think twenty-five individuals, not a block of twenty-five students. In September it didn't look as though there were many differences. They all looked summer-fresh, autumn-ready.

But that was a deception. I learned the illusion of September had best be broken immediately while I had some advantage. Seeing differences meant mounting a reality campaign:

- Learn names the first week.
- Practice consciously eyeballing every student during each class.
- Be aware of students who are and are not eager to take part.
- Be ready to talk about matters other than course business, keeping a wary eye out for students who regularly try to distract the teacher.

These simple practices transmit definite signals, sending the message that this teacher is interested. The effect is to elevate class consciousness, enhance development of rapport, and encourage participation.

It wasn't long before the hour was regularly comfortable and positive. Individuals begin to seek me out. Many class discussions bubbled beyond the bell. It became easier to talk with students, in and out of class.

Opportunities arose to hold serious talks with individuals about their work, their problems, or their plans. Sometime during the course of the year, I let the following question arise:

In your future career, do you want to be in a job that primarily takes advice or gives it?

In this discussion, students began to consider the nature of their vocations in terms of their own personal characteristics. High school seniors have a lot to think about, and this fact added a dimension to the classroom which I would have been foolish to ignore.

Assessing Students' Learning

How does a teacher know students are learning? How do we know some-one with whom we are talking face to face is listening?

In order for education to take place, students have to pay attention. They must be interested enough to engage the subject matter. Many high school students learn in a hurry the minimum required to get by. A teacher cannot settle for that.

Teachers have to develop methods for indicating whether students are being fully engaged or not. Implementing such methods requires per-sistence, perseverance, and documentation. Here are a few of my methods:

- Reflect on how well students carry things over from one class to the next.
- Note how eager students are to move into the class routine.
- Assess students' motives behind their questions.
- Assess the quality of responses to new material. Just observe and cultivate an efficient memory bank.
- Note how students respond to a concerted eye-contact campaign.
- As a matter of practice, look at each student sometime during every hour.
- Carry on a long-range collection of bits and pieces of things that happen, e.g., attend to the paperwork on absences and tardiness.
- Answer and ask questions that aid understanding. Note details.
- Work more on understanding your students than staying on the lesson plan.
- Describe the ways students are adjusting to the class. Are students comfortable and able to concentrate for long stretches of time? Are they active participants? Why do they participate? Are their motives of a cooperative nature? Or are they selfish?
- Note how persistent students are when you give instructions for an assignment.
- Learn to read expressions, particularly in students who do not ac-tively participate. The face is a dead giveaway among most adolescents.
- Tend to be positive about things that demand criticism.

These observations seem like common sense. Sustaining interest in students as individuals always seemed to me a prerequisite to understanding them, to say nothing of teaching them anything. Teachers may become so enamored of their subject matter that they forget the two-sided, give-and-take nature of the process.

Teachers can't make students learn. The trick is for teachers to generate thirst before they lead their students to the water. Thirst for learning can be a potent force. I became convinced students really want to learn, but not all were thirsty.

Tests are not the best way to assess how well students are learning. Teachers have to use them because documentation of student progress requires it. A stimulating review, for example, will tell teachers all they need to know, though it is hard to document personal observations. I learned a great deal from observing how actively students engaged new material, and particularly how they related it to the old. Just because students are "with you all the way" does not mean they are learning well. English teachers have a tool that other teachers usually do not or cannot fully adopt. That is composition.

Critiques of student writing need to provide encouragement which should be personal, private, and profound. Compositions and students' response to critiques indicate how well they are learning. Their responses to critiques are as close to sure-fire method of evaluation as there is.

Student evaluation is a multifaceted process. The better we understand students, the fairer the ultimate assessments. The idea is to keep evaluations in a secondary role as the teaching and learning develop. This goal is hard to achieve because students have been influenced by many other teachers and all kinds of attitudes about tests and evaluation. But we teachers have to work at it. Knowing how well our students are learning is rewarding, even when we cannot always do much to change it.

Dialogue: Of the Intangibles

Usually, I listened more than made suggestions about student concerns. At other times, I shared some of my own life experiences:

Me: Hi, Todd! How are you doing today?

Student: Oh, fine. I'm not interrupting anything, am I?

Me: No, I'm ready for next hour, and besides, I need a break.

Student: Do you really think talking to me is a break?

Me: Of course. Conversation can stimulate and still be relaxing.

Student: I enjoy talking to you, Mr. Johnson. I hope I'm not interfering or anything.

Me: Have you done anything more on plans?

Student: All I can do. I sometimes wonder whether I should apply to so many schools.

Me: You wouldn't want to be in the position of not trying for some college and then be sorry you didn't.

Student: I'm tired of paper work, tests, and reading college bulletins.

Me: Are you learning anything from all this?

Student: I guess so, but whether it will do me any good or not …

Me: These things have a way of taking hold years later.

Student: I hope so

Me: Do you know what your problem is? You don't really know what you want to do.

Student: Tell me about it.

Me: Is there any reason to think you should know at this point in
your life?

Student: You can answer that better than I can.

Me: At eighteen, I had no choice in the matter. I was off to service.
That's the way it was in the spring of 1945.

Student: Maybe it would be better to have someone else making
decisions.

Me: Could be. I didn't look at it that way at that time. I never
realistically thought of running my own life. Someone else
always took care of that. After service, I went off to college because Uncle Sam paid the way. Then someone else decided I
needed to be drafted when the Korean Conflict started. By that
time, I was so used to others' decisions that I couldn't initiate my
own—and I was almost twenty-seven.

Student: We have too many choices.

Me: Well, you must decide, but just remember, it's not life and
death. I can vouch for that.

Student: But people make it seem like that.

Me: I don't know. It's true it took me eleven years to find my
vocation, but those years were not really wasted. I think of my
brother. He got his first clarinet when he was in fourth or fifth
grade. His life has been nothing but music ever since and golf.
That seems a little narrow to me. I don't think there is any rush.

Student: Something tells me I have to keep at it.

Me: Of course, and you'll recognize your opportunities when they show up. And between your head and your heart, you'll do OK.

Student: Those words you have up there on the divider. I've noticed them before, and I've been thinking about them.

Me: Go ahead, read them out loud.

Student: Perhaps the most valuable result of all education is the ability to make yourself do the thing you must do, when it ought to be done, whether you like it or not.

Me: Isn't that what education should do? Knowledge, information and training are important parts of it, but how you use your mind and heart in the process is also important. Discipline, compassion, confidence, that sort of thing.

Student: Mr. Johnson, isn't that what is missing in school today? Aren't we ignoring some important stuff?

Me: Yes, of course. But the bells are ringing, and the break is over.

Student: It was more than a break, Mr. Johnson. See you sixth hour.

Boys and Girls: Favorites and Encouragement
The American Association of University Women commissioned studies on how schools shortchange girls. The reports concluded that girls face discrimination from teachers, textbooks, tests, and their male classmates.

My impressions, which have persisted since, have been the reports are essentially correct, though this issue is complicated business. To cite one of the report's conclusions: "Teachers pay less attention to girls than boys." Anyone who has taught in coed classrooms knows that boys tend to demand more attention. They are more aggressive, and whether they are excellent, middling, or poor students, their active nature creates attention.

In my early years of teaching, I found it easier to encourage girls because they were more cooperative, accepted rules more readily, and worked harder. Boys tend to extremes. Since their physical development lags that of girls, boys are on the defensive more. Their active natures make them stand out, whether their actions are good, bad, or indifferent. Teachers are more likely to meet frustration with boys than with girls.

Because they require more attention, all things considered, boys are often responsible for the way a teacher is forced to work, the tactics used, the general tone of the classroom. The aggressiveness of boys often determines who receives attention. Though this outcome seems unfair, anyone who has tried to manage twenty-five adolescents knows that aggressive, outspoken, troublesome students have to be dealt with; otherwise the majority will receive little attention at all. In most cases these troublesome students are boys.

Seniors exhibit a broad range of physical maturity. Most girls have not only reached physical maturity they have long before adjusted to this social fact.

Boys are in various stages of physical development, but most are not fully in sync with the social aspects of their development. Therefore, when they succeed academically, they succeed big. When they cause trouble, they stand out in their troublemaking. The barometer for reading boys is an unpredictable game, and it demands close scrutiny.

Girls seem more willing to accept classroom rules and are more active about academic success. Though not always true, their uncertainties seem less demanding than those of boys. If teachers pay less attention to girls than to boys, it is likely that necessity contributes significantly.

Another factor which applies more to male teachers is the natural attraction to females. The same attraction no doubt exists between female teachers and male students. When boys frustrate and girls cooperate and seem to work harder, equilibrium is more difficult for a male teacher to achieve. Teachers cannot favor boys because they are aggressive or are troublemakers, nor can teachers ignore them, for the same reasons. Teachers cannot favor girls or boys when they are successful students. The problem is that encouragement can sometimes be interpreted as favoritism.

We as teachers must, however, demonstrate that classroom achievement is the goal of education. The opportunity for favoritism is great, but the destructive results should be so obvious that most teachers consciously fashion their approaches to be scrupulously egalitarian. At least one assumes they do.

Teachers are obligated to establish a balance in their relations with boys and girls. Only those who have taught can know how difficult it is to achieve that balance. Teaching adolescents is a tough course in human relations, but also a grand, exciting adventure.

An Embarrassing Moment

One morning, I was well into preparations for the annual research project. The research essay flows from a thesis statement developed early in the process. Ah, the key word – "process." But I'm getting ahead of myself.

My students and I were talking about seven steps of the research process. I emphasized that the thesis statement will become the directing element for all of the steps. The idea was to encourage students to decide early their controlling ideas and, then, to do research in pursuit of them.

This kind of lesson can be deadly. We can't let it become too mundane and somber, or we'll lose students, who are pretty easy to lose in February and March of their senior year. This research project is a serious discipline, important to anyone hoping to practice a responsible profession. We have to lighten things up.

During the first twenty minutes of instruction, I noted signs of distraction developing among my charges. At first, these seemed innocuous, but something was going on. Attention seemed to be centered around a student named Bob, who otherwise seemed to be following me closely. Indeed, he was, as it turned out.

Another student named Mike, who sat across from Bob, and two or three girls seemed to be as interested in Bob as they were in what I was saying. I glanced at my two class barometers, two girls, but they seemed to be out of the loop on these goings-on, whatever they were.

I could understand why a group of girls might pay special attention to Bob because he was a tall, handsome young man who looked mature beyond his years. Any high school senior boy who could maturate a cool black mustache had to draw some attention. But this scene did not involve adulation. Something else was going on, and it was beginning to bother me. We were well into the lesson when I became convinced that I was part of whatever this dynamic was.

First, I thought of all the cosmetic problems that could be responsible. Was there something on my face, am I repeating certain gestures, or heaven forbid, something worse?

Whatever it was, it was drawing more and more attention, and Bob was clearly the center of it all. I continued my instruction through all of this drama, while the class was now paying strict attention.

Well, at some point, I had to find out what's going on. When I was sure that some force was affecting what I was trying to do, I stopped.

I had to be careful because even though I've always been able to generate interest and then hold it for an extended time, there was always room for slippage. It would be embarrassing to question somebody and then find out nothing untoward was going on.

I looked my friend Bob in the eye, all the while assessing the reactions around him through my well-developed peripheral vision. I don't recall the exact words but must have added up to "What the hell is going on?"

Quickly Bob answered. "We're counting, Mr. Johnson."

What are you counting, I wanted to ask. But he beat me to it, informing me that I was repeating one particular word. "You keep using the word 'process," he said, "and we're counting. We're up to twenty-six."

I did three things fast. I breathed a sigh of relief, swallowed hard, and passed through several shades of crimson. I tried not to show frustration, but I did.

If I managed a retort for the enterprising Bob, I don't remember it. All I recall is the embarrassing impact of it all. In front of twenty-plus high school seniors, here I was, doing one of the things I scold them for in red in their writing.

I learned that I can't let such things get the better of me. I was very careful about using the word "process" from then on.

An Especially Memorable Classroom Experience
No one has asked me what my most memorable classroom experience was. If someone would, I probably would cite the experience with my 1968-69 first hour class. That morning I used the "eagle" examples in my annual attempt to stimulate thinking about personal expression and to

generate some understanding and motivation about its power and possibilities.

It was an idea I picked up in a publisher's bulletin for English teachers. It involved a dictionary definition and Alfred Lord Tennyson's impression of the great bird.

I wrote the two excerpts on the side board, side by side. I had developed a number of ways of using these contrasting descriptions, but I usually chose a time when whatever we were doing would lead to the necessity of an example that illustrated the difference between the literal and the figurative.

I sometimes left both excerpts on the board, out of the way, but in plain sight, for several days. It was more important to choose the right moment than it was to choose a particular way to use them.

I cannot remember the circumstances that particular morning. But it is well to point out that the Class of '69 at Badger High School was the last of the romantics, daydreaming idealists who believed in school spirit, and whose class play was *Brigadoon*.

They exhibited high imagination and positive demeanor despite the age in which they were growing up. They were willing to be different, original, in their approach to anything. Their cynics were buried in the jolly juices among the majority.

This first-hour class contained the progenitors of that spirit. They were bright and happy and not about to let all see they were influenced by the world's having gone sour, despite the events of 1968. It was inevitable that eagles would soar.

What I did was coax oral readings from two students. I looked at the old seating chart and encouraged persons whose styles would match the excerpts, but I could only guess who read them. Whoever they were, they were in sync with the two styles. Listen. And imagine.

An eagle is any of various large diurnal birds of prey of the falcon family, noted for their strength, size, and graceful shape, keen eyesight, ability to fly. Typical eagles have their legs feathered to the toes, although there are several other types.

The first was read as the matter-of-fact presentation that it is. No emotion. Deadly straight. Cold and calculating.

The second came, as all poetry does, not telling exactly what it is, but transmitting a feeling, a mood, atmosphere. Then the great bird dives toward the sea. The breathless nature of the experience was as clear as anything could be:

> He clasps the crag with crooked hands:
> Close to the sun is lonely lands,
> Ringed with the azure world, he stands.
> The wrinkled sea beneath him crawls;
> He watches from his mountain walls,
> And like a thunderbolt he falls.

I'd give anything to know how that experience entered each of those twenty-five adolescent psyches. Their reactions were instantaneous, and then there were those two ways of experiencing. There was what we learned, and there was the emotion of what we learned.

Then the silence broke. A confident male voice from stage left intoned, "Cool!" The leader of this auditory breakthrough was Gary. With that one word the intellectual spokesman of the Class of '69 converted the silent fusion of feeling into oral response. One after another they snapped out responses. Details escape me, but I recall the tone and texture of each. They are still etched in my experience. A spirited exchange of visions and fancies followed.

The convivial Pete bubbled and broke into musings. Poet Linda was beside herself with satisfaction. I thought Cherie might break into song. Terry performed a dance of the mind all around the room.

Cheerleaders Lynette and Cathy threw smiles into the action from their front row seats. Even the back-of-the-room folks were drawn into the midst of things. I can still see all their faces and hear their voices. The serious warmed in the glow generated about them.

Jorjanne went along with the happiness, quiet Julie smiled knowingly, and Jane finally came around. Even bashful Alleta looked as if she was going to say something. Cathy, Mary and Terry seemed to exude what makes the Irish poets. Even class skeptic Bob had a glint in his eye.

230

Indeed, one symbolically boomer word, which means to have survived its fifteen minutes of fame, set off the explosion. These 69-ers were documenting orally their ideals and hopes. Eyes spoke eager ideas. Bodies animated, the air ecstatic. And the bell rang.

First hour was over, and its passage, the group, the experience, all were frozen, to be remembered as such adventures are. Something had generated out of the routine of the moment, which grew and grew, and then was gone. Will we ever know why we feel the way we do or why such group identity is possible?

This event happened over fifty years ago, but I remember it and that group of individuals clearly. This fusion of feeling is the stuff of continuity, of culture, of civilization. We came to realize we were together in physical presence and somehow in spiritual community. This fragile stuff of life must be part of existence. Civilization depends on it.

Teaching, Learning and Fun

I had never thought of teaching as fun exactly. But having taught the generation which could easily and accurately be labeled the fun corps, I learned a lot about fun in thirty years of trying to convince its members that learning is important.

Many students measured classroom activity in terms of fun, so one of a teacher's perennial tasks is developing the atmosphere in which learning is important, though there is nothing wrong with enjoying it. Making circumstances right for teaching sometimes takes more time and effort than teaching itself. High school seniors are not easily fooled.

A positive approach, consistency, persistence and patience will usually lead to cooperation and trust. Most students will come around to the process and blend into the rapport that develops with every class. Staying on course with a certain plan is less important than developing the atmosphere in which dynamic teaching and learning take place.

I remember classes in which I was a student that were hopelessly predictable, uninspiring, endless. It was difficult to generate a desire to work in those circumstances, to say nothing of the work which must follow outside class.

I've had all sorts of comments about me and my classroom from former students. Here is the bittersweet acknowledgement one departing student left on my bulletin board on the last day in June: "This is a wonderful place to work if you're inclined toward that sort of thing." Another said to my face years later, "I'm sorry I wasn't ready to work for you." And a number of others admitted that all they really wanted in high school was fun. Some students apologized for not applying themselves.

I am not against fun, though personally I am by nature a serious sort. But that is the point. Why can't one's work be fun? The business is serious, but thinking of it as enjoyable makes the seriousness attractive, too. I did not find teaching drudgery – trying, unfair, frustrating, at times, but never far short of invigorating. I agree with Noel Coward, "Work is much more fun than fun."

Conferences with Parents of Baby Boomers
I'd like to be in a silent and invisible presence as baby-boomer parents confer with teachers about how their children are doing. I was an English teacher when those same parents were the subjects of conferences in my classroom. Many times I wondered how a generation that was present at the birth of instant gratification would handle the demanding business of raising families.

I also wondered how teachers would go about discussing problems today's high school students are having: the short attention spans, the ever more intrusive distractions, and the exposure to such social hazards of alcohol, adolescent sex, drugs, and violence. I don't mean only physical violence; I also mean violent language and activities, that are, the lack of civil behavior.

Boomers learned their freedoms were important, but often they did not learn that shared responsibilities are what make a democratic society work. Now these students are parents, and increasingly single parents.

How do we educate a child in civil behavior when we did not learn the lessons ourselves? How many parents are in the unenviable position of instructing sons and daughters in subjects like alcohol abuse, health risks of tobacco, marijuana trips, and other symptoms of social dysfunction?

Society needs rules and enforcers of rules. Most important, society must see that rules are carried out and enforced as a truly community affair. These understandings are very difficult in a society in which fifty percent of families are dysfunctional. Civil societies are impossible without functional families.

When I was making my way to maturity, I did not encounter such society-wide social problems. We were preoccupied with surviving economic depression and fighting a world war. Society needs things that unify it. With self-discipline we could achieve unity and solve our problems, but history seems to teach that catastrophic events are required to make us pull together.

Many parents came to talk to me about the progress of their children because they felt it was their duty, not an automatic family function that was in the same league as providing food, clothing, and shelter. The greater dangers to our democracy are subtler and slower working than we can know.

On Writing References

Writing references is an art because so much depends on the subject, the receiver, and me, the writer. It often made me feel as though I had someone's future in the palm of my hand.

The trick for making reference-writing work was three-fold:

1. Never write a negative reference.
2. Allow a liberal amount of time between assuming and concluding the task.
3. Insist on confidentiality.

I usually told students, who were probably pressing deadlines anyway, I wanted six weeks. That in itself is a test for the student. If he/she loses patience or has been tardy in beginning his preparations, I already have fodder for the process. At that point, my students understood I was serious. They should expect to be observed closely, be asked questions from time to time, and furnish information when asked.

References require candid and precise appraisal. Confidentiality is one way of assuring that. It is just one of many ways a teacher can develop trust with students. Trust takes time, which is why requiring references in the first semester is a dubious policy of colleges. Those schools that require character and academic references are particular about the students they accept, and they must realize that "your current teacher of English" has only known you for a couple of months, and to be able to write a useful reference requires knowledge and familiarity.

With all the other complicating factors, January was as early as I could be comfortably ready. Besides, that was when the first permanent grade was entered for the course, and I needed to think about formal evaluations anyway. If I was not reference-ready or student-friendly, then there must be other factors.

If I didn't feel I could write a reference for a student, I found a way to refuse. It would not be an out-and-out no. My major concern was the person as student. He or she would continue in my course whether I wrote a reference or not, so that relationship was the one to protect. A lot of ways to say no were available. It's just that I couldn't always think of them when I needed them, and of course I could not afford to wait too long. It's when I could smile and say "I'd love to" that the function of the reference was most useful in terms of the classroom.

The crucial question in accepting or rejecting a reference revolved around the question, will this letter be a positive reference? If I could not make it so, I wouldn't accept it. The real challenge came when negatives needed to be woven through in such a way that they become part of the overall appraisal, which in all other important ways would be positive.

I wanted to write the kind of reference that someone will read and take seriously. I put a great deal of time into the process, and I thought it reasonable to expect a full hearing at the other end, whether it be a college admissions officer, an employer, or a Rhodes scholarship committee.

Every applicant for anything has academic and character weaknesses. I needed to face that fact. At the same time, I wanted to see these problems in terms of the subject's positive traits. If those traits dominate the subject's impressions, then I wanted my reference to reflect that.

Supposedly, one negative factor will be seen as a rejection automatically. I did not agree. There are no perfect people, and anyone who reads testimonials as part of his professional duties, knows that to be the case and is likely to discount entirely, those statements of unqualified acclaim. I have always thought that acclaim balanced by other realistic elements was a useful, if difficult, thing to do.

Writing references is an art because judgment and ingenuity are required. In the end, it is no more than the written expression of an evaluation which goes on in a teacher's mind all year. That sort of evaluation far surpasses the grading mechanism used in schools for a long time. If I issued five A's in a class, how can I show the differences that exist among these five (or twenty-five, or one twenty-five) students. I cannot. The only way is by the written report or evaluation.

A reference is different because it is a specific, isolated subjective tool which has a rather narrow application. And a third party will read the reference. I am evaluating an individual, for an individual.

References are serious business and quite personal. My students' future may be advanced or hindered by the references I write.

Interacting with Colleagues

Teaching at Badger High School for nearly thirty years yielded several professional bonuses: working in a new school building, working for Superintendent Vernon Pollock, and working with several of his administrators and master teachers. They greatly influenced my development and effectiveness as a teacher. I had some challenges too.

CONTENTS

Superintendent Vernon Pollock
Principal/Superintendent Karl Reinke
Counselor/Assistant Principal Jim Graf
Vocational-Education Coordinator Don Anderson
Metals Teacher Paul Rauhut
Social Studies Head Bob Petranek
Social Studies Teacher Bob Guth
Band Director Ron Krause
Business-Education Head Don Kutz
Two Colleagues in the English Department
Teachers, Secrets and the Lounge
The Influence of Athletics
Those Uncertain April Field Trips
How Badger High School Affected My Development as a Teacher

Superintendent Vernon Pollock

One thing my teaching years proved true... Mr. Pollock was a credit to his profession, and his influence profoundly touched many students, families, educators, and community groups in the Lake Geneva Area.

I have never given any conscious thought to the idea that Vern Pollock would die. Someone who is as important in one's life as he was in mine is not thought of in that way. He will always be there somewhere.

We would see him in the summer, write to him on his birthday, and greet him for Christmas. He might have shown up on a warm summer day and spend a few hours in the backyard helping shuck corn and telling stories. How my family and I wish that we could have him over for another feed. How some of my colleagues and I wish that we could drive on another summer afternoon with him to Wrigley Field.

But die? The man of magic, die?

Maybe it is because he was such a strong presence in all our hearts and minds that death really didn't make much difference – he was an integral part of what we are. He will never really leave us.

When I say "we," I am talking about my family and two generations of teachers whose professional and personal lives were enhanced by having worked for him. It's funny, I never thought of it as working for him. He was not an employer or boss or administrator in the general sense of those words. Mr. Pollock was the magic responsible for the environment that let teachers work, thrive, or fail.

He hired us, treated us as professionals, left us alone, never put us down. He made us feel important. When hiring, he knew all about prospective teachers, sometimes more than they knew about themselves. He was interested not only in credentials, but in the person, the personal qualities. And he had a gift for reading character. We could grow and succeed at what we were there to do.

He worked primarily in his office and was visible through a large plate-glass window. We looked beyond the window and saw him conferring, talking on the phone, or doing office work.

It was not a pleasant feeling to fail Mr. Pollock. How do we return the favor of the environment that Badger High School offered in those days? And all the while, somehow, he knew how we were doing.

He wanted no spotlight, only the satisfaction of serving the profession he loved. He may have been misunderstood at times, usually because he declined center stage. But those of us who understood him knew that the spotlight was really in each heart he touched.

One of the real disappointments of my twenty-eight years at Badger High School was the institution's lack of consciousness about its past. Exhibits of this amnesia occurred regularly, the latest being the night when Mr. Don Anderson reminded me of the Vernon Pollock Scholarship.

Don had contacted a school counselor in charge of the upcoming honors convocation and referred to the man for whom the scholarship was named. The response was, who is Vernon Pollock? This is like a Ford employee not knowing who the company founder was. Who says history is not important?

People who work for school districts do not need to know who the originators were to do their jobs. Yet a sense of the institution's roots, of how it got to where it is, and its traditions will yield community continuity and build the civil cohesion society needs.

Those of us who were hired by Mr. Pollock knew as soon as we began that support and the freedom to innovate were givens. He created an atmosphere in which we could thrive.

We had our share of effective teachers who worked in a healthy, thriving, and competitive spirit. We felt we had a superior staff, that the community's children were exposed to the influence of seriously dedicated teachers. Mr. Pollock hired them. Whenever I think of my colleagues, I marvel at what it took to find and hire such a staff.

In addition to playing the key role in organizing Union District #1, he built the groundwork for a useful functioning high school. Architects like Mr. Pollock are still performing their unsung work. Thank you!

Principal/Superintendent Karl Reinke
Badger High School opened its signature orange doors for the first time in September 1958. An interesting aspect of those first days was the direction and clarity of the new school's philosophy. Superintendent Vernon Pollock and Principal Karl Reinke left little doubt that the new high school administration would allow its teachers the freedom to practice their skills. It was "freedom to teach" principle which, as it turned out, led to an environment which teachers found inviting and encouraging. Thinking back

over those years, it becomes clear the Pollock-Reinke administration developed a strong, deeply dedicated group of professionals.

Though Mr. Pollock was responsible for assembling the new staff, Mr. Reinke brought character to the endeavor. It wasn't necessarily his character that brought this character about – rather he allowed it to develop school-wide. His style was always in character. He was approachable with firm jaw, measured prose, reserved manners, and consistent follow-through. If anything or anybody was getting to him, it was often hard to detect, which is a good quality in a principal. The freedom to experiment was always there. Fortunately, most Badger teachers understood how that worked. Mr. Reinke was easy to like and respect… so long as we were not in his discipline sight lines. I can't remember that I ever was. That was the idea. He gave my colleagues and me the gift of the "freedom to teach." I respected him deeply during my teaching at Badger High.

Counselor/Assistant Principal Jim Graf

Mr. Jim Graf came to Badger High in September 1959. I am sure he was older, but he looked twenty.

Jim was a counselor for seventeen years and assistant principal for another seventeen years. As counselor, he came to my senior English classes in late September to talk about applications, tests, financial aid, and career planning. Away from school, we often talked about the changing circumstances for students on college campuses. Sometimes we discussed schools, administrators, teachers, and how important understanding is among the participants.

One of the amazing facts of Jim's professional life was how he came to grips with being a career vice-principal. Seventeen years was a long time to be the main target of devious adolescents.

I always thought being an assistant principal was a rite of passage, like basic training. Once this period of fire, of initiation, was over, one could move on and up. The assistant principals are the point persons, the lightning rods of the public high school. The problems come to them. They draw the fire.

With Jim, we have extraordinary circumstances here. His experience as counselor gave him access to the nature and variance of adolescent problems. His modest, restrained bearing made him a good listener. He was forever giving kids second chances. His hallmark was understanding.

A key to his success was that he could shut out the flak from colleagues and concentrate on students' welfare. The influence he commanded by having the confidence of marginal students and effective teachers was impossible to measure. Jim was grossly under-appreciated and underpaid.

He used to tell me when he was counselor, "I have to justify my job every day," meaning, one day's success does not guarantee tomorrow's success; meaning, one day's failure can make tomorrow's triumph; meaning, every day will bring different problems, each one unscheduled.

I'm not sure he was jealous of classroom teachers who met the same students every day and had the luxury of a more specific focus. Yet he certainly understood the broader, schoolwide picture, which many teachers did not. Counselling was the basic training for his principalship.

He must have developed an inner strength and confidence which made problems appear less severe to him, problems which sometimes appeared insurmountable to the rest of us. There was something good in what he did. Humanity in education is possible. Jim was testimony to that.

Jim's philosophy was up front, working all the time. Listen. Be Fair. Be ready to give a break. Believe in humanity. Then you will sleep well. What more could one expect of professional life? No wonder I respected him deeply.

Vocational-Education Coordinator Don Anderson

Mr. Don Anderson worked in the mold of his mentor, the man who hired him, Superintendent Vernon Pollock. They were kindred spirits when it came to the business of educating high school students. Don created one of the best high school vocational programs in Wisconsin. Even though we worked in very different departments, we collaborated often on behalf of our students and became good friends.

Don came to Badger High in 1960, serving as one of two industrial arts teachers. He served as the head of a large, diverse department for thirty-two years and as vocational-education coordinator and work-experience supervisor for twenty-five years. An enterprising and faithful community leader, he was active in many professional and community organizations and has held offices in most of them. He returned from retirement in 1997 to serve for two years.

Don was offered opportunities to "move up" through the ranks of education, but he always declined those opportunities. Don said often, "The best part of my job is the direct contact with young people and the creativity they bring to the classroom."

He had a seriousness of purpose which produced high expectations. His students respected his dependability. He treated his students as professionals. He developed solid relationships with business and industry, just as he was able to do the same between himself and his students. They learned a lot about architectural drafting, but a whole lot more about personal values and life's principles.

Don has been an invaluable teacher, administrator, and community resource. He was an educator leading important changes in education.

Metals Teacher Paul Rauhut

Our subjects were at opposite ends of the scholastic spectrum, just as our teaching quarters were at opposite ends of the Badger High complex, well over a tenth of a mile apart. Yet, Mr. Paul Rauhut and I identified as teaching colleagues. We believed that when teaching and learning are kept in perspective, subject matter and process will follow naturally.

The closest thing to an automatic reflex I ever saw at Badger High School was the metals students putting on their safety glasses before operating a machine. I've seen football players run on the field without their helmets. I've seen home economics students reach for hot dishes or pans without potholders. I've seen Bunsen burner abuse. But I never saw a student who didn't put on his safety glasses before reaching for the switch.

About head high on his office window was a rectangle of paper with this message: *Stupidity is forever; ignorance can be fixed*. The message seemed clear: just because we do not know something does not mean we cannot learn it.

Paul did not hang out in his office. He was on the move. He looked over shoulders, asked questions, and dispensed crisp advice in that clipped, direct language of his. He let students know metals was serious business. He was never distracted, making it his job to know always where and how his boys were working.

One of his former students told me, "I never saw him angry. He did

241

not get upset… but I remember once he took me aside and talked about my work ethic." Shop problems were never public problems. They were solved in private.

Paul carried these same qualities into work for his colleagues and the school district. "At a time when many school districts were turning the job of negotiating and teacher welfare over to expensive outside sources, Paul played a key role," according to Don Anderson. "He was the main contact with legal counsel and was able to clearly articulate issues to the benefit of both sides."

Paul never sought the spotlight. I admired him because he was serious, disciplined, self-taught, aggressive, human.

Social Studies Head Bob Petranek

Both Mr. Bob Petranek and I along with several others joined the faculty when Badger High School opened in September 1958. He was best known for his seemingly endless inventory of comedic skills and a delivery system of almost superhuman quickness.

Bob's classes were always interesting. Mostly, he taught economics which does not suggest a lot of humor. His use of humor was not only possible but necessary.

His ability to keep a lesson going in a straight line was close to absolute. Bob had a way of absorbing distractions, or more likely using those distraction to advance his subject's context.

He never sought the spotlight, but his influence worked in wondrous ways.

Social Studies Teacher Bob Guth

The dean of Badger's classroom teachers was Mr. Bob Guth. He taught history over six decades.

As a UW-Madison undergraduate, he completed his student teaching at Badger High School under Mr. Russ Otto in the spring of 1969.

"One day, Mr. Pollock called me to his office," Guth said, "and we chit-chatted for a while about his dogs and hunting." It was small talk, casual. "Then suddenly he asked me if I was ready to be a Badger teacher in the fall." Bob did not realize it, but he was being hired on the spot, in less than ten minutes.

A calmer, more confident teacher you could not find. Bob was an assistant coach for football and basketball for twenty-five years. He gave up coaching when his boy began competing in sports at Burlington High School.

Guth says kids really haven't changed over the years, but the faculty community is not as close-knit as it once was. "We're getting too big."

Band Director Ron Krause

Mr. Ronald Krause directed Badger's band for twenty-five years. The sounds emanating from the band room, the auditorium stage, the Broad Street parades, and the many contests in which his musicians excelled – all these bestowed a richness to life at the school and the community it served. Most observers would agree it was his jazz ensembles that caused electricity to flow from their Badger Experience. Ron shared his professionalism with his students.

Business-Education Head Don Kutz

Major Don Kutz served in the United States Army. I often addressed him as the officer he was in World War II. He was in the quartermaster corps and grave registration. We won't go there. Don was head of our business-education department and taught accounting. There we will go.

Don never lost his military bearing. He was always in the hall opposite his room during passing time. School policy required teachers be in the halls between classes. Only a few teachers did this duty with any regularity.

Don was always strict about following rules. For his twenty-five years at Badger, he did jobs that demonstrated his business and organizational skills. He oversaw the running of the school store and athletic ticket sales. Students also remember him because he was the attendance officer. When they missed school or were tardy, they had to report to the very serious-looking and rules-oriented Mr. Kutz, who had a great eye for ferreting out fakery.

Don was a faculty leader without ever holding an office. The officer bearing didn't hurt him one bit. I recall the year I was president of the Badger Education Association. As a conservative, he often led the charge against attempts to change things. As a liberal-tending soul, I tried to promote an endorsement of an NEA-sponsored code of ethics. Don saw little need for changes or promotions like that. He had no need for a code of ethics. He already had one, and a superior one.

Don was a member of that civic generation which survived the Great Depression and helped win World War II. He was another member of that heroic group which steadied, fathered, and mentored many who followed, including almost two generations of students. Here was a teacher who was a credit to our profession, our community, and our country.

Two Colleagues in the English Department

I worked with several excellent English teachers, but two knew how to reach students and gain their attention and effort.

As a speech teacher and drama coach, Mr. William Hintz knew how to attract and engage students. He produced large events for the school and community. Once a play or musical was in production, his focus naturally had to be on the few and for as long as eight weeks. Bill was constantly challenged by and addressing important questions of task, mission and ethics. He also chaired the English Department.

Mr. Robert Pavlik was a prophet and an innovator. He recognized that schools needed to be changed. He went about launching and sustaining the Study Skills Center, the Cross-Age Tutoring Program, and the Communication Skills course for non-college prep seniors. Since these projects were all innovations, they required leadership and planning. The effects of the Bob Pavlik period were profound and personal. I rethought my professional life more than once because of his efforts. He made a difference with students who regularly got the short end of things in the public high school.

These two real giants of their profession kept me honest in their inimitable ways. Each in his own way was a kind of conscience. I measured what I did by what I thought they were doing. In them I saw what happens when a teacher gains heavyweight stature. They were in a class by themselves.

Bill Hintz and Bob Pavlik were my barometers. I spent a great deal of time reading them. Their effects no doubt were stronger than I knew.

244

Teachers, Secrets and the Lounge

One secret to being an effective teacher is knowing how to keep a secret. That is hard to teach as one of the great principles of pedagogy, but in the long run, gaining the confidence of colleagues and students depends on it.

Most of us, when we learn something interesting or startling, generate an itch to tell someone. The determined traffic to the teachers' lounge was always a good indicator of that intent; teachers always look as though they have something important on their minds. But daily routine can generate boredom, and the gathering of the pedagogues offers temporary isolation from the adolescents and a chance to be the center of attention with the latest reports and rumors. Time to relax and let it all out.

Often what transpires is gossip, but not always. The important thing to remember in the teachers' lounge is that it is not the place to yield up professional secrets. It is, however, a good place to listen. I learned a great deal about teachers there, but relatively little about students. So that might cast doubt on the value of the teachers' lounge.

Yet this place, the modern equivalent of the "boiler room," was necessary. If there was a need to be able to keep secrets, it should not be at the expense of communication. I have had more classroom problems eased, placated, or solved by talk with other teachers, and there must be a place for that kind of conferring to happen. The standard teachers' lounge once was the boiler room. It held regular all-male convocations. Men teachers went there for breaks to chat and to smoke. Superintendent Pollock knew about boiler rooms, and apparently concluded that if there must be a place for teachers to congregate, let it be a small one.

At Badger High School, not only was there no appropriate space in which to meet visitors, the teachers' lounge was really an unfortunate postscript, an afterthought, which turned into something which served no useful purpose. The room was twelve by twenty-two feet, hardly a spacious living room. Two adjoining restrooms were tiny. The lounge served thirty-seven teachers when the school opened in 1958.

Some departments had office areas, but they were never private because students could come there. Since student teaching assistants were common, their presence was common. It was where they prepared, corrected papers, and did whatever else they could to serve teachers.

Fatigue does generate in the classroom after several hours. Useful relaxation can only take place in a space where students cannot freely go. One colleague once told me he couldn't relax until he went out the front door. Even those teachers who were perfectly at ease with students all or most of the time need a change of pace.

Not many teachers did their work in our lounge. I tried to in my early years at Badger High School. It was a question of whether my preparation hour would produce more work in my room where students had access or at a work table in the lounge where consistent chattering and choking smoke were constant companions.

The need for a place of relaxation does not automatically lead to idle chatter and storytelling. If teachers have a place where they can relax, they will do just that, and their work will follow them. When I needed to talk to another teacher about a student, I needed an atmosphere of privacy and something approaching comfort. When communication is possible, the rumor mill is unlikely to reach serious proportions because the atmosphere will be associated with the job of educating. It will be part of it.

The Influence of Athletics

One of the first revelations a teacher encounters in the public high school is the extent to which athletics dominate the education enterprise.

Three seasons of sports cover the academic year. Fall sports span the first quarter; winter sports, the second and third; spring sports, the fourth. Athletic schedules dominate the school's master schedule, which are controlled far in advance and from the athletic conferences and the Wisconsin Interscholastic Athletic Association, widely known in the public schools as WIAA. As a result, schools must plan everything else around these schedules.

We had an unwritten school-wide understanding that no activities would be scheduled during the first three or four weeks of the school year so that classes could be firmly established, and continuity developed without interruptions and outside pressures. The exception was, and still is, sports. Varsity football, for example, was well underway (two weeks of two practices daily) by the time classes begin. And the first game was usually at the end of the first week of class.

The first all-school event, homecoming, was not scheduled until the last week in September or early October. Since its existence depends on football, the date was determined by the football team's home schedule.

Many teacher-coaches gave the impression that their consuming interest was sports, and teaching was a requirement to be fulfilled so they could be coaches. I remember a basketball coach who diagrammed plays and talked incessantly of his sport in his academic classes.

When I was in high school and the possibility of coaching was before me, I probably sensed the inequities. I remember a math teacher who could be persuaded to talk football in class. He had been, of course, a football coach. As a student in his algebra class, I remember this grid talk. I also remember being uneasy about it. But math was tough for me, and I saw no reason not to go along with it. That was over seventy-five years ago at Fennimore High School.

The influence of athletics was ubiquitous. For example, the principal's office was one place where I thought privacy was assured. But for many years, right across a narrow passageway, was the open door of the athletic director's office.

Of all the extracurricular activities, athletics offered the most choices. Thirteen sports in all: football, cross country, volleyball, basketball, swimming, wrestling, gymnastics, baseball, softball, track, tennis, golf, and soccer. Seven are offered to both boys and girls. Each required a basic outlay for equipment and uniforms and salaries.

Some sports seemed to involve little outlay yet were the most expensive in the long run. Swimming pools, tennis courts, and tracks were expensive. Their maintenance and upkeep involved regular expenditures.

Football had high-cost equipment requirements. Because of the physical contact, medical costs needed to be provided for.

Schools which have gone to the extreme of dropping athletic programs are unwise, even though the reasons are practically always finances. Athletic programs are important. They aid conditioning; they encourage cooperation, team and school loyalty.

Something must give when students are playing a varsity sport. Today it is big business. Commitment is physical, tangible, and daily. Academic education is mental, often quite intangible, and should be engaged in daily. A sport pays off with winning or losing, success or failure, and tangible results on the sports pages. An academic classroom subject will pay off some time in the future, after an accumulation of experience and maybe some oblique occurrence to let the students know it was all worthwhile. Very intangible stuff.

Some intelligence and perspective are in order. Everyone knows language competence should be the skill around which the academic program is built. Start with the calendar, and we'll see the public high school is not structured that way.

Activities that allow tangible student and community participation are those that thrive. They allow students to perform and the community to observe. They have immediate physical manifestations.

Academic disciplines are not like that. They are investments. They are part of the future. They bring satisfaction to the minds of individuals. The schools, since their academic training should be their primary missions, should be structured primarily to accommodate their investments.

Playing football no doubt gave me an underlying attitude about health which remains with me to this day. No one made me play football. I volunteered. No parent pushed. No coach pressed. It was all my idea. I did not understand how important reading, writing, and the academic disciplines were. I did what I had to do, and I had my share of trouble. The rewards of mathematics, history, science, and the arts were not all that clear to me.

But football was very clear. Practice was regimented. Physical conditioning and contact were realistic facts. Cooperation with teammates was necessity. Friday was the pay-off. We played before a cheering crowd. We could be heroes or goats. What did we play for? Better question is who did we play for? Perhaps it was some young lady we hoped was watching. This social game was for social consumption. It was the central part of my life for four autumns in high school.

I later became an English teacher and have often wondered what that was all about, back in high school. Many times since, I have wished to have back some of that prime learning time. But it had disappeared with the cheers, the sore muscles, and hectic social chemistry of high school.

It is a memory. To the beginning English teacher, it is an enigma. Reading and writing are not as important as Friday football, basketball, plays and concerts. They weren't when I was in high school in the early 1940s, and they aren't with teenagers today.

Those Uncertain April Field Trips

Badger High School and high schools across the nation have what are called field trips, and April is the month for them. That's primarily because by administrative ruling they are not allowed in May. Between the changing weather and teachers who just waited too long, the field trips simply stacked up like unpaid bills. After all, it is spring, and it has been a long year.

The field trip must be of recent vintage since only one of the three dictionaries consulted even mentions it: "a trip away from the classroom to permit the gathering of data at first hand."

Students look forward to field trips eagerly, primarily because they are passes out of classes. As one advisor stated curtly in a memorandum to colleagues about a forthcoming excursion, "If you feel that any of these students should NOT miss your class, please let me know immediately."

One never knows for certain why some field trips are held. One permission slip read, "The following Soph.'s will be gone on a Biology field trip to Milwaukee all day Thursday April 1st. If there are any complications, please contact me."

Another permission slip read as follows: "The following students will be on a field trip to Farm Power and Equipment Show Friday, all day, March 19. If this will cause inconvenience for any student let me know."

And how about, "Teachers will you please excuse the following girls, sixth and seventh hours, Friday to attend a Physical Education workshop at LaCrosse."

Some of the follow-ups to directives are curious. "The following boys did not go with us on the Career Opportunities field trip yesterday and should not have been excused from classes all day."

Field trips are conducted for many reasons. Witness:

- Please excuse the following students who will be attending a play in Milwaukee on Wednesday, April 14.
- The following students will be attending F.B.L.A. Convention at Green Lake this Friday, March 26. (Future Business Leaders of America.)
- Please excuse the following students all day Monday, April 19 for the state FFA judging contests at the Univ. of Wisconsin.

- Please excuse the following students on Wednesday, April 14 so they can go to Whitewater State University for FTA. (Future Teachers of America.)

Must have been what Shakespeare had in mind when he wrote, "The uncertain glory of an April day."

How Badger High School Affected My Development as a Teacher

When I came to Badger High, the administrative policy of trusting teachers to be able to work on their own was very important. This liberal atmosphere was excellent for me. I thrived on my own. We had plenty of obstacles and problems, but the general ethical tone was perfect for my development as a teacher.

The same ethic, however, allowed some teachers to take advantage of what to them must have appeared to be a license to leisure. Personally, I found the environment positive, generally encouraging, and healthy. I loved Badger's cosmopolitan flavor and broad socio-economic society.

I often wondered why one of the richest of school districts in the state could not get in step with the state. Badger High School is one of only five or six schools which are still union districts. What the financial, political, ethical ramifications of that are, I do not know. But it certainly has cost in more than financial ways.

At other times, the community could have rallied to initiate and support change. Lake Geneva has more organizations and less unification than other communities of its size. Community loyalty would be very difficult to prove. If it exists, it is in isolated pockets. Socio-economic extremes, though they are in the minority, are factors. The rich of the north and south shores and beyond are not benefactors of Badger High School.

Unionism in our teaching ranks became a significant issue. When the Wisconsin Education Association became a labor union in the late-1960s and early-1970s, the professional foundation and a chance for unified professional thinking and ethics went away for good. When Badger's faculty split on this matter in 1972, a new organization formed, made up essentially of the most experienced of teachers. That organization itself became a union, so that during the last twenty years three groups emerged. The old Badger Association, which is the local of the Wisconsin Education

Association Council, never claimed more than thirty percent of the faculty membership.

The newer Badger Professional Education Association was a clear majority but had no ties with a larger state or national organization. The third group was mostly those who disagreed with BEA's approach but saw little improvement in the new group. I have no problem admitting I was of the latter group. That probably stigmatized me with both groups, and I probably suffered in ways of which I am not even aware. The rift caused by that 1972 division was major factor in faculty disharmony for years.

I cannot say this school and community impeded my growth. Its liberal thinking about a teacher's prerogatives was too strong. I grew, but I was to a large extent responsible for that.

The temptations to assume leadership roles were dissipated early as I served in association roles and positions. As president of the BEA (1960-61), which when it was essentially a professional organization that had little political clout but enormous potential for growth as an organization of professional teachers, I was frustrated because colleagues only wanted what teachers used to call "S and S." If the association could provide nominal representation at salary time and could sponsor picnics and parties, that is about all one could hope for.

That year the National Education Association had passed on and recommended to its locals a code of ethics for the teaching profession. I worked hard to get it passed in our local chapter. We did accept it. But I learned then and there that teachers were not going to change and actively support, beyond their votes, any such standards. The criticism ranged from buttering up the administration and doing their work for them, to "Johnson, what are you trying to do, be a goody, goody?" I had no problem getting lost in my classroom.

Badger High School was the institution carved out of a rather arbitrary territory made up of diverse socio-economic parts. It has always seemed that the loyalties generated by this school district were about as digressive and distracting as such things could be.

Nothing seemed natural about the evolving of "Union District No. 1 of the City of Lake Geneva, Village of Genoa City and Towns of Bloomsfield, Geneva, LaFayette, Linn, Lyons and Spring Prairie." A tangible enmity formed between the two incorporated entities.

How these developments affected me is difficult to assess, though one fact stands out. I was on my own to develop as a teacher, as I saw fit. That is very good, if the teacher is truly disposed to develop himself. It was. I welcomed the considerable freedom.

When I tried to collect the impressions of teachers in other schools and the extent they were permitted to develop themselves, I found some real horror stories. Many teachers are self-starters to the extent that it is necessary to organize a class and make it appear to be working. Of course, that is only the beginning of real education.

Then some teachers never moved beyond that minimum in their teaching careers. Teachers like that discouraged me. The reason is that if all teachers are not pulling together at roughly the same rate, the school's effectiveness will be inhibited. No individual teacher can possibly make enough difference to overcome the cumulative effect of the group.

However, if teachers can block out the various influences that work outside their classrooms, there is no end to what can happen inside. To that extent, Badger High School was a solid influence on my development. I thrived with freedom to work on my own. My development took place at a rate determined by me and my experience each year. I set my own pace, set my own standards. I expected more of myself than the school did.

My only taskmasters were my students. I learned to understand them, serve them, communicate with them. Each student was a representative from the school district. I had been hired to facilitate the growth of each of them. That is what I did to the best of my ability.

That is easy to say, "the best of my ability." But no one else said it. I determined the rules, the work, the goals. And in my heart of hearts, I felt I did well. Badger High School gave me the freedom to work as I saw fit. And I think most of my students would agree it turned out just fine.

Retiring

Teachers leave teaching for lots of reasons. I retired at age fifty-nine and thought that was early. Now fifty-five is a common age to leave the classroom.

I know I could have taught several more years at nearly the level I did for twenty-nine years, assuming continued good health. I worked at a pretty stiff pace during my career, but I began to feel I was completing a cycle. Then losses of my father, mother, and sister Carol in the early 1980's caused me to reflect on my life and career.

Three other factors appeared formidable during the closing months of my last school year and played parts in my retiring:

- The ever-accumulating department difficulties
- Talk of a bureaucrat, not an educator, being hired as superintendent
- Consistently large class sizes challenging my ability to reach students

In addition, right from the beginning of my career, I wanted to write about teaching and my place in the profession. But my pretty stiff pace was simply too much to maintain as well as attack writing seriously.

On the last day of the 1985-86 school year, I handed my letter of resignation to Mr. Dean Dare, my principal, whom I respected. I have never looked back on my decision to retire.

CONTENTS

My Original Plan for Retirement
When I completed my twenty-nine-year run as a classroom teacher, I determined to read a lot and get into a physical program to guarantee, as much that is possible, good health in succeeding years. Two years into retirement, I commenced my long-overdue writing regimen that eventually became the major thrust of my retirement. On April 1 (no comment please), 1988, I began to make entries into my first Cambridge steno-pad journal. By 2016, I filled one hundred steno-pads with well over a million words yielding nearly fifteen-hundred manuscripts and well over two-hundred published pieces in local newspapers.

I would describe my writing as eclectic. In addition to writing about my teaching career, I wrote several essays on each of the following topics:

Cultural Icons	Democracy	Generations
Media	Music	National Events
Nature	Numbers and the Odds	Photography
Presidency	Reading	Technology
Sports	Time	War
Community Newspapers	Family History	Military Life
Life in Fennimore	Life in Lake Geneva	Travels
Home and Daily Life	Finances	

With all of my writing, I have done more than glance back a few times. Now that I've had "breathing space," the profession looks very different. I still miss high school seniors fiercely.

Retiring and Sorting Stuff
As a senior English teacher engaged in the promotion of writing skills and the study of the English language and literature, I gathered quite a large collection of resource materials for my students and me to use. Teaching journalism also required organizing lots of resource materials.

I became a pretty good organizer when I was in the classroom because I had to. Five classes, each with its own demands for resource materials, created a need for different systems of organization. If I didn't keep up day by day, week by week, managing those materials could, and occasionally did, get out of hand.

254

When I retired from teaching and began to concentrate on my own writing, it was difficult to cut back on all those resource materials. Although I tossed a lot of files, notes and articles back in 1986 when I moved out of my classroom, I kept enough to serve as a substantial base for my writing activity.

Upon retirement, I had no demand for the immediate organizational systems. It doesn't take a brilliant mind to figure out that when left to organize one's own resources and time, that a new level of self-discipline is required. Though I practiced it, slippage did occur over time.

Let's face it, it's time to get rid of stuff. Throwing things out is actually the easy part. It's the assessments, the decisions about what to keep and what to pitch, that cause the difficulty.

I've been filling plastic bags with paper of all kinds. The problem is everything I tossed has some connection to my experience, and the question is not whether it is valuable or not, but whether or not I will ever use the materials again. I understand I could only use a very small percentage of any material saved, filed, and kept.

So, I have been making choices. I have gotten far enough along that throwing things away has become harder. I've pitched stuff I never thought I could, but I don't think about it! It's on to the next decision.

Another factor in making such decisions is my age. I'm already in my early 90s. What on God's green earth makes me think there is a reasonable possibility of using even a miniscule fraction of what has been collected?

I'll bet there are teachers, especially English teachers, who could use some of these resources, but here I am, filling plastic bags, then filling the recycle cart outside. And off it goes to wherever.

So here I am, trying to decide what to keep, how to organize files. I think of all those student editors I had who could see forests, while their mentor only could see trees. I need assistance from one who could work the upper echelons of organization, who understands me, who is computer-literate-plus, and who could tell me where to get off once in a while. A half dozen or so could fill that bill.

One of the unfortunate factors in my professional life has been that I have had too many interests. And I still try to keep them all going. In an age of specialization, it has been easy to feel a victim of variety. Every time I think about it, I can't bring myself to regret it. I can still practice my interests in writing, photography, music, history. Also, I have entirely too many projects waiting to be done. Realistically, I'll not get to even a tiny fraction of them.

I didn't only toss out or keep resource materials. I did acquire one major resource shortly after I retired. I bought a copy of the *Merriam-Webster International Dictionary*. It cost about $85. What are the odds that I would ever use everything stored in that huge volume? I know, very unlikely. But when I get on the trail of a word, the big book with its hundreds of thousands of entries has become valuable indeed.

Making Choices

As a non-salaried, "not-working" person, I regularly felt the pressures from some friends, family and former colleagues who suggested I should volunteer for things. No one was pressing me hard, though my pastor came close some Sundays. Many had fancy ways to make me feel badly if I did not volunteer, give of myself, or do whatever they wanted to call it.

I am not at ease in most social circumstances. I do not seek out such situations. When necessity arises, I gird my faculties and wish I were somewhere else. When I create the necessity myself, I still feel discomfort, though I have come to the conclusion that it ever will be so.

I can't say I don't have the powers of social contact. I felt the same reservations about the classroom teaching at first. But as confidence and devotion increased, I felt the kind of control that generates not only perpetual interest but also persistent energy.

Someone will say, well, now do it again with something else. I am, really. But the writing business is notably private. In fact, interruption of any kind causes consternation.

My writing is an outgrowth of my classroom teaching. While memories and saved files have sustained my interest in writing, I miss the daily inspiration of meeting classes. That's what classroom teaching was for me, daily inspiration. It wasn't always so at the outset, but by the time things got going, the phenomenon renewed itself.

My argument that the classroom was all-giving, all-consuming, and always challenging to take a step further, does not hold with some people. However, I think I used up my altruistic self during my thirty years of classroom service. The institutional aspects of teaching degrade personal standards. They level us off as teachers to safe, unionized conformity. Teaching is not for the innovative, and incisive, the incandescent of spirit. Like the armed services, one's urge to change things is dampened, dulled, discouraged. But any effort on my part to alter those facts and conditions was expended in the classroom.

I don't think I have become cynical, but the vitality of what is possible is withered by the way things were and are. I have packed up my teaching experiences and brought them to bear in my writing. The problem is that I know society works in large part by the volunteer efforts of a few, especially with some activities that make our society essentially good. I cannot help thinking that I gave twenty-nine years to one long volunteer effort in a line of work whose majority looks askance at spontaneous and unforced work of any kind.

I think of Shakespeare's eight-word line at this moment:

Necessity delivers us from the embarrassment of choice.

To Change or Not to Change

I am no longer a child, but much of my childhood has made the trip with me. I still have unreasonable expectations, uncertain resolve, and numerous hesitations. I understand that my childhood was far from expansive and uninhibited.

Through my first thirty years of life, the things that went wrong outnumbered things that went right. When I landed in my profession, I was satisfied to be a classroom teacher, nothing more. For twenty-nine years, that is all I did. That is all I wanted to do.

The confines of my classroom produced their own kind of release and expansion. I tuned in on the generation I taught, and I have never quite tuned them out. I abhor yuppie simplicity and directness. But I admire their candid, flexible, relaxed tendencies.

My own generation has become narrow, limited, and is still standing for unrealistic, inflexible remnants of Depression-WWII times, which like it or not, have changed. Yes, the confines of my classroom produced their own kind of release and expanse. With that came confidence. Post-teaching experiences accelerated my social consciousness. I understand what I have missed.

257

Underlying everything else was a powerful desire to change things. But as a creature of habit and limited in many ways, I tended to stay the course. These two forces, one on the move, the other almost an immovable fortress, were increasingly competing for the center of my life.

Maybe this internal struggle was a manifestation of my age, which I had not recognized as such yet. Maybe it was only a product of the life of the mind. I did carry on a majority of my activity there. Maybe I recognized that I had lived in a groove, which others perceived as a rut. Maybe I was unconsciously reacting to those pressures. Maybe in generating a new vigor for life I had discovered a desire to do other things.

It was reasonable to think that since I came to my life's work by unusual means from an unusual direction and at an unusual time, that I would ease out that way.

Visiting My Classroom Years After Retiring

I visited room 207 late one afternoon. I looked around and saw a clean slate. In fact, the room looked immaculate, orderly and, I'm afraid, unused. No active walls and bulletin boards advertising course content. I couldn't see that jostled look of desks or the clutter of the last class hour. Whatever was done in the last class did not show.

I expected a classroom at 3:30 in the afternoon to look used with echoes of action in the air. While I used to hate the clutter of my room, I have to admit that the clutter was an active testament to academic action.

I felt like going to someone in authority and asking if I could have my room back. Someone needs to mess up that clean slate, put notes back on the board, and plaster those walls and bulletin boards with questions and quotations to make students think. Oh, and put the dictionaries back underneath the desks.

There, you see? You can take the teacher out of the classroom, but you cannot take the classroom out of the teacher. And therein lies the importance of the teaching profession.

Reflecting on My Career as an English Teacher

Language is so close to our beings that the teaching of it would seem to demand top priority. Few people master language to the point of competence. Fewer still can teach English. Most start their careers far short of the minimum knowledge and skills needed to teach English effectively, including this teacher.

I was ten years into professional practice before I acted without reservation regarding my ability and experience, and before I did things, without hesitation and that telltale lack of confidence. If there is one quality an English teacher needs after competence, it is confidence.

During my career, I grew to understand the complexities and privileges of being an English teacher. Along the way, I hoped that our communities and country would understand, not just support, more deeply how important English teachers are for the quality of our being.

What English teachers need to have is understanding, reasonable class loads, and most important, an upgrading of the public's attitude toward the place of language integrity in the lives of educated people. If these needs were met, no effective English teacher would think of doing anything else.

CONTENTS

Influence and Power

As an English teacher, I became aware that I exerted influence. As one does the job, there isn't time to reflect on how it works. But teachers are influential. It was only when I retired and began seriously to think and write about education that the nature of a teacher's influence took shape in my mind.

When a teacher's personality engages what he or she is teaching, students take notice. Until then subject matter and its presentation are held at a kind of arm's-length market transaction. If a student wants to learn something badly enough, it matters little how it is taught. However, most students did not come to my classroom that way. I consciously had to work at generating their interest. The subject matter alone did not do that. The subject matter and I did that. I was the vehicle that transmitted whatever made students see importance in what I was teaching.

I became conscious that my ability to generate this learning fervor was improving. It seemed that I could reach a larger number of students and bring a larger percentage of classes to the point of real engagement.

Influence means power, no question. But they are not the same thing. I never thought of my influence as power, but as a vehicle for generating the desire to learn. If we do not learn willingly all our lives, the world will leave us in ignorance. I found many students indifferent to learning.

Making students want to learn does not come from formulas or panaceas. It's a question of teacher, student, and a given circumstance. But I can testify that the vigor with which I approached the task, consistency and persistence of the process, all had something to do with it.

This influence was a gratifying experience and one of the features of teaching I miss most. Although the classroom is gone, the habits developed in this process are not. I continually attempt to achieve the same results in my writing. I am trying to do it right now. An audience is out there ready to be my class in a different kind of classroom.

Now this may be an unrealistic assumption, but I had pursued it for several years. Somehow, I still think I can influence others with my vigor, my experience, and the methods that have worked. Every once in a while, opportunities arise that allow me to work that old magic. At high school reunions, I see the whole process in a different dimension.

Just as great revolutions are necessary in public schools, why cannot they take place on the personal level, too? Mostly because we do not have the courage to try to change things. What I see as possible may be personally too costly. How I feel may not be enough to initiate action.

Maybe influence is always power.

Building Trust in Language Use

Why did I want to teach English? That is not easy to answer. Not because I have doubts, but because I don't. The problem is that most everyone does. There is nothing like one's language to set the nerves on edge. What a difference it takes to be able to use language, spoken or written, without inhibitions, confidently and comfortably. I doubt there is anyone who can do that fully, all of the time, but the attitudes that come out of our language experiences are often not good.

In company which demands linguistic competence, we become something less than ourselves, trying to make language work right. When we watch this phenomenon in others, we can see how it affects whatever content and communication are intended. Language can frustrate a person when everything else is perfect.

The language of English teachers is not perfect, nor should we expect it to be. Yet it is hard to be natural in the company of a former classroom English teacher, particularly one who got through to us. It is not perfection that causes English teachers to create such mental chaos in students.

Rather, it is what the idea of being an English teacher means. He or she is a symbol, a badge, for the bungling, battling and blustering that went on in his or her classroom. That teacher becomes a perpetual symbol for our language failures. I do not think it should be that way, but somehow our attitudes about language create this perception of the English teacher. I suppose there are those who do not approach their classroom with the characteristics necessary to understand, trust, and teach students. Part of the problem is the nature of English teachers as a group. Why do we stand off from teachers, especially English teachers? It is as simple as not wanting to face the symbol for our failures in learning. It is fear of making mistakes, misspeaking.

When I began teaching, I found my mind was more occupied with setting a good language example myself than with establishing strategy through which I could trap erring students. In fact, I was always uneasy

261

about student mistakes, particularly in class. I always wished they had not made them and looked for gracious ways of getting them off the hook without over-accommodating them. I'm sure that on the whole students recognized this as a kind of sensitivity on my part. Some may even have felt worse for having erred.

Language problems are not corrected overnight. Parading a student's language weaknesses before a jury of his peers is not the way to gain his confidence. Neither is waxing sarcastic or laboring the matter. So, if in class I feared making language errors myself and was unnerved by student mistakes, I developed great care about such matters.

Eventually I developed confidence about my own use of language, and I admitted my mistakes quickly and without hesitation. Once students saw I had their language welfare at heart, they were less fearful of their own mistakes. I have been told by former students that being called on mistakes was a new experience for them; apparently in some cases I was the first to do it.

Also, when a class began to recognize that they were all in this to-gether, they were more indulgent of peer criticism. As this chemistry developed in the course of the year, we all began to look at language usage as something to be attacked together rather than at anyone's expense.

It is this casual-appearing but serious tone which generates language respectability. It is also one of the reasons I wanted to teach English, one of the reasons I learned to revere the profession. This kind of rapport in the classroom allowed us to attack even the severest of language blunders.

So, when a student slipped in his "ain't" to propel his verb phrase, I would shoot back, and I mean shoot back, the correct, or a correct, con-traction. I tried to make the correction as firm and matter-of-fact as possi-ble. Often the student would accept the criticism and interruption, state the word I offered, and proceed.

But it is its effect upon the student using it that I observe. Sometimes students use the word deliberately to gain attention. Sometimes it is plain ignorance. But it is the ignorance I want to "fix." Attitude is as much of this problem as any rule is. "Ain't" is a symbol of uneducated speech. As far as I am concerned, it is the symbol. It is widely used, but those who do not use it, never do. It is those students who slip and use it who can gain from the attention.

If students recognize that I am not ridiculing them or making them feel uncomfortable, they accept the criticism or at least tolerate it.

What more could a professional who works with over 100 students per day ask? So, there is nothing secret clouding a student's linguistic horizon. It is the nature of the relationship between the teacher and her students. However, despite the fact that I have no doubts, students always do – until we reach a rapport through mutual trust and understanding.

By the way, did you know "ain't" can stand for "are not," "is not," "am not," "have not," and "has not"? Any Anglo-Saxon monosyllabic utterance which can have that many uses must lack precision.

How We Assess Learning and Teaching English
Of all professions, the results of teaching seem hardest to measure. That doesn't mean we cannot tell when teaching has worked. We just cannot reduce measurement to SAT scores.

When teaching has succeeded, I know it if the conditions are right. Students have to do something overt in order for me to know. That does not happen often. I don't mean tests. Tests are what we use, but I don't have faith in them. Administrators have to have some sort of an idea of whether I am doing my job or not. The problem with that thinking is I could go through the motions and turn in my lesson plans, grade reports, and grade book at the end of the year, and no one would know from these alone that I was doing my job.

Now the students, that is another matter. They know whether I am doing my job. They know when there is a relationship between what is done in classes and what gets to the report card. But students cannot do much about it. They are in no position to complain about teachers any more than they can openly praise teachers.

Everything is against the student taking part in the process. First, there is the age difference. Students are underage, immature, apprentices. Teachers are adults, mature, skilled professionals. Authority must be maintained, so a distance is established and maintained. How a teacher develops this territory between himself and his students is the important factor of any classroom. Some teachers are so sensitive about their authority that business of the class is all one way. The teacher gives, the student takes. The only time the student can give back is on a test. Even questions are discouraged. No interchange or as little as possible.

On the other extreme, some teachers become too close to students. There is little recognizable line between students and teacher.

All sorts of middle ground are possible, and success depends on how the teacher allows this relationship to develop. If all teachers were skillful and persistent in establishing and maintaining their relationships with students, education would be far different from what it is now. We wouldn't even need principals, only some sort of coordination of efforts. This is the part of teaching that is difficult to measure.

One must develop rules to follow in pursuit of these relationships. It must be general enough, so any student neatly fits into it. This aspect of teaching is personal. How I may have gone about it probably has little bearing on how someone else goes about it. What a teacher does in September, however, determines the ground on which the year's action takes place. It is important and impossible to measure.

Although the students are in the middle of this process, they do not think about it in a way that suggests evaluation. They are not adults. Adults will not trust them as peers. Those who are the direct benefactors and are the subjects of the whole process, are never consulted or trusted in judgments of teachers. Over time this is a frustrating relationship for teachers, some teachers.

Inferior teachers love it because they can control their circumstances with the only people that matter, administrators and school board. Any teacher trying to do the job right regrets this arrangement because he or she can expend effort all out of proportion to one's return and no one in authority really understands the predicament. Even other teachers cannot understand it, because their territory is developed from their own personalities and experiences. In fact, if they judge another teacher based on relationships with students in their own classrooms, the whole thing will be misread, because they cannot know what another teacher really does.

Teaching English in an American high school was a satisfying experience made tolerable by a progression of adjustments and sacrifices. I wonder if there is another job anywhere in which we are trying to coordinate behavior and mental processes at the same time. This activity is difficult to control, much less measure.

Value of the Liberal Arts

I hold to the importance of liberal arts. We citizens need to understand the underlying promises of science and comprehend the sweep of history. The rudiments of mathematics, the skills of the English language, and appreciation of art in all its forms are fundamental to being truly educated.

The focus of the current generation is specialization. Why waste time on disciplines we will never use? What does history have to do with engineering? What does mathematics have to do with law? Why should we learn to read and write when we will probably be doing something that depends on physical dexterity and one's mind?

I believe understanding the fundamentals of disciplines other than those in which one specializes will still help a person grow, to gain perspective. Take for example, chemistry. As we read and listen to all of the messages in our lives, we will be exposed to facts, ideas, experiences, which have to do with chemistry. We will relate them to the fundamental factors of chemistry which we learned in high school or college. We learn to view chemistry in all sorts of practical ways. Though we will never be chemists, we are able to appreciate how it fits into the rest of the world, something we could never do had we not studied chemistry.

That's roughly the way the liberal arts work. We gain a perspective on the main elements of life. To learn how to see things in perspective.

Teaching English, Job or Profession?

Those who have successfully made careers in the classroom, and there are lots of them, will tell us that useful teaching requires "can do" qualifications, that it is a quality of mind and spirit that begins very early in life. It starts with reading, develops into curiosity about the world and the people in it, and that is followed by a desire to make the connection between what one learns and other people. Sounds like a liberal arts education to me. There develops a kind of built-in social compassion. People like that will make superior teachers.

Psychologist and philosopher, William James, who knew something of the mind, said about teaching, "When all is said and done, the fact remains that some teachers have a naturally inspiring presence, and can make their exercises interesting, while others simply cannot."

But the distance between students sitting in the classroom and the teacher who appears before them, is not all that far. Everyone is a teacher, and many more than are, should be. I can name dozens of former students who would have made effective teachers, but simply did not think along those lines. They did not develop a passion for sharing their learning with others. In our society teaching is not economically advantageous.

Every society needs a profusion of teachers. Competition would not hurt public education at all. But one truth no one will deny: we need a powerful system of education and an enthusiastically committed corps of teachers. And Henry James must have been talking about teaching when he argued, "The ultimate test… of what a truth means is the conduct it dictates or inspires."

Until the best minds and spirits can be drawn into the profession, American education will remain a good deal less than it ought to be.

Former Students Teaching English

I am told I made the study of language appear very important. I must have done that by demonstrating an interest in the folks I was teaching. Somehow these motives led to an intense experience which caused students to believe me and believe in me.

Now it makes me cringe to think that there are people in their own classrooms consciously or subconsciously imitating me. I did pass something along. It was such a chaotic, hard, demanding task that I could never think of it as something graceful. It pulled and strained and caused me to think I was losing my bearings. But through it all came something which made me look up and reach up.

I never looked upon myself as inspiration for prospective English teachers. I know that a number of former students are teaching English. I don't know how many, but most left my classroom without the slightest hint of teaching, much less teaching English. It probably wasn't. But I remember being pleasantly surprised a number of times after the fact.

But only once do I remember a high school senior coming up to me and declaring, "Mr. Johnson, I want to be an English teacher. Do you think I could do that?" I eagerly looked Jessica in the eye and blurted, "Of course you could." But as I bid her be seated, I began to think of what she was really asking me. Within a few seconds, I decided what I wanted to say, but obviously could not: that if she could generate energy in proportion to the interest she induces by simply being in the company of others, she will succeed well enough.

I wanted to say that, but I asked instead, "What book are you reading currently?" She answered, "Mr. Galbraith's *New Industrial State*."

It was predictable she would say that. The book was ubiquitous at that time of year. She was in contemporary American history and was carrying it everywhere.

If Jessica was on an English kick, she was probably reading from my reading list. Maybe she was, but who has an appetite for Shakespeare when huge bites of a tough economist must be taken every day?

Me: What caused this sudden interest in being a teacher?

Jessica: It isn't the teaching so much as the language. I'm really beginning to see what language is.

Me: What do you mean?

Jessica: Well, I love being around people, especially children. I like working in groups. I'm thinking more about how I talk and write. I'm using the dictionary more often, because I want to. And writing, you've really got me interested in writing.

Me: OK, OK, I believe you. You're a fighter, Jessica. You're willing to learn. You're pleasant to be around. You don't take any nonsense from people. And you love to solve problems. Those are all characteristics English teachers need.

Jessica: Do you think I would make a good English teacher?

Me: Jessica, I would stake my teaching certificate on it.

Jessica: Oh, thanks, Mr. Johnson.

Me: You're welcome, and if you want to talk more …anytime.

Jessica: Thanks, thanks.

Me: See you tomorrow.

That was the only time we talked about teaching. I remember thinking, what right do I have to be so sure of something about which I do not know enough. How can I know any student well enough when 110 of them come through my classroom every day?

Jessica seemed to understand what teaching involves. Even as a student she understood. Imagine what that must have meant when she became an English teacher. How important it is to be able to sense a student's point of view. To stretch beyond ourselves, to understand someone who can be kept at a distance and a little below us. That is the way a teacher wants it. That is the step which makes a teacher the teacher.

It didn't matter administrators piled bodies into my classroom over the class hours of the day; I stretched a bit further, trying to understand someone a little better. I could take the paperwork and the meetings and those projects the office dreamed up to keep teachers out of mischief. I strained to understand students, even though the problems they had were more severe as the years went along.

One afternoon, about the time I was preparing to leave for home, Jessica came back to see me. No announcement, no phone call, no note, no letter. She just stood there in the doorway at the end of an eighth hour one day, smiling.

Jessica: Hello, Mr. Johnson.

Me: Hi. What a breath of fresh air.

Jessica: I thought I'd drop in to see how you're doing.

Me: Sit down, sit down. Gee, you look great. What are you doing?

Jessica: I can't stay, but I wanted to tell you I am teaching. I work
    with seniors and am finally getting the hang of the writing game.

268

I was interested in hearing about that, but the world is in a hurry and off went Jessica to who knows where. About all I'm left with is the memory of things I wanted to say, things I want to understand. The only certainty is that the fire I lit in Jessica has since burned vigorously.

I feel civilization and continuity in all of this. Some years ago, one of my students presented me with a small framed piece of parchment paper inscribed, "The teacher is like the candle which lights others in consuming itself."

I wish I could get together all my former students who are now teaching and ask them why they are teaching. I don't have any idea how many there are, but enough of them surface in the reunions, random conversations, and reading, to let me know there are a good many. I am told I had something to do with it, just enough to raise some curiosity.

What did I do to cause a number of former students to become teachers, much less English teachers? I felt I was a pretty good ad for teaching, but there are so many possibilities of reasons I cannot tell where to begin. Thinking back over the years hasn't done it, and various conversations have not produced the clues.

I know my endeavors at communication were more important than my knowledge of language. The ability to keep records, to be consistent, and to be fair-minded all had something to do with it. Being uncomfortable with always starting a lesson or instruction the same way kept me digging and changing. This practice probably had the effect of a fresh approach, which probably had something to do with it.

I also always had a fear that I would lose students, that they would not stay with me through the process of a class hour. I remember some classes as being particularly trying that way. Each of the twenty-six of them had the capacity to challenge me, whether out loud, by eye contact, or by body language.

Most other classes were just the opposite. Their animation was more directed and unified. Individuals seemed to have more of an idea of class mission or group objectivity. We should not ignore the fact that there were seventeen in this class. Somehow, I also was more at ease and comfortable with the smaller groups. Trying to figure out what made it work, however, was a complex matter.

I don't think the disparity in class sizes had too much to do with it.

Students who have spent many hours, many years in classes together develop certain relations affecting the character of a group. So, the groups take on certain characteristics. Each senior class had a personality all its own, and each academic class within each of these senior classes took on its own makeup.

I suppose the fact that I was interested in this chemistry had something to do with my understanding groups of students. I never in thirty years of teaching English was bored, indolent, or felt there was something out there more interesting to do.

Stuff like this probably shows in a teacher. Students recognize it as something beneficial to them, maybe in a few, as something they would be interested in doing. Assuming determination, energy, and, most of all, patience, a reasonably well-educated person can succeed in the classroom.

We can't be passive, and I don't mean passive about organizing, preparing and teaching itself. I mean we cannot be passive about our interest in, and desire to increase the facility of our students. We must be active about them individually and as a group. Though terribly time-consuming, it is a fully engaging activity.

My first and only serious battle was class size. As we can readily imagine, potentially powerful teachers are destroyed, particularly early in their careers, by savage class loads. To expect a strong academic high school teacher to work with more than one hundred students a day is slowly killing the best chances we have for developing the best teachers in the world.

So, it is surprising to see a considerable number of former students carrying on this noble mission. It would be interesting to examine their experience, motives, and decisions to see why

Reforming Schools

I frame my twenty-nine years of teaching between two significant national events: the success of the Russian Sputnik in 1957 and what it meant to American education, and the failure of the American space shuttle Challenger in January 1986. The first beeps from space began during my first full year of teaching. My last semester took place with the explosion leading to the deaths of seven astronauts including the first teacher to attempt space flight.

To say that the changes in education since 1957 have been dramatic would understate the facts. From my point of view, the changes have altered, transformed and diversified society, shifting many values and rendering students less seriously and soundly educated than two generations ago. Many especially important factors can be cited. Our schools need to anticipate and respond to the significant events and changes in education.

CONTENTS

Changes in Social Influences
Changes in School Traditions and Customs
Changes in Career Options
Attempts at Teaching Efficiency
Insisting on High Standards
Universal vs. Specialized Education
Education and Democratic Societies
Teaching and Learning Are Not Regimented Processes
Priorities in Education
Public Conversation on Education
Getting Serious About Education
A Long-Range Planning Survey

Changes in Social Influences

Social influences on the boomer students became more diverse and powerful than for previous generations.

Was it possible for students to be academically successful and still hold jobs that kept them occupied twenty hours a week? Some students could manage school and work effectively, but not without some sacrifice to their education.

Television became an influence on students and teachers whether they watched TV or not. Whether one was drawn by prime-time escapism, sex, or violence, or by television that can inform and educate, the consumption of time was enormous. Add the uses of TV in the home and classroom, and the chances to develop passive, detached citizens increased greatly.

The automobile also consumed a great deal of some teenagers' lives. Most were distracted and inhibited by automotive aspirations. But they all took driver education. I know of no other high school course which was anticipated as early by more students than the driver's license course.

Some students stayed in school until they were sophomores for that reason. Owning a car was one of the common reasons given by students when we asked them why they did not have study time. "I have to work to make the payments," they would say. Unless disciplined, students earned money to spend – now!

Certainly alcohol, tobacco and drugs were major influences. Alcohol became a sinister influence because adolescents were merely copying a habit which had consumed adults all along. Alcohol, the automobile, and sex were problems. They became even more complicated because of other factors, especially divorce.

The weakening of social institutions likewise weakened the ability of teachers to harness the energy of youth in the classroom. Marriage was the most important of these institutions. I don't mean to be harsh, but it's a trade-off. Parents in order to maintain their own perceived autonomy or rights, through separation and divorce, denied their children's opportunities and social senses.

Students going through the severe crisis of identity associated with the breakup of the family were still expected to weather the rigors of the academic classroom and survive. Some of them did it marvelously well. Their difficulties fueled their academic appetites. Others were unpredictable, undirected. I didn't know what to expect of them from one day to the next. Others were in disorder, confused beyond help. Then there were those about whom I did not know, whose moods changed unpredictably, and I would wonder why.

Changes in School Traditions and Customs

As in the other social institutions, the decline of unifying traditions and customs in schools accelerated. When I was a student and when I became a teacher, anything that brought a feeling of community to the school was encouraged.

Students were practically always against them. In my first teaching job, I was required to attend school events and take my turn ushering, monitoring and generally taking part in that general principle of education that says wherever teachers are present and circulating, trouble will not arise. When I came to Badger High School, teachers were assigned seats in the auditorium among the students. The teacher union would not allow that. So, what happened to the unifying, the feeling of community? Teachers no longer needed to attend school functions. Students certainly didn't. School concerts, plays, athletic contests were sparsely attended.

Homecoming, a misnomer to begin with, had fallen on hard times. Yet it was that first all-school event of the fall which could generate unity as well as release youthful energy. Many teachers wouldn't do anything for the school unless it was in the contract. It's as though teaching were a job that can be set up and blocked like an assembly line. It was impossible to expect students, who could sense this adult hypocrisy, to participate with much more than a passive assent.

Some students did participate in school events. Some students would go out and cheer for the red and white. But there was something sad about seeing cheerleaders leading empty bleachers in cheers. Something cheerless took place for a well-rehearsed play produced by sixty people performing to an audience of forty. Something forlorn took place when well-prepared athletes competed in front of a handful of peers and a few parents. The participation was gone. The community was bound to lose.

Changes in Career Options

The nature, the number, and the necessity of career choices have changed significantly in our society. My high school years, 1941-45, were taken up with World War II. Any choice had to do with which service I would enter. If I didn't do something about an alternative, I would be drafted into the army. So, the process was left to chance, or else it was so controlled that there was no choice.

As a teacher however, I always found it difficult to comprehend, much less deal with, how complex the process of choosing a career was becoming for my students. The challenges to the guidance process were appalling.

While I was student teaching, someone pointed out to me that the English teacher by the nature of the job has the best opportunity to serve students in personal matters. It was true. The noble and honorable nature of guiding young people in their choices has always attracted me.

When a student meets with a teacher, he or she is meeting because of course work or the rapport of the class. The student may not ever perceive it as counselling.

One time I looked in Barron's big book on careers. The entries were in the thousands. How can a teenager possibly approach the task without an inspiration of some kind?

If any conclusion can be drawn from this discussion, it would have something to do with participation. We do not give enough time and attention to our youth, as a society and as individuals. Our objectives are not clear and direct. Our societal reflex is to veto taxes for education without examining the substance of proposals.

These factors lead to a neutral, noncommittal tone which confuses youth.

Attempts at Teaching Efficiency

Some of the most hateful words in education are "tracking," "grouping," "leveling," and a phrase like "homogeneous grouping." Placing students with similar problems, talents, or habits together in classes dates back to the 1960s. The process was called progressive. It came at a time when the World War II baby boomers were over-running high schools.

At Badger High School, we called it "grouping." For several years it was accepted, or at least tolerated, by all academic departments. Socially, the practice is segregation; academically, it can be prudent. No one liked the idea. I didn't.

As happens with fads, its fading found me hanging onto the practice. Maybe I was the one who was selfish, but teaching language literacy made me do things which may well be termed survival tactics.

Most students considered classes and teachers socially, not academically. Some students signed up for classes in groups so they could be together. Some did exactly what their parents tell them, even though age eighteen is well on the way to adulthood. The motivation of many students was to find the classes which will bring the most interest and the best grades. Students who had not become academically aggressive, but should have, tended not to knock on doors, or complain, or attempt to communicate with teachers that they need something more challenging. There were those who would do anything to avoid an academically challenging class, signing out of it before signing in.

The social pressures on teachers were immense, especially if the teacher had academic standards. Her classes were in demand. Her load was already too great. She knew she could effectively work with only so many students at a time.

Classes which could be called middle or intermediate groups, had, in their majority, students who were not particularly inspired with the course work. Those classes tended to be taught by teachers who are not particularly inspired with the course work either.

Academic development is not a whole lot different from physical development. Those students who take care of their bodies, train regularly, and discipline these activities, will surely dominate a list of successful athletes. This process in students is easy to see and measure.

Those students whose minds have been developed consistently, who read as readily as others stretch and run, will achieve academic success as certainly as disciplined athletes achieve their success. This process, however, is not so easy to observe. It is private and develops privately.

Academic characteristics are observable. When I had a class with two or three truly disciplined scholars, I could count on having a generally serious class demeanor. With four, that direction was even more pronounced. With five, the class will tend to be dominated by those five, and the rest will tend to be audience.

The view of the scholar as being quiet, private, and to him or herself more often, is not all stereotype. Developing the mind is essentially a quiet activity. Its growth occurs best under conditions where reflection and thought thrive.

Students at Badger High School came from a wide range of socio-economic backgrounds. Such diversity produced general classes of extremes which were often hard to manage to the benefit of all, unless class sizes were within reason.

Imagine how a class can accelerate if it contains students with similar facility and experience. But that is not panacea. A class full of achievers is more difficult to manage than other classes, because the students represent a force that keeps coming at us. Preparations, observation, and execution must be consistent, actually never ending. Unpredictable turns in plans occur almost daily.

Active minds have a habit of carrying their activity right through class hours, and often beyond. The competition among achievers is intense, just as it is in other classes and activities, and just as it always has been. If something came up, I did not know, I had better find out by the next day. Earning the trust of an aggressive, achieving student is more difficult than with others because their expectations of their teachers are high.

It is true such bright students will probably learn no matter who is teaching, but that would not reflect the spirit and scope of what classroom learning is designed to be. The community aspects of learning are important in this society, not only because of size, but because of diversity. The classroom is the focal point of society's designs on how informed and educated its citizenry is to be.

Is it any wonder students who have learned to love learning have high expectations of teachers? Part of a generation's mistrust of society must be borne by its teachers. Now another generation has arrived, the sons and daughters of that generation. What kinds of expectations do those students have? The teacher is still the key to addressing those expectations.

Acceleration of learning is desirable because there is so much more to learn. In fact, in those classes of strong academic students, I insisted they be called accelerated classes and not some of the other names they were given, like fast-track, top group, or advanced placement.

But these accelerated classes were not always successful. I often had better results with other classes. Since the accelerated class absorbed the scholars, high achievers, leaders, whatever we want to call them, the intermediate classes took on a character of their own.

Several things happened. A more relaxed, less intense atmosphere developed. Students known for their reticence and nonparticipation, now took part. A more cooperative system of support grew among the students. They were more likely to volunteer to help each other. But what I thought to be the most promising development was that new student leaders emerged.

In heterogenous groups, these new developments would never have occurred. The same old "smart" kids would have continued to dominate. And as my accelerated classes proved, those bright folks are going to compete and dominate no matter where they are, because they have been doing it for twelve years.

There is the argument that not having the entire range of students in each classroom flies in the face of the realities of society where everyone competes. I disagree. School does represent society, but adolescence is a special time and we need to recognize that efficient learning is the first priority.

I am the last teacher to defend tracking or grouping as a standard for the academic classroom. On the other hand, enterprising teachers when working with reasonable numbers of students can achieve miracles. The enrollment numbers of the 1960s caused tracking to be developed.

Insisting on High Standards

Separations, divorces, and other forms of child neglect simply meant that children were not ready to be students when they came to school. Their training had not disciplined them to accept the cooperation and responsibility necessary to allow classrooms to function well.

So, schools became something more than schools. I never minded the advisory aspect of teaching language to eighteen-year-olds, but I can note that clear and precise advice went out about the time long hair and flowers came in. Now a teacher must make very sure he knows a student and his or her motives before proceeding with advice of any kind.

Earning a student's confidence became increasingly difficult through the years. Many were on guard because they have learned not to trust adults. That probably began with their parents, but in the schools, it certainly made humanity a difficult condition to maintain. For teaching and learning, that was and is an absolute requirement.

I always encouraged students to develop self-discipline. Strong language skills and self-discipline can take a person a long way in life. Students who have never been held for word-form accuracy before were appalled by my rule.

Student: You can't make me look up every word on that paper to check spelling.

Me: Oh, yes, I can!

Student: I won't do it.

Me: Do you really think your spelling is so bad that you have to look up every word?

Student: Yes, I do.

Me: You think that because you have never thought about it, you haven't developed a sense or an eye for words.

Student: I can read all right.

Me: The difference between reading words and writing words is the difference between eating Thanksgiving dinner and making Thanksgiving dinner. Or driving a car and servicing one. Someone writes the writing you read, and anyone who has tried it knows it isn't easy or automatic. Do you want to read and take instructions all your life, or would you want to write and give instructions? You have to develop an eye for words if you expect to call yourself educated. When you have your draft ready for final copy, go through it and circle words you think may be misspelled.

Student: But Mr. Johnson, you know what I mean, even if I have wrong spellings.

Me: I can buy and wear that shirt I saw in a store, too. I saw some sloppy stitching, and the weave looked crooked, but I could buy it and wear it. Would you buy a shirt like that and wear it?

Student: I probably wouldn't have noticed if anything was wrong.

Me: That doesn't make any difference, does it? You can buy it and wear it. It serves its purpose, despite poor workmanship. It seems to me that the problem in education is still teachers that want to teach and students that want to learn.

Student: I suppose I'd have to learn more about buying clothes.

Me: I expect so. But I say it's more important in language, because language is you. It's you expressing yourself. Accuracy, clarity, feelings, and integrity are at stake. Spelling isn't everything, but it is a signal that other language problems lurk. If you train your mind to spot, and then remedy your language problems, you are not only training your mind, but you are training the vehicle which allows you to express what is in your mind, the means by which you share ideas. Your language. If you can do that clearly and accurately, you will be one of those people it's so easy to admire. You know the people I mean. They say things so smoothly. They not only know what to say, but how to say it. Their words just flow out. They sound intelligent.

That standard of learning is what school and education are all about. We need to train our students' minds to function, to learn, to express themselves. It makes sense. Somehow, we are not paying enough attention to it.

We are not promoting the important things – family, self-discipline, responsibility. The reform needs to be done within each of us. What I am afraid of is that education will change, by the sheer gravity of its problems, into something that will alter the definition of mastery.

I recall when learning the periodic table of elements was a staple of chemistry. I also recall when reading a book was the bare essential of a reading assignment: it was what we did with it afterward that counted.

Mastery, no matter in what form or what discipline, brings us closer to the essence of the discipline. I'll never forget the satisfaction of having mastered the periodic table. In the many applications that followed over the years, I could picture where each element was, place its valence and other characteristics in some perspective. Think what that mastery means to a chemistry major.

And the *Prologue to the Canterbury Tales* – well, I gave my students the same assignment for over twenty-five years. Teaching a respect for one's culture is intangible business, and, of course, important.

From 1957 to 1986, students were often reluctant to take on the burden of mastery, no matter what form it took. I know adolescent reluctance is natural, and that if what we adults have to pass on is worth anything, we certainly can inspire the interest and desire necessary. That is what teachers are for.

I know enough about the fires of learning to understand what happens when they are kindled. Learning cannot be stopped. All the teacher does is help commence the process. This one engine will run by itself. All we have to do is think of an experience when an adult turned us on to some activity or interest.

However, we do not require the degrees of mastery we once did. And that is too bad because loss is unavoidable. I don't know whether classroom A's carried the same weight they once did, whether the mastery they represent is the real thing or not. All I know is to master is to understand and be able to apply readily and accurately.

Universal vs. Specialized Education

How can a society require universal education and not make some sort of allowance for the immense differences among individuals?

I felt I could not reach all students who came to my classes without altering my essential mission. We act blindly when we expect all students to receive the same education. It isn't that we do not allow for differences. What happens is that differences are not a major consideration when we set up curriculum. They become a consideration only as a result of applying the curriculum. We always are reacting to the problems that become obvious as we teach.

In the 1960s, the trend was to group students in academic courses with the idea that we could serve them better. I thought it unfair at the time, but problems being what they were and colleague pressure being what it was, I was swept up in the idea.

Student habits and attitudes are almost set in stone by age eighteen. I developed the idea that classes could be better served if students were grouped in rough proportion to what sort of instruction they needed.

In relation to its importance to life generally, the practice of the English language receives short shrift. Much more of our resources and teaching energy needs to be put into training students in their native language. That can be said of the other academic disciplines as well, mathematics in particular, but also science and social science and foreign languages. So, as the world becomes more complex and learning is more diverse and extensive, the pressure on school officials to decide priorities about curricular content has been increasing.

High schools offer too many courses which do not enhance the basic curriculum. To what extent should public high schools be responsible for physical education, driver education, the learning of vocational skills, competitive athletics, developing musical talent?

At the time I retired from teaching, Badger High School offered band, orchestra, and chorus. In addition, each of these had an extension course for advance or more proficient students. The extension of band was jazz ensemble; of chorus, pop singing; of orchestra, the Bach group.

If a student happened to have talent and ambition in two of these areas, he or she could occupy four of the eight class hours of the day with music classes, which had the reputation of being "sure-fire A's."

In academic requirements, it is expected that students will study English, math, science and social science courses in all four years.

It doesn't take much to figure out where the pressures are on students. I taught a journalism course which would pass as one of the extensions of a basic course in English. But no matter how one goes about journalism, it is not an academic English course. It is in extension of language training and a whole lot more. It is a good but narrow application of language.

The students I had in both journalism and English were never left in doubt about which course was academically important. Smart students understood that one should be the training ground for the other, that English covered far more than the narrower focus of journalism. I rode herd on journalism students who thought that was the only course they had.

One year a girl wanted to enter my first-hour accelerated English section. That was not unusual, but her record demonstrated no strong reasons why she should be on that level of language application. Later I found out she was one of those students who was "majoring" in music with four hours scheduled for music courses, and in order to fulfill her English requirement had to be placed in my first-hour class so that she could take the music courses, which were scheduled during the hours when my other English classes met.

I approved her request after a conference or two with the music department head and a promise that the student would have to apply herself to justify such a move. The girl promised me, too. The characteristic trait of her work for me was periodic lapses in attention to deadlines, which seemed to correspond to demands of concert and contest dates in her music work.

It takes no genius to see how adolescents, who are driven by specific, specialized interests, cannot see the overriding importance of academic training. Their interests have become specific and specialized, which is fine. However, they must have mastery in academic disciplines.

It is costing a great deal to keep education universal and practical. High schools cannot be everything for everybody. Decisions about priorities are impossible to avoid forever.

Just what a high school should be has never been decided. It certainly cannot continue to play to the whims of teachers who think they have all-important specialties and students who have the impression that their choices are the most important factors.

Education and Democratic Societies

*The schools ain't what they used to be
and never was.*

Will Rogers

Should the fact that we live in a democratic society make a difference in what our schools are like? Universal education is a marvelous idea. To be able to state unequivocally that all American citizens are or are becoming educated, and know it to be a fact, would indeed be miraculous. It would prove beyond a doubt that democratic societies work.

The twentieth-century American phenomenon of universal, compulsory education unquestionably was a marvelous idea, but like so many aspects of American education it overlooked realities. Anytime something is made compulsory, especially for adolescents, questioning and resistance can be expected.

Education is a natural human inclination. Learning permits survival. Raising children to love learning seems fundamental. That schools must be different in a democratic society seems obvious.

I always thought it a near tragedy that a high percentage of high school students were (and are) not truly engaged in the business of their own educating. Many are in school because they have to be; they stay around because it is the law. Others remain because high school is where they get their driver's licenses. School is also the social center for each age group. In fact, universal education means every young person between five and eighteen is in community schools.

To learn, we must want to learn or be reasonably disposed to the influence of teachers. Learning under compulsion is not in the spirit of liberal education. Some students who come with a desire, a necessity to learn, are going to learn despite the shortcomings of classroom methods.

A major problem of public education has always been the reluctant learner, who because of the hundreds of pressures from without, does not come ready and eager to learn. With many students, teachers must exert efforts beyond what is expected, to motivate students to pursue course requirements.

Children are not naturally drawn to academic life. Adolescence

283

teaches them to test and question. Teachers must not only be experts in their disciplines but also salespeople and first-rate persuaders.

The atmosphere in our society is not conducive to academic pursuits. Few are the parents who develop the skills and attitudes in their children. Few are the parents in whom these skills and attitudes were developed. The odds are against their children. Liberal education that is verboten. Reading is not a society rule – television is. Scholarship is not a top priority – quick one-liners are.

Today's most popular prime-time television program produces nothing but silly repartee, yielding little more than a rapid sequence of one-liners which go nowhere, add up to nothing. The fact that *Seinfeld* is a comedy and a release from life's troubles hardly justifies its silliness. It hardly seems a representative demonstration of a society that calls itself educated and advanced. What do adolescents learn from the TV entertainment we call primetime?

The kind of culture democratic societies produce often does not demonstrate what they should or could produce. When students came to my class in the morning after an evening of stimulating but empty prime-time and late-night television, they were anything but alert and ready for the serious business of the classroom.

We're all in this education process together, and when we don't live the examples we expect our children to follow, we have chaos.

Should living in a democratic society make a difference in what schools are like? Of course, if we remember that responsibilities are the price of freedoms. However, we must make it the business of our lives to exact balance between the two. The problems of American education are very serious, yet as simple as can be. All they require is being more selfless and less selfish.

The responsibility of seeing to it that learning is sustained effectively among adolescents is just as important as maintaining the flow of electricity to all those conveniences we take for granted. Electricity serves immediate needs; education serves long-range needs. And that is the problem. We're consumed by today.

Who and what are we going to do to serve the needs of the future? We are so absorbed by the ease and greed we've created that the fundamentals are left to chance. We sometimes exercise economy in the wrong things.

President Franklin Roosevelt, made democracy's priorities clear: "The school is the last expenditure upon which America should be willing to economize."

What schools are like does matter. The life of this democratic society depends on it.

Teaching and Learning Are Not Regimented Processes

Keep them busy. Don't allow gaps in time. Be certain that structure is in place and apparent to all professionals. Free time is a waste of time: it only encourages chaos. Instead, we need order and homework. Students need to be kept busy. Teach things that can be mastered, which can easily be transported into the A-B-C structure of grading. Attendance report, lesson plans, periodic reports on students (only accounts on problem students are required), all these practices help keep us attuned to how efficient and persistent teachers are.

Let students take many courses. Doing so fills up their day and means fewer study halls, which means fewer control problems. Students must be in the classroom mastering facts. They must memorize them so they can pass tests on them. It is the grades that really count, so they can do well on their SAT's and ACT's. In order for this regimen to happen, we must focus on facts. Thomas Gradgrind in Dicken's *Hard Times* advocates for mastery of unemotional facts:

> Now, what I want is, facts. Teach these boys and girls nothing but facts. Facts alone are wanted in life. Plant nothing else and root out everything else. You can only form the minds of reasoning animals upon Facts: nothing else will ever be of any service to them. This is the principle on which I bring up my own children, and this is the principle on which I bring up these children. Stick to facts, Sir!

Who says a good education cannot be measured? Work for mastery. Work for good grades. Work for the facts. This mastery can only take place in an orderly, controlled atmosphere. This kind of schooling is not education. This is regimentation of the strictest order. And that will not promote the willing growth of minds and spirits.

I liked it better when teachers were hired on their merit and promoted that way. Union lockstep is not going to attract the kinds of minds we needed in education. Neither is the idea that teaching is an easy 8-to-4 job that can still be called a profession.

Somehow the ingrained attitude that learning is rote, memorized, to be achieved by the passing of tests, must be changed. Otherwise reform in education will never work or only seem to work.

Priorities in Education

What would happen if annual schedules for schools were built around something other than athletic activities? The Wisconsin Interscholastic Athletic Association appears to have more control over the way the school year is structured than any other social entity, even the Wisconsin State Department of Public Instruction.

What would happen if basketball and other winter sports, instead of being scheduled over the long stretch of two academic quarters, middle November to middle March, were scheduled over one academic quarter the way fall sports and spring sports are?

What would happen if some of the activities which represent student emotional peaks were disassociated from athletic events, for example, homecoming in football?

What if academic considerations determined the way weeks were organized? For example, hold athletic training in practice periods three afternoons a week instead of five. Then academic work can be pursued more vigorously and consistently during after school hours at least two of the middle three days of the school week.

Such alternatives might also aid students who hold jobs outside school. When it comes to holding jobs or playing sports, participation seems to indicate that job-holding students outnumber student athletes.

These questions and suggestions are not to state that physical training is not important; it is. But it is also a manner of individual volition. Again, I do not intend to deprive physical well-being of its appropriate place. If people do not desire to keep themselves in good physical condition, what will make them do it over the mature years of their lives?

The amount of leisure time people have now, compared to forty years ago, is considerably higher. We seem to support the idea of increased leisure at the expense of the development of academic skills. We forget that the skills called for in the workplace are academic, that it is the failure in language skills and mathematics that causes the most trouble for businesses.

If high schools were organized in such a way that it appeared academic skills were the most important function, things might start to change. If the current secondary school curriculum were examined with these new priorities in mind, some courses would begin to appear inappropriate, unjustifiable, even silly.

There are two chief problems that public education, particularly on the high school level, must begin to resolve. One is the general low esteem in which the typical student holds his or her academic experience. The other is to find a reasonable way to fund public schools.

A stronger teaching profession will enrich the experience. High school will yield a more positive experience and supporting it financially will be seen as a necessity. This whole process could turn into a powerful, perpetual social engine.

Public Conversation on Education

> *Education is not the filling of a*
> *pail, but the lighting of a fire.*
> William Butler Yeats

Discussions of education could hardly be described as public. Rather, they are private. People run for school boards when their children reach school age. Business people more often than not look up on school districts as potential markets. The public generally thinks and talks about education when referenda arise and when property taxes come due.

The public activates toward education when athletic teams win. Nothing arouses the public power faster than having a basketball team on the verge of winning a berth in the state tournament. How much space local newspapers give to competitive sports? Yet, thinking of the high school and its mission, athletics is on the periphery of importance.

No, the discussions have to involve the nitty gritty of education itself, the process of teaching and learning. That simply does not happen. Sadly, the teacher's territory is sacrosanct. The assumption is that teachers are thoroughly trained in their specialties, and who are we to question that?

If specialty were all there were to it, the education problem would not exist. There is more to it than that. Teachers must love children, not simply tolerate them in the names of their specialties. In addition, teachers must be skilled in the psychology of convincing children that learning is the most important mission of childhood and adolescence, and that education does not stop with degrees. In fact, as Emerson put it, "The things taught in schools are not in education but the means of an education."

It's unfortunate, but education must compete. What does it take to compete with television, the computer, the games, the automobile, in the high levels of product pitch to which children are exposed? How do we fight a society which bombards our youth with the idea that one must be forever stimulated?

Education is a community activity. It is the one function on which the community must agree. Certainly, disagreements and distractions will occur, but the function of community is to disagree, study, debate, and compromise. Until citizens agree about the importance of education and participate with conviction, all other social forces, these competitive elements, will not be brought to serve the community's youth.

What is missing in the public conversation about education is the conviction that such public conversation is the community's most important function, and that until the citizenry believes and acts upon that belief, private priorities will continue to suppress good education.

Getting Serious About Education

Why can't we Americans get serious about education? We enjoy the fruits of the hard work and effective education of earlier generations, but we cannot seem to understand that we must also prepare and apply ourselves for the next generations.

Is education really the nation's top priority? Do the sharpest and most innovative young minds take to teaching? Are our high school and college students devoted to education? Is it really the first of their priorities? How are our technologies and their distractions affecting the graduates who emerge from the school pipeline?

A gradual erosion has taken place in our system of educating. Diversions and distractions abound. The urge and persistence required to earn the rewards of self-discipline seem to have waned.

All of these changes add up to a kind of loose societal resolve toward the serious and constructive life. Leisure trump's vocation. Passive entertainment dominates our lives. Making money seems more important than developing relationships. Conversations, dialogue, are often superficial, sketchy. We cannot stay at one task for long. Attention spans become abrupt. Multi-tasking is now a common verb.

All of these changes seem to be leading to chaotic, unstructured lives, to a society with little purpose in declining unity. We live to consume, work to fulfill our private lives. How else to explain cell phones in public?

Increased facility in communication is good, assuming we have something to say. I make it a point in public to edge closer to cell phone responders, and what I usually hear is far below the urgency and utility one would expect of such conversations. People sometimes use that form of communication so they don't have to talk face to face. And a lot of the content is not urgent or even constructive.

Movies and television have made us slaves to passive entertainment. Americans have to get their fix of shock and surprise. We can't wait to be horrified or outraged, and sometimes offended. We can't wait to get all shook up. Somehow this frenetic life commenced in the 1950s when the likes of Elvis Presley "shook" things up. Talk about culture shock! We have become receivers, not givers. Unsettling social changes do not seem to bother us. We do not give back.

Our way of life demands we contribute. Democracy is not run from Washington. It depends on main street America. And the chief symptoms of ominous change are in our schools.

To move forward, we have some significant questions to answer. Are we thinking about other strategies than the property tax to support schools? As parents, are we the main supporters of public education? Have we really educated ourselves, making us models for our children? Do we actively promote teaching as career options for our sons and daughters? Do we have skills which can be useful to local schools? In a period when there is so much more to learn, are we inclined to read more? Are we really able to tell the difference between our wants and our needs? Does the Internet settle us down to serious, single minded goals?

Is conserving a fundamental skill? My generation is at some

advantage here because we grew up in a time when conserving and making do were mandatory. That habit is lost on later generations who, relatively, have everything they need. Yet the satisfaction we would expect to see if people who have everything appears to be lacking. Instead we live on hectic, unsettling schedules. But what are those roller-coaster lifestyles getting us? What do we really want?

What are our expectations? They are, for the most part, private priorities and do not relate to the sustenance and sustaining of democratic society.

No wonder U.S. education is in trouble. Schools are a reflection of society, but they are also a crucible for change. We need to steer their priorities in new directions. We must make it possible for students to take charge of their own learning. Give them the tools to learn aggressively on their own. Then all teachers need to do is provide the spark.

> *Education is not the filling of a pail,*
> *but the lightning of a fire.*
> William Butler Yeats

A Long-Range Planning Survey

A "Long Range Planning Survey" on the front page of the current *Lake Geneva Area Schools Community Report* on June 8, 1992. It's the clip, fold, and mail-in type of questionnaire.

Question 4, the last one, was "If you could invent the perfect school, what would it be like?" There is one line of space on which to respond. That space is 4 ¾ inches long and ¼ inch wide.

I never spent much time speculating about perfection in schools, much less the unreality of "inventing" one. If we could manage to commit perfect people to teaching careers, there might be a possibility. But there are no perfect people (even if we could agree on what perfection is).

If I could develop an effective school, I would pay close attention to the people I hired. I would identify high school students who showed interest in teaching and try to find out what appealed to them. I would hire teachers whose personalities engage others easily, who have patience, humanity, and social consciences. Without teachers, we have no schools. Without good teachers we do not have good schools. Effective teachers

290

can make effective schools.

What other institution has such direct access to the talent it needs to propagate its profession? It has always seemed strange to me that schools do not actively pursue good teachers and actively develop the ones they have. There is no direct link between the people who hire and those who teach. Teaching is a private activity, but that does not mean those who hire and fire must depend on rumor and second-hand information to learn how their teachers teach and how their children learn.

As a teacher, I only came close to the public professionally when I was hired, when parent-teacher conferences were held, when the annual budget was made public, and when we complain about how much is spent on teachers' salaries. As I suggested, without teachers we have no schools, and without good teachers we do not have good schools.

The single most serious morale problem in teaching: not being recognized, and when we are, it is in lockstep with the harmless drudges, the non-teacher teachers, and dangerous, inefficient fools.

Money isn't everything; in fact, it is a miniscule part of the task. I remember being told, don't worry, you're recognized even if you don't hear about it. That is not very satisfying or morale supporting when you're in the middle of one of those bad, bad days in the much-advanced age of permissiveness.

What I needed was not so much direct support or money for a job well done, but rather a sense that someone out there and up there in the institution was not simply supporting me, but also understanding me.

Effective teaching is turning boredom into stimulation. Effective teaching produces students who are passionate, not passive. Effective teaching develops students who are not resigned to routine and who recognize the value of self-discipline. Let's affirm the importance of effective teachers and figure out how we can get more.

I don't know how I will get all of this thinking in that 4 ¾ x ¼ inch space. Let's be realistic. I can't. That is precisely the challenge.

The Gateway Arch, National Park Service, St. Louis, Missouri

Conversations for Our Nation's Future

President Franklin Roosevelt made one of democracy's priorities clear: "The school is the last expenditure upon which America should be willing to economize." I believe that the life of our democratic society depends on high-quality education, and yet our community and legislative bodies continue to "economize" in ways that jeopardize the quality of learning our youth experience.

In *And Gladly Would He Teach*, I encourage the general public to learn how society's changes are affecting schools, how language integrity is essential for our democracy, and how we can support our schools. I promote ongoing dialogue on such questions as these:

- **How well is our community and country addressing our children's hopes and challenges?**

- **How can we employ and retain well-prepared teachers?**

- **What communication skills should citizens in a democracy have?**

- **What does mastery of high standards look like?**

- **How can our schools balance academic, athletic and special interests of youth?**

And Gladly Would He Learn

And Gladly Would He Learn

Dedication

To the artists,
musicians,
thought leaders,
entrepreneurs,
athletes,
writers,
journalists,
media personalities,
singers,
photographers,
scientists,
astronauts,
architects,
military leaders,
and political leaders
who inspired my personal and professional life.

On Cultural Icons

I must be looking for something in other people. My attraction to people with exemplary talents and minds continues to this day.

In the thirty-plus years since I retired, I have read over six hundred books. Though some were fiction, most were not. I approached every book as a potential writing source.

Each essay in this chapter contains my reflections on people who have been cultural icons during my lifetime. I studied their personalities and minds through their biographies, autobiographies, and feature stories. I am still looking for something in others. I try to find it, and then move on.

CONTENTS

Lawrence Peter "Yogi" Berra
David Brubeck and Van Cliburn
Art Buchwald
Noam Chomsky
Samuel Clemens
Bret Favre
Bill Gates
Charles Kuralt
Ernie Pyle
Christopher Reeve
Cal Ripken, Jr.
Norman Rockwell

Fred Rogers
Will Rogers
Mike Royko
Charles Schulz
Albert Schweitzer
Frank Sinatra
Mike Singletary
Jimmy Stewart
E.B. White
Ted Williams
Frank Lloyd Wright

Lawrence Peter "Yogi" Berra

Baseball's different today, but it isn't.
Yogi Berra

Lawrence Peter Berra represents what baseball means to many Americans. The passing of the Hall-of-Famer is a reminder of what he meant to the game. His nickname reveals a great deal: Yogi!

He was a catcher, probably the most demanding position physically. Later he was a coach and a manager. But that is only the beginning.

Yogi Berra played in more World Series than anyone … fourteen. His career began in 1946 and concluded in 1963 when the New York Yankees dominated major league baseball. He was as good a catcher as baseball has ever produced, and it is important to note that catchers have considerable control over the game. Yogi was a three-time American League Most Valuable Player. He was the catcher for pitcher Don Larsen's perfect game in the 1956 World Series.

The name Yogi explains a lot since his reputation seems to rest as much on "his unique wisdom" as it does on his Hall-of-Fame baseball career. His language produced a wealth of unusual axioms, off-the-cuff aphorisms, which have become as famous as his baseball heroics.

Though many of these utterances didn't seem to make sense, there was more sense than was initially apparent. One reporter used the phrase "linguistically dizzying" to describe Yogi's sayings. Probably famous was "It's déjà vu all over again."

About a popular nightspot, he declared, "Nobody goes there anymore. It's too crowded." It is easy to see what he meant, but the humor of the contradiction commands attention.

In describing how to find a teammate's residence, which involved a cul-de-sac, Yogi said, "When you come to a fork in the road, take it." There is truth there – hidden beneath.

In the early-1970s, his New York Mets were several games out of first place in August. Yogi declared, "It ain't over til it's over." The Mets made it to the World Series.

Yogi's semantic slips often smothered his baseball smarts:

- Ninety percent of the game is half mental.
- I wish I had an answer to that, because I'm tired of answering that question.
- The other team could make trouble for us if they win.
- I knew exactly where it was. I just couldn't find it.
- I double-checked it six times.
- You mean now… Yogi's response to someone asking, 'What time is it?'
- Put the convertible top down so the air conditioner can work better.

His odd and zany aphorisms displayed "unique wisdom." We all say things intended one way but taken another. Most of his sayings bear an inner logic often lost to the humor. Baseball remains our national pastime. Yogi Berra contributed more than his share to its legacy. It would be hard to forget the language lore.

In one of the Yogi collections, he expressed useful advice about work:

Whatever job you have, do it with real energy and effort, or else you won't get it done or done right… The more zest you have, the better job you'll do, the better you'll feel about it, and the better you'll make others feel.

Not everyone finds a love, a zest for his work, but Yogi did.

Lawrence Peter Berra, baseball winner, Hall-of-Famer, loveable linguistic loser was a considerable credit to humankind. Thanks, Yogi!

David Brubeck and Van Cliburn

How is it possible to discuss two great musicians when they seem to be such opposites? Both were pianists who made significant achievements in the 1950s.

Is it necessary to discuss both in the same context? In this case, yes, because each produced his own form of artistic revolution. As a point of pride, I recognize both as examples of American genius.

Dave Brubeck, who died in December 2012 a day short of his 92nd birthday, had changed the sound of jazz and made it mainstream.

Van Cliburn died in February 2013 at age 78. He was the twenty-three-year-old Texan who won the International Tchaikovsky Piano Competition in Moscow in 1958, becoming an American hero. His recording of the *First Piano Concerto* was the first million-selling classical record, eventually reaching over three million.

It's hard to write about art without waxing personal. The existence of these artists has caused me to reflect on why music means so much to me.

The irony is I am no musician; I love music and have done what is possible both in and out of my profession to encourage it.

The 1950s were years of fundamental change in America and in my life. Two music events influenced American culture:

- Van Cliburn's winning the Tchaikovsky competition
- Dave Brubeck Quartet released the album *Time Out*, and *Take Five*, the first jazz single to sell over a million records

Commercial considerations aside, it is hard to describe the way music stirs emotions and demands all of our senses. When Van Cliburn's recording of the Tchaikovsky concerto went public, we fell in love with our fellow American who was beating the Russians at their own game. He played with animation and ardor. He allowed Americans to share in the power and energy of Russian music at the height of the Cold War and eight months after Sputnik. I still recall the renewed sense of pride and élan his performance generated.

Things worked a bit differently with Dave Brubeck. I've never quite caught on to his unusual rhythmic ways. *Take Five*, as it took the pop world by storm, seemed an anomaly. Brubeck performed the song in 5/4 time, which has been called "a defiant time-signature." Just try to keep all that straight. You can easily lose your way in quintuple rhythm. Yet there is a provocative, irresistible tug to the piece.

But the piece has ironies too. The first is that Brubeck does not have a solo – he always has solos. Alto-saxist Paul Desmond's first and last choruses frame the tune's centerpiece, which is Joe Morello's drum solo. But something's missing: it's that figure Brubeck keeps playing over and over and over through the five-minute piece (get it? Take five!).

I can't explain how and why it works. I could not recount the number of times I have heard it. Each time I play *Take Five*, it comes on as fresh as spring.

It is impossible to compare the music of Brubeck and Van Cliburn. Why should anyone want to? Music is its own invention, and it doesn't matter who the musicians are as long as they are well prepared and give us something. The music of these two American icons will surely survive the twenty-first century too.

Art Buchwald

While assembling the contents of a box of books to sell or give away, I included two of Art Buchwald's collections, *While Reagan Slept* and *You Can Fool All of the People All the Time*, columns written during the Reagan years.

I've had a number of his collections over the years and have read three or four. But when my three local dailies did not run Buchwald's Pulitzer Prize winning work, it was easy to lose the connection. After all, his columns appeared in over five hundred newspapers worldwide.

The *PBS Jim Lehrer News Hour* featured a segment about Buchwald's experience in a hospice where he was living out his days. The eighty-year-old decided not to submit to dialysis.

He was delighted that family, friends, colleagues and the French government have been bestowing all kinds of honors upon him. The French ambassador was shown placing one of its prestigious medals around his neck. Buchwald began his journalism career in Paris in 1948.

In the second half of the segment, a national journalist interviewed him. He had lost none of his mental vigor and sense of humor in his eighty years. I wondered why he was giving up this precious talent when his essential tools were functioning well. He had done two columns the week before and one during the current week.

What made Art Buchwald an effective social commentator? First of all, he was funny. In a column about his French years, he wrote, "I always got along with the French. I once asked a French friend, 'Why do the French dislike Americans?' He said, 'The French don't like each other, so why should they like you?'"

The man had heart and also a stiletto urge to puncture the high and mighty. He knew how to penetrate the innards of problems and the people

300

who have them. He worked outward through mazes, puzzles of motivation, and contradictions. In the process, he managed a fine balance between the heart and the urge. In the preface of *Beating Around the Bush*, one of his latest collection of columns, he suggested, "There are no bad guys in Washington, there are only good guys doing bad things."

At the heart of his art was his ability to say things that were utterly common but seasoned with elements that surprise, contradict, or send the reader off on unexpected excursions. Accompanying Buchwald's latest collection was the following from the *Library Journal:*

> Buchwald is a pitiless chronicler of human folly, particularly as it manifests itself in public officials; the targets of his satire are pretension, inconsistency, and hypocrisy. He makes his readers laugh out loud, then leaves them wondering whether what they laughed at might not equally well have made them weep.

Born in 1925, Art was a Depression child. He never saw his mother. He and his father did not connect very well. His three siblings were older sisters. He spent his childhood in a Seventh-Day Adventist shelter, New York's Hebrew Orphan Asylum, and several foster homes, all before he was fifteen.

In his autobiography *Leaving Home*, he said, "I must have been six or seven years old and terribly lonely and confused, when I said something like, 'This stinks. I'm going to become a humorist.'"

By the way, reading his words means more if you have heard his voice.

The last choice in the hierarchy of vocations one would expect to see for Art Buchwald was the armed services. But he was reaching draft eligibility at a time when every male faced the prospect of military service. Not only was he in the service, he was a Marine. He wrote, "At seventeen I was young, I was unhappy, and most of all I was undisciplined. The Marine Corps was the right service in the right place at the right time."

Read the chapter "The Marine Recruit" in *Leaving Home* to understand Private Buchwald's dilemma. Even I, who weathered two periods of basic training (Navy 1945 and Army 1951), cannot understand how he survived.

301

His drill instructor was Corporal Pete Bonardi, who "was the toughest, meanest…" Sorry, I can't use those words here.

But as the service often does for males, it makes men of them. It also makes enduring relationships. "I began to realize that the Marine Corps was the first father figure I have ever known," Buchwald writes. "From early morning to late at night they took care of all my needs. It was a love-hate relationship, as many father-son ones are. I mentioned this to a master sergeant who said, 'Fifty percent of all recruits coming through here feel the same way.'"

Buchwald wound up with life-long respect for the DI who had made his life so difficult. The touching exchange near the end of Bonardi's life released some of those "weeps." The respect turned out to be mutual.

If ever there were a self-made man, Art Buchwald was he, having earned the right to be the universal humorist, satirist, and social commentator that he was. In a column called "Four Lettered Words and More," he demonstrated a disdain for entertainers who depend on expletives to get laughs:

> Cable TV has been a boon for writers because the F-word had made it easier for them to write script. Every time one of the characters has nothing to say the writer gives them a cuss word.

That speaks volumes about contemporary entertainment (and education).

Buchwald had a social conscience. In the preface to *Beating Around the Bush,* he reflected on the dilemma we face in the Middle East. "I also deal with the Iraq War. It is not my position that it was a good war or a bad war, a just war or an unjust war, a smart war or the dumbest war we have ever gotten into. My position is that it is the only war we've got, so we have to support it."

I have missed the zestful, savvy Buchwald all these years, but I'm making up for lost time. And I wish, Monsieur Buchwald, you had more of it. I wish we could travel some more on your journalistic junket. Again comes that human, even-handed attitude of mind, "Whether it's the best of times or the worst of times, it's the only time we've got."

Noam Chomsky

Something about Noam Chomsky will not go away. The grandfatherly, soft-spoken man, who is about a year older than I am, keeps turning up.

I've been reading references to his work for at least fifty years. His connection with causes is ever present. I've seen him being interviewed and put on the defensive so often that it is easy to simply ignore him. But that grand, wise man with an understated voice keeps chipping away.

Chomsky is a much-practiced author, linguist, and America's most consistent dissident. He knows something and can see things the rest of us prefer to ignore or cannot see. He won't go away because he is certain of himself. What he sees that is wrong, he can isolate from everything else. That is what is so important, frustrating, and amazing, about genius – it sees on a higher plane.

I checked out *The Oxford Companion to the English Language*, and the discussion of his linguistic experience shows more of what is familiar than what is not. His transformational grammar is logical, but adapting it to the practical, daily classroom routine is not so easy. Chomsky concerned himself with how the linguistic structures and processes work in the mind. That sounds familiar.

He maintains that current grammar is only concerned with how sentences grow out of phrases and phrases out of words, but it does not relate sentences of differing structures. That, too, sounds familiar.

Grammarian Chomsky is concerned with knowledge of the language, not performance. As the *Oxford Companion* points out, the standard approach "distinguished between a speaker's competence (knowledge of the language) and performance (actual use of a language)."

What transformed Chomsky the grammarian, into Chomsky the dissident I was not sure, until recently. PBS ran a two-hour program called *Viewpoint: Manufacturing Consent*. It explored the life and times of the well-known linguist. The program delineated his belief that democratic freedoms cover up irresponsible use of power. He is particularly severe about the media and their serving the country's power brokers.

It was a convincing examination. Of course, it is all very familiar. Chomsky will not go away, and it is probably a good thing.

Samuel Clemens

The mind of Samuel Clemens was unusual. He had a delightful sense of humor, playful satire, and rousing skepticism about life in general. In his twenty years as a journalist, he often pressed reader credulity. It's almost as though he expected his readers to question his integrity but recognize truths.

In the *Stolen White Elephant*, he wrote about the detective squad trying to locate a runaway white elephant. The effort expended to locate a subject that would be extremely hard to hide was monumental. The beast was not located until inspector Blunt stumbled onto the animal in "the dim remote end of a vaulted basement where sixty detectives played cards and slept."

Somehow through all of this dubious stuff, law enforcement personnel of the time must have felt some uneasiness. Silly as it was, details must have come close to reality. Man's tendency to expand upon the privileges of duty are well known.

His approach to subjects was consistent. He used an underlying value system, which, though often overwhelmed by exaggeration and implausibility, remained constant, like a working conscience.

I recall Twain's famous line about books and reading: "The man who does not read good books has no advantage over the man who can't read them."

I recognize that "rousing skepticism" about life because I have it. Most of us do. It is at once a defense against the inequities, pressures, and the general unfairness of life. That conscience goes to work, and we still get along despite all.

Brett Favre

Brett Favre has become a standard by which the ideals of grid battle can be measured. His attitude and spirit were as much at play as his physical abilities. They made him a dynamic team leader with whom fans could intimately relate.

For most jobs, just showing up every day can be a challenge. But on the battlefields of the NFL, it is different. Consider these Brett-stats:

- Most consecutive starts, including playoff games – 275
- On injury lists – fifty times
- Most passing yards in NFL history – 61,655
- Different receivers caught Favre passes – 44
- Touchdown passes – 442
- Consecutive games with at least one touchdown pass – 36
- Victories coming from behind in the fourth quarter – 40
- MVP awards (1995-97) – three (only player ever to do that)

It's hard to understand what it means to have started 253 consecutive conference games at quarterback. As much as it pains a Bears fan to say it, during the sixteen years Favre produced his 160 victories, the monsters of Midway had twenty-one starting quarterbacks.

Brett Favre attempted 8,758 passes, completed 5,377, a 61.4 percentage. His passing yards would reach almost twelve miles.

While concentrating on locating and connecting with his receivers, number four had to deal with harsh, hulking brutes bearing down on him, sometimes from four directions. No matter how you look at it, that's a tough job.

Despite fan adulation, the millions in salary, and the respect of peers, the salient fact of Brett Favre's football life was his love of the game and how that love infected others. *Newsday* writer Johnette Howard put it this way: "It was this human touch that attracted fans. They knew Brett was truly in touch with them."

As I listened to Favre deliver his valedictory to the press, I wrote down some words that occurred to me as he spoke:

- Authentic, down-to-earth: 'I'm not going to sit here and say I won't miss it because I will, but I just don't think I can give anything else.'
- Fair-minded, humble: 'I've come a long way.'
- Genuine, no fakery: 'Mississippi and Wisconsin – how can you beat that?'
- Passion: 'You rely on each other more than in any other sport.'

I have tried to describe how Brett played quarterback. I can't. Mike Reiss of the *Boston Globe*, however, came close: "The laser throw. The exuberance. Put them together, and it was a snapshot of vintage Favre."

An editorial in the *Milwaukee Journal-Sentinel* around the time of his retirement ended this way: "And, oh, yeah, the toughest guy on the field wasn't afraid to cry."

Bill Gates

How does one understand what it means to command nearly one-hundred billion dollars? Our age is filled with extraordinary numbers, but the idea that a sixty-four-year-old man accumulated such extensive wealth is mind-boggling. The facts in the case make such wealth predictable.

The computer has taken over the world. Its development and sophistication have been staggering. But it is the software, the stuff in the computers that offered the real opportunity. The company called Microsoft developed to the point where its co-founder, Bill Gates, became one of the world's richest persons.

David Frost interviewed him on PBS. Nothing in his looks, language, or demeanor gave away what must be a powerful mind. What was striking was his rational but measured discourse. He sounded like a man on his way to controlling his segment of the world, and that is a goodly share.

In their conversation, I was looking for hints about what this extremely wealthy man plans to do with his considerable wealth. The persistent impression was that here is a man who understands the world he has helped create and will see to it that the computer controls every aspect of our lives that it can.

Bill Gates is certainly recognized and has acted upon what he saw as a world-changing opportunity. He seems to understand the world he has helped create.

The idealism of the boomer generation will be tested in this man. I hope the world is not moving too fast for rational judgment. Those numbers keep overwhelming us. I have trouble understanding $1200.

Charles Kuralt

The idea of driving a big motor home around the country looking for human interest stories to tell on television, is a fascinating, romantic idea.

The man who did it was not a swashbuckling, fast-talking network type. He was not a made-for-TV face and figure. He was, rather, the down-to-earth, authentic, and somewhat physically roundabout, Charles Kuralt, the most convincing of television's reporters.

Kuralt died on July 4, 1997. What an appropriate day. If ever there were an American with his finger on the country's pulse, it was Citizen Kuralt. Telling stories was his art, and he traveled every state to paint portraits of common folk who distinguished themselves in different ways.

After a reportorial tour in Vietnam in the 1960s, he managed to obtain a "yes" from CBS officials to this question: "Why don't you let me wander around the country, do some feature stories?" Later, Kuralt described his work:

> I haven't had an assignment from that day to this. For story ideas I rely on dumb luck and letters from viewers. I have moseyed back and forth across the country, pausing in every part of every state, with CBS paying all the bills. My bosses, preoccupied with coverage of politics, wars, and calamities, don't even know where I am. They don't care where I am.

Kuralt began his odyssey on a three-month trial basis in 1967. On the very first stop, he sent back a piece on Vermont's fall splendor: "It is death that causes this blinding show of color but is a fierce and flaming death. To drive along a Vermont country road in this season is to be dazzled by the shower of lemon and scarlet and gold that washes across your windshield." Kuralt was "on the road" for the next thirteen years, clocking as many as 50,000 miles a year.

Charles Kuralt did many of the things I enjoy doing: writing, photography, travel, working with people close up, and the opportunity to put all these elements together. CBS colleague Dan Rather described Kuralt as follows:

> Charles's essays were miniature movies, carefully scripted, filmed

and edited. They told of our life and times. They had breadth, depth and sweep to engage the eye, ear, and mind. Charles was the first correspondent to take his typewriter into the editing room regularly. Let the film talk to you ... listen to the pictures, hear what the pictures are saying, then write them as you would write to music.

I'm sure Kuralt would agree. He was practicing them in television, the toughest of all media, while insisting on his standards.

Above all, he was a writer, a poet. Colleague Eric Sevareid knew that:

Among the very few poets in 'electronic journalism' there is, first and foremost, Charles Kuralt. He has given the craft a different dimension. Normally, in television, the thought and the word merely attend the picture. He has made the picture attend thought and word. The poetry of America is in his soul and he makes it manifest through the camera's eye.

The meat and potatoes of Kuralt's art was the feature story. One important skill is writing good leads. Following is his lead for a story about a horse trader, Ben K. Green, from Cumby, Texas   (*On the Road with Charles Kuralt*):

Thanks to the Interstate Highway System, it is now possible to travel across the country from coast to coast without seeing anything. From the Interstate, America is all steel guardrails and plastic signs, and every place looks and feels and sounds and smells like every other place. We stick to backroads, where Kansas still looks like Kansas and Georgia still looks like Georgia, where there is room for diversity and small miracles.

I'll bet you want to find out what is so miraculous about a Texas horse trader.

Speaking of miracles, following is the introduction to a story about the changes in people's work (*On the Road with Charles Kuralt*):

Drive across the country and you find that hardly anybody makes any thing. I think of my friends and neighbors. One of them sells insurance, one of them takes pictures for a living, one's an actor, one's a lawyer – none of them makes anything. I talk on television. I don't make anything either. This may be the most fundamental change in this country. Years ago, nearly everybody in the cities made something – harnesses, wagon wheels, hats, violins …

Across the TV screen slides the impressive panorama of the Golden Gate and its famous bridge. Kuralt's interview with three men who worked on the massive undertaking (1933-1937) illustrated the dangers of the job and the power of the Depression in people's lives.

Kuralt's ability to write anecdotally was absorbing and incisive:

Before I was born, I went on the road. The road was U.S. 17, south from Jacksonville, North Carolina, through the Holly Shelter Swamp to Wilmington, where the hospital was. My father backed the Chevrolet out of its place in the hay barn next to the farm cart and helped my mother into the front seat on the afternoon of September 9, 1934. He made the trip in a little more than an hour, barely slowing down for the stop signs in Dixon, Folkstone and Holly Ridge. I was born the next morning with rambling in my blood and fifty miles already under my belt.

Quick, to the point, with a perspective most would not think of, Kuralt's work was a never-ending study of humanity and effective communication.

How about one more lead for the road? A recent Kuralt piece was a commentary published in the November 1996 Female Icons Issue of the *New York Times Magazine.* Its subject: Eleanor Roosevelt. Here are the first few sentences:

I unbuttoned Eleanor Roosevelt's dress. I was very nervous, though she did her best to make it easy for me. I had grown up persuaded that Eleanor Roosevelt was the greatest living American, not excluding her husband.

I know what you're thinking. You <u>are</u> going to tell us where this story lead leads. No, Charles Kuralt had done his job arousing your interest. I have done mine introducing you to his. The rest is up to you.

Charles Kuralt, our best itinerant journalist, joined the likes of Alexis de Tocqueville, Mark Twain, and John Steinbeck as one of the great travelers and interpreters of America.

Ernie Pyle

Ernie Pyle has grown on me. That war, which I sat out as a high school student, still affects us all. I was old enough to sense the importance of, and to identify with, World War II, half in fear and half in envy. An adolescent will catch the heroic stuff, but he will also understand that the day may very well come when he, too, has to go to war.

I remember the name Ernie Pyle from that time, but I doubt I had a precise understanding of who he was and what he was doing. Ernie Pyle was the war's most famous reporter, and he lived like a soldier, with soldiers, in their dirty, dreary, dangerous circumstances. That probably had something to do with his being such a good reporter.

At the time I certainly knew the war was important, but I was in high school. It was easy to isolate myself in my little world. The war was the routine that guided community life. It is only now that I can understand some of what was going on and can appreciate the gravity of those years.

Ernie Pyle turned out to be a means to that end. Not the only means, but an effective one. He identified with the people whose lives that epic struggle affected, the people who fought in the war. In *Brave Men*, he focused on the privates, lieutenants, corporals, and captains so much that no one would suspect there were generals.

That was, until it came to Omar Bradley, the lieutenant general who commanded U.S. troops in the D-Day invasion of June 1944. Pyle wrote:

As you may know, I am concerned mainly with the common soldier, the well-known GI. I usually let the exalted high command shift for itself. But now I want to reverse things and write about an American general. For three days, back in Sicily, I rode and sat around with Lieutenant General Omar Nelson Bradley and at times I was so engulfed in stars I thought I must be a comet.

I make no bones about the fact that I am a tremendous admirer of General Bradley. I don't believe I have ever known a person to be so unanimously loved and respected by the men around and under him. It would be toying with the truth to call him handsome, rather than good-looking. His face showed the kindness and calmness that lay behind it. To me General Bradley looked like a schoolteacher rather than a soldier. When I told him that, he said I wasn't so far wrong, because his father was a country schoolteacher and he himself had taught at West Point and other places. His specialty was mathematics.

The general was just the opposite of a 'smoothie.' His conversation was not brilliant or unusual, but it was packed with sincerity. He still had the Middle West in his vocabulary – he used such expressions as 'fighting to beat the band' and 'a horse of another color.' There was no pretense about him, and he hated ostentation.

His troops universally admired and respected the general who was responsible for the actions they were about to take. Pyle's characterization of Bradley sounds like the sketches he did of many GI's.

D-Day was a time when we remember exactly where we were and what we were doing when we found out about it. The dimensions of the engagement were such that no one soldier or general could possibly comprehend its totality. Even seventy-five years later, that is hard to do.

But Ernie Pyle brought the individual soldier's struggle to the light of day, even though those days were uncertain and dark. Through his accounts, I have come to understand the range, the reality, and the deadly dimensions of World War II. Ernie, his *Brave Men*, and his war are indeed growing on.

Christopher Reeve
Still Me, Christopher Reeve's autobiographical account of his fight against life-threatening injury, is captivating and convincing. It is hard to believe he could record this story at all. It is articulate, thorough, and essentially of his doing. He used no ghost writers or collaborators. The writing conveys a consistency that comes from a single mind and heart.

Considering all that Reeve had gone through, an unusual, even-tempered quality permeates his book. He not only understood his predicament of being a quadriplegic, but was able to view it in an even, objective manner. One cannot help being in awe of Reeve's achievement.

His book was not a Pulitzer, but it was a winner in that it transmitted a very difficult narrative in a straightforward, lucid manner.

A great deal of Reeve's material had to come from those who helped him during his struggle. Think of all the chances to misinterpret and misunderstand, over-emotionalize, and rationalize. It would be easy to lose faith in human nature during such a time. It must have been difficult, but no more so than recovering from an injury of deadly proportions.

Christopher Reeve, the Superman hero of the movies, fractured two vertebrae. He was engaging in a riding competition on Memorial Day 1995, and as his horse began ascending a jump, Reeve said, "He just stopped." Reeve was thrown forward, coming down on his head. Reeve wrote, "I only fell a few feet, but I shattered my first cervical vertebra as I landed on the top rail of the jump."

His book is also a penetrating study of the human spirit. The battle lines were drawn in the book's first paragraph:

A few months after the accident I had an idea for a short film about a quadriplegic who lives in a dream. During the day, lying in his hospital bed, he can't move, of course. But at night he dreams that he's whole again and is able to do anything and go anywhere.

Reeve's childhood and adolescence produced a highly disciplined young man, his physique and disposition leading him into many athletic activities. "I never felt that I was courting danger, because I always stayed within my self-imposed limits. In all aspects of my life I enjoyed being in control, which is why my accident was a devastating shock not only to me but to everyone who knew me."

Upon learning how serious his condition was, he told his wife Dana, "Maybe we should let me go." She cried, but told him, "I am only going to say this once: I will support whatever you want to do, because this is your life and your decision. But I want you to know that I'll be with you for the long haul, no matter what. You're still you. And I love you."

Reeve recalled watching his wife when he talked about wanting to slip away:

> If she had looked away or paused or hesitated even slightly, or if I had felt there was a sense of her being—being what? —noble, or fulfilling some obligation to me, I don't know if I could have pulled through. Because it had dawned on me that I was going to be a huge burden to everybody, that I had ruined my life and everybody else's. Not fair to anybody. The best thing to do would be to slip away.

Christopher Reeve had not slipped away. His life prepared him for such a battle. He drew from his experiences to demonstrate the dimensions of his struggle.

One was his Broadway role as a Vietnam veteran in *Fifth of July* in which he had to learn to simulate walking on artificial legs. He played Ken Talley, a former teacher and soldier who is now a bilateral amputee. The research for *Fifth of July* took Reeve to a VA hospital where he was introduced to "the world of the disabled."

> A Vietnam vet named Mike Sulsona became my coach. In 1969 Mike was an eighteen-year-old soldier finishing his second tour of duty and scheduled to go home just one week later. Then he stepped on a mine that blew off both his legs.
>
> At first, I was awkward and self-conscious around him, but he put me at ease. He explained that before he went to 'Nam, he was a high school dropout hanging out on the street. Now he was married, the father of two children, and a budding playwright. The accident had given meaning to his life. He taught me how to stand up, sit down, and move like an amputee. Braces were made to keep my legs rigidly in place. I had to be especially careful not to move my toes and spoil the illusion.

Reeve describes one particular scene about his fear of falling backwards:

> One of a bilateral amputee's greatest fears is of falling backwards,

because the amputee has no way to protect the back or spinal cord. In Act II, a character bumps into Ken, and he falls straight back.
That scene produced unexpected results at every performance.
Even though the words were always the same, my experience was different every time. Sometimes I felt anger and denial. Then my attitude was: Don't help me, I don't need anybody. Sometimes I cried and would reach out for help. Sometimes I tried to pretend it hadn't happened.

The dialogue never changed; but you can say 'pass the salt' and load the words with any number of meanings, depending on what's happening within you.

Reeve's learning to act "in the moment," an acting term which means the opposite of planning in advance, served him well in his recovery.

His most anxious times occurred when he was alone. One particular image served him well at those times. Someone had sent him a picture postcard of a Mayan temple in Mexico, the Pyramid of Quetzalcoatl.

After reflecting on the card, he wrote:

There were hundreds of steps leading up to the top. And above the temple were blue sky and clouds. I taped this postcard to the bottom of the monitor where it was always in view. I let it become a metaphor for the future. Even as I watched all those sobering numbers on the screen, I began to imagine myself climbing those steps, one at a time, until finally I would reach the top and go into the sky.

Within his physical limitations, he has "climbed the steps." Most of us would say he was limited, but in the three years since his accident he had established a charitable foundation to enhance research on spinal cord injuries, testified before Congress on behalf of health insurance legislation, lobbied for increased federal funding for spinal cord research, directed the HBO film *In the Gloaming* which earned him an Emmy nomination, and delivered inspirational speeches to the Democratic National Convention and the Academy Awards. As the dust jacket of *Still Me* says, "The man who cannot move has not stopped moving."

Reeve learned to comprehend the realities of his life without ignoring

314

the power of the mind's inventions. In 1975 he was cast in the play *A Matter of Gravity*, opposite Katharine Hepburn. In it she (as grandmother) taught him (her grandson) how to see the differences and act on them:

> Hepburn often said to me, 'Be fascinating, Christopher, be fascinating.' That's easy for you to do; the rest of us have to work at it. But over the course of rehearsals, the out-of-town tryout, and the Broadway run, I learned that she was talking about unpredictability, about revealing contradictions. She told me that if you're playing a character who's usually drunk, you have to find moments of complete sobriety in order to add dimension to the role. Not even a chronic alcoholic is drunk all the time. And she talked about how important it is to bring your own life experience to the work. She once said, 'You are already real; the character is fiction. The audience must see your reality.'

Reeve does not shy away from the realities of his life as a quadriplegic:

> Until Memorial Day 1995, my body had never let me down. I thought I was pretty indestructible. But I had to be aware of my body all the time. I was forced to become a serious student of myself…
>
> Gradually I realized I had to learn to think of myself the way I used to think about a new hobby or a new sport. I had to be as disciplined about my body as I had been about learning to fly a plane, or sail a boat, or ride a horse. I had to understand exactly where I was now, and how I would be for the foreseeable future. How could I master my situation? Who would I become?

We all ask ourselves those questions, but Christopher Reeve was required to deal with them on a different level. His courage never failed him, and "Courage," as Sir Winston Churchill put it, "is rightly esteemed the first of human qualities… because it is the quality which guarantees all others."

Christopher Reeve died in 2004. His supportive wife died in 2006.

Cal Ripken, Jr.

When Cal Ripken, Jr., took his position for the Baltimore Orioles the 2632nd time without missing a game, he broke the record for most consecutive games played by a major-league baseball player. Somehow Ripken's extraordinary attendance is not the stuff out of which real records are made. But that is not the idea.

When was the last time you missed a day on the job? How many different reasons can you think of for missing work? How many days when you wanted to call in sick, but didn't? With all the distractions, how hard is it to focus on your job? Are you motivated toward your work, or away from it?

Translate those questions into the life of a baseball player. Other sports are more demanding of the body, but none as demanding of the mind. Baseball's pace can generate a dulling tedium that invites thinking about everything but the game. The distractions are everywhere – the fans, the press, the money people. Also, baseball action comes in spurts. Sometimes the time between pitches is enough to induce dozing.

But when the action comes, the nine players on the field had better have thought about the possibilities and their options. That is particularly true of infielders, especially shortstops. The longevity-casualty rate for shortstops is in a class with pitchers and catchers. Keeping the mind on the game and staying in tune with its rhythms are priorities for infielders, particularly shortstops.

That is not to say playing shortstop is not demanding physically. In fact, it is probably the most demanding of all positions, except for catching. Quick reflexes are needed to initiate movement, to bend for the ball, low and long, again and again, to be able to make an accurate throw.

If there is ballet in baseball, it is the melodious movements of a good shortstop. If you've never seen Ozzie Smith of the St. Louis Cardinals dance his way through a double play, or run half the distance between bases to field a ground ball and throw out a runner by two steps, then you've missed something of the art of the shortstop. Those runners, sliding into second base, spikes first, try to break up double plays. Baseball is demanding enough physically.

For the mind, the challenge is to stay focused. One of my favorite pastimes at Wrigley Field was watching Ryne Sandberg play second base.

How many balls are hit to the second baseman? As a percentage of at-bats, not too many. On every pitch he must be ready, ready for a smoking liner, a slow dribbler, the ground ball that is just out of reach to the left or to the right, or the Texas leaguer that could be caught. Because Sandberg's mind was on the possibilities and options, he seemed to get where he needed to be quicker and surer than others. He seemed to be able to reach ground balls others could not.

When Ripken readied his glove and positioned himself for that first pitch, he did it for the 2131st time without missing a beat. With all the demands of the game, to go 162 times over a seven-month period every year for fourteen years must take something out of him.

Back in the spring of 1988, the Orioles lost their first twenty-one games. Ripken went 0-29 at one time during this infamous team slump. His father, Cal Ripken, Sr., was fired as Orioles manager after the first six losses. It must have been difficult for Jr. to keep his mind on his work.

Playing 2131 games in a row takes more than simply showing up. Look at these facts: To date, Cal Ripken, Jr., has batted 8488 times and made 2348 hits for a batting average of .277. He has hit 323 homeruns and batted in 1249 runs. He was the winner of two American League Most Valuable Player Awards, in 1983 and 1991. He is the only player in major-league history to start twelve consecutive All-Star Games.

During his streak, Ripken played in 19,167 of the Orioles' 19,329 innings (99.2%). He once played in 8243 consecutive innings, beginning June 5, 1982, and ending Sept. 14, 1987. That's six seasons.

He made only three errors in 1990. A record for a shortstop.

In the fourteen years Ripken has played for the Orioles, the other major league teams have used a total of 525 shortstops.

He has played with thirty different Orioles' second basemen.

Ripken was never on the disabled list since he began playing professional baseball in 1978. Since his streak began, more than 3700 major-league players have gone on the disabled list.

Among other accomplishments, he demonstrated a determined and worthy work ethic. The record is "all the more remarkable at this moment in baseball history," says a *Chicago Tribune* editorial (9/7/95), "when seasons are longer, night games are common, coast-to-coast travel is frequent and grueling, and seductive salaries and player selfishness make Ripken's brand of devotion seem quaint." Ripken was in many ways like the rest of us, minus the notoriety.

New York Times columnist Claire Smith wrote that Ripken, Jr., "made history out of longevity." Many of the rest of us try to do so as well, but we do not receive awards, standing ovations, and the kind of money professional athletes receive.

I would never think to ask what Ripken's salary was. I have no idea. What did he think the key to his longevity was? He has been quoted as saying, "I always believed in a weird sort of way that if you play hard, you're always alert, you're always ready and that way you insulate yourself from problems."

The key to his success seems to be his attitude, his everyday desire, his work ethic. If ever a man earned his way, it was Cal Ripken, Jr.

Norman Rockwell

Remember those Norman Rockwell *Saturday Evening Post* covers? I've often wondered what it was about Norman Rockwell's work that generated almost immediate response from readers. I suspect it was the same things that appealed to the rest of us.

The *Post* cover (Dec. 29, 1956) graced the front of my room for years. It depicted a little boy in pajamas with his back to a dresser, the bottom drawer open. Hanging over the edge of the drawer was part of a red and white costume. Even if you've never seen the painting focused on the boy's face, you know the young man is learning the bitter truth about Santa Claus.

Most of us want to believe life is the way he painted it. All of us have certain corners and crevices in our psyches which allow for the way life could and should be. I understood that because my students let me know when they commented on things like "The Discovery." They were high school seniors contemplating their last Christmas before life's adventure took them away from the friendly confines of home.

The mind behind those paintings once discussed contemporary art with his son. Rockwell was pointing out how today "freedom has become license. There's no discipline anymore. There's not enough idealism. We're going after culture, but not as something that would help the country or the world but as something for ourselves, to satisfy our own little cravings." We pursue our agendas. Somehow society has gotten to the point where monetary well-being is more important than moral well-being. We're taking Christ out of Christmas. One of the most religious of observances is the most commercial.

For me, the lure of Rockwell was his clinging to values that seem fundamental to life, values we know we should be living by.

Fred Rogers

Fred Rogers was known to have very tough personal standards, his own and those pertaining to the quality of television, not only for his show.

An interviewer on ABC's *Nightline* asked him to be a guest on the late-night program. He declined because he had to speak to a kindergarten class the next morning, and he felt he had to be rested so he could give the children his full attention.

Will Rogers

The telegrams of the last days read as all of his other pieces did. They had a relaxed, off-the-cuff style with insights regularly popping out, his Oklahoma twang tending to mislead readers about the socially and politically attuned brain functioning behind it all.

Rogers' final, longer-than-normal telegram, published the day after he died on August 15, 1935, focused on the Matamuska Valley Colony in Alaska, designed to provide opportunity for families done in by the Great Depression:

> Plenty food and always has been and will be. They can always get that in, but it's homes they need right now and Colonel Hunt in charge realizes it (LeRoy Philip Hunt Sr., U.S. Marine Corps served as first director of the project).

Will Rogers' last sentence: "You know after all there is a lot of differences in pioneering for gold and pioneering for spinach." Will's clincher sentences seemed to clinch. They deposited reflection, insight, and lightness in one fell swoop. Here maybe was a touch of tragic irony.

Maybe Will wasn't always taken seriously because of that straight-arrow, civil approach spiced with a down-home tone and a signature lightness of spirit. A more serious political intellect would be hard to find. One can understand why the line "I never met a man I didn't like" has stuck. He lived by that idea.

Mike Royko

One of the easiest things to possess is an opinion. Though easy to have, they are not always easy to substantiate.

People whose business it is to express opinions publicly must possess certain characteristics and skills. Curiosity and persistence are two of them. Public developers of opinion should also be fair-minded and patient in their research. Two other important factors are a competence with the English language and a strong sense of civic responsibility.

Four of these traits are personal. Individuals develop them as they mature. The other two are learned through practice. It is a measure of success of our democratic society the degree to which we learn them. Civic responsibility in the hands of a competent practitioner of language can exert a broad influence.

On April 29, 1997, America lost one of its great journalistic exponents of these qualities. What made Royko effective was his ability to say socially valuable things in language that everyone understood. After reading one of his columns, you wanted to run right out and talk to someone.

If we could have peered into the Royko mind during his daily routines, we would have been impressed by how he went about choosing and directing his subjects. Having a private opinion is one thing; publishing it for millions to read is quite another. He thought what he had was instinct. So, we can add skeptical, tough, and courageous to our list of characteristics. Royko was original, authentic.

The *Denver Post* got it right when they once called him "baloney-proof." His aggressive, direct style caused him to write in a realistic, dramatic fashion. The following excerpts from his columns show how he marshaled language to make a subject stick:

Most countries don't have flag-burning laws, including such nationalistic societies as England, France and Japan. But I suppose that if you had wars fought in your front yard, back yard, and living room, you tend to shrug off minor irritants. (7/13/95)

We entered the Age of the Jerk sometime in the 1960s. That's when screamers decided they could dominate any public discussion, slobs decided that all the world was their litter box, and droolers began forcing this boom box noise on innocent ears. (3/3/95)

We're in trouble. Schools give diplomas to borderline illiterates; corporations hire them for 'service' jobs that should require at least an 8th grade grasp of fundamental English. And they are turned loose on the public. (2/9/96)

Mike Royko had an instinct for the gritty middle of a problem. He could express it in language Joe and Mary Public could understand. Columnist Clarence Page, whose office was near Royko's, said, "He used to say his job was simply to 'explain things.' That's like saying Duke Ellington's job was to play the piano."

At the end of the 1996 election campaign, Royko scolded national commentators for suggesting low voter turnout was a national disgrace:

Not me. I'm proud that in more than thirty years at this job I have never once urged people to vote or chided them for failing to do so.

My belief is that someone who must be nagged into voting hasn't been paying attention and doesn't have any idea what the issues are or what the candidates will or won't be trusted to do.

In other words, a civic klutz. So why is it important to the future of this nation for a klutz, or millions of klutzes, to punch holes in a ballot? Think about that. If you are the kind of thoughtful, involved person who really studies the issues and the candidates, do you want your vote canceled out by some klutz who doesn't even bother to say eenie, meenie, miney, mo?

Royko put the issues in terms everyone can understand. Readers may or may not have agreed. Whatever the problem, it was out in the open, discussable, debatable, and maybe even a step closer to solution. No preaching, no criticizing. Nobody wants to be a civic klutz, while in fact many of us are. Chalk up another, Mike.

Royko's was not the intelligence of the editorial ivory tower or the university research center. It was, rather, that of his resident hangout, a place called the Billy Goat Tavern on Chicago's Milwaukee Avenue, where working folks gather to talk things over.

His bar companion was Slats Grobnik, Mr. American Workingman and, as some insist, Mike Royko's alter ego. Grobnik is the embodiment of release that comes with an afternoon beer and camaraderie of friends.

A *Tribune* letter-to-the-editor (5/2/97) explained him this way:

Slats was…Mike Royko's other self: his regular guy persona with rough dirty hands, the guy with the 7 to 3:30 job trying to get by without getting squashed, yet a guy able to articulate a common sense philosophy without getting over-reflective or longwinded.

Mike Royko did a balancing act of a universal view and a neighborhood view. He seemed to be connecting all the levels and range of humanity. But always he was Chicago, the neighborhoods, Milwaukee Avenue.

Tribune columnist Mary Schmich sized up Mike Royko:

His was the world view of the ordinary guy unafraid of power and pretension, who leavened common sense with wit, who anchored wit with guts. Royko talked to you, not at you. He was a teacher but not a preacher. His aim was as straight as a ruler but he seldom rapped you on the wrists.

Royko's essence was a combination of personal qualities, civic responsibility, and the mastery of language. And always, conscience was at work. No matter how aggressively readers agreed or disagreed with a Royko's opinion, if they reflected on his underlying motive, more often than not, they found an honest attempt to right a wrong, topple an outrageous human foible, or eliminate silliness from the world.

How are we ever going to replace that huge gap on page three of the *Trib*? The *Albuquerque Journal* understood the importance of that question:

Newspaper columnists fall into five general categories. Those categories, in ascending order, are: 1. Bad. 2. Good. 3. Very good. 4. Outstanding. 5. Mike Royko. He is the best; God made only one Royko, and that's too bad.

Royko's writing is about the frustrations, joys, values, and predicaments that everyone goes through. (*San Francisco Chronicle*)

From the headlines, I learned the world was a serious place. From Royko, that I needed a little perspective. (*Tribune* letter, 5/1/97)

Royko had the righteousness of the best liberal and the skepticism of the best conservative. (*Tribune* editorial, 4/30/97)

Charles Schulz

Peanuts, Charles Schulz's famous cartoon strip, has been saying incisive, entertaining things about human nature for over fifty years. I am inspired to share a bit of my experience with Schulz and his work, and to point out how it enhanced my understanding and communication with my students.

As a teacher I continually tried to identify characteristics of my students. I noticed that certain traits and habits recurred regularly. So, I tried to recognize these traits as we became acquainted. Learning what makes students tick is important if you want to teach them anything.

These people patterns are handy, but they need to be made realistic and tangible so that you can see them in your mind's eye and thereby relate them to students. There are many devices for accomplishing this, but one of the best was Peanuts. The art of Charles Schulz was never far away. It spoke to me personally and still does. His characters are real in the sense that they are consistent in their personality patterns.

Life dilemmas take on dimensions of childhood. Or is it the dimensions of childhood take on life's dilemmas? It simply seems natural to accept these children on adult terms. Schulz has figured out how to make the line between child and adult very thin. He understands we all have the child in us still. One of the Peanuts characters can zap a problem in four frames and one cool punch line.

Schulz's humor encourages civility. No violence; no crude, demeaning language; no off-color humor. We identify with the characters because they are people we know. For example, I recognize Charlie Brown. He wants to be liked so much that he bores people. He doesn't mean to be naïve – he is trying to learn. Then, when he makes the same mistake again, and again, I not only recognize him but I find he is many of my high school seniors. He is also me.

But Lucy is perfect, anyone can see that. Her heart is subordinate to her mouth. I always wondered how many others she cheated out of learning because of her toxic tongue. However, she can be understanding.

Linus is not perfect, but he has a well-rounded personality. He is typical of eighteen-year-olds, bright but innocent. He says high-minded things and reminds me of Don Quixote. I always feel Linus is a metaphor for the maturing process. Try. Fail. Try again, but don't embarrass us.

Peppermint Patty is a primal boomer. She is independent and wants what she wants – now. She speaks out no matter what the consequences. Did you ever notice that she and Lucy seldom meet? Maybe "like" poles do not attract.

Schroeder is a musician and an athlete. It seems incongruous he can play Beethoven and can be a baseball catcher. He does both. He is not ready for girls.

Sally doesn't know what is going on and is too demanding for her good. How can Charlie Brown be her brother? She inherited all of her family's gall.

Don't you wish all students were like Marcie? Yes and no. Yes, she is intelligent and cooperative. No, I never cared for students whose eyes I could not catch and hold. And she says "sir" all of the time.

Snoopy is a real person in disguise. He is innocent, but proud. He'll satisfy anyone's alter ego. He knows his bounds but is always looking for a chance to race his imagination. He has a few hero-worshippers, but they watch from a distance. He is an everyman. He loses more than he wins, tries more than he gives up, and really wants to succeed.

Occasionally, Charlie Brown and Linus have philosophical discussions, dozens of these discussions over the almost fifty years. One in particular seems to typify the dilemma of adolescence. In the first frame the two are pictured thoughtfully leaning on their elbows over a stone wall. I've often wondered why it is a stone wall. Charlie Brown says, "Perhaps you can give me an answer, Linus."

In frame two, Charlie asks Linus, "What would you do if you felt that no one liked you?" The next picture has the two facing each other with Linus replying, apparently rather eagerly and definitely, "I'd try to look at myself objectively, and see what I could do to improve… that's my answer, Charlie Brown."

In the last frame, both are looking at us across the wall again, with Charlie Brown stating rather emphatically, "I hate that answer!" How many times have students looked at me and thought that, I do not know. But it is at that point that communication and teaching commence.

Albert Schweitzer

Finally I read *Out of My Life and Thought*, Albert Schweitzer's autobiography. His words are full of thoughts about life and its decisions and about hard and direct reasoning aimed at the dilemmas which lie between the ideal and reality. Those decisions we all face to one extent or another.

Anyone who considers Schweitzer from a distance certainly wonders how he made his decision to give up the academic life of Europe for the life of a general medical practitioner in the African Congo.

He was driven by a desire to help humanity on the most immediate, basic level. He had been teaching, writing, and preaching for some years. Then he began medical school at age 30. His reason seems to be reflected in these sentences:

> I wanted to be a doctor that I might be able to work without having to talk. Anyone who has gone through the process of justifying his work in terms of humanity knows how this works. I had been giving myself out in words. It was with joy that I had followed the calling of theological teacher and preacher. By this new form of activity, I could not represent to myself as being talking about the religion, but only as an actual putting it into practice.

My experience with this dilemma has worked in different ways. As a teacher, I was doing a good deal of talking about reading and writing, but I was not truly practicing them. Remember George Bernard Shaw's infamous line, "Those who can, do; those who cannot, teach."

Now I am practicing these skills as a major priority, and I keep looking back and thinking I am no longer serving and practicing what I am writing about. Oh, the dilemmas between the ideal and the real.

Frank Sinatra

"Old Blues Eyes is gone." Those were my first words upon hearing the news. Some significant segments of my life are affected by the passing of Frank Sinatra. As one of a number of elder entertainers who added substance and meaning to my growing up, he understood the profound influence he was having on many of our lives.

One journalist wrote, "The generation that came of age during World War II embraced Sinatra, and his music became the accompaniment for their lives." For over half of the twentieth century, he sang away our blues and helped us celebrate life's upbeats.

Right from the beginning, Frank Sinatra was personal in my life. He was all I could never be ... talented and appealing. He was blessed with a voice that was natural, strong and rich, and he did my singing for me.

He understood what I was going through – at eighteen, at twenty-one, at thirty-five, at sixty, and still. He was singing songs the way they were meant to be sung. Sinatra could sing anything that had quality. That is why he was hip or cool to every generation for whom he performed.

Sinatra began recording about the time I achieved adolescence. I was interested in music but was never a musician. My first experience with popular music was the big bands and their recordings. Somehow adolescence forces the findings of outlets for the many feelings associated with "adolescing," and music is a major one.

Band leader Tommy Dorsey was noted for his ability to find good musicians, good arrangers, and then evolve marvelous combinations. When Sinatra became Dorsey's lead vocalist, he was often blended with a trio called the Pied Pipers, two male voices and one female. The woman was Jo Stafford, who later became a hit-producing vocalist herself.

I remember many of the Sinatra-Pied Pipers collaborations: *Stardust*, *There Are Such Things*, *Street of Dreams*, *Once in a While*. These were the last dark days of the Depression and the ominous early stage of World War II. The ballad I recall best, and Sinatra's first No.1 single, was *I'll Never Smile Again.*

These Dorsey-Sinatra ballads were a temporary elixir, a stay against the chemistry of growing up in a crucial period of history. I was unsure and naïve, so I often retired with my 78 rpm records, among which were vocals by this young man whose voice somehow made the pangs of puberty more tolerable. I related easily to *Be Careful, It's My Heart*; *Everything Happens to Me*; *Do I Worry?*; *We Three (My Echo, My Shadow, and Me)*; *Night and Day*; *The Things I Love*.

I underwent a number of "from-a-distance" affairs during those years. Sinatra recorded *I've Got a Crush on You* a couple of years after I finished high school. I recall wishing he had done that sooner. I also wondered why I couldn't be like the person behind the voice in *All or Nothing at All*.

Without a Song and *The Song Is You* linger as testimonials to the importance music was assuming in my life. I figured out that Frank Sinatra was something special, something about his voice and the way he conveyed a lyric that penetrated to the core of consciousness. He almost became part of one's psyche.

I collected records with abandon during my college years. Those red-label Columbia's that said, "Vocal by Frank Sinatra, arranged and conducted by Axel Stordahl," were numerous: *S'posin'*. I did a lot of that. *Body and Soul* was not simply a Sinatra song. It was a cry for compassion. *I Guess I'll Have to Dream the Rest* followed my July 1950 draft notice.

My only real love affair was with the woman who became my wife. But our marriage got off to a rocky start, through no fault of ours. Thanks to Uncle Sam, we spent only two of our first twenty-five months together. I spent the next two years at a job for which I was thoroughly unsuited.

It seemed that during this time Sinatra was singing songs that measured the meter of my bewilderment. *They Can't Take That Away from Me* and *All of Me* seemed to have my initials on their dedications.

I Could Write a Book. I can hear the mellow Sinatra laying out the lyrics which caught the spirit of the first years of our family.

When I came out of service the second time, Sinatra began his career with Capitol Records. He recorded songs that were upbeat, uplifting. It was the only time I had trouble relating to his tunes. Apparently, he was going through a happy time. I know I was struggling. *Young at Heart, I Get a Kick Out of You*, and *I've Got the World on a String* were marvelous, and they probably helped a little.

These were hard years. My life lacked direction. I was discouraged, and I had little time or money to collect records. Now, seven decades later, if I had to choose one Sinatra song (which is almost impossible), it would probably be *I've Got the World on a String*.

327

But then came my life's turnaround. I was almost thirty, that age which, a decade later, would become the "all-washed-up" age. You know, "don't trust anyone over thirty." I became a teacher. From the start I loved it. Two women in my life made it possible, and my metaphorical turn of mind assigned Sinatra songs to them. They were my wife Beverly, *Someone to Watch Over Me*, and my student-teaching supervisor, Miss Edythe Daniel, *Too Marvelous for Words*.

Both of these comforting renditions came out during this crucial period. In fact, radio stations began playing *Too Marvelous for Words* when I was halfway through my student-teaching semester with eighth graders. I didn't have time to pursue my musical interests for a number of years. But every once in a while, a Sinatra tune struck close to home.

One of the most popular was *All the Way*. It became a kind of metaphor for my teaching and its dreams. It was released in the fall of 1957, as I began my first full year of teaching in Osseo, Wisconsin.

Before we moved to Lake Geneva in 1958, *Come Fly with Me* appeared to be a justification for moving a family of six 225 miles.

My first high school seniors at Badger High (1959) graduated as *High Hopes* was released. Sinatra was a kind of punctuation to what I was doing in my classroom. When he formed his recording company, Reprise, his music took on new dimensions. Some of those popular tunes seemed tailored to the detail of professional life.

The year I took on more activity than I should have (1960-61), there was *On the Sunny Side of the Street*. The year I grew the fastest in my teaching (1963-64), there was *The Best Is Yet to Come*.

As the turbulence of the 1960's took its turns, I could not help being introspective, wondering what was to happen next. *But It Was A Very Good Year* (1965).

As I learned to understand students better, I felt teaching had become an elixir of youth. *You Make Me Feel So Young* (1966).

When *My Way* came out in the late-60's, I woke up to how important it is to have confidence. The tune became the theme for a generation.

This progression of Sinatra songs and performances continued, right up to 1996, which begs the questions: How can one artist maintain a level of general popularity for over fifty years? How can appeal persist even through the evolving of generations? What does Sinatra do to songs that makes them consistently touching and authentic?

He took lyrics which otherwise seemed mediocre, shaped them, and made them his songs. The fact that he did not read music seems to have liberated him. He lent his style and interpretation. In fact, Sinatra seems a lesser singer when he is not improvising. His fashioning of lyrics made them his – and mine. He seemed to sing to and for me.

Sinatra did little things to seal his relationship with audiences. He always mentioned the composers of songs he sang. It indicates that Sinatra was serving the music and his listeners. He also insisted on only the best supporting musicians. His arrangers and conductors read like a who's who of quality maestros. In addition to Axel Stordahl, there were Nelson Riddle, Billy May, Don Costa, Gordon Jenkins, and Quincy Jones.

Sinatra made his audiences comfortable because his gestures, body language, and his discerning, mischievous eyes were intended for them, and they recognized this friendly aura of confidence and cool.

But Frank Sinatra was not without his faults. There was his Rat Pack reputation, his connections with Mafia figures, his multiple marriages, his fights and often feisty stubbornness, the improper-appearing influence on two U.S. presidents, and the unforgiving force of his ego. Even his recurrent retirements became tiring.

I for one have learned to be tolerant of the idiosyncrasies and off-beat habits of geniuses. Their powers and the cost of their service to society are not really such a burden. Fifty years from now, in the case of Sinatra, only "The Voice" will be remembered.

Mike Singletary

Is it possible for me in my ninth decade to still have heroes? You bet it is. We have seventy-year-olds who have more experience, thereby having more by which to measure current experience. Besides, who says we can't think young?

Several recent occurrences have caused reflection on Mike Singletary, the famous, former Chicago Bear linebacker. Singletary, the man, as well as Singletary, the football great, was about-to-be Hall of Famer.

These "occurrences" brought back reasons why I believe that playing middle linebacker is about as demanding a job as there is in football, requiring mental alertness as well as a tough physical constitution.

The first of these events was the January announcement of Singletary's election to the NFL Hall of Fame. He was chosen in his first year of eligibility, having entered the league in 1981 with such other notable defensive stars as Lawrence Taylor, Ronnie Lott, Howie Long, and E.J. Junior.

Singletary's statistics are impressive. Voted most valuable defensive player in 1985 and 1988, he missed only two games in twelve years. He made 1488 tackles in his career, 885 of them solos. That averages out to eight per game, almost five single tackles per game. In playoffs, he made eighty-three tackles, thirty-eight solos. Singletary was voted to ten straight Pro Bowls and was All-Pro eight times.

The second event was the death of Ray Nitschke, the former Green Bay Packer middle linebacker and Hall-of-Famer. That has generated talk about other great linebackers. New York Giant Sam Huff was certainly partly responsible for creating the position.

But the great tradition of middle linebackers is a Chicago Bear story. Bill George and Dick Butkus established an act which would have been hard for anyone to follow, but Mike Singletary followed it and became the acknowledged team leader when the Bears made the Super Bowl in 1986. Tough, single-minded defensive coach Buddy Ryan said Singletary was "the leader of the Bears, no question about that, on both sides of the ball."

But Mike Singletary was only 5'11" and weighed 228 pounds, not big by NFL linebacker standards. But dogged determination led to durability. Teammate Gary Fencik, who despite his size was known as a tough hitter, said recently Singletary "willed" himself to play every down.

He was smart, prepared, a hard hitter. Randy Cross, who played on three San Francisco 49er championship teams and is quoted as saying, "He was one of these guys who wasn't really big, but he knew how to explode right on contact."

Singletary had a reputation for alarming opponents. His nickname "Samurai Mike" demonstrates something about his style. He is said to have even shouted out plays the opposition was going to run – he was that familiar with other teams' offenses. You could say he was what good linebackers must be – masters of organizing confusion.

A caption under a picture in a special *Tribune* section during Super Bowl week in '86, demonstrates how Singletary's energy could sometimes

backfire: "Bear linebacker Mike Singletary screams 'Samurai stuff' at offenses and was penalized for unsportsmanlike conduct at Green Bay for
screaming at himself after a complete pass."

Singletary was intense, his mind always on the game. Anyone who
watches NFL football on television remembers those shots across the line
of scrimmage at those fierce and furious eyes.

Singletary learned to expect a great deal of himself. Growing up in a
Houston ghetto and constantly told he was not good enough to play, he developed a discipline and a determination that would not be denied. Singletary himself said, "More than anything else, I was just a player who
made the most of his ability."

He was a good but not superior athlete. He wasn't a first-round draft
choice (second in 1981). He was able to turn some tough "nots" into "why
nots." But curiously, despite being surrounded by great athletes, everything gravitated to Singletary. As his position coach for seven years, Dave
McGinnis remarked, "He was the focal point."

He was the inspirational leader of the Bears. He has also been called
"the team's conscience." Mike Singletary played with his heart as well as
with his body and mind. Mike Singletary – the tough gentleman, or should
it be the gentle tough guy? In a 1986 Super Bowl cover story, *Time* suggested that Singletary appeared "strangely civilized out of uniform."

Football is a game that strains the extremes of the human persona.
That brings me to the third of recent occurrences. Mike Singletary had another side too. It was his humanity.

One time, he heard a radio report that Bear player Alonzo Spellman,
who has a history of personal adjustment problems, was in his publicist's
home and would not come out. Singletary drove there and after several
hours convinced Spellman he needed help, and a crisis was averted, at
least for the moment.

Singletary and Spellman were teammates for only one year, but Singletary has remained a loyal Bear supporter and holds moral high ground
when it comes to his former team. He earned that because of his conduct
off the field as well as on.

Occurrence number four. A couple of days after the Spellman incident the *Tribune* carried dates for three book signings Singletary was holding. I began to think I should go. I called my musician son, but he had a

rehearsal scheduled.

At the last minute, I decided I should attend. It is not hard to spend hours in a Borders bookstore, so I drove to Deerfield early so I could look at CDs and books, keeping an eye on the line forming.

Book signings, especially with celebrities, are not exactly private affairs. After talking to a few people in line, my turn finally came. With a hundred pairs of eyes on me, I walked up to the seated Singletary, shook his hand, and said, "You are a courageous man."

What came next was so much drivel. I could not think of anything original. In fact, I couldn't think of anything.

After he signed my two books, he rose, and we shook hands again. I looked him squarely in the eyes and he did the same, but "courageous" was the best I could do. I nodded, turned, and left. But I felt good. My years were telling me I had met a good man.

Jimmy Stewart

Jimmy Stewart was part of my youth, and he followed me into adulthood. Of all the movie stars of the last eighty years, his was the marvelous persona that penetrated my spirit. He was the neighbor down the block, the friend always within reach. He accepted his style, his fragilities, and so did the rest of us.

The *Chicago Tribune's* tribute caught the essence of the man. No matter what part he played, he "will always be the vulnerable hero, the brace and folksy dreamer, the stammering romantic, the man not afraid to cry." He was like our friends and neighbors, and he brought the world out into our local theaters.

I remember well his first film *Mr. Smith Goes to Washington* (1939). As an idealistic twelve-year-old, I thought what an adventure the nation's capitol must be. George Bailey in *It's a Wonderful Life* (1946) reminded me of the people in my hometown of Fennimore, WI.

The tragic story of baseball pitcher Monty Stratton (1949) and *Harvey* (1950) seemed a sort of summary of my years at the University of Wisconsin-Madison with its handicaps and delusions.

Stewart was convincing as the lead in *The Glenn Miller Story* (1954), and he played the hero of my birth year, Charles Lindbergh, in *The Spirit of St. Louis* (1957). The movie adaptation of *Anatomy of a Murder* (1959) was released as I was beginning my teaching career.

In all of these films, Jimmy Stewart was the same honest, homey person, while convincing in a wide array of roles. I doubt I saw more than a dozen of his seventy-five movies, but I saw him at his best; and like a good friend, he was consistent in most all his roles.

I can't think of another actor who was always himself as he was portraying different characters. The Stewart persona became the character; the believability he brought to an astonishing variety of roles was incredible. He brought us his characters through his character.

Jimmy Stewart will be a metaphor for the age in which he lived. He was true hero of the hero generation. He was true-blue Stewart in everything he did. I never met him, but I feel I've known him all my life.

E.B. White

E.B. White was a kindred spirit who followed me through my professional life. I didn't know his work as well as I should have. I knew him by reputation, and in that process, something grew through to me and took seed, to grow and regrow every academic year. It was as though I knew him. He was that dependable professional writer who worked by standards, whose sentences were fashioned of sweat, rules, and integrity, ever glowing with what the rest of us wished was happening to us.

With style and class, he stood for what we all know language can and should be. Now don't tell me he was not a kindred spirit. His little book entitled *Elements of Style* could never pass as the great and comprehensive solver of language problems, but it was a sign of what could happen if you allowed the process to take hold. It led to habits, good habits. It led to consistency, predictability in language use, which is good because then language, the tool, becomes the constant and ideas become variable.

But a discipline is involved. On page 49 of "the little book," a section called "Misused words and expressions" targets the word "hopefully."

This once-useful adverb meaning 'with hope' has been distorted and is now widely used to mean 'I hope' or 'it is hoped.' Such use is not merely wrong, it is silly. To say, 'Hopefully I'll leave on the noon plane' is to talk nonsense. Do you mean you'll leave on the noon plane in a hopeful frame of mind? Or do you mean you hope you'll leave on the noon plane? Whichever you mean, you haven't said it clearly. Although the word in its new, free-floating capacity may be pleasurable and even useful to many, it offends the ear of many others, who do not like to see words dulled or eroded, particularly when erosion leads to ambiguity, softness, or nonsense.

That is pure White. He knew, as I learned to know and some students came to know, that as language is directed and refined, so thought is focused and expressed. He knew that words which do not contribute to that process are excess sound and take up space as clutter, as this last verb phrase does. What does "take up space as clutter" say that "excess sound" does not.

One of the most serious of writing problems is wordiness. In drafting anything, the mind focuses on ideas, so that sentences tend to be over worded and exaggerated. As a teacher, I knew the cause nine out of ten times to be first-draft syndrome. Students simply refused to reread and revise first drafts. Turn it in, as is. The student does not think enough of his ideas to see them through allowing the orderly process to take place. There is nothing automatic about it. It is voluntary and entirely conscious. So, having a good idea is only part (a small part) of it. The key to successful writing is how the whole process is carried out. Eventually some parts of the process become automatic, at least easier, but every good idea required diligence and discipline.

Now do you see how E.B. White is a kindred spirit?

One final word. And that word is "finalize." In discussing the adopting of coinages too quickly, White says, "...the writer will discover in the course of his work that the setting of a word is just as restrictive as the setting of a jewel. The general rule here is to prefer the standard. "Finalize," for instance, is not standard; it is special, and it is a peculiarly fuzzy and silly word. Does it mean "terminate," or does it mean "put in final form"? One can't be sure really what it means, and one gets the impression that the person using it doesn't know either, or doesn't want to know."

Slapping "ize" on any noun does not necessarily make it a useful verb. Words without a history of use and acceptance will have difficulty communicating clearly. Verbs ending in "ize" are common. When they become established, their meanings settling precisely, they become useful words; but with no purpose other than a laziness which keeps the writer from looking for a more precise verb, then the magic of man's unique ability to communicate is diminished.

Bringing students to the acceptance and practice of this discipline is difficult, chancy at best. You can see why I valued a kindred spirit.

Ted Williams

Ted Williams, the last to hit over .400 in a season (1941), could put a bat on a ball with more authority than most any other player. I sat in the Wrigley Field stands in 1947 when he and a batch of future Hall-of-Famers played in the All-Star game. Joe DiMaggio, Stan Musial, and the like. But when the "Splendid Splinter," who could uncannily eye a pitch earlier than other hitters, went into that longsome, graceful swing, it was a sight to behold—even when he missed.

I used to dream about that swing. I saw Williams over and over again in the theater newsreels, and it is no wonder his lifetime batting average was .344. I recall his loping gait as he rounded the bases, running out some of his 521 homers. He took running bases seriously, even though he was not quick afoot.

Homerun hitters today don't vigorously run out four-base hits. In fact, it strikes me that they often traverse the 120 circuit in ways calculated to indicate achievement. But running out a homer signals the hitter is all business. It's over in a hurry, so the next hitter can take advantage of the breakdown in the pitcher's concentration and continuity. Ted Williams will always be remembered for that kind of on-the-field seriousness.

He once said that making a rounded bat hit a round ball squarely is the hardest skill in sports. Williams, who never claimed to be a homerun hitter, hit 521 of them while carrying out his normal routine hitting duties.

As he was settling into his prime, his career was interrupted by service in World War II (1943-45). Then in the early 1950s, he missed most of two more seasons to serve in Korea. He returned to the game each time as though nothing had happened. Had he played those five full seasons, maybe he would have had another .400 average. There's no telling how many homeruns he would have hit.

I have trouble thinking of Ted Williams without considering how the game has changed. Baseball is the national pastime, though it may not always be in the form of major leagues as we know them now. How would Ted Williams fit into the game today? With his unusual and sometimes problematic behavior, he probably would not be as disciplined and directed as he was then. He was of a generation that forced personal discipline. His development as a hitter certainly was enhanced by this social necessity of the times.

Think of today's social forces, not known for encouraging self-discipline. For example, salaries that are not in proportion to talent. The average annual major league salary is two million dollars or $12,300 per game. I don't care how good any player is, $26,000,000 for a 162-game season is a ludicrous mis-assignment of priorities.

Then there was team loyalty. Williams played his entire career with the Boston Red Sox. Though Boston fans and he were not always on the same page, the loyalty was unquestioned. Trading players almost randomly was unheard of.

How many competent fielders are there in today's game? How many players think the game as they are playing it? As TV cameras pan dugouts, it is easy to see that concentration is often not on the game.

I can see why he left the game early. Those around him were not of the same dedication. Team effectiveness became something less than it should be, and the hope of improving was slight. Discouragement was bound to set in. After all, he was playing in the major leagues with the cream of the talent who should be fully engaged in the game.

Yes, Ted Williams' leaving has triggered thought about the game. Where are the students of the game today? *Boston Globe* columnist Bob Ryan shed some light on the success of this famous Hall-of-Famer:

Williams studied hitting as if he had been assigned to the Manhattan Project. It is frightening to think what he could have been in the years of videotape, because he was so far ahead of everyone in his day simply by using his five senses. Nothing about either hitting or pitching escaped him, and nothing was deemed too trivial. He studied pitchers, umpires, and wind patterns.

Players were students of the game. Dugouts were often observation posts and strategy camps. Imagine the information Williams passed to teammates.

Baseball is a much more interesting, profound game than it appears. Certainly, it was for this fan, and there is some pain in seeing it in decline.

Frank Lloyd Wright

At age seventy, his greatest adventure, his Taliesin experiment in teaching architecture, was only becoming known. Some of his greatest work was done in the twenty years after age seventy.

Frank Lloyd Wright was a fascinating man. His autobiography is a marvel of singular experience. It is probably not the way the world sees (or saw) him, but I have to say one thing: his private life is marvelously consistent. Others could have not seen that in their relationships with him. He stood on very high ground, from which he observed in a creative and objective way. Others saw an individual who stood above them, and to some the higher ground seemed like dominance.

He used the autobiographical format to his ends. For example, his account of the tower, the famous Romeo and Juliet windmill, does the telling. It was a naturally awkward stance for a writer doing autobiography to be a third person and try to make himself convincing. That did not keep his account from making an impression, however.

When a person like Wright is right most of the time and is effectively vocal to boot, he is going to alienate a great number of people. Sometimes it is difficult to knuckle under to a bright and right peer. His inherent and persistent logic overwhelms, and it is difficult to tend one's affairs without becoming entangled in his.

People in his position need to be even-tempered and fair-minded. But that is difficult because they see so much of the illogical and unreasonable in things. In fact, they are experts at spotting inconsistencies, because their minds are clear and practiced at logic and reason.

I'm sure the world's geniuses will go right on being misunderstood, much as Frank Lloyd Wright was. Almost as long as I've known the name, my fascination with Frank Lloyd Wright has persisted. Growing up, I heard tales of Taliesen and what went on there. The extraordinary genius with an ego to match ran a school in practical architecture.

I recall one or two family Sunday drives that took us near the wondrous structure built into a Wisconsin River bluff near Spring Green. There was always talk of scandal, wild dreams, and unpaid bills. I don't think I understood at the time. All I remember was the fascination with the mind that dreamed up all of this.

Wright's mother wanted her son to be an architect even before he was born. Imagine the powerful influence this desire must have had on him, to be ordained an architect before birth. All of the influence a mother could bring to bear was with the idea that her son was to be an architect.

Did Wright ever document his recipe for learning? What did he expect of the process? What did he think of the education of his day?

I have always thought a boy was sent to school to find out about himself... (for) the proper study of mankind is man...(but) when he goes to school, he's left to find out about himself as best he can. It's not in the course, it's not in the curriculum. He is conditioned rather than enlightened. The enlightenment is left for him to get, somehow, as he can... It costs a lot to achieve enlightenment by experience. I don't know that there is a short cut. I don't know that culture could do it. But if culture and education were on speaking terms today, there might be some hope.

Our educational system has let the country down and has not given to the youth of America the sense of American freedom. What it is to be American.

The way we get our teachers is ghastly, unbelievable – especially the teachers of architecture. A teacher should be somebody, should have achieved something.

I did not write that. Wright did. But I could have.

On Democracy

I grew up with the idea that democracy is not something you believe in, or a place you hang your hat, but it's something you do. You participate. If you stop doing it, democracy crumbles and falls apart.
Abbie Hoffman

The greatest blessing of our democracy is freedom.
But in the last analysis, our only freedom is the freedom
to discipline ourselves.
Bernard Baruch

Principles of democracy have inspired me throughout my personal and professional life. My readings, writings, and teaching celebrated my dedication and delight for living in a democracy. While I worry often that we citizens forget the lives lost and lessons learned in the history of our democracy, I remain hopeful that our balances of power over the years will keep our democracy vibrant.

CONTENTS

Evolution of Democracy
Participatory Democracy
What Democracy Requires
Candidates for Leadership in a Democracy
On Committees

Evolution of Democracy

I was an adolescent during the Depression and World War II. As a father of five children, as a grandfather of seven children, and as a great grandfather of eight children, I cannot help being alarmed by how world affairs and particularly events in this country are inclining.

As a democracy, we are committed to aiding nations fighting dictatorships and other forms of oppressive behavior. Our economy and the technology have given us more than anyone could have dreamed possible fifty years ago.

We are the most powerful nation on earth. Our heritage and the democracy which has grown with it are the envy of the world.

The personal freedom we have inherited and which many Americans fought and died for, has brought us miraculous opportunities for personal growth and service. The results of these opportunities have produced many individuals who have given themselves to serving others in such areas as medicine, the ministry, teaching, research, human services, organizations like the Peace Corps, world relief groups, the Red Cross, and many humanitarian organizations.

These organizations are products of the freedom which is our birthright. These people have accepted responsibility, which, of course, is the other side of freedom's coin.

Some of us are not accepting the responsibilities that accompany citizenship. In many cases, we are not even learning the basic tenets of American democracy. When it comes to history, most of us need to know more of our history in order to appreciate our given rights and responsibilities.

Participatory Democracy

One day, out of the ubiquity that is the media, a voice rendered the following: "Democracy is slipping away from us because we are no longer participants."

That statement has stuck with me. At first, it seemed invalid, though provocative. Well, it's still provocative, but, unfortunately, it is true. In our liberty we are becoming independently but unwisely detached from our institutions. Those institutions, free to solve society's problems, often without citizen consensus, take a little more of our liberty, by default.

This trend is especially noticeable in the electoral process. How can we can elect a president with less than a majority of the votes and, at the same time, acknowledge that less than half the electorate voted?

Isn't there something of a millennial tension and discomfort in the idea that the potential of the Internet may be at the disposal of people who could wish for nothing better than wreaking havoc on others from the privacy of their residence?

Institutions – families, schools, government, community, services, corporations – are no longer the objects of our loyalty and service. We seem to believe we can survive by our ingenuity and energy.

How long can participatory democracy serve under such conditions? Oh, I can hear you now, "As long as the economy stays strong...." Anyone who understands the economic system under which this society functions, knows it will not always be strong, and that it only takes some event of uncertain significance to destroy the balance that is the economy in a democracy. On Wall Street the people who make it work do not always appreciate and understand the reality of the lives of those whose money they so nimbly and impetuously juggle.

Our liberties have taken us in such diverse and seemingly irretrievable directions that one cannot help speculating where it is we are heading. The fact that it is hard for Americans to speak with a single voice anymore will someday be significant, if it isn't already.

We acted singularly in World War II because another nation practically destroyed our navy one Sunday morning. Most Americans knew that hideous things were going on in Europe and Asia, but we were not of a mind to try to stop them. Not until someone struck us in the back.

Is such an attack unlikely today? Yes, maybe in those forms, but what about the bevy of nations that don't like the idea that only five nations are allowed nuclear weapons? What about groups who try to terrorize others into submitting to their demands?

But the real dangers for our participatory democracy come from within. Have we gained our economic advantage at the expense of others? As an open society, do we really welcome immigrant peoples? Are we using some of the immense wealth generated by the current economy to solve social problems that always seem to grow more serious? Are we bending every effort to see to it that children are provided the means to an adequate education?

341

Are we still capable of speaking with one voice? Or must we undergo a catastrophic event before we comprehend? Robert W. Hutchinson, an outstanding educator of the twentieth century, described the elements of this dilemma: "The death of democracy is not likely to be an assassination from ambush. It will be a slow extinction from apathy, indifference, and undernourishment."

What Democracy Requires
I am indebted to my thoughtful friend Vern Stephan for reminding me of a process which is important to every American. It operates out of sight and out of mind for most of us most of the time. Vern's reminder was that a democratic society must be worked at, even slaved at.

Years ago, around election time, Vern wrote a brief letter to the editor of the *Lake Geneva Regional News*. What prompted it was low voter turnout in the November election. He quoted professor Alexander Taylor:

A democracy cannot exist as a permanent vote of government. It can exist until voters discover that they can vote themselves largesse (excessive gratuities) from the public treasury. From that moment on the majority always votes for the candidates promising the most benefits from the public treasury, with the result that a democracy always collapses over loose fiscal policy, always followed by a dictatorship.

The average age of the world's greatest civilizations has been two hundred years. These nations have progressed through the following sequence: From bondage to spiritual faith; from spiritual faith to great courage; from courage to liberty; from liberty to abundance; from abundance to selfishness; from selfishness to complacency; from complacency to apathy; from apathy to dependency; and from dependency back again to bondage.

Now this issue would only be of passing interest had it been written today. But it was composed over two hundred years ago when America was still thirteen British colonies. Our crowded and stressed lives are overwhelmed by details. We are allowed to see a lot of trees, but not the forest. The specifics of our days drown the plans of our lives. We need to be reminded

342

that democracy requires effort to maintain the balance between freedom and responsibility.

Democracy does require effort, sometimes even slavish effort, but most of the time it is as simple as honoring the ballot box.

It is easy to forget that each day we are helping to fashion the past… our history. It's a short trip from greed to complacency to apathy to dependency. Bondage could be but a ballot away.

Candidates for Leadership in a Democracy
In an ad for a PBS program about the presidential election, several citizens were making short comments. One of them was a gentleman who kind of swept into a closeup pose and said in a matter-of-fact tone, "If God had intended us to vote, he would have given us candidates." The sentence stuck. I heard it three days ago, but it is sticking.

We can assume that the candidates are no different from schools in their relationship to society. Society produces both. The qualities of both reflect society. It is no secret that both are letting us down.

The reasons are no secret either. As a nation, we simply do not want vigorous, intelligent leadership. We also do not want superior education. I don't think effective leadership will be directed from heaven any more than I think effective schools will.

Maybe a little guidance wouldn't hurt, but we the citizenry will improve schools and candidates. It means looking at both as though they were essential. It means shifting some priorities. How can we have a vigorous, stable economy without understanding it and being a lot less self-serving? How will social equity occur without intelligent perspective about humanity and the ever-more-crowded planet on which we live? Effective leaders will help us answer these questions.

How will we get those leaders? From an intelligent, well-educated citizenry. Being cynical about elections and their candidates will not yield worthwhile ends. We must do something more substantial.

No one from above will give us candidates. Effective education will not just happen. We all know what to do, but it requires focus, leadership, and a marshaling of what we know to be the best in us. A democratic society depends on its citizens to bring freedom and responsibility into balance.

On Committees

It is doubtful this republic could function without committees. If we are to live by democratic principles, there must be consent, at least majority consent. That means people must work together and agree together. Maybe not unanimously, but so majority is served.

I am a faithful and abiding citizen, but something about committees bothers me. How are committee members chosen? I would also like to know whether committees made up of hand-raising volunteers fared as well as those appointed by individuals or by other committees.

I've served on committees which I was certain were appointed by people who knew that a judiciously chosen group could reach a predetermined objective. Someone wanted something done, but needed consent, at least of the majority of a committee. Usually a force on a committee has done all it can do beforehand to determine the way a committee will act.

Even volunteers have a tendency to a predisposed end. Some committees will never act, no matter what the impulse. "Progress" is what most inactive committees report, some acting only when members tire of meetings. Oliver Wendell Holmes, Jr., American jurist, whose pronouncements on free speech are regarded as landmarks, said, "I hate being placed on committees. They are always having meetings at which half are absent and the rest late."

A committee is a group of people who individually can do nothing, but collectively can meet and decide that nothing can be done. Well, maybe it isn't that serious, but unless leadership develops within the group, not much will happen. A committee is "only as good as the most knowledgeable, determined, and vigorous person on it. There must be somebody who provides the flame." Right on, Lady Bird Johnson.

Committees are a good example of security in numbers. "The genius of committees is that they can make decisions that no one would want to make alone" (Tracy Kidder in *Among Schoolchildren*). So clearly there must be a balance of minds when it comes to committee effectiveness. Good faith, determination, and a definite objective are basic ingredients.

Committees are essential, but I am thankful my work did not depend on working within committees. I am also thankful for those whose temperaments and dedication equip them for quality committee work.

There is a sign on a church bulletin board in Benton (Wisconsin) which says, "For God so loved the world that He didn't send a committee."

Could there be a connection between this succinct observation and the fact that the first Wisconsin state capitol was near Benton?

On Generations

One of the most thought-provoking books in my life has been William Strauss and Neil Howe's book, *Generations: The History of America's Future, 1584 to 2069*. The volume treats in detail the thirteen generations since the colonial period commenced. The authors maintain that these generations have gone through five cycles beginning in 1584 when the first "idealist" generation, which sent people to America, developed.

The Fourth Turning is Strauss and Howe's sequel about twentieth-century generations. Both books make so much sense that I am surprised we do not require knowledge of it in general education. I have heard little about these social patterns from anyone except these two authors.

Every time I enter a conversation, a serious one, I wind up invoking something from Strauss and Howe. It turns up in my thinking and writing. In public affairs television, speakers often allude to things that verify the idea that there are patterns in the generations, that each one has its characteristics induced by its experience, particularly with the generation preceding any specific one.

In this chapter, I describe the silent generation; the boomer generation which I taught; and the impact of those generations on change and character.

CONTENTS

Generations: How Do We Fit In?
"Boomers"
History, Change and Character

Generations: How Do We Fit In?

(World War II) bred caution and sensitivity
among Silent children, lending them a persona
that produced a lifelong preoccupation with
process, fairness, and artistic expression.
Generations, William Strauss & Neil Howe

Most everyone living today is in one of four groups: GIs, the elders, born between 1901-1924; the silents, the mid-lifers, born between 1924-1943; the boomers, the rising adults, born between 1943-1960; and the 13ers, born between 1961-1981. The very youngest is called the millennial generation, born starting 1982.

I was born near the beginning of the silent generation. Since I was near the beginning of this group, I am now into "elderhood."

It appears my generation is out of luck, trapped, can never lead the nation. For example, the GI generation has provided all of the presidents since 1960. In 1992, William Jefferson Clinton, a boomer, was elected.

We provided society with few heroes in the traditional sense of that word. We grew up respecting, caring, and being careful.

Other well-known silents are Woody Allen, Martin Luther King, Elvis Presley, James Dean, Andy Warhol, Gore Vidal, Clint Eastwood, Phil Donahue, Marilyn Monroe, and William F. Buckley, Jr.

We are not so much defined by what we did as we are by those who preceded and followed us. We are stuffed between the over-achieving GI (civic) generation and the self-absorbed boomer generation. We were too late to help win "the good war" and too early to have had our adolescence celebrated. We were instrumental in founding organizations of dissent that the 1960s boomers would turn radical.

It is interesting to note what was going on when we were at various ages and how those events influenced us. For instance, we were between birth and thirteen years when *Snow White* and *The Wizard of Oz* appeared.

When WWII ended and the first atomic bomb was dropped, we were three to twenty years old. When the Korean Conflict came along, we were eight to twenty-five. The climax of the McCarthy period found us twelve to twenty-nine.

We were fifteen to thirty-two when Sputnik orbited the earth and when rock and roll was oscillating. We were nineteen to thirty-six when John Kennedy inaugurated the Peace Corps in his first year as president.

When JFK was assassinated and *The Feminine Mystique* was published, we were twenty-one to thirty-eight. In 1968 when Martin Luther King and Robert Kennedy (both silents) were assassinated, and the Vietnam War was at its climax, we were twenty-six to forty-three. When Neil Armstrong (also a silent) set foot on the moon, we were twenty-seven to forty-four.

When Watergate forced President Nixon's resignation, we were thirty-two to forty-nine. The Carter "malaise," the energy and Iran crises found us thirty-seven to fifty-four. When our second candidate for president lost in 1988, we were forty-six to sixty-three and pretty much out of luck.

Midlife was a major crisis for us. We were buffeted by unpredictable and defeating changes. At the very time our power should have been greatest, we observed the fragmenting of families, cultural diversity, institutional complexity, and widespread and messy litigation.

Entering our elder period, we knew affluence, but our reputation was indecision. Some of our cultural milestones should convince any doubters about our nature and contribution: *Portnoy's Complaint* (Philip Roth), *One Flew Over the Cuckoo's Nest* (Ken Kesey), *Unsafe at Any Speed* (Ralph Nader), *Cosmos* (TV series, Carl Sagan), *Ms. Magazine* (Gloria Steinem), *Playboy* magazine (Hugh Hefner), *Future Shock* (Alvin Toffler), *Megatrends* (John Naisbitt), and *Sesame Street* (PBS, Joan Ganz Cooney).

We silents continue to do what we do so well – be observers, share our wisdom when the younger will listen, and wish we inherited better.

How history will see us is not for us to decide. Also, part of the wisdom of age is recognizing that we are partly responsible for what the generations that follow become.

348

"Boomers"

It seems boomers are a duplicitous lot. Some are not consistently honest. They wear many hats. As circumstances shift, they shift.

I can't say that people of other generational groups are not the same, but for some reason the current working-adult generation often turn out to be duplicitous. That is, marked by "contradictory doubleness of thought, speech, and actions." *The Merriam-Webster Tenth New Collegiate Dictionary* goes on, "as the belying of one's true intentions by deceptive words or actions."

It seems more people have double standards today. When they earn their livelihoods in the public eye, exposure of their actions can take on enormous proportions. Corporate crime at the highest levels, for example, has altered trust in our economic system.

Speaking of the highest level, a U.S. chief executive had a reputation of deception, of being duplicitous. His successor loudly said things that were soon contradicted, also loudly. Diplomacy and its Paris aplomb was sacrificed for Lubbock loudness.

These jolts to public trust have occurred in many areas of American life. Sadly, it has now happened in journalism, where trust is the basis of the job.

It sets a panic process in motion. If one trusted journalist has slipped from his moral structure, how many more have done the same? As my mother and my wife would say, if you see one undesirable insect in the house, how many more are there you can't see? One wonders how many meandering consciences there are. If journalism requires one characteristic over all others at this time, it is trust.

The idealism of our boomers needs the discipline we were forced to develop, and it is a helpless feeling to realize we cannot simply bequeath it to them. Heaven knows they need it.

As is all too evident, the idealist boomers are not exactly producing the ideal society. By their idealism and sheer numbers, they are the dominant generation.

Boomers are turning moralistic, and their children have become alienated. The Xers say, who needs someone else's experience? Their parent boomers say, it didn't do <u>us</u> any good. How can it do our children any good? James Baldwin observed, "It seems to be typical of life in America, where opportunities, real and fancied, are thicker than anywhere else on the globe, that the second generation has no time to talk to the first."

> *I don't know who my grandfather was; I am much*
> *more concerned to know what his grandson will be.*
> Abraham Lincoln

> *Every generation revolts against its fathers*
> *and makes friends with its grandfathers.*
> Lewis Mumford

History, Change and Character

> *Character is destiny.*
> George Eliot

We learn where we're going by understanding where we've been. That is part of the tragedy of humanity, that we do not learn from history.

Today's young people seem to know little history. I don't mean a knowledge of facts, notions, and impressions gained as fragments with no connections to the whole. Rather, we need to understand history's impact and lessons. Like a jigsaw puzzle, it's hard to understand the whole by looking at the puzzle pieces.

Change has been the hallmark of the span of my life. The month of the year of my birth saw one of the major achievements of the twentieth century, Charles A. Lindbergh's solo flight across the Atlantic. That doesn't sound like much a decade into the twenty-first century, when thousands of people are flown across the Atlantic daily.

Every time I see the "Spirit of St. Louis" hanging in the Smithsonian and think of the stage to which aviation had developed in 1927, I remind myself that this was a solo flight. "Lucky Lindy" did it by himself.

A Lindbergh biography stands on one of my "to-be-read" shelves. Its title is *The Last Hero*. In my ninth decade, I am convinced we have not had a real hero since. Our heroes, or at least those who capture and hold our attention, have had limited appeal. Singers Frank Sinatra and Elvis Presley struck the fancy of youth. Generals Eisenhower and Patton inspired the generation that fought World War II. Astronaut John Glenn and activist Rachel Carson were heroes, but they did not reach the national conscience in the way Martin Luther King did.

For sheer outpouring of worldwide adulation and acclaim, there has never been another Lindbergh. I don't remember the event, but my childhood was replete with impressions associated with the Lindbergh. Why we do not, cannot generate such heroes escapes me. Something about our national unity and societal spirit might provide reasons.

Recent generations have placed high priority on personal liberty and independence; however, I find no one who demonstrated those qualities more than Lindbergh. The younger generations trumpet the importance of freedom, the more interdependent we become. There is an eerie, almost robotic element in our so called "free" society. Try calling a business of any size and you're talking to machines. That's a long way from the telephone operator one had to go through when making calls in the years of my growing up. Yes, change is the hallmark of our age. So maybe I will be able to articulate some of the factors that have characterized the ninety-plus years of my life.

"Character is destiny" penned novelist George Eliot. She knew whereof she wrote. No matter what skills and experiences one brings to a profession, if we don't pursue that elusive quality, what is the use?

On Media and Communications

In my mind, effective communication involves meaning, shared interest, intimacy, thought, patience, reflection, and adequate feedback.

Communication is becoming more important all the time. That may sound like superfluity carried to extremes. Oddly enough, we shall need much more communication about the issues of our emerging communications and media. The essays in this chapter reveal my respect and concerns for the rapid changes taking place in communications and media.

CONTENTS

Common Sense

A former student called attention to a piece by Wendell Berry entitled "Why I Am Not Going to Buy a Computer." He said it was in a collection of essays called *What Are People For?* I told him I had to read one of Berry's books, but that I couldn't remember the title. I told him to hold on the phone while I checked. Sure enough, it was *What Are People For?* and the essay in question was in there.

Since I have reread it, I am newly perturbed and energized by the subject. Berry is an outspoken opponent of many of the methods by which we use our resources in the name of progress and economic stability.

His stand against computers is simply part of a larger problem. Berry's reasoning is guided by a number of principles. One principle is our dependency on and overuse of energy. Another is the expense of it all. He asks, are computers bringing us nearer to things that matter?

He cites "peace, economic justice, ecological health, political honesty, family and community stability, (and) good work" as things that matter.

In citing his fourth reason, Berry wrote this:

> I do not see why I should not be as scientific about this as the next fellow: When somebody has used a computer to write work that is demonstrably better than Dante's, and when this better is demonstrably attributable to the use of a computer, then I will speak of computers with a more respectful tone of voice, though I still will not buy one.

Despite Berry's protests, I acknowledge that computers allow the marshaling of material facts on a large scale and more rapidly than ever before. I suppose the day could come when anyone anywhere could command any fact any time. But having knowledge available does not guarantee, or even suppose, its use. How much can one person know? To what use could such volumes of information be put, except by agencies of government and large corporate entities?

An emerging necessity of the world and this country is reducing consumption. A finite earth with finite resources inhabited by a population that is looking more infinite all the time, will eventually be uninhabitable.

One of many shocking thoughts is the possibility that China, a nation of over one billion people, will become the kind of consumer society which we are. We are in the process of showing the rest of the world how to live. The apparent excuse is that we are the place where democracy succeeds, and the world wants to follow us.

But are we really teaching democratic principles? Aren't we selling our products and our way of life in the name of corporate profits? Something is terribly wrong with the way we are doing things.

Internet as Playpen

The Internet is a huge invisible but universal playpen. That also goes for accompanying iPads and eToys. World-wide, people are exchanging messages, most of which are unessential. A couple of decades ago, we had a minimum of devices to establish immediate contact with other people, and we seem to have gotten along all right.

Speeding up living is not necessarily a good thing. After all, life is where you are, not off in someone else's space where your presence is lacking. This gossipy intercom is indeed a giant fun fiesta.

Allowing that much of what goes on in cyberspace is useful, one must also allow that most of it has become necessary. Burning life's minutes off in someone else's space seems less than important. As my children say when we travel, be sure you carry a cellphone in case of trouble. Beyond that I see little utility in most of these miracles of technology.

Speeding up the world isn't necessarily an advantage. Believe me, from this perch in the middle of my ninth decade, quality of life is not a great deal better than it was sixty years ago. When the new-toy effect of the digital age wears off, reason may restore a measure of maturity. We can bring our new playthings into realistic focus and in time for the new civic generation to save us again.

Movies

Sometimes the real movie hero is the one who sits through it. Moviemakers really have it made. The same goes for TV producers. People will sit and stare at screens endlessly, then over and over again.

They love it because it is passive. They don't have to think or become engaged. The only interplay is with an electronic image, which will be replaced by the next one, and the next, and on and on ad nauseum.

Viewers look as though they are doing something, while they may be thinking about something else or about nothing at all. This habit is probably more common with television, but it also applies in movieland.

People get into a kind of electronic cocoon. Whatever happens to minds in this sort of state is anyone's guess. It is probably different with each person. I may be odd man out on this, but I cannot watch images flashing by unless something of substance is generating.

The difference between movieland and TV-land (which is often also movieland) is that movieland requires you to get up, transport yourself to a theater, and plunk down a fair amount for a ticket. I've never been convinced these sacrifices guarantee the moviegoer's undivided attention. It is well to remember that profit is the real goal of movies.

The quality of films is a factor. Can you remember a time when movies were rated by how good they were, not on who was allowed to see them? This criterion says something about the substance of flicks.

Seeing a movie over and over again seems to run counter to logic, but it is a common practice. How many films are of sufficient quality to warrant repeat viewing? You could probably count them on the fingers of your remote-control hand. It is probably well to state the obvious: people really want to be stimulated physically usually with violence and sex.

As an adolescent, I found movies a way to pass the time. It was easier to be off to the theater with the boys. I didn't have to do or think anything.

What was so appealing about the silver screen? Humor, of course, was always welcome. Fights were exciting and sometimes so badly done we would laugh our way through them. Then there were car chases, speedy horses bearing gun-toting pugilists, heroes of various sorts tracking down and capturing villains, and the omnipresent violence. Today we should show violent movies in black and blue.

Our language has been reduced to the lowest common denominator. Long ago, Hollywood moved from the smart set to the smut set. Will Rogers' succinct appraisal of the movies seems as relevant today as in the 1930s: "There is only one thing that can kill the movies and that is education." Among other talents, Rogers was a popular screen star.

The question is how much entertainment can we endure? How much is simply the passing of time? Whether it is the silver screen or the tyrannical tube, both are capable of consuming vast quantities of time.

How much electronic image-watching is useful or productive

entertainment? At what point are we simply wasting time? Maybe it's time to redefine entertainment and determine how it relates to other aspects of our lives. How much entertainment is advancing the human condition?

When the Academy Awards are the talk of the town, one cannot help wondering what impels the makers of movies. Are they advancing film art? Is that their goal? Or is it to titillate or terrorize? Or to aid us in passing time while they make their millions in the name of art? What was it that Will Rogers said about movies and education?

Some cinema movies are well worth the time and money. Seniors, who are generally seasoned movie-goers, were quick to defend their film habits.

I worked at the fringes of the film art. I did everything but go to see them but used this fact to advantage when the topic came up in classes. I actively encouraged comparing movies to other forms of entertainment. When students learned I was not a movie-goer, they easily became movie storytellers. Of course, I played devil's advocate to the hilt.

I read reviews and occasionally watched Siskel and Ebert, the TV movie critics. So, I wasn't exactly ignorant about the movies.

I regularly asked questions about the difference between watching a movie and reading the book on which it might be based. I used any strategy to stimulate the imagination and encourage reading. Which actors, for example, did their characters justice? I recall more than one discussion about George C. Scott's characterization of General George S. Patton.

There were exceptions to these classroom campaigns. I did learn from several movies after seeing them. Probably the most notable was *Butch Cassidy and the Sundance Kid*. This rambling, tongue-in-cheek, Western-Eastern-Bolivian flick was full of quality work. Clever dialogue produced humor and satire. The photography was exceptional. When I happen to notice the film on television, I decide to watch it again.

Journalism and Cyberspace

A breakfast without a newspaper
is a horse without a saddle.
Will Rogers

I am not a professional journalist. As a late-comer English teacher, I saw the need for an outlet for student writing skills. I learned my journalism by practicing scholastic journalism … by playing the patient observer. I have to confess as I look back on the experience, it was a bit scary.

Our society has no more important mission than helping to encourage an informed citizenry. All we have to do is consider our community without its newspaper(s).

Granted, technology has brought the computer and the Internet into play, but I find it difficult to believe keeping a community informed with anything less than a newspaper to be foolish wish-wash. The integrity of the printed page means somebody is responsible, a direct, tangible, real way to inform. Cyberspace, as we regularly learn, has indirect, intangible, unseen elements that are by nature impersonal and virtually unreachable.

The new phenomenon, the blogger can never provide the consistent, trustworthy, dependable service an established newspaper can. Not that newspapers are always consistent, trustworthy, and dependable, but it is hard to say what a newspaper's competition would be. Most of the time they serve their communities in stalwart, effective ways.

Don't expect always to agree with your newspaper. It would be sad if you did. As someone once put it, harmony seldom makes a headline.

Fundamental Communications

Despite what technology wizards say, two forms of communication are not going away soon. One is the book. The other, the newspaper.

As a woman being interviewed recently on television said when told she could find books and newspapers on the Internet, "I cannot read off a computer screen for any length of time. You can't relax over morning coffee staring at a screen," she said. And you can't curl up in an easy chair or in bed with a machine.

When I went walking for my *Chicago Tribune* one morning, I was

357

told there was none to be had. By the time I got home empty-handed and back into routine, it was clear something was missing.

No one seemed to know what had happened. When I picked up my Tuesday morning *Tribune*, it didn't take long to spot the "Note from the Publisher" (4x6 inches in size) on the front page. The first sentence read: "We are very sorry that a computer system failure caused by a software coding error delayed production and delivery of Monday's print edition of the *Chicago Tribune.*" Maybe it wasn't as bad as one fifteen-word letter-to-the-editor put it: "Monday morning with no *Tribune* on the doorstep is like a death in the family." Nonetheless, something was missing.

Newspapers provide services that are immediate, timely, and diverse. They are a connection among the world, the community, and us. When they are missing, a good share of the world's goings-on is missing. No doubt about it, the substance and detail of news can only be gotten consistently through newspapers.

Or books. What other format allows long, intense periods of reading? How else to achieve penetration and depth of a subject? With books, glitches and power failures cannot stop them. By the way, candles still work in the dark.

I try to think what life would be like without newspapers and books. Our society requires its citizens to keep in touch with the world and each other. It would be a pretty dull place without those daily doses of the world's goings-on.

Effect of Media on Education of Children

What is the effect of media on the educational experience of children? The effect is significant, probably overwhelming, maybe even incalculable. In fact, the media are responsible for a frightening preponderance of children's education. This fact assumes we understand that more learning takes place away from the classroom than in it.

The media have made life away from life more important than ever. That is, young people find themselves more occupied with experience that is not part of their lives. These events can be real, imaginary, or as the new phrase has it, virtual reality.

The term "media" covers a lot of territory. The media are many. Television, movies, newspapers, magazines, music, the telephone, the computer, and the newest method for escaping life. The Internet.

Life also now provides considerable means by which children can physically "leave life," so to speak. Cars, buses, trains, and planes reach across the country, the world, and fast. America has become notorious for its mobility. We can leave life temporarily with alcohol and drugs. There are also easy ways to leave life permanently.

We can lose ourselves in data-gathering processes. The very tools of communication, information, and access have made record-keeping universal. A lot more about me than I would ever want to admit is available out there in the space we call "cyber."

That's "cyber" as in "cybernetics." The word derives from a Greek verb meaning "to steer," or "govern," which when turned into "cybernetics" means "the science of communication and control theory that is concerned especially with the comparative study of automatic systems" (i.e., computers).

It's the "govern" part that bothers me. The world of cyberspace makes accessible far more than will ever be used. But the computer has not made us focus on society's problems. It has simply made boundless information available. It is a little scary to think of the uses to which such accessible information can be put, and by whom.

Growing up today must seem endlessly confusing. The options for activity and learning are many and diverse. The most important skill in utilizing such masses of stuff is self-discipline which is easily smothered by it all. Self-control in a world that offers such diversity must seem pointless, or at least impossible. It is really more important now than it has ever been. We don't access self-discipline: we practice it, we master it. We restrain it. We control ourselves.

A liberal education is no less important now than it was one hundred years ago, but the idea needs redefining. What are the essential skills? What are the requirements for increasing the quality of culture? Are all branches of knowledge equally important? At what point do we leave the essentials and begin making decisions about which curricular activities to pursue? How can we make available the experience of those who have it to those who do not? Will the technological marvels improve the quality of the communication that takes place among us?

The choices and dilemmas which young men and women face today are far more difficult than ever before. Those students lucky enough to have well-educated, communicative, and compassionate parents are in a better position to find their way than those who do not. Those students fortunate enough to meet energized, tough, in-touch teachers are more likely to be prepared to understand the world into which they are growing than those who are not.

The effect of media on children must be positive and well balanced. But there must be folks along the way to point out factors that foster good judgement and allow young people to relate constructively to society. If they do not learn how to communicate and develop strong ethical habits, what good are the boundless resources of cyberspace?

My Three Sustaining Skills

> *Be not the first by whom the new are tried,*
> *Nor yet the last to lay the old aside.*
> Alexander Pope

Age and wisdom do not always harmonize. The technology revolution has not caused me to abandon three significant skills: writing, photography, and music. I have sustained each beyond what some might call the bounds of reason.

I write. In fact, that is what I am doing right now, pen in hand on the page of a good quality, 140-page steno pad. Then if all goes well, I will revise and type a manuscript. Yes, I said type – on my Smith-Corona Galaxie 12.

I also shoot pictures. The camera is a Nikon N90 SLR. It uses film, and I have a dependable processor who does good work and gets paid.

The third is music. I am not a musician, which allows me freedom to listen to music and consult sources. It also allowed the building of a considerable collection of recordings. I mainly collect LP's, long-playing records, which have been around for over sixty years. I prefer the analogue sound, and I do not mind expending considerable effort to keep the collection in good shape. The period of great jazz and the big band coincided with the period of the long-playing record. All of it was recorded analogue, and the playing format was the LP.

Part of the reason I have stayed with these three currently out-of-favor formats is habit. Why change things that work? I might add we don't have to go far to find opinion that supports this thesis.

On writing. I stick with the pen, pad, and typewriter because thinking is essential. Writing longhand and typing manuscript on a manual typewriter lets the mind work at a pace consistent with revising, rejecting, and reworking. I often read about some well-known writer who composes in the same way.

Concerning photography. If I am going to produce worthwhile images, deliberation and care have to be involved. Film photography requires both. If I can't reproduce in a print what I see in my SLRs viewfinder, then photography is fakery. The temptations of digital photography, the ease, the supposed simplicity, the choices, the manipulation to produce something that was not in my viewfinder, are all something different from the photography I practice. If you want to see this practice carried to its natural conclusion, read about and view Ansel Adams' work.

In terms of music, digital sound is edgy, thin, harsh. Music should be natural and, like writing and photography, involve the practice of patience. Handling LPs is an art. Cleanliness, time, and care are essential. Listening to music also has requisites. If I can't listen to the music, I mean really listen to it, there is no point in playing it. Finally, LP liner notes are readable and in good supply. Some of the cover art and/or photography is as good as the music inside.

Conclusion: These words may very well add up to "What's the hurry?" Expressing one's self, recording what one sees, and enjoying music, do require time and patience.

On Music

I am not a musician, but I have always loved music. My first recollection of buying records goes back to the middle 1940s, almost seventy years ago. It was 78 rpm records then. In fact, when the microgroove revolution began about 1948, I had already invested quite a bit in those breakable, noisy, shellac discs.

However, when LPs came on the scene, my collection grew very slowly because of the navy, college, marriage, the army, a restaurant business, back to college, and then raising a family on a teacher's salary. Buying LPs was down the list of priorities, but gradually I began collecting. Today, I have thousands of LPs and CDs, especially in the classical and jazz fields.

This chapter reflects some of my passion and delight for the importance of music in my life.

CONTENTS

Antonio Vivaldi

Antonio Vivaldi must have been some teacher. This Italian clergyman was a music teacher during the Baroque period. He instructed students on their individual instruments, and he composed pieces for his student groups and particularly for blossoming soloists. They performed Vivaldi's works in something resembling our recitals.

He wrote hundreds of pieces for ensembles and a variety of solo instruments. A music pundit once commented that Vivaldi rewrote the same concerto 500 times.

There are many stories about the temperament of the man. We have this fascinating circumstance of the cleric teacher who wrote music for his students to perform. One cannot help wondering what his life was like.

The only link was the music itself. What a wonderful thought. Imagine! Writing music for one's students, and then having the music become eternal.

Mozart and IQ

Do you think there is anything to the idea that listening to Mozart can give your brain power a boost? Some years ago, newspapers reported that such research had indeed been conducted, and what's more, it was true.

Researchers at UC-Irvine had students listen to Mozart's *Sonata for Two Pianos in D Major (K. 448)* for ten minutes before taking an intelligence test. Thirty-six students were given standardized IQ tests after listening to Mozart, after listening to a relaxation tape, and after meditating in silence for ten minutes. All students scored higher after listening to Mozart than they did after the other two.

This sonata is an animated, intricately structured piece. I don't know which ten minutes the students heard, but the composition is twenty-two plus minutes long and has three sections. The first is an "allegro con spirito," meaning brisk with spirit. The second is an "andante," a slow and thoughtful segment. The third is back to brisk, brisker than the first.

Which ten minutes of the twenty-two-minute sonata did the students hear? Could it have been the animated complexities of the first movement, the slow, meditative strains of the second, or the vigorous driven quality of the third? It seems to me the effects of each might be different.

I have never thought of Mozart's music as cerebral as much as

363

ingenious. He was more likely to use his powers to stimulate emotional responses than to develop an academic puzzle. Technical prowess always seems to be present, but its purpose runs far beyond mere difficulty. There is always the pull toward the emotional center of what he is doing.

I have yet to hear a Mozart composition in which every stitch and fabric is not part of a tighter focus, which, when once discovered, is as dependable as the dawn of day.

Hearing Mozart is always pleasing and accelerating because his music transmits a finished, fulfilled quality. It seems pure, elemental, a kind of lowest common denominator of music. It seems to be a balance between the technical and the emotional. Of course, there are exceptions. After all, the *Kochel Catalogue* contains 626 of his compositions.

Clarity and simplicity mark Mozart's music. It stimulates. It is civil. It is universal. There are reasons it persists. Mozart may be the only artist to have brought the objective and subjective into approximate conjunction. I feel as though the basic elements of emotion are right there before me, but, ironically, only in sound. The mind and the heart have to do the rest.

Some in Mozart's time thought *Sonata for Two Pianos in D Major* was little more than entertainment. Mozart authority Alfred Einstein defended the sonata thus:

> … the art with which the two parts are made completely equal, the play of the dialogue, the delicacy and refinement of the figuration, the feeling for sonority in the combination and exploitation of the different registers of the two instruments – an entertaining work is at the same time one of the most profound and mature of all Mozart's compositions.

His music appeared simple and light while being profound and mature.

Now, about measuring intelligence. If a generation has grown up which could not do academic work without the accompaniment of music, then discovering Mozart indeed would be electrifying. The differences between the music of Mozart and the music of most of the twentieth century are as hash and steak.

I have a theory about the appeal of this sonata, but I can only describe it in emotional terms, because that is how it touches me. It is more heart than mind. Granted, it is as Einstein wrote, technically attractive. It is its craft which lays the groundwork for its emotive power …

> … when I feel strongly about something and have an itch and ache to do something about it.
> … when high barometer readings match good internal rhythms, and I feel as though I can do anything.
> … when I have trouble waiting my turn to talk.
> … when I can't wait to show someone something I have written.

In all these cases, there is a powerful urge to act. Particularly in those brisk movements of Mozart's sonatas does this latent energy burst the brain barrier and demand action.

Clear, pleasing, natural music seems to be in a better position to move us. The product of this sonata's complexities is a release. It makes us want to do things.

As a teacher, I found the problem with intelligence was motivating it, not increasing it. Take note. Mozart the motivator.

---

* Musicians will no doubt take exception with the simplicity. As a non-musician and listener, I can only report how it seems. But I have talked to musicians and read about how difficult Mozart often is.

Canadian Brass in Elkhorn, WI

My family and I went to Babe Mann Park, which runs alongside the free-way at one end of Elkhorn's industrial park, to hear and see the Canadian Brass. I guess it officially became an annual event tonight when the mayor of Elkhorn said it was so and people surveyed the sign on stage: "Horn Fest – The Brass is back. See you next year."

The Canadian Brass is one of the few musical organizations which consciously and consistently attempt to bring music to the people. I mean literally, so I cannot miss it.

They even began their concert in the audience. The only figure on stage was the man who introduced them. All of a sudden here were two Brass members a few rows in front and to the right of us, and the other three were coming through the crowd from the left. In tee-shirts, red suspenders, and dark slacks, they met a few feet in front of us, and worked their way toward the stage, playing *A Closer Walk with Thee.*

That's the idea. Close relationship among musicians, music, and the rest of us, who hear more than music. These five artists enjoy entertaining. They have so mastered their music that their major preoccupation seems to be communing with their audience. That is important because to the novice, classical music tends to intimidate.

None of that with the Brass. Their music is as music ought to be-accessible, uninhibited, explained. They always provide context for their work. I have attended five of their concerts, and I always learn interesting information about music. The programs vary. Music is arranged for brass that you would not think brass would or could play. Good humor accompanies everything they do.

A drum and bugle corps aided the Brass in this concert. They were introduced as a horn and percussion ensemble called "Star of Indiana." They provided a rich stereo effect, as sections of the unit flanked either side of the stage, creating the ultimate surround sound.

Pachelbel's *Canon* was played with an add-on embellishment, a proliferation of tubas. The performance illustrated the fact that this baroque composer introduced the bass line which runs through the piece.

The stereo effect came through richest in *Pictures at an Exhibition,* Modeste Mussorgsky's series of tone impressions. The Brass on stage provided the solo and lead ensemble work, while the dispersed units of Star of

Indiana brass and percussion played general ensemble parts. I thought such a rich orchestral piece might lose something in restricting it to brass. But it didn't. It had its rich and tasteful flow.

The same can be said for Gershwin's *Rhapsody in Blue*. The unique opening seemed destined to be forever clarinet, gleamed in trumpet tones.

The weather had to cooperate because the "Summer" section from Antonio Vivaldi's *The Four Seasons* was on the program. Over the top of the stage a soft, cloud-filtered, yellow sun descended, dissolving into orange, then darkening into shades of red, as it approached the artificial horizon which was Interstate 43. A long jet-vapor trail headed eastward, arcing overhead. As the last strains of *Summer* echoed, the final sliver of crimson sun slipped over the freeway. Talk about timing.

A balloon rose as Pachelbel's *Canon* commenced. The vapor trail was a long, wide cloud. The variety continued with Verdi's *Rigoletto* in parody, a talented young percussionist from the Star of Indiana, and *Strike Up the Band*. Later, after darkness had settled, a tastefully thoughtful arrangement from the movie *Schindler's List* and *America the Beautiful* led toward the evening's climax, *1812 Overture*, fireworks and all.

As the horns echoed into the night, I thought this event was authentic America. Elkhorn, a small, rural county seat, with companies that make band instruments. The Getzen Company makes them for the Canadian Brass, who decided they owed something to the community which has contributed to their success. So last summer they gave a free concert. An enterprising chamber of commerce took hold.

So successful was that concert that another was planned, this time at nominal ticket prices. Again, success. Now it looks as though Horn Fest may become a permanent fixture. What a success story!

Brahms and Beauty

> *Einstein said that "the most beautiful experience*
> *we can have is the mysterious." Then why do so*
> *many of us try to explain the beauty of music,*
> *thus apparently depriving it of its mystery.*
>
> Leonard Bernstein

Bernstein was correct because it is mystery that not only attracts us, but also holds us. The latter because we are driven to sharing like the successful thief who is so elated with his success that he has to tell someone about it. It is not good for him that he does, but his humanity demands it.

I want to try to explain anything that touches me deeply. Things that touch me deeply have those characteristics that cannot be explained. I need to try to explain them because their attraction, their mystery, force me toward familiarity and understanding.

For example, as a non-musician who loves Brahms, I marvel at the incredible ways in which idea fragments cascade into larger elements, which become the beauty of Brahms. How can something so complex be assembled to be so beautiful? How can unity be achieved from such complex mechanics and such strength of feeling?

One Saturday in October, I went for a walk late in the afternoon down along Geneva Lake. High clouds blowing off a storm system far to the southwest were arcing across the western sky. The sun was about to disappear, and I knew beauty was at hand. As I walked along the shore and peered through late autumn's bare branches, I watched the great artist move through many moods, tones, and skyscapes.

While I observed this phenomenon of nature, I was listening to the last three movements of Brahms' *Fourth Symphony*. I don't understand the master's mechanics and techniques, but I know I did not think about those things. Instead, I listened to the perfect complement of sound for nature's activity. I never thought about how my mind was working in response or how the emotions welling from within were inspired.

It was as though Johannes Brahms had written his *Fourth Symphony* for me to hear as I walked along the shores of Geneva Lake on a Saturday evening in October.

368

Was I taking part in that synthesis which Georg Szell, the famous conductor, described:

> Music is indivisible. The dualism of feeling and thinking must be resolved to a state of unity in which one thinks with the heart and feels with the brain.

Don't fool around trying to figure out how it works. Enjoy it while it lasts, for it will never return. It will only be retained as a memory, which itself is a mystery.

Orchestral Music With and Without a Conductor

Listening to orchestral music, I have come to the conclusion that the conductor is of supreme importance. He plays no instrument and gives a lot of advice. The musicians are perfectly capable of playing without him. One might conclude that, other than keeping time, the conductor performs no serious function. That conclusion is simply not true.

If you've ever listened to the same music that three or four leaders conducted, you could not possibly believe that. It isn't that they instruct musicians in their skills; rather, the conductors interpret what they believe to have been the composer's intent. In the process, they harness all those musicians to a singular end.

On television or on record, I have listened to several conductors rehearse orchestras. Although each had his or her style and method, each managed to institute real changes in the way the orchestra was playing. I am not a musician. I cannot read a note, but I can sense the adjustments they brought about. I could hear the differences. I would not argue against the importance of the conductor.

Then along came the Orpheus Chamber Orchestra. Somehow, I found out that they play without a conductor. About thirty musicians play together with no one person advising them on how to play. I don't mean how to play their instruments; rather, I mean how to bring a unified measure of interpretation to the music.

How do they do it? Do they assign committees of orchestra members to make decisions on how to interpret? Do they have bull sessions during rehearsals? Or is there really a leader who conducts incognito? Maybe they set a big metronome up in front and everybody follows.

When I listen to the OCO play Franz Josef Haydn's *Symphony No. 78,* I sense no lack of direction and purpose. The playful last movement trots along quickly and leaves no doubt about its objective.

Someone or something is in charge. Who or what, I do not know? In one of his National Public Radio Shows, Peter Schickele, referring to the orchestra's leaderless condition, pointed out that they possessed "a good collective soul." There is something holding them together.

I've heard them when I thought they were not of one interpretive voice. The Orpheus Chamber Orchestra manages the art of leadership without a conductor. I'll bet each musician knows a lot more than his or her instrument.

Max Morath: America's First "Popular" Music

Not many entertainers teach while they perform. There is no reason why they could not do both in equal measure. But most do not.

One Saturday in May at the Woodstock Opera House, an attentive audience was thoroughly entertained, while learning a great deal about American music. The entertainer was Max Morath, and the education involved the observance of one hundred years of ragtime.

First off, the Woodstock Opera House was a perfect place for a one-man show. It was intimate, ten rows of seats on the main floor, which was really the second floor. There wasn't a bad seat in the house, about two hundred downstairs and two hundred more in a wide, sweeping balcony. A grand piano took up a goodly portion of the stage.

This was a perfect marriage – a building of 1890 vintage and an entertainer known for his expertise in turn-of-the-century popular music.

Anyone who can entertain alone – no other folks to help, no music, no notes – has always impressed me. Max Morath doesn't need a microphone. What he was doing was conducting a class in early twentieth-century popular music.

His voice was spritely and had a snap in it. It even seemed to crackle. It had an edge, penetrating every nook and cranny of the old opera house. His was a friendly, intimate voice.

Here, well along in his seventies, Max Morath was playing Scott Joplin's *Maple Leaf Rag* with the zest of a thirty-year-old, and he did it up-

370

tempo. He said he plays it at every concert. He appeared to be a happy man, whose smile was his trademark.

Morath has been playing the Woodstock Opera House for seven years, always in the merry month of May. So, there you have the place and the entertainer. Now the music.

After doing *The Real American Folk Song Is A Rag* (1918), Morath pointed out that George and Ira Gershwin wrote the tune when they were starting as a team. Ira was born in 1896 and George in 1898. They were "just kids" when they composed this piece.

The first rags were published in 1897, so the Gershwins grew up during ragtime's heyday. The first one, published in Chicago, was *Mississippi Rag* by W.H. Krell. The second, published in St. Louis, was *Harlem Rag* by Tom Turpin.

As a good teacher would, Morath demonstrated an example of "the music ragtime drove out." It was the ballad *Mother Was A Lady*, which exhibited "the triumphs of virtue." It was a three-minute melodrama. While singing and playing, he pointed out how the standard melodrama plot unfolded. "More sinned against than sinning" was the phrase he used to characterize women's dilemma at the turn of the century.

Max Morath's audience was made up primarily of people whose parents grew up during that time and must have known the music.

Morath said the composers of *Mother Was a Lady* were Edward B. Marks and Joseph Stern, but he was quick to point out that they were young when they wrote it, so they were probably known as Eddie Marks and Joey Stern, emphasizing that pop music has always been a game for the young. He added that "popular music is folk music that shows a profit." Times haven't changed much, have they?

It was syncopated rhythms of the rag that began to influence popular music. Morath used a ballad called *Come After Breakfast* (1909) to demonstrate how popular ballads changed after ten years of ragtime. The key lines were "Come after breakfast, bring your own lunch, and leave before suppertime." You can almost sense the rhythmic energy that would accompany a piece with lines like that.

The new music was criticized, as new music always is. Morath said that "no good could come of ragtime. It was scurrilous … reeking of excessive syncopations." However, it "brought life and verve" to popular music, much as jazz did in the 1920s and swing in the 1930s and 1940s.

The first decade of the 1900s was distinctive, and "its music labeled (the) times." As Morath put it, the 1900s was a time "when sex was dirty and the air was clean." But ragtime "liberated popular music … released and energized it," influenced the music that followed, even as the new century begins.

Two of the best-known exponents of ragtime were Scott Joplin and Eubie Blake, whose first rags were published in 1899. Joplin's was called *Original Rags* and Blake's *Charleston Rag*. After playing both of them, Morath discussed the divergent paths the two men followed. Joplin composed over fifty rags but died in 1917. Blake composed less and played publicly all his life, right up to his one hundredth birthday in 1983.

The work of both men came into renewed popularity when rags were the rage in the 1970s. Joshua Rifkin recorded over half of Joplin's rags, and the movie *The Sting* energized the revival. Who knows what originality will spur the twenty-first century?

This lively music with its persistent syncopations was to be America's first "popular" music. As Morath stated, "Most everything since has emphasized those ragtime syncopes—embellished and embroidered them to every generation since, as American popular music has become the soundtrack for Main Street, and lately, the Global Village."

One of Scott Joplin's most popular rags, *The Entertainer* (1901), was Morath's last number. It was also the encore. Let me explain. Like most of Joplin's rags, it had no lyrics, that is, Morath said, "until I wrote them." So, the last number was *The Entertainer*, the piano solo; and after enthusiastic applause, *The Entertainer*, the encore, with words.

The lyrics tell of a piano man who tries to accommodate late-night patrons who seem preoccupied by matters other than his efforts. The lyrics recall the way times and the music used to be. The last lines were:

C'mon and let him play like he used to play, seems to him it was yesterday, the entertainer…passing the night away.

As the last phrases melted away, the lights faded. The entertainer's profile was the last to disappear. Max Morath: musician, historian, teacher… and entertainer.

Bill Evans to the Heart of Things

Did you ever listen to rich and interesting music, but you couldn't explain what made it that way? As frustrating as that may be, think of all the other life-enriching things that cannot be explained.

Bill Evans' music certainly falls in this category. Paul Pettinger has been explaining to me in his biography of Evans, *How My Heart Sings*, how some of his music works. However, not being a trained musician, I can't understand it.

As Duke Ellington said, "If it sounds good, it is good." Then why should I worry about what makes it sound the way it does? But I have the urge to explain things to people. After all, I have been and remain a teacher. I have some degree of means to share what and how I feel.

The Evans piano draws the listener ever closer, because the music is unusual and nothing like it has been heard before. His music is also penetrating. It gets to nerve ends I didn't know I had. I must say his music is rich: it relates to more and more of my experience. It conveys how I often feel. That's it. Evans feels and communicates feeling. Once you understand that and can manage the cerebral path of the structure and substance, you got his music.

But then the next time it is different. Of course, when did music ever sound the same the next time? When did you ever feel the same twice?

When you get to the heart of a real artist, you must be ready to follow his context, his mind, and his heart. The freedom this later permits is quite astounding. You realize you not only know the artist, but your understanding helps open personal vistas.

Music is a universal language which allows an artist to communicate directly, if you are willing. With Bill Evans, it's all willingness.

(L)et's (P)lay Music

In every attempt to organize my music collection, I reach that point of wonder – where will this all end? There are now thousands of LPs. That's long-playing microgroove phonograph records, for those who don't know—thousands of them in the two rooms where I keep them.

I take considerable pride in doing more than storing, stacking, and sticking them in places where they should be. The sound you can get from a well-produced LP on a reasonably high-quality sound system is superior to anything else in sound. Like a fine restaurant, you cannot really know until you try it. Then it's hard to stay away.

But you have to take care of LPs. By that I mean returning them to their jackets when not in use, storing them on end, and keeping them clean. You learn to handle LPs without touching playing surfaces. You also learn to hate warping.

Like anything worthwhile, there is a price. It isn't the cost. The price is time, effort, and care. Don't misunderstand, I have CDs. At the moment, it's the only universal music format.

Something in CD sound isn't natural to me. It can be edgy, thinly metallic. This is the age of amplified instruments – the guitar being the chief culprit – brought about by the rock movement of the last fifty years.

I became locked into the LP. In addition to the sound quality, there was the timeliness of the format's demise. During the mid-1980s, as the CD claimed the market and LP declined, the CD became very costly, but LP prices went down. It was my chance to have music at reasonable cost.

When the CD came to popularity, people began selling their LP collections. I began filling in the twenty-year gap during which I knew great music was being recorded, but when I couldn't afford it. I began to close the gap with retail stores such as Half-Price Books and philanthropic endeavors such as the ALS Music Mart tent sale in Skokie's Old Orchard Shopping Center.

Though these enterprises are selling used records, they are examined carefully and priced accordingly. Between three and five dollars gets you discs that, if they were reissued on CD, would cost from nine to fifteen dollars. LPs, depending on their musical content, can bring hundreds of dollars, but a significant library can be collected without breaking the bank.

Another advantage with LPs is a reassurance in understanding how the mechanics that produce it work. I'm not a recording engineer, but it is easier to practice care and discretion with recorded music formats if you can understand what is going on. I don't mind saying that it takes a leap of faith to play, much less understand, CDs.

Unless you're a modern-day technician, there is no way to appreciate what is going on inside a CD player. Making music out of 0's and 1's is beyond me. Not that I understand how music gets from those squiggly grooves through a stylus to loudspeakers, but at least I can appreciate what is going on. I can correct problems in the LP process. Correcting problems with a CD player is beyond my understanding.

The LP has a couple of other advantages. We can read LP liner notes without a magnifying glass. There is often a music education to be had in the notes on the backs of LPs. Then there are the album covers, which sometimes are more artistic than the music.

Criticism of the LP usually takes the form of timesaving. CDs are handy, convenient. No puttering. The music plays longer. You can program hours of it. You can also walk off or become absorbed in something else and forget the music.

These behaviors are part of what I call instant gratification syndrome. If it isn't handy and convenient, don't bother me. But don't we have to be willing to spend time with it and concentrate on it?

It isn't the imperfections of the medium that make me persist; it is the perfection of the message. For now, and as long as my critical senses function, I will enjoy this elevated level of communication. A hint of eternity emerges from listening to the music and storing the music for future use. We cannot leave the message or the medium alone. Victor Hugo said something close to the truth: "Music expresses that which cannot be said and on which it is impossible to be silent."

How Music Works

All kinds of answers materialize when I ask people why they do not appreciate Mozart or Miles Davis. Most answers suggest that the music does not make much sense. When someone declares that jazz sounds like a noisy clutter, it says they haven't taken time to investigate.

When someone observes that Beethoven and Ellington are too complicated, it has to be because of tin ears or cultural lag. If these musical giants generated genuine interest for me, you cannot blame me for asking why so many others have not learned about them. As Longfellow wrote, "Music is the universal language of mankind…." But as in language, music that endures differs vastly from music of the moment.

I have always been interested in how composers and musicians express themselves. What, in the makeup of each, manifests itself when they compose or play? How can two violinists, for example, make the same composition into such different entities? They will play the same piece with the same notes and directions; yet, their performances will be altogether different in effect.

An example is in order. A few years ago, after traveling to Germany, I took part in the preparations for a family reunion. I learned that several German composers were born and raised in lower Rhine River communities, not far from the village from which my great, great grandparents emigrated to America in 1846.

One of these composers was Max Bruch, born in Cologne in 1838. His concertos are standards in violin repertory. Hungarian violinist Leopold Auer (1845-1930) proclaimed, "From the standpoint of the violinist, who plays these (concertos) in public, they are artistic Declarations of Independence...eloquent and inspiring documents...."

I have several interpretations of the first of these concertos, *Adagio*, including probably the most famous, the one of violinist Jascha Heifetz. Right from the beginning, though, I was drawn to American violinist Isaac Stern's recording. Why? It was the most uplifting, gratifying, and exhilarating. He is "admired for his vital, expressive performances, with warm tone and impeccable style" (*Grove Encyclopedia of Music*).

I put Stern's recording on cassette and took him along on my morning walks. Its magnetism drew me in. Later I took the audiotape along to Grant County (Wisconsin) and listened to it as I drove in the area where my great, great grandparents settled.

Now when I hear Max Bruch's *Adagio*, I see the village on the Rhine bluffs in Germany and the rolling farmlands of Grant County, the places where my great, great grandparents carried out the bold changes in their lives.

A cousin, who still farms in Grant County, accompanied me to the farm where our fourth-generation grandparents settled in 1847. We considered the bluffs eight miles to the south and west where the mighty Mississippi flows. I thought of the Rhine and the village high on a bluff scarcely a half mile away. We thought of how our lives are different because of what our ancestors did – as *Adagio* filled the air!

One of the three themes in the concerto was called "a melodic glory of the nineteenth century." How fitting. Cousin and I looked at each other and the rich Grant County farmland, and we felt the power of the moment.

The moment provided a narrative texture to life.

I have tried to figure out why this interpretation of the same collection of notes could become so dominant in my experience. I checked the *Grove Encyclopedia* again, and there were those words about Isaac Stern's style: "...admired for his vital, expressive performances, with warm tone and impeccable style." There you have it. Stern was doing more than playing notes well. He put himself into the music. He elevated Bruch's work.

In case you need more proof of Stern's stature, he was the man who spearheaded the drive several years ago that saved Carnegie Hall. Isaac Stern died at eighty-one on September 22, 2001.

There is more to music than meets the eye, ear, or mind. Classical music penetrates the depth of my being. That's how music works for me.

Girl Names in Songs

In that great period when American popular music was peopled with composers and lyricists writing imperishable tunes and memorable lyrics. It is not surprising to find women's names recurring regularly in song titles, or as song titles.

In organizing my music collection, I have noted over eighty tunes with milady monikers. The one that turns up most often is Laura. But that's not the only "L" lady tune. There are Liza, Louise, and Lisa.

The D's have it too: Dinah, Daisy, Dolores, and Diane.

Or the C's. Carla, Charmaine, Cheryl, Clair, Coquette, and Cecelia.

Mark the many M's. Mandy, Marie, Melinda, Melissa, Michelle, Margie, and Mame. There is the Maria of the *West Side Story*, and the Maria of *The Sound of Music*.

Sometimes the names run in combination, like Lida Rose, Rose Marie, Marie Elena, and Donna Lee. At other times they are only parts of titles: *Celia's Waltz; Song for Ellen; Waltz for Debby; Lulu's Back in Town; Hello, Dolly; Peg O' My Heart; Georgy Girl;* and *Have You Met Miss Jones?* There's *Daisy's Dream, Rachel's Dream, Stella by Starlight,* and *Jeanie with the Light Brown Hair.*

You could almost waltz through the alphabet with titles that are girls' names. Amy, Beverly, Celia, Donna, Emily, Francesca, Gigi, Judy, Lorelei, Marilyn, Nancy, Penny, Ramona, Sunny, Tangerine, and Wendy. You could pretty much do a second run through the alphabet.

We have a lot of "sweet" ladies. Start with *Sweet Georgia Brown*, then *Sweet Sue – Just You, Sweet Lorraine*, and *Ida! Sweet as Apple Cider*.

To wind up this meandering through women's handles, here are a few more. We wouldn't want to leave anyone out. So, here's to the ladies: Genevieve, Josephine, Catherine, and Jean. And Natalie, Rosaline, Eloise, and Kim. Ruby, Audrey, Nola, and Rosetta. Can't think of a way to end this, except to say thank goodness there are ladies and songs about them. Some guys wrote *Noreen's Nocturne, Portrait of Jennie,* and *Song for Anna.*

It's the Music

Jazz has been part of my life for most of it, and since I am in my ninth decade, that is a while. Though most of my experience has come through recorded music, I have been in the audience of Louis Armstrong, Chick Corea, Woody Herman, Louie Bellson, Dave Brubeck, Count Basie, Dizzy Gillespie, and the Modern Jazz Quartet.

No doubt the most personal contact occurred during a noon hour in a downtown Madison record store, when, between classes in UW days, I met Stan Kenton. If there was a single impetus for my interest in jazz, it was that chance meeting with this well-known, controversial band man.

Kenton was easy to talk to. He seemed interested in listening to a drifting college student who loved the big band scene, but had trouble directing his collegiate career.

I discovered seven decades later that Kenton was having difficulty keeping his band intact at the time. The easy flow of conversation bore no hint of troubles. The big band era has pretty much run its course in the mainstream of popular music. This progressive, enterprising spirit continued to front a band, and later Kenton even started his recording label. There was quality. Jazz was working its way into the mainstream.

We've lost something since those days, and I know what it was. It was trouble, hard times and war, depression, and World War II. Mainstream popular music seems to reflect social conditions. When we really need a boost, music can give it to us. During difficult times, music comes to the rescue, not only in quantity, but also in quality.

One hates to admit it takes a depression or war to bring out the best in the arts. The twenty minutes or so I spent with Stan Kenton reassured me that fine art is worth seeking. When you meet the practitioner, who wants to share his time with you, you cannot help being impressed.

Jazz is still an important part of my arts life, and I feel good about that. We still have the recordings of those jazz giants, but we miss the excitement of living in such times.

The Power of Popular Music

The fact that the mainstream of American popular music has abandoned the "American Songbook" is as difficult to understand as it is unfortunate.

As I was preparing to go to the local supermarket, I heard the opening strains of *Star Dust* on River Walk Jazz from San Antonio. They were celebrating Hoagy Carmichael tunes, and of course *Star Dust* was bound to be on the list. I caught the opening lines of the verse as I was leaving:

And now the purple dusk of twilight time
Steals across the meadows of my heart…

You see, I lost my wife a few years ago, and it doesn't take much to make memories manifest. I got to thinking about that tune and the era that made it possible. I also thought of the years I courted my wife and the music that was all around us. Granted, those times had their share of silly adolescent tunes, but the mainstream popular music was usually hummable, singable melodies which touched the hearts of young lovers with something approaching substance.

Beverly and I had many musical moments. Certain songs were associated with familiar places and memorable occasions. For some reason, the one that comes to mind is a Sammy Cahn-Jule Styne song, *Let It Snow, Let It Snow, Let It Snow.* It made the pop charts right after the war in 1946, but Woody Herman's big band made a recording that returned for a few years during Midwest winters.

In the year of our engagement (1950-51), we drove to my parents' house after a movie on one of those winter nights. A light snow was falling. We listened to music, and as the night wore on, we wished the moment's natural wishes.

But the reality was I had to drive Beverly home, seven miles down into a valley where increasing snow would certainly be accumulating. I played Woody Herman's *Let It Snow*. The lyrics bonded the moment:

Oh, the weather is outside is frightful.
But the fire is so delightful.

My parents' home had a fireplace:

And since we've no place to go,
Let it snow, let it snow, let it snow.

I have never felt any closer to another human being as I did that snowy night. That no doubt is why I remember it so well.

See what songs can do? They become integrated into our lives, our inner lives, and our relations with others.

Music to Die By

Some months ago, my musician daughter asked me what music I want played during my last rites. Complex factors go into questions like that, to say nothing about answering them. My children, like their mother, tend to anticipate life's obstacles and the bends in the road.

Another factor of course is my age. After all, I am in my ninety-second year. The tendency of my children to be realistic about life's cycle is reasonable enough. I am giving some thought to this matter, though it is not easy.

This sort of request has some surreptitious elements. Are we really able to know how others think about us? May I speculate about how those I have known think about me? Music personal to me may not have any relating power to those who know me. Does it matter? After all, these songs would be my swan songs, and shouldn't I have such choices in any case?

Funerals are not for the deceased; they are for the living.

Though I am not a musician, music has played an important role in my life. Choosing favorites is hard enough. Selecting pieces to accompany me out of this life has, to say the least, tough tones.

It is an advantage to approach music from the outside, that is, as a non-musician. There is something fascinating about perspective from the outside. I figure that most music is for audiences, and I am audience. Why can't I take part in its various components? So, if I want to choose music to be played or performed at my life's egress, that seems appropriate enough.

The music that drifted into my consciousness first was the second movement of Franz Josef Haydn's *String Quartet No. 3* from his *Opus 76*. Its simplicity endures. Two violins, a viola, and a cello play the same melody over and over.

Usually variations follow, but here there are only embellishments. The different instruments state the melody. The effect is striking. It seems much like the proposition that one's profession can be interesting, even inspiring, if one learns how to make repetition interesting, even inspiring. That was pretty much what teaching was all about. Haydn achieved it in spades. His famous melody is today the Austrian national anthem.

Another attractive piece of music has been bestowed with all the ironies of which World War II was capable. The igniting of this melody's impact on me goes back to a PBS program whose theme is long forgotten, but which produced a scene forever impregnated in my experience.

In the Russian soldiers' memorial in Moscow, there is a solemnity producing monumental overtones. Twenty million Russians died in the four years of Germany's invasion and retreat. Yet the music playing constantly in this solemn place is Robert Schumann's *Traumerei*. The composer lived his life in the same Rhine valley not far from where my mother's paternal family originated.

One of the crowning joys of life is my love for that early twentieth century outburst of song, now referred to as the Great American Songbook. It was a time when real melodies and real lyrics made the pop charts.

George Gershwin was the leader of this clan of composers. In 1927, the year I was born, he wrote *The Man I Love*, which survived my ninety-plus years and is still performed by jazz groups, big bands, and vocalists.

I will never forget carrying that heavy Sound Mirror tape recorder up UW's Bascom Hill in 1950 so I could present a script timed to the Benny Goodman Quartet's recording of *The Man I Love*. Needless to say, that radio project in my speech class was a harbinger of things to come.

The lyrical bounty of the songbook has so affected my life that choosing favorites seems futile. Some of them I associate with personal experiences. *Because of You* came along early in my marriage as well as in my temporary separation due to military service. Tony Bennett will remain deep in my memory.

Following are other tunes I associate with life experiences. All I can do is list them hoping that some idea of who I am and what I was may filter through.

Ain't Misbehavin – I could write at full emotional throttle with this song. Fats Waller! OMG!

On the Sunday Side of the Street – I do not know how to put in words how Tommy Dorsey's big band and the vocal group the Pied Pipers made this tune express happy, happy happiness.

Happy Days Are Here Again – As a very young boy, I remember this tune which was the upbeat theme of Franklin Roosevelt's presidential campaigns in 1932 and 1936.

In a Mist – Not just because it was recorded about the time of my birth, but because Bix Beiderbecke's horn, though absent, was present in spirit in this piano solo by the great Davenport, Iowa jazz man.

Pennies from Heaven – This marvelous tune will always come to me through the voice and vibes of Louis Armstrong and Jack Teagarden in their famous Town Hall concert recording. What extraordinary happy yet subdued stuff.

Night and Day – The ultimate in sophistication, mystery, and beauty in a song. Sinatra did it best. Percy Faith's studio band arrangement is close. Indiana's Cole Porter knew what he was doing when he wrote this song.

Autumn Leaves – I once put color slides to the Mantovani recording of this enduring song. Autumn has not been the same.

Pick Yourself Up – How a blind man can play piano is amazing enough, but here in the George Shearing Quintet recording, somehow the words "So take a deep breath, Pick yourself up, Dust yourself off, Start all over again," have personal character inferences.

How High the Moon – This song plays constantly at the Lake Geneva Museum, 124 slides sequenced to the Modern Jazz Quartet's *Moon*. The slide presentation is called *Lake Geneva Portrait*.

Memories of You – If I had to choose one favorite, this is it.

The Song Is You – I mean the song is Sinatra. If it weren't for 'The Voice,' this song would be much less. Memories of magic!

What a Wonderful World – Vietnam, Louis Armstrong and my son David (aka Smilin' Dave) are responsible for this song being on this list. Dave is an entertainer, and I think he almost killed his voice learning to do his interpretation of Louis performing this song. With pride and tears.

As a final stroke for the American songbook, I declare that the last four lines of *Sunny Side of the Street* do a spirited job of describing what my life has been:

> If I never had a cent
> I'll be rich as Rockefeller
> Gold dust at my feet
> On the sunny side of the street.

I have to remind myself what this writing is all about. We need elegy. Edvard Grieg, the chief figure of Norwegian musical art, wrote *The Last Spring*. It seems to have all that is necessary to remind me of the land from which my father's parents emigrated in the nineteenth century. I inherited the country, Norwegian spirit, and a deep respect for life. When the "last spring" descends, I am sure I will know I have lived and understood the connection.

I thank my musician daughter for posing the question. I'm sure courage was an ingredient.

On Numbers and the Odds

Ever stop to think how numbers rule our lives? We worry about them, praise them, and are awed by them. Often, we don't understand them.

Are you fascinated by the odds? I mean do you ever wonder, for instance, what the chances of winning the lottery are, or what the possibilities are of two people writing identical poems?

This chapter contains six essays, ten pages, 3,333 words, 16,096 characters, 23 paragraphs and 292 lines. What are the odds of this chapter expressing my fascination with numbers and the odds?

CONTENTS

A Plethora of Numbers
What Are the Odds?
The Lottery – A Do-Nothing Moronic
Playing the Lottery Without Playing the Lottery
Hitting a Baseball – Not as Easy as It Looks
And Kilometers to Go Before I Sleep

A Plethora of Numbers
We track twelve months and 365 days each year. Then, one-quarter of a day each year translates into 366 days every fourth year.

Twenty-four-hour days, sixty-minute hours, and sixty-second minutes mark our progress through life and time. In my ninety-two-plus years, I figure I've traversed some 33,580 days, over 805,920 hours, about 48,355,200 minutes. The idea that the heart, that life-essential pump, has beat continuously all that time is amazing indeed.

We count our longevity by years, which are caused by the earth's turning: its rotation, the twenty-four-hour day; and its orbiting the sun, the four seasons. These annual cycles seem similar and endless.

Certain years become milestones: sixteen, eighteen, twenty-one, thirty, forty, fifty, sixty, sixty-five, seventy, seventy-five, each with a different kind of relationship in life's chronicle. Some of us remember comedian Jack Benny practically institutionalizing thirty-nine as a permanent milestone (or maybe a year stone?).

Other numbers stick with us through life. I've had a Social Security number for about seventy-five years, and I still can't extract it from my brain on demand. The same is true of bank and credit card numbers. I can still recite my U.S. Navy and U.S. Army service numbers instantly.

All of us have to remember certain phone numbers or have them recorded in handy places. It's hard to get comfortable with phone cards. The last phone card I used involved entering thirty-one numbers. That's a lot of digits, increasing the chances for error and frustration.

I don't have an e-mail address, and I don't have to worry about numbers and passwords to access databases, but a lot of people do.

I have a chart to compute heart rate for exercise. I record numbers when buying gas so I can keep an eye on miles per gallon. Three-dollar gasoline really gets our attention. I have noticed a difference driving since I changed my car's license number to letters.

Some things cannot be done without numbers: paying bills, figuring a budget, preparing taxes, playing a sport (any sport), telling time. Try "springing" forward or "falling" back without numbers.

How about keeping track of birthdays and anniversaries? Our family has thirty-one members.

How about weather? Barometer readings, rainfall amounts,

temperatures, wind chill factors, heat indexes, wind speeds, dew points, humidity. Endless numbers.

If we are using the metric system, we probably wonder why everyone else isn't. Since we are not on the English system, we can't conceive of relating to metric, much less learn it. Can we remember now to convert temperature Celsius to temperature Fahrenheit? Or vice versa?

If we mind our money, we know about consumer price index, the gross domestic product, unemployment rates, Dow Jones averages, and interest rates.

Let's not forget highway speed limits, ACT and SAT test scores, and casualty lists. Numbers are blamed for a lot of things: Friday the 13th, 9/11, April 15.

We also keep track of other kinds of numbers. The Walworth County Fair is 170 this year. Though many are not particularly interested in history, we seem to relish numbers from the past. As always there are numbers.

Roger Bannister ran the first four-minute mile that year. The U.S. exploded the first hydrogen bomb – six hundred times more powerful than the Hiroshima blast. Speaking of blast, *Rock Around the Clock* was recorded in 1954.

It seems that certain numbers mark normalcy and neutrality, e.g., temperature 98.6 degrees Fahrenheit.7, 20/20, IQ 100.

Speaking of IQ, one of my brighter students left me this note one day on the subject of procrastination: "It would only take a second to do it, and yet from the 31,536,000 seconds in a year, I just can't seem to find the time." I don't know what this fellow is doing today, but I'll bet it isn't counting seconds. Maybe minutes and hours – eight-hour day and all that.

Imagine how many numbers play into computers and the Internet—and wouldn't you know, it all comes down to 0s and 1s.

What Are the Odds?
I never play the lottery, but I am curious about what happens sometimes with numbers. As an English teacher, I wouldn't give the time of day to the idea that two people could, independently, write identical pieces of anything. But as most would agree, unusual things sometimes happen with words.

First, the numbers. A couple of years ago I began to notice that in the big lotto games, consecutive numbers turned up a great deal, more than I thought reasonable.

Well, think of what is involved. From fifty-four numbers, six are drawn. If, let us say, the number ten comes up, what are the odds that nine or eleven will come up? Of fifty-three numbers remaining, there are two chances out of fifty-three that nine or eleven will be drawn. That is 3.8 percent. How many times will nine or eleven be drawn? The odds increase as more numbers are drawn. After five non-consecutive numbers, the odds increase to twenty percent, one chance in five that the sixth number will be a consecutive with one of the other five.

As I watched the numbers with increasing regularity, this frequency of consecutive numbers continued. Finally, I began to record the results. I found one of four results occurring:

0 – when no consecutive numbers appeared
1 – when consecutive numbers were drawn
2 – when two sets of consecutive numbers turned up, e.g., 12, 13, 14
    or 12, 13 or 27, 28
3 – when three sets of consecutive numbers occurring in one lottery

I've been recording these numbers on 3x5 cards for over a year and a half. I record every six-number lottery that I see reported. That includes Illinois Lotto, Wisconsin Megabucks, Super Cash, and the Indiana and Michigan Lotto's, which are reported in the *Chicago Tribune*. Most are fifty-four number games; two are fewer, one is thirty-six and the other forty-eight.

During this period, I recorded numbers for 649 drawings. Of these drawings, 378 had at least one set of consecutive numbers. That is fifty-eight percent. But some had more than one. Ninety-six of the 378 had two sets of consecutive numbers. On twelve occasions, three sets of consecutive numbers occurred. That means out of 649 drawings 498 cases of consecutive numbers occurred. That is seventy-six percent. Something in my reasonable self tells me that this high percentage should not happen. But it does, consistently.

Now, about words. An unusual story appeared in the *Janesville Gazette* in 1994. Two women, both Janesville natives, single mothers, and graduates of Parker High School, wrote identical poems. With numbers, certain phenomena can occur, but with language, and particularly something as personal as poetry, I am in disbelief. The facts are that there was no collusion. The song is entitled *Sometimes, I Wonder*:

> Who you are
> What you're like
> And what you think of life
> Sometimes…I wonder
> Who I am
> Where I am going
> And what life means to me
> Sometimes…I wonder
> Who we are to each other
> What we need
> And where our dreams will lead
> Sometimes…I wonder.

Several factors struck me about poem(s). It has little of the substance that makes poetry complex. The rhythms are restricted to parallel phrasing. There is no rhyme, and one is not swept up in a predominant rhythm.

Look at the words. None require thinking or relating. They are common words, and very few have more than one syllable.

There is no metaphor. Everything is straightforward and literal. It is clear that the poet(s) has some questions about what life has wrought, but nothing beyond the simplest of concepts.

These facts seem to increase the likelihood that two women could have written this independently of each other. Maybe somewhere someone else wrote it also. Maybe a dozen people have. Is it possible for a man to have written it, too?

As poems go, this one is simple and direct. The order of ideas is such that more than one person could have developed it. Not a single word that is different. Even the punctuation is identical. What are the odds?

Can you blame me for wondering about the odds, chances, and the phenomena that numbers and words generate? Of course not. We all observe such phenomena and are fascinated. From our limited viewpoints we can be shocked, not understanding all there is to be understood about what we are observing.

But that will not stop me from marveling at the liberties of lottery probability and the idea that two young single-parent mothers, living in the same area, could write the same fifty-two-word, sixty-two syllable poem.

The Lottery – A Do-Nothing Moronic

> *One of the weaknesses of our age*
> *is our apparent inability to distinguish*
> *our needs from our greeds.*
>
> Don Robinson (1963)

A Frenchman defined the "lottery" as "a tax on morons." Let's not get into the deeper implications of that.

I have never bought a lottery ticket because I don't like the fifty-five million-to-one odds. I don't know where I picked up that number, but when we get to millions, we should come to recognize that winning is futility. I know someone has to win.

But we must maintain a certain reality about numbers. Any game of chance, even when the government runs the game, has a built-in set of limitations. Our minds have a difficult time considering any limitations when all we can think is "What if I win?"

When you get to thinking this way, remember how many other people are thinking exactly the same way. Our possibilities are so severely limited that winning is but a flurry of excitement in our minds. I know, someone has to win, believe me, it will not be you or me.

Those millions of others in competition with you make you and your chances insignificant and remote. Do nothing moronic.

Playing the Lottery Without Playing the Lottery

I am interested in the lottery, but not for the usual reasons. I don't know a great deal about odds and probability, but I've discovered numbers can create unusual twists and turns. I'm staying with letters and language. The odds are better.

The odds against winning a lottery are so overwhelming that it is hard to understand why people play. Maybe it's because the odds in life are steep, too.

I also play the lottery, but in an entirely different way. I don't spend any money, but I figure to have almost as much chance of winning as the players do.

Some years ago, I noted that successive numbers turn up regularly in six-number lotto games, including Megabucks and SuperCash. With the mix of fifty-four or forty-eight balls, the chances of rolling out successive numbers would seem to be rather small. It is hard to believe they turn up as often as they do.

It occurs in over half the games. I know because I have been recording their frequency for some time now.

On 3x5 cards I record a zero if no successive numbers occur, a one if one case of successive numbers occurs, two if two occurs, and so on. The maximum on a six-number game is five, but the odds are that will never happen. But on two occasions, four successive sets have occurred in the Michigan Lotto game. The numbers were 39, 40, 41, 42, 43, 44, 45, 46, and 47. Think of all the numbers that could have come up, preventing this phenomenon. Forty-four to be exact.

Speaking of odds, what are the chances of four sets of successive numbers turning up? This finding may surprise you, but up to the date these figures were tabulated (about Sept. 1), 2385 lotteries out of 4299 contained at least one set of consecutive numbers. That's fifty-eight percent. Over half of six-number lotteries contained at least one set of consecutive numbers.

One set took place in 1796 games, two sets in 525 games, and 63 games had three sets of consecutive numbers. So, when you play, you'd better include at least one set. Of all 4299 games, 41.8 percent had one set of consecutive numbers.

Keeping track of the frequency of consecutive numbers in six-number lottery games sounds pointless. The activity is no more "duncical" than gambling against substantial odds that you might win one of them.

Probability is a tough game to play. Chances to win are hopelessly small. The media give a great deal of publicity to winners, downplaying the tens of thousands of losers.

My experience with gambling in any form is zero. For me, it has no redeeming reasons. I understand that nagging inner urge that suggests I have a chance of a lifetime to hit it big. However, the odds are stacked heavily against it.

That's as close to real odds-fighting as I will ever get. Exceptions would be for the lines in the convenience stores, waiting for folks to juggle numbers and relieve themselves of their money. We have more serious forms of gambling, but the lotteries make gambling comfortably acceptable, so that more virulent forms may more easily prosper.

Hitting a Baseball – Not as Easy as It Looks

If you've ever tried to hit a baseball, you know it is not as easy as it looks. The ball is round, and the part of the bat you want to hit the ball is also curved. To make the ball hit the bat squarely, you have to contact that "sweet spot," where the center of the ball strikes the center of the curved surface of the bat.

Having played baseball, I can attest to these truths. So, when a thirty-seven-year-old major leaguer manages his 3000th hit, it is a sports deed of major proportions. That's what New York Yankee Derek Jeter did the other day (7/9/11). He not only hit his 3000th; he got four other hits. His 3000th was a homerun.

Let's look at the odds. If a major league batter could attain an average of two hits every game for ten years, he could have his 3000 hits. Looking at the list of players who have reached these heights, it becomes clear you have to play a long time to have a chance.

Which is harder, hitting a golf ball straight or a baseball? With only twenty-eight players ever making 3000 hits, one would guess the latter. Over half of them were outfielders. Though alertness is desirable, outfielders are not in a class with catchers and shortstops. Catching is the toughest position in baseball. No catchers are on that list of twenty-eight.

Derek Jeter is only the second shortstop to make 3000. There are reasons for that. It is the toughest fielding position and must have some effect on the ability to hit consistently.

Jeter is the first Yankee to reach 3000 hits, the first who played his entire career as a Yankee. Some impressive Hall-of-Famers were Yankees: Lou Gehrig (2721 hits), Babe Ruth (2518), and Mickey Mantle (2415).

Joe DiMaggio (2214) holds that seemingly untouchable record of fifty-six consecutive-game hitting streak. Think what it takes to get at least one hit in fifty-six straight games

But we're forgetting the most important factor of all. The pitcher has something to say about whether the batter can hit a pitch squarely. That is the pitcher's job, to make the batter fail to hit successfully, or at all, for that matter.

Other factors affected his hitting longevity. A player has to be relatively injury-free to accomplish such heroics. When a batter is on a hitting spree, pitchers will often walk him, and walks don't count as hits. Then there are those days when pitchers dominate, and no one hits. How did Joe DiMaggio ever manage a hit in fifty-six straight games, to say nothing about accumulating 3000 hits in a career?

And Kilometers to Go Before I Sleep

It's been over twenty-five years since the federal government began a campaign to convert the United States from the English system of measurement to the metric system.

Well into the twenty-first century, we are still talking degrees Fahrenheit, inches and feet, ounces and pounds, and pints and quarts. All nations of the earth except Myanmar, Liberia, and the United States use degrees Celsius, meters, kilograms, and liters. It's obvious we Americans are not ready for metric.

These examples seem convincing proof for the power of tradition, of established practice. Most everything else changes, but not how we measure things.

Sometimes this contradiction means trouble. In a space probe of Mars, the vehicle in question missed its objective because of an error that an English-metric conversion caused.

The English system is so rooted in our culture that alteration would require more than executive edict or legislative action. We love those words that evolved from our English past and actually much beyond that.

Funk's *Word Origins* for instance states, "our 'inch,' earlier spelled 'ynce,' stems from the Latin word 'uncia,' which denoted both one twelfth of a foot and one twelfth of a pound."

But it is not measurement application that gives the word its character. It has become part of our linguistic and literary heritage. Phrases from our literature give the word a secure place in our culture. For example, we say, "give an inch," "budge an inch," "every inch a king."

In Shakespeare's *Coriolanus*, "give him death by inches."

English poet Arthur Hugh Clough penned "no painful inch to gain," and John Dryden, "For every inch that is not fool or rogue."

In *Don Quixote,* the Spanish classic that has become part of our heritage, "He's a good man and a true Christian every inch of him."

Words of the English system have extended themselves far beyond measuring things. You have to admit that "kilometers per liter" instead of miles per gallon isn't American.

Can't you imagine a sportswriter describing a sixty-meter run for a touchdown? OR a goal-line stand on the five-meter line?

What if Robert Frost used "kilometers" in one of his famous poems:

The woods are lovely, dark and deep.
But I have promises to keep,
And kilometers to go before I sleep.

Americans are perpetually experimenting and precipitously changing. While we would not be world conquerors or rulers, we are proud of our freedom and will fight when threatened.

On Photography

Photography has always been an avocation for me. As a youngster, the idea fascinated me that I could hold a little box up to my eye, flick a lever, and be reasonably sure that in a few days I would see that same view trapped on a piece of paper.

But that was only the beginning of the fascination. How could that strip of celluloid stuff carry that image, hidden from view? Then even more mysterious, the camera had to be taken into a dark room, which is still called a darkroom, before the film could be taken out. Many years later this mystery still fascinates me, though I know about the latent image, silver halides, developers, and the mechanics of the darkroom.

In this chapter, I included essays about my technical and artistic experiences with photography.

CONTENTS

My Photographic Voyage
Angels in the Air
An Enduring Image
Grand Scheme of Things
Henri Cartier-Bresson
Kodachrome
The Color-Print Game
Importance of Images
The Ability to See
It's All in the Light
Visual-Musical Portrait of Lake Geneva

My Photographic Voyage
Color photography has become universal, and my fascination with photography runs even deeper because of the dyes and complex processes of color film. I know very little about them. That lack of knowledge has not prevented me from making over 90,000 color transparencies since 1952 when I went into a U.S. Army post-exchange in Japan and bought my first 35mm camera.

I have owned five cameras, the last one costing more than the other four put together. I paid less than forty dollars for my first camera; an Argus C-3, the first 35mm camera that reached the mass market.

I was a PFC in the U.S. Army, stationed in Kobe, Japan, in 1952. I expended a goodly portion of a payday to buy the Argus C-3. I knew it was not the sleek, expensive mechanical marvel that was the Contax or the Leica, but it made beautiful slides.

In the months before I finally bought the camera, I took an Army Special Services course in basic photography. When the big day came to make my investment, I was ready to use my Argus C-3.

The rangefinder gears were on the outside of the body. The shutter had only five settings. The f-stops ranged from 3.5 to 16. The shutter release protruded from the top of the camera and was easy to trip accidentally. Compared to today's technological miracles, the Argus C-3 was primitive. It was the means, however, by which film captured me. Photography became a major avocation and persuasive fulfillment.

Bruce Johnson with Argus C-3 camera, mid-1950s

My advice to beginners has always been, study first, then shoot simple. One of the problems with all the computerizing and automating is that new photographers do not learn the principles behind the action. Then they become an automation too, making intelligent photography difficult. No, let's make that impossible.

Today, I own two cameras. One is a 1968 Nikon F. Its mechanics are much like the Argus C-3, except that things work smoother and have more features. It also is a single-lens-reflex, which was one of the important developments in photography.

The other is a Nikon N90, which has all the automation ad gadgetry one could ever want. A photographer can find advantage in sophisticated gear. Worthwhile photography is created through the mind and control of three variable factors. It is definitely an advantage to have shutter speed, f-stop and focus working properly. The rationale is that you can concentrate more on composition and any artistic opportunities that might not present themselves when all is automatic.

These features, no doubt, are handy. But they are not enough. The mind and an alert awareness of what is out there in front of the lens are the master ingredients to successful photography. I find myself regularly overriding photography. I find myself regularly overriding the automatic readings on my N90's displays.

My interest started with the simplicity of the Argus C-3 back in 1952. I have been ever thankful for this introduction to 35mm photography.

The Nikon was aging, and in 1990 its light meter went berserk. The worst kind of berserk because one minute it would work fine; the next, it was feeding me false readings. You'll never believe where I was when the first failure occurred: walking the Golden Gate Bridge.

Finally, it was obvious I was wasting film and frustrating myself. For the second trip to Germany in 1992, I bought an inexpensive handheld meter. All this time, my enthusiasm and patience for photography were running low. Would I ever do enough photography to warrant new equipment? And, once a Nikon user, always a Nikon user.

In April 1994, I purchased a Nikon N90, a 35-80mm zoom lens, and a speed light. I had not used a flash since 1968, but all of the automatic stuff was tempting, and I had to get photography off dead center.

In the first year, I shot about ten rolls of film. Improvements in cameras have picked up, and I still don't know how to use even a fraction of the features. I'm pretty much point-and-shoot so far. The basic automatic features are a godsend.

As a further attempt to increase the photo urge, I began having transparencies printed into 5x7s, 8x12s, 11x14s, and a few poster sizes. That eventually led to framing with mattes and everything. It has gotten to be a big operation, but still an avocation, and still fascinating.

Angels in the Air
The daily life in Eau Claire, WI, were abruptly interrupted one lazy June afternoon. Into a partly cloudy and peaceful sky roared the U.S. Navy's flight demonstration team – the Blue Angels. Their exhilarating, intoxicating power charged the heavens for miles around with an eye-popping, ear-spitting electricity.

An estimated 50,000 people experienced such power at the Eau Claire's Chippewa Valley Regional Airport that summer. My daughter, Dorie, and her husband, Steve, combined a belated birthday and Father's Day gift to the biennial Jaycee-sponsored airshow. We've been doing it ever since.

These disciplined young fliers and their machines were a study in co-operation and inspired some pride for a short time. What they did seemed miraculous, though as English novelist Arnold Bennet once pointed out, "When a thing is thoroughly well done, it often has the air of being a miracle."

As I stood atop our van to record images of these swarming and storming Hornets, it occurred to me that men do not really fly. They instead sit in their cockpits and control their machines. The machines fly.

What manner of man is capable of such skills and strains? They were men with diverse American names like Wedemeyer, Silkey, Dunleavy, Beare, and Verissimo, led by a commander named Dom.

They controlled F/A-18 Hornets. Specifications included: length 56 feet, height 15.3 feet, wingspan 40.4 feet. Their maximum speed was Mach 1.8-plus, which was nearly twice the speed of sound, or about 1,500 miles per hour.

The plane could perform combat at 50,000 feet, about 9.5 miles up. The jet was described in the official program of the *Upward Airshow* as a

U.S. Navy's Blue Angels at Chippewa Valley Regional Airport
Eau Claire, Wisconsin

"highly maneuverable supersonic strike fighter." It was really a maneuverable rocket.

Its F404-GE-402 General Electric Enhanced-Performance engines are each in the 18,000-pound- thrust class. We no longer talk about horsepower.

The forward thrust of these planes was so great they can use small wings, their surfaces being only 400 square feet, or 200 square feet, per wing. That seems like a lot, but a square with sides of 14 feet yields about 200 square feet.

Though they were military strictness par excellence, something generated beyond that, something involving the human spirit. Maybe it's pride that we are members of the species that can do such things, or simply satisfaction from observing activity that reflects extraordinary accomplishment. Maybe it was the roar of American persistence and technology, or maybe it was the wits and courage of finely trained and disciplined men.

One moment they fly by like a roar of lions, and the next, you can hardly see them with binoculars. They soar, boring into the atmosphere as though they were drills penetrating steel, but with supremely efficient results, no sparks, and little resistance. Some impressions remain with me:

- Two planes stabbed the air at 400 miles per hour, hurtling directly at each other, winging over at the last second, to pass within feet of each other. Then they rose, straight up, defying gravity, roaring at full throttle until they were but specks against the sky.
- All six, bunched tightly in formation, made an ear-shattering, bone-tingling pass, and I wondered how one learns to make six powerful machines huddle so close together at 400 mph.
- After another harrowing pass, two Angels climbed and banked, demonstrating what a tight turn really is. The sound arrived a little later, making its turn exactly as its source had.

Then there was silence. All six jets were scrambling and scurrying far off, beyond sound and out of sight. Every once in a while, a distant jet whine or a whistling could be heard, telling us they were out there somewhere. It was an eerie quiet, because you know what's going to happen. The waiting and anxiety are part of the show. Then the thunder and roar returned. After one final rumble, the Angels climbed, banked, and peeled off single file, signaling the show was almost over.

These men fly literally inches apart, daring, trusting, and moving fast. They come into view before you can hear them, an eternally powerful presence.

I remember Tom Wolfe's description in *The Right Stuff* of the search team in the Everglades coming upon the remains of a jet fighter and its pilot, part of whom was dangling from the massive foliage of the Florida swamps. But all these experiences tell something about the human endeavor, discovery, and progress. Understanding nature has its cost, but the fruits bring a tasteful, harmonic vibration which reminds us we are still one with nature.

As the miraculous machines moved along the runway, louder than most other aircraft at full throttle, I again thought about man, flight, and these storming symbols of power. We Americans have always loved machines. We are thrilled by and take pride in power, speed, and freedom of movement. We like to think we can go here, there, everywhere, whenever and however we choose.

We also admire the discipline of young men who can learn what has to be learned to charge the heavens thus. They represent us at our best. Their intensely provocative engines get into our psyches as well as our eyes and ears.

I believe we are like them in our lives, our private and public lives. We do not pilot the F/A-18 Hornets with the Blue Angels. However, understanding that we put them there, and that we, in our lives and in our work, are the fabric of society that made such pilots and machines.

An Enduring Image

> *I really believe there are things nobody*
> *would see if I didn't photograph them.*
> Diane Arbus

One of the most enduring images my camera has produced is of the Washington Monument, taken on a family vacation in the summer of 1965, as national unrest prevailed.

It is not a standard look at the towering obelisk, which is always difficult to compose. The monument is a simple form, but it stands out there in the mall all by itself, so there is little available to frame it.

I have tried to use tree branches across the top and down the sides, but since the image is about as vertical as a subject can be, that leaves something to be desired. I have tried to shoot down the Reflecting Pool from the Lincoln Memorial, but that was before I had a variety of lenses from which to choose. It has always seemed pointless to do the subject all by itself without any framing devices besides the ground and the sky.

I suppose I could have placed a person in the foreground and position him or her to guide a finger so it looked like he or she was a giant holding down a rocket by appearing to press down on the pinnacle. I've never cared for freaky stuff like that, especially with national monuments.

On that 1965 journey to the east coast with four children, ages thirteen, eleven, nine, and eight, it was something of a challenge to maintain a focus on the national shrines. At the Jefferson Memorial, which is a circular structure supported by pillars with the third president seated in the center. I strolled outside the pillars, weaving in and out among them. As I passed two of them, I glanced across the Tidal Basin, and I saw the Washington Monument framed in a different way. The long shaft of light between the pillars presented the monument, a brief show of dark green trees, the Tidal Basin, and at the button, white marble steps.

Eighty-five percent of the total image was pillar, the one on the left appearing as a darker-shaded green. The one on the right exuded the color we recognize was marble. Neither was in the sunlight, only that fifteen percent through which the Washington Monument appeared.

I remember being enthralled by the image. I varied the factors by moving closer, then farther away, and changing exposures, and doing more studying. I didn't have an SLR camera, a zoom lens, or any other lens than the standard 50 mm. Considering the circumstances, I'd say I lucked out, even if I did have to work fast. I made only one frame. But I wish I had stopped down so that the monument would have increased its definition. On the other hand, I've been told that having the obelisk and the sky so close in exposure adds a bit of mystery.

National shrines seemed to mean more in those years of civil-rights and Vietnam strife. The 1965 photo still inspires a deep personal response.

Washington Monument, National Park Service, Washington, D.C.

Grand Scheme of Things

>*Who are we? We find that we live on an insignificant*
>*planet of a humdrum star lost in a galaxy tucked away*
>*in some forgotten corner of a universe in which there*
>*are far more galaxies than people.*
>
> Carl Sagan

Every once in a while, events take place which make us aware of the universe and what small part we play in the grand scheme of things.

I've been reading about the grand conjunction of heavenly bodies expected to take place in late April. The waning crescent moon and the planets Venus and Jupiter were going to spend a little time together in the early morning sky.

I've not had good luck with viewing and recording these celestial events. I've tried my luck, but too many things can go wrong.

First is the weather. It is hard to get through a day with dawn-to-dusk sunshine and dusk-to-dawn starlight. Second is the times when the events occur. Often, they are late in the day or early in the morning. Too late to be alert, too early to be awake.

But *Astronomy* magazine said of this event, "This is one morning conjunction you certainly won't want to miss." So, I marked the date on the calendar, watched the weather reports as the day approached and went to bed the night before, certain the weather would be perfect.

Rising at 4:45 AM, I peeked through the front window, and the crystalline sharpness of the objects in the eastern sky startled me. Already the morning's dusk-in-reverse was in progress. So, I hurried through my bathroom routine, grabbed the camera already mounted on a tripod, and headed out the back door.

Pulling out of the driveway, I wasn't sure just where to go. But I sort of gravitated to "senior hill," the place at the north edge of Lake Geneva where adolescent couples used to go to contemplate the world and each other. I located a spot where I could frame some earthly foliage around those celestial subjects.

Things can go wrong at various settings. I thought about what it was I was photographing. Here was a sliver of crescent moon, 225,000 miles away, low in the eastern sky. To its right and slightly above was bright Venus, and less than one degree to its right, Jupiter the largest planet.

These celestial bodies shone brightly against the ever-increasing hues of the dawn. Venus, 83,000,000 miles away, seemed to be perched on the moon's shoulder. Jupiter, at 500,000,000 miles away, appeared to be just a jiffy to the right of Venus. Venus has a diameter of 8,000 miles, and Jupiter, 88,000 miles.

This view can be sort of shocking to an inhabitant of this minor planet. Here they are, the three brightest features of the night sky all lined up, reflecting the light of our approaching daystar, having their bright crystalline moment together.

Meanwhile, back on senior hill, I was reviewing my photographic mistakes. However, they seem insignificant against this ethereal, elysian canvas of the universe. This phenomenon, which, like all of nature's components, was disappearing quickly into the blanket of diffused light that is the earth's atmosphere. Emperor Sol was ascending his throne to reign again. Another of nature's delights gone, vanished.

I should have learned by now what photographer Henri Cartier-Bresson understood a long time ago. "Photographers deal in things which are continually vanishing, and when they have vanished there is no contrivance on earth which can make them come back again."

Although Venus and Jupiter remain relatively close through May, the crescent moon is in the western evening sky where it will cavort with another of the planets.

I'm back in my routine, one of those folks, who like most Americans, "cheerfully assume that in some mystic way love conquers all, that good outweighs evil in the just balances of the universe, and that at the eleventh hour something gloriously triumphant will prevent the worst before it happens" (Brooks Atkinson).

Henri Cartier-Bresson

We've all seen still action photos which make us wonder what will happen next. For the photographer, this attention is more than minimum success.

One of Henri Cartier-Bresson's most famous images is called "Behind the Saint-Lazare Station" (Paris 1932). This print has been reproduced many times over several decades, and I confess initially I did not understand why. The print had nothing really important in it, so I thought.

But I was forgetting a significant principle: subject matter is not always key to a successful image. "I hate exoticism—everything is interesting," Cartier-Bresson said. He took his famous photo in a courtyard near Paris railroad station. In fact, it was out "behind" the station.

Random refuse is strewn about. The yard is not apparent because it is covered with water. A man is in the process of dashing across the courtyard and has just negotiated a crude ladder lying in the water. As he took his first step beyond the ladder, the camera recorded his heel as it was about to splash into the water. But it didn't. It never will.

Permanently recorded is the man suspended in the air. Since the almost perfectly still water reflects everything, there is a second image of the man inverted with his heel about to touch its opposite. In fact, the two heels are so close that one is tempted to lean forward to observe just how close. There is a ballet quality about the figure's suspension over the temporary courtyard pool.

The man is near the right edge of the frame almost ready to leap out. Other shapes and figures offset his figure. A metal fence in back extends across the scene. Its pickets look like spears reaching skyward.

Note the other four figures. Three figures look at first like humans, then like gravestones, but they probably are neither. The fourth is a man who is moving, but first impression is that he is standing still. Also, on a wall near the fence, are two posters which show what appear to be two ballerinas gracefully soaring. All these forms reflect in the water, providing a real and a reflected backdrop to our man leaping.

One of life's unremarkable moments in a plain, unremarkable place is frozen in time. Taken eighty-seven years ago at 4:05 PM (there is a clock tower in the background), it survived as a fanciful, quixotic fragment of life.

So, what happens next? Does the man splash his way out of view and continue hurrying to wherever he is going? Does he slip, lose his balance, and fall flat on his face? Where is going? What is he running from?

Cartier-Bresson's photography seems to symbolize this dilemma of deluge and "what happens next." Man, in his whimsical but often destructive course through time, frets and fumes about the future. He forges ahead. Is this comedy or tragedy we are watching?

- A sort of haze, partly shrouding roofs in the background, balances very well the light reflected in the water of the foreground.
- The random refuse does not seem so random after some study.
- The photo is in a vertical format.
- Though not mentioned, this a black and white print.
- The scene is cluttered yet orderly.
- The journey from confusion to insight was a long, slow one.
- This is a hazy-bright day. That is why so much detail can be seen.
- Subjects are back-lit. That is one reason the subject, with some blur caused by motion, appears to stand out as sharply as he does.
- The whimsy of a middle-aged man leaping over a pool of water stands out in bold relief from the rather gray, somber surroundings.

We have learned to record images for posterity, if you will. We have done so well that we sometimes have trouble distinguishing reality. The overwhelming avalanche of television, movie and print images makes it difficult to sort out what is real, unreal, true, untrue, valid, invalid.

His modus operandi should shed some light on his work:

- Always used a Leica, the best of those first 35mm cameras. It was small, inconspicuous, accurate.
- Always worked with black-and-white film.
- Never used a flash. It was available light for everything.
- Never developed his film.
- Never set up a photo. All pre-exposure planning was done in his head as his subjects shaped up before him.
- Always insisted on creating a complete picture on the spot— then no altering or cropping of prints.

Settings for his photos were always natural. Asked when do you press the shutter, his answer was, "It's a question of concentration. Concentrate, think, watch, look and ah, like this, you are ready. But you never know the culminative point of something …. But you shouldn't overshoot." He shared additional wisdom:

> It's like overeating, overdrinking. You have to eat, you have to drink, but over is too much…by the time you press, you will arm the shutter once more and maybe the picture was in between.
>
> You can't have freedom without discipline. There is no such thing as complete freedom, just as nothing in the world is completely good or completely bad. Everything is relative. There must be freedom, yes, but always with a sense of form and structure behind it.

Cartier-Bresson's photographs have the same planning that artists' paintings have. That's because his main interest was art. He studied with artist Andre Lhote (1927), whom he credited with teaching him "everything I know about photography." He used an analogy to explain the difference: "Photography is a sketchbook. Drawing is meditation."

Somewhere I read that he had "an instinct for extracting the most telling moment from the scene before him." It has been called "the decisive moment."

After hunting experience in Africa, he developed a metaphor for shooting. You must "approach tenderly, gently … on tiptoe—even if the subject is a still life," he once said. "A velvet hand, a hawk's eye—these we should all have."

Ubiquitous and all but invisible, he was the unchallenged master of unpretentious, unretouched reportage—winning for its seeming lack of guile as for its ability to communicate directly with enormous impact.

Cartier-Bresson once noted, "Photographers deal in things which are continually vanishing and when they have vanished there is no contrivance on earth which can make them come back again."

Kodachrome

Sixty-seven years ago, I aimed my Argus C-3 camera at my fourteen-month-old daughter sitting in a multi-colored inflatable pool in the yard of my father-in-law's farmhouse on a sunny summer day. The resulting image has stuck for several reasons. It was taken shortly after I had seen my daughter for the first time, which is enough by itself to make it memorable.

In 2009, Kodak made an announcement that affected a lot of us who were active in color slide photography. Kodak decided to cease the manufacture of Kodachrome. Anyone close to the changes going on in the world of photography should have been surprised.

I hadn't stopped using Kodachrome, but certainly the opportunity to do so was now considered more carefully. Cost is one thing. Other factors were availability and the reduction of labs that process Kodachrome. I did continue to use it, but with great care in choice of subjects. Now Kodak, the old photo granddad of color photography, was going to yield to economic realities.

My first impulse was to call the Camera Company, Madison's fellow photo friends. Since I read the news in the *Chicago Tribune* early in the morning, I called the Camera Company seven minutes before they opened at 9:30.

Keith Power, one of the dependable folks employed there, answered. "How much Kodachrome do you have on hand?" I asked. He responded, "You heard!" Everyone has a sense of humor at the Camera Company.

Keith told me they had twenty-five 36-exposure rolls. I had them hold twelve. They did, and the next day before a UW clinic appointment with our daughter, I dropped off film and some reprint work. As I came in the door, storeowner Ward Lundgren thought for sure I was going to break out to the lyrics of Paul Simon's *Kodachrome*. He said they had something over a half dozen calls on the subject after I called the day before.

They had the dozen rolls all bagged for me and eight more if I wanted to buy them. I told them I'd decide when we returned from the clinic.

I was told they could still order Kodachrome. The important factor was the expiration date. That turned out to be August 2010. Kodachrome will last a lot longer if it is kept refrigerated until it is needed.

That's a lot of film. The cost did not seem to be a factor. After all, the

Kodachrome era was coming to a close. Who knows how long processing will be available? I could not ignore expense, but Kodachrome film and the processing have long been expensive. At this point, each roll of thirty-six costs $8.99 and $8.09 with discount. That's 22¢ per slide. I still consider cost a factor, but my love affair with Kodachrome was ending.

All I could think of was photographer Steve McCurry. He was the *National Geographic* photographer whose portrait of an Afghan refugee girl appeared on the cover of the June 1985 edition. This Kodachrome image was one of the most stunning I can remember. Those haunted eyes, conveying the fear refugees experience. It was vintage Kodachrome.

Kodak requested McCurry shoot one of his last Kodachrome rolls and donate the images to the George Eastman House. McCurry told the *Tribune*, "I want to take the last roll with me and somehow make every frame count – just as a way to honor the memory and always be able to look back with fond memories at how it ended my shooting Kodachrome."

So, I figure this investment can be my way of saying goodbye to a beautiful relationship. It is also opportunity. I am always looking forward to the next challenge turning up in my viewfinder. Recording moments could be considered art I suppose, but it is the chance of capturing for eternity a special moment, an evanescent image, which will never return.

In color photography, and more especially with the rich, deep, warm colors of Kodachrome, the reward of capturing a moment is particularly satisfying. If this photography were culinary, it would be the most delicious dish ever tasted.

How many moments have you captured which could enlighten family experience three generations from now? Only photography can do that.

Here's how Paul Simon said it in his popular *Kodachrome* – "They give us those nice bright colors. They give us the greens of summers. Makes you think all the world's a summer day."

The Color-Print Game
Now that I have turned the color-slide game into the color-print game, it is time to reflect on what this shift means.

Being a practical and frugal sort, I see the first factor as money. It is expensive; making prints costs money. The way I am going about it you'd think there was only so much time to do this. Today it was $117, and a week ago over $160. I have never turned many slides into prints, so it's like finding a treasure. But assuming expense and excitement, there is also the artistic, qualitative angle.

I have been surprised in a number of ways. One is how blowing up an inch by one-and-a-half-inch piece of film to 8x12, 11x14, or 20x30 inches can maintain a sharpness that would seem to be unlikely, if not impossible.

Another factor is what comes through larger prints. Of course, making larger images is going to allow one to see more detail, relationship of parts, and the dynamics of the image. These benefits seem to leap out at a far greater rate than the increase in size would seem to warrant.

I have developed a good eye. My composition surprises me sometimes. Those little pieces of cardboard contain far more than can be seen, even when blown up on a screen. I am seeing thing in these prints which I did not remember were present. Sometimes I wonder whether I was factoring them into my original shooting of the image. If the general principles are taken into account, the details will take care of themselves. It certainly appears that way, and quite often.

Importance of Images

> *Life is not about significant details,*
> *illuminated in a flash, fixed forever.*
> *Photographs are.*
>
> Susan Sontag

I am fascinated by images. Always have been. Though my experience has been mostly photography, I include images of all kinds. Maybe that is because I concentrate hard on them, knowing they cannot be recorded.

Image-making accelerated to a frenzy during my childhood when *Life* magazine became the chief source of the world away from my world. Their great photographers gave the pre-television generation its image lift. The Depression, World War II, then the Cold War, and all the interesting people and the catastrophes of nature and man: all of these images were almost the exclusive bailiwick of *Life* magazine.

An early interest in photography must have had something to do with my recognition that the still image can stand eternal in the mind. The

412

Alzheimer's Association sends out greeting cards with its appeals for donations. One of the most common subjects is Monet and his art. I save those cards. When I have occasion to use a note requiring a more elevated purpose, I look through the Monets and choose. For some reason these scenes from nature, as uplifting and abstract as a Debussy prelude, make a penetrating statement in their not-quite-real impressionistic scenes. They are real but allow the view to fill in gaps, indeed if there are any.

That is what happens with photographic images. I have always desired to share what I see with others. Though that opportunity is limited, I carry on the practice of framing enlarged prints and even clipping images from publications, pasting them on cardboard, then posting them in conspicuous locations to view and study or just stare at.

By one's ninth decade, life's perspectives have changed. I always conduct my thinking beyond myself. Though I can do little about it, I consider man's place in the universe as well as his place on earth. Though I am convinced we are cosmic accidents, looking over at the image of the blue earth rising above the moon's horizon continues to send chills through me. Looking at our blue marble, I understand all of the world's experience is and has been conducted on the surface of our tiny sphere seemingly alone amid the blackness.

Images can stir the mind's higher energies. I'm not sure if my experience is any different from those of others. I am sure photos have had a lot to do with it. When traveling, I tend to see things as potential photo subjects. I'm composing all the time. So, when I see a striking photo, finding its essence is an immediate goal.

Imagine you've been at sea for several days, and all you've seen is water and sky. Then, someone says a ship is appearing on the horizon. You're so excited to see something besides sea and sky that you hurry to record the event. But the human eye's capacity for concentration is such that the ship looks larger than the eye of your camera will see it. When the film is developed, I have a print that is ninety-nine percent sea and sky.

The secret to a successful image is a memorable connection. It may come from the image itself or something with which that image is associated. Or it may come from the dramatic realization of an earthrise, or the unexpected impact of a distant skyline.

Images come at us constantly. Very few images stick. Those that do become permanent parts of the fabric of our experiences. They help elevate life's meaning. They are integrated into our very beings.

Is it possible to imagine what life was like before photography? Are we better off for having instant access to pictures? What is the constant bombarding of images doing to us as humans? Are we fortunate to have the means to always recall where we have been and what we have done?

The Ability to See

Alfred Eisenstaedt, the great German-born American photographer, who really was *Life* magazine, became a master of the candid.

He could quickly put a subject in a context that made photos look planned. He studied subjects until he knew something of how their minds and emotions were related to the way they looked. Every time I see a collection of Eisenstaedt's work, the meaning of patience comes to mind.

His photos always looked casual, candid, unplanned. But like all good photography, something draws us in, and we can see the planning.

The famous August 1945 photo, for example, of the sailor in his dress blues kissing a nurse dressed in white. He has her bent backward in a dance-like pose, which will forever convey the joy and relief of V-J Day and the end of World War II. Have you ever noticed how the people in the background of that picture form symmetrical half-circle which seems to be closing in on the couple? Did you note the buildings in the background receding toward each other ending in the famous Times Square corner, which appears right over the couple's heads? Still this sharply contrasting couple stands out in bold relief.

Planned, the photo looks planned. However, I know it is as candid as photography can be. Eisenstaedt called this gift "the ability to see." He told this story to a *Christian Science Monitor* reporter in 1973:

At my Chicago exhibition there was a man and a young boy, and the man said, 'My boy, I'm going to buy you the same type of camera, the same lenses and I'm sure you will do the same type of pictures as Mr. Eisenstaedt.'

I did not want to belittle him so I said, 'Of course you will in time, but it isn't as easy as it seems. Look at me (he held up his hands). I have two hands and I can't play the piano. Cliburn, Rubenstein can.

414

Where does it originate? The piano or the camera doesn't do it. It must be still here (He tapped his head). It takes time, naturally, to learn to see.

Eisenstaedt was probably best known for his candid portraits of famous people. He made well-known people look common in their popularity. He made Marilyn Monroe look like the girl who lives down the block. Most photographers made her look unreal, unknowable. He made Marlon Brando look like the "American Olivier" he could have been. He almost had Brando smiling.

Eisenstaedt had a photo of Albert Einstein at his desk. The picture was taken through the vertical frame formed by the partially open door. I am made to feel as though I am intruding on the great mind's privacy. I have sense of participation in one of the twentieth-century's great forward movements. Eisenstaedt seemed to have another worldly alertness. He must have seen all that was important.

I wish I had Eisenstaedt's ability to get to the heart of things. He had a splendid sense of reality and how to turn it into art. Though the exposure was made in a split second, there is no way to measure the larger genius, the patience, the sense of timing and reality. The product of that genius will live on.

It's All in the Light

You can make decent pictures if you understand and utilize light. Notice I said "make," not "take," pictures. Ansel Adams, the extraordinary photographer of American's Western landscape, always said he made pictures.

Adams believed in what he called the zone system of photography. This system trains photographers to anticipate or previsualize specific textures and contrasts of the desired photograph and then expose the film with this previsualization in mind.

I have to admit I had trouble when it came to consider the photograph before the fact. Photography becomes an exercise of the mind in Adams' thinking. Indeed, if photography is to be an art, the mind needs to be at work in all stages of "making" a picture. Of Ansel's work, one critic said, "With camera, mind, and heart, he explores the ocean of light that floods the continent each day."

It's all in the light. If I were going to select a photographer whose work could be used in demonstrating the elements at work in photography, it would be the prints of Ansel Adams.

One of the most widely circulated of Adams' prints is entitled *Mt. Williamson, Sierra Nevada, from Manzanar, California, 1944*. In the foreground is a massive field of boulders extending to the base of the Sierra mountains several miles away. The main peak of Mt. Williamson rises among the cliffs and chasms of the lesser peaks. The later afternoon sun shoots shafts of light obliquely through the unstructured clouds of a mountain thunderstorm.

The sharp contrast between the ethereal light through the clouds among the crags and peaks, and the field of eternally stationary stones, convey a powerful truth about the earth. Adams caught the elemental feel of nature, its hard, stony composition. He captured the sun's incessantly changing influence, the earth's ever-changing as well as its never-changing face.

How do you "make" pictures like this? Ansel Adams wrote about his photographic methods in *The Making of Forty Photographs*. Here is a segment of his discussion of the Mt. Williamson print:

The eye and mind gather the splendors of this region into wonderful ideas and anticipatory visualizations. The camera is not very cooperative without exciting foreground and skies. Our eyes scan only a small angle of view at any moment; as we move our direction of sight, our visual memory holds and builds impressions of larger and larger areas, while bringing each point concentrated upon into clarity and detail …

The Sierra slopes back from desert edge to summit at an angle of forty-five degrees or less; seen from a frontal distance, it appears a gray rise of land engraved with clefts and gorges of vast proportions. Early morning shadows give way to flat sun-glare; this, in turn, yields to the complex confusion of midday sun and shadow, which is better remembered in the mind than on film. In the afternoon, the shadows lengthen, and the range finally becomes a giant wall of subtle textures and jagged crests.

It IS all in the light. People with cameras in their hands often forget that factor.

Adams comments further about what photographs share with all art:

As with all art, the photographer's objective is not the duplication of visual reality. Photographic images cannot avoid being reality in direct relation to the placement of the camera before the subject, the lens chosen, the film and filters, and the exposure indicated, the related development and printing; all, of course, relating to what the photographer visualizes.

I think you will agree, we "make" pictures, not "take" them.

Visual-Musical Portrait of Lake Geneva

Starting in 1970, walking became a regular part of my daily routine, and I did a good deal of slide photography along and near the lake. The vagaries and chances of my walking routines determined which elements of the community were photographed.

At one point, I sequenced about seventy slides over the six-plus minutes of the Modern Jazz Quartet's *How High the Moon* (Hamilton/Lewis, 1940). The blend of vibraphone, bass, piano and percussion rendered the tune in a manner seeming to catch the feel of the locale.

By 2007, I tightened up the sequencing and wound up with one hundred twenty-five slides cued to the same six-plus minutes of the MJQ recording.

The major elements of the project involved the four seasons, the historic district, and many aspects of Geneva life that no longer exist (e.g., the railroad, Geneva Inn, Paint Spot, Gargoyle). Contrasting community elements corresponded to changes in the rhythms of the music. The upbeat center section pictured the active downtown life of the city, while the first and last sections suggested a lyrical, more thoughtful mood.

I hope my DVD entitled *Portrait of Lake Geneva* transmits a little of the feeling we all get at times about this place I began to call home. I convey a degree of pride when I show it off to visiting friends and relatives. The pride side is the natural beauty.

On Presidents and the Presidency

Our presidents represent us, and we trust them with a great deal of responsibility. Though I was not always aware of it, our presidents have had a direct effect on the mood, temper, spirit of daily life. I judged their abilities, successes, and failures by how I related to them as individuals.

The first essay in this chapter describes a visit my family had to the little-known but inspirational Presidents Information Center in Rapid City, South Dakota. Then I share my brief and sometimes much longer impressions of thirteen presidents who served from 1927 to 2016.

CONTENTS

The second set of essays contains my reflections on campaigning, building trust with citizens, and bringing about change.

Presidents Information Center

On the weekend of July 4, 2010, my wife, our youngest daughter and I attended the ordination of our granddaughter's husband, the ceremony taking place in his father's church in Rapid City, South Dakota.

Those events were planned. Not in the plan was meeting all of the U.S. presidents. While we had seen the four faces on Rushmore's mountain twice before, we weren't prepared to see all of the presidential faces at once on the streets of Rapid City.

On downtown street corners are realistic portrayals of all of America's presidents. The life-size bronze statues convey faithfully both physical and personality traits. I can't recall how we learned about presidents taking up residence on Rapid City street corners, but it sounded like a must-see. So, on the afternoon of July 5, between our visit to a cousin and the daily afternoon rain, we went to have a look.

Expecting crowds, we found few tourists, and parking was easy. We parked the van on Sixth Street off St. Joseph Street and looked for the men who have led America over the last 240-plus years.

At the end of the first block was the smiling, waving figure of President Jimmy Carter. We asked Denise to drive her wheelchair beside the thirty-ninth president so I could take a picture. Maybe we shouldn't have done that because by the time we walked a block, Denise was already parked, ready to have her picture taken with another executive. This happened a dozen times so that a subsequent photo album has its first section filled with "Denise meets the president" photos.

The Presidents Information Center was an immense project, and why it has not received media attention beyond South Dakota is hard to figure. The only information I've found so far was a short piece in the South Dakota travel book and a listing of the statue locations on a downtown city map.

The Presidents Information Center is located at Seventh and Main Streets. Curiously, the center was closed on the Fourth of July weekend. With that address and the zip code, I later sent a note, but it was returned marked "insufficient address." My cousin called the center and learned that the lady in charge was out of town, but they would have her call my cousin. We have heard nothing further.

The five sculptors were Western artists who completed four statues a

419

year from 2000 to 2010. The artists are Lee Leunding, John Lopez, James Michael Maher, Edward E. Hlavka and James Van Nuys.

Studying and photographing the statues, I found myself wondering who these men really were and why they spent their maturity in the tough business of national leadership. Why did they want that complex, mind-bending job? It is safe to say most gave their lives to its mission.

I thought I perceived the essence of what they brought to the task. I've been a student of the presidency and have never felt as close to these men as I did on the streets of this middle-American town.

The presidents have come to middle America. The statue of President Reagan stood in front of a restaurant, President Eisenhower near a parking lot, President Van Buren in front of a law firm, President Carter by a bridal store, and President George H.W. Bush at the Elks Building.

They seemed to blend in, though we tend to visualize them above and beyond reality. On the Main Street of Rapid City, SD, they seemed approachable, understandable. I recognized traits and characteristics I'd read about, heard enacted, or otherwise learned during my life.

Of all the presidents in my lifetime, President Roosevelt made the strongest impression on me. He served just over twelve years.

Today, in Rapid City, FDR stands before a bank of network microphones. Clearly, he had difficulty standing. I will never forget that warm, patrician voice that spoke confidently as Americans lived in the throes of depression and during the war that produced over two hundred ninety thousand American deaths.

Our presidents have for the most part been dedicated, determined men. Their intelligence, personalities, and the nation's circumstances during their terms combined to produce their experience. The connection between president and the people was joined to varying degrees. FDR and his fireside chats were partially successful. It may be well to note I was an impressionable pre-teen during that time.

Some connections seemed especially real in Rapid City. The uniformed general stands resolute, hands on hips, in the midday Dakota sun. David Eisenhower gave the D-Day orders and later became our thirty-fourth president.

The actor, corporate spokesman, California governor, and fortieth president, Ronald Reagan, has one foot perched on the marker bearing his name. He is in cowboy attire, and he projects that famous Hollywood smile that won over the nation.

Someone who was not a president said, "People want to be taken care of; they place ultimate responsibility for that on the president" (James David Barber, a political science professor).

Someone who was president said, "The president is the representative of the whole nation and he's the only lobbyist that all the one hundred and sixty million people in the country have" (Harry Truman).

Now we are three hundred million, and leadership is even more challenging than ever before. During our Fourth of July weekend on the streets of Rapid City, I felt the spirit that our presidents transmitted, each to his times and challenges. Our unplanned meeting with twenty-one of the presidents was as intriguing as it was unexpected...something thoroughly American about that.

Franklin Delano Roosevelt (1933-1945)

> *A radical is a man with both feet planted – in the air.*
> *A conservative is a man with two perfectly good legs who . . .*
> *has never learned to walk forward.*
>
> *A reactionary is a somnambulist walking backward.*
> *But a liberal is a man who uses his legs and his hands*
> *at the behest – at the command – of his head.*
>
> Franklin Delano Roosevelt

President Roosevelt was in the White House for twelve years. I was five when he was elected and about six weeks from high school graduation when he died on April 12, 1945. I first heard the news of Roosevelt's passing when I was in Mr. Roy Gustrowksy's science class at Fennimore High School. Though I was about to turn eighteen, I could not recall another president. I had vague recollections that there was trouble in the world and that a savior had arrived. One Depression and World War II later, the president was about to celebrate the fruits of his long, difficult twelve years. The war in Europe would end less than a month later; and the war with

Japan, four months later. He died before he could see the fruits of victory and renewal for our country and other countries.

The sad news came on a routine Thursday afternoon. I recall not specifics but a gradual overwhelming sorrow. At the time, my life was filled with all those things that consume high school seniors six weeks before graduation. The only difference was that I was senior having no choices beyond military service. After four years of anticipating service, it was almost time.

But now the hub, the central pivot of it all, was gone. President Roosevelt's strong political and moral leadership had characterized American life for twelve years, and now it was gone. Leadership during those dozen years demanded much. Roosevelt communicated and generated trust in the American people during difficult and desperate times. Those radio fireside chats seemed to make him part of our families.

Since April 1945, I have had thousands of occasions to compare other men, other times, other causes, and other crises and catastrophes to those of FDR's time. He has worn well. He is now an unquestioned icon. That was not always so. In fact, he and what he did were widely despised.

My father and mother trusted President Roosevelt. I grew up trusting him, too, because he fought the Depression and became one of the two most influential leaders in World War II. I might say that I had a family father and a national father. I could have done a lot worse on both counts.

Over seventy-five years as an adult have taught me a great deal about the New Deal, national responsibility, and what leadership involves. Deep down, I know that national leadership has not been the same since. Maybe it takes real national crises to bring out the best in us.

My feeling about bad economic times and episodes of violence reminds me of the person who knows his body is sending out signals that there is trouble, but like many of us he ignores them or treats them in superficial ways. Then at some unannounced moment, the body erupts. We talk as though this trouble is something out of our sight and control. Common sense told us regularly that trouble has been building for a long time. Now we must pay the price of heavy emergency treatments.

In the case of a democracy, those heavy measures are paid for by the people. If we had only had a plan, someone's vision of how such a serious problem might have been solved. If only our measure of responsibility had been as bounteous as our measure of freedoms. What has happened is we have insisted on the latter and left the former for others.

Even the Congress and the President are acting that way. Our democracy comes up for grabs under such attitudes. The greatest social experiment in the history of the world up for grabs? Someone must turn up with a vision and the ability to relate it to the nation. Someone must generate a union, an accord about fundamental human concerns.

When I think of presidents who did that, two come to mind: Abraham Lincoln and Franklin Roosevelt. It is easy to say that we do not have the problems they faced. I am not so sure. The events of recent years seem to say differently. Because of the events in one city, a whole series of social dilemmas sharpened their focus. We do not need a civil war or a great depression to tell us we have serious problems.

I've studied Lincoln and his times. I grew up hearing and feeling the reassuring words of FDR. One was from a privileged background; the other, from stark poverty. One was educated in the best eastern schools; the other, strictly self-educated. It didn't matter that one suffered a life-limiting attack of polio, or that the other split rails, told stories, and matured on the frontier. We don't have those kinds of leaders today.

Something of what this country stood for was fundamental in these men. When their time came, they provided leadership to deal with their society-splitting problems. I think our problems are every bit as serious today. We can see and feel the symptoms; the prognosis is quite clear. A doctor would not want to wait any longer.

Harry S. Truman (1945-1953)

President James Polk said a moving thing on his retirement,
'I now retire as a servant and regain my position as a sovereign.'
He was right. I've been through it and I know.
Harry S. Truman

Harry Truman was president for almost eight years, during my service in the U.S. Navy, the first years of my undergraduate studies at the University of Wisconsin-Madison, and my service in the U.S. Army. Since those years, my opinion of President Truman has evolved from questioning the intricacies of "Harry's war" (Korea) to the belief that he was one of the most important and influential of all U.S. presidents.

Truman was honest and direct, and he had the welfare of the country in his heart. He was the twentieth-century president most likely to be called the commoner among us. He did not attend college; yet he was as well read as any president.

In my first turn in the voting booth, I voted for Thomas E. Dewey. Yes, I did. You may be saying, "Thomas E. who?" In 1948, six months after I turned twenty-one, I voted for the New York governor and former state's attorney who said he was going to clean house in Washington.

As it turned out, Dewey's opponent, Harry S. Truman, the vice-president who assumed office when Franklin Roosevelt died just before World War II ended, won the election and became a good chief executive.

By 1948 Truman was succeeding at an almost impossible task: the transition from a full war footing to a peace-time economy. But the accelerating Cold War, the economic growing pains, and assorted other problems were making him look weak to the electorate. The favored Dewey was expected to perform a landslide. I guess as a twenty-one-year-old, I wanted to be part of a landslide. Truman is now considered one of the most effective of our presidents.

I have concluded that I did not dislike President Truman, but I regretted the situations I was forced into, and upon which I (or we) had to live, e.g., the Korean Conflict and the draft. My personal life was uncertain; my college education was uninspiring. Then there were the issues of General Douglas MacArthur, the atom bomb, the ugly loyalty problems which led to the specter of Joe McCarthy, and the Cold War. These problems affected my morale and view of the world.

President Truman, in the case of Korea, did draw a line on the advance of communism. Then Douglas MacArthur, U.S. commander in the Far East, was assuming an overly aggressive military posture in Asia. Civilians do still govern this country. Truman probably set the stage for McCarthy in his zealous pursuit of "un-American activities." These were matters in which a thoughtful person could not remain neutral.

No matter what one thinks about atomic power, the only part Truman played was the decision to use or not to use the bomb. It is terrifying to think Vice-President Truman was told nothing about the Manhattan

Project in the interim between his November 1944 election and April 12, 1945, the date of President Roosevelt's death. Then less than three months later, he had to decide whether to employ this awesome power or not. After almost six years of world war, the prospect of invading the main Japanese islands was horrifying.

Now here is some real honesty exhibited by the thirty-third President of the United States. The following anecdote comes from Ralph Keyes' *The Wit and Wisdom of Harry Truman,* when Truman was a senator:

> Following a driver who'd done the same thing, Truman went through a stoplight in Washington. A policeman pulled them both over. After examining Truman's license, the policeman asked if he was 'the Truman Committee fellow.' Truman said he was. 'You've been doing a good job in there, Senator,' said the policeman. 'Just let me get this other fellow out of your road till I give him a ticket, then you can roll along.'
>
> Truman responded, 'Officer, I'm a citizen like anyone else. Give me a ticket.' The policeman did so, reluctantly, but never sent him a summons. When he heard no more about the matter, Truman sent a contribution to the Policemen's Fund for the normal amount of a fine.

How many people today, or any other time, would pursue a truthful end as persistently as Harry Truman did? You would trust someone like that.

Dwight David Eisenhower (1953-1961)

Politics… excites all that is selfish and ambitious in man.

I have one yardstick by which I test every major problem – and that yardstick is: Is this good for America?
                              Dwight David Eisenhower

The decade of the 1950s was not a stable time in my personal and professional life. Within a few years, I completed my degree from UW-Madison, married, served two years in the U.S. Army, failed in the restaurant

425

business after two years, completed my teaching license at the Wisconsin State College-Platteville, started a family, and began my teaching career. The end of the decade found me in my second year at Lake Geneva's Badger High School as a teacher of senior English. The president during most of this momentous decade was Dwight Eisenhower, hero of World War II.

Dwight Eisenhower was an American hero who did not seem to want to be president. When you do something only for the honor of it, it shows. Ike's smile seemed less infectious after he became president. Ike transmitted a father image when I needed a drill sergeant.

John Fitzgerald Kennedy (1961-1963)

> *When I ran for the Presidency of the United States,*
> *I knew that this country faced serious challenges,*
> *but I could not realize, nor could any man realize*
> *who does not bear the burdens of this office,*
> *how heavy and constant would be those burdens.*
>
> John Fitzgerald Kennedy

The two and half years of John Kennedy's presidency demonstrated promise, but his assassination left emptiness for many of our hopes and dreams.

Curiously, on Friday, November 22, 1963, I was not in my classroom. I was at home. The school board was preparing to present a referendum for a building project. Superintendent Vernon Pollock asked me to write an essay representing the facts for the presentation in the media and for those citizens attending the public meeting which was a week away.

I agreed to do it. The research and writing demanded some privacy. A substitute was engaged, and I spent Wednesday, Thursday, and Friday at home working on this assignment. On Friday morning, I could see I was going to be pressed to finish so I turned no radio on. I was isolated. I finished about 3 PM and decided to take the draft to Mr. Pollock to read before the weekend.

When I walked outside our home for the first time that Friday afternoon, I began to feel a gray, overcast day, misty and depressing. As I drove down Broad Street, I turned on the radio and heard the familiar

426

symphonic strains on two of the three stations I tried. One was the funeral march from Ludwig van Beethoven's *Eroica Symphony,* and the other was the somber tones of the fourth movement of Tchaikovsky's *Symphony Pathetique.* Strange fare for commercial radio. As I drove through a fine rain toward Badger High School, I knew something had happened.

I don't remember exactly how the news came to me, but I learned that President Kennedy was shot in a motorcade in Dallas and that his body was being flown back to Washington. I don't recall I felt anything until I entered the east door of the school and heard classroom activity.

I had been working quietly in private when the event was reported over two hours before, so I had not shared the experience with others. For that reason, remembering the moment has always held a private meaning for me.

What I remember most is the walk down the two long halls to the office, feeling the hundreds of people on the other sides of the walls. The halls were empty. People needed each other at that moment. I encountered no one until I was in the office about 3:25 PM.

By this time, I understood what had happened and began to know the pain of public mourning. People wanted to be around each other, but few words were spoken. Fear of the unknown, subdued anger, and helplessness intensified. That gray day was forever etched in our innocent minds.

President Kennedy could communicate his youthful idealism. His demeanor always seemed positive. His thirty-four-month presidency of youthful idealism seemed to be rubbing off on us. He made teaching and country seem important, right up to and including "The Four Days" of the precarious Cuban Missile Crisis.

We knew him as a work in progress. We will always remember him as the fond hope of an idealistic generation. He will always be more symbol than substance. His death signaled a 1960s revolt and brought the great mission to the moon.

At forty-six, which is no time to die, he seemed to represent all the positive, optimistic traits we associate with the American character. We'll never know Kennedy's legacy could have been because he didn't have sufficient time to develop one.

I was not going to watch the steady stream of JFK remembrance programs. The problem was avoiding starting. The magnetic power of those sad, profound days was overwhelming. The memorial was a *CBS Reports* presentation of some original footage. What was presented was carefully threaded together so the continuity of those long, leaden days was caught and held, and tears were hard to fight.

Barren trees, the stone edifices of the capitol, military men doing their duty, the courageous Kennedys, the long shadows cast by a low November sun. My imagination, then and now, was forced to fill in the missing pieces, the colors, the thoughts of the people I saw, the meaning of it all. Something changed with the crack of that rifle in Dallas. Americans can never be exactly the same again.

Each November 22nd since his passing has been poignant. Even as my students came along who could not remember the events, there was a melancholy, somber, thoughtful discussion that connects the generation which experiences, to those that do not. As years went by, it became harder and harder to convey the immediacy, the piercing quality of the event, but its meaning somehow was apparent when we finished.

The sad rusts and grays of a late November contrast with the ebullient January day when the bright snow, Robert Frost's white hair, and the hopes of the inauguration of an engaging young president, brightened our future. Something of American innocence and virtue was undercut that day, wherever we were, whatever we were thinking, however our surroundings appeared. Whether we are for better or worse today, November 22, 1963, is forever frozen in our minds and history. I doubt that the changes and effects could be better experienced than in the country's classrooms over those fifty-five years.

The turbulence begun in the 1960s is part of the changing of political and social attitudes. Depending on a person's age in relation to the event, each American has come to view our institutions, our rights, our society, ourselves, differently.

Lyndon Baines Johnson (1963-1969)

> *Now there are many, many people who can recommend*
> *and advise, and a few of them consent,*
> *but there is only one who has been chosen by the*
> *American people to decide.*
>
> Lyndon Baines Johnson

The style of President Lyndon Johnson can pretty much be described by one word: Texan. He brought a wheeler-dealer style to the U.S. Senate where he was Majority Leader for six years. It is easy to recall photos of LBJ right up in some politician's face trying to induce his will.

In his presidency, that characteristic was a large plus and a larger minus. A plus mainly because of social legislations, much needed, but always hard to achieve. In this case, it took his arm-twisting senatorial expertise to bring it about. The minus was just as important, but in the opposite direction. One word should suffice – Vietnam.

The Senate was where Johnson was in his prime. However, as "Master of the Senate," Lyndon Johnson was something less as president. His social legislation was remarkable, but Vietnam was his Waterloo. He was the backslapping, arm-twisting Senate leader who got things done as president, especially for things he understood, such as social welfare and education. For Vietnam and the new generation, no.

President Johnson has always seemed an enigma. One minute you want to pat him on his hill country back and congratulate him on the good he capably did. The next, you want to kick his Texas shins for his overbearing, self-serving character. I doubt he spent much time wondering how he might become a suave, sophisticated social type.

Johnson was ambition personified, and he devoted himself to fulfilling it. He is known to have proclaimed his ambition a number of times in his youth, "I'm going to be the president of the United States." He made these proclamations often beyond the age of childhood.

Lyndon Johnson drove me into a new kind of idealism, but it wasn't the kind that made me feel good, with his loud, awkward syntax and all that stuff going on behind the scenes. The Vietnam period was no time to turn forty. I never was comfortable knowing LBJ had been a teacher.

Richard Milhous Nixon (1969-1974)

When the president does it, that means it is not illegal.
Richard Milhouse Nixon

The Johnson-to-Nixon process of change was about as chaotic as anything could be, short of civil war. Many citizens will remember 1968 for many reasons. Richard Nixon won the presidency that year. After twenty-two years of trying, he inherited a lot of trouble. As we later were to learn, he also caused a lot of trouble. Watergate was a historic sequence of events, driving the dour Nixon from office.

Not enough Americans trusted him. He was not a crook, but we were regularly reminded of it. No president was more misunderstood. Re-elected in 1972, his difficulties leading from the Watergate break-in overshadowed his foreign policy successes and entire presidency. He resigned in August 1974.

I made the mistake of looking in on PBS's *The American Experience* focusing on President Nixon. Three hours later, I was spellbound by Richard Nixon's journey through tough American years. The question remains for me the same as it was after I saw the program the first time. How much did Nixon have to do with the way America is today?

This California Quaker son just never quit. That is good in a person. No doubt he was steadfast in his pursuit of America's best interests. That, too, was commendable. You would think that combination could not fail.

But Nixon's problems were means, not ends. If ever there were someone whose methods were faulty, it was Nixon's. Somehow his career as senator, vice-president and president set an example which has helped create an unhealthy atmosphere. Could it be that 1968 was an American turning point? What was it that changed? Did America lose its innocence?

Johnson and Nixon were two of the most controversial figures you could find in twentieth-century America. Both were not beloved by their countrymen. Both had personalities which could be abrasive. Something in them made Americans skeptical. Neither's typical pose was a smiling countenance. Something made Americans distrust them.

Through sheer grit and determination, both survived the great social and world conflicts to become president. If World War II made Americans unify in a way not realized before or since, the 1960s caused deep divisions.

Both Johnson and Nixon served as president during these turbulent years, as each matured during the Depression and World War II. First, Johnson succeeded President Kennedy when he was assassinated. Then, Nixon became president with forty-three percent of the vote and a divided nation. Nixon propagated the sourest atmosphere of all presidents I remember, but he lit a new fire under journalism.

The Vietnam War drove Johnson not to run for second complete term, four years after a great electoral victory. Nixon was forced to resign within two years of winning a great landslide victory in 1974.

Johnson was a rancher from the hill country of central Texas. Nixon was born in a poor Quaker family in southern California.

Each was characterized by the strongest of ambitions. Each was politically astute. Each learned political savvy through tough campaigns.

Johnson's towering ego and Nixon's private, inaccessible self caused them to draw enemies as they learned how to win. Johnson overwhelmed people. His record as Majority Leader in the U.S. Senate equipped him for many of his successes as president. Nixon was uncomfortable in public, but his ambition and intelligence made him an effective combatant. His idealism and interest in foreign affairs lifted him to victories that seemed to assure his place in history.

Though Johnson's greatest contribution was social legislation, his inability to solve the Vietnam problem led to his withdrawal from the 1968 presidential campaign. Though President Nixon achieved significant breakthroughs in the world, he allowed subordinates to assume tactics prior to the 1972 elections which led to the inevitability of impeachment in 1974, a chapter which will forever be known as Watergate.

As personalities and politicians, both dominated their worlds for many years. History will assign them their places, but their misunderstood, enigmatic natures will forever leave them as fascinating studies.

I admired neither of them. There was an overwhelming, awkward presence about Lyndon Johnson which made admiration difficult. Nixon seemed to trust no one and disliked social amenities. Neither seemed the

431

type that could win elections, yet both won consistently.

The years from 1963 to 1974 were some of the most uncertain, disruptive years in American history. Those were the years of the presidencies of Lyndon Baines Johnson and Richard Milhous Nixon.

I wanted to understand who they were and why they were as they were. The fact that they were controversial guarantees interest. There was something in them and their humble backgrounds that is profoundly American. Studying them helps me understand what we are as a nation and who we are as Americans. We elected them, gave them the power to become what they became. They were both products of us.

Gerald R. Ford (1974-1977)

I am a Ford, not a Lincoln.
Gerald R. Ford

Vice-president Gerald Ford served out Nixon's term. Gerald Ford's mission was to restore trust to the White House. Like Kennedy's term, Ford's term was just over two and half years. Following a tortured presidential period and never being elected to the office, Ford was in no position to succeed. His decision to pardon Nixon was controversial.

Jimmy Carter (1977-1981)

A simple and proper function of government
is just make it easy for us to do good and
difficult for us to do wrong.
Jimmy Carter

Former Georgia Governor Jimmy Carter was elected president in 1976. He always struck me as a sincere, serious, well-meaning man, who was not prepared for the presidency. Carter led not, when leadership was absolutely essential. There was hesitation and a moral wavering. His smile and even-handed ways helped equip him to be a public servant extraordinaire, especially after he was president. I always think of the marvelous contrast in his impact between when he served as president and what he has accomplished since he lost to Ronald Reagan in 1980.

Ronald Reagan (1981-1989)

Republicans believe every day is the Fourth of July,
But Democrats believe every day is April 15.

I've often wondered how some people in positions of this kind manage without having any acting experience.

Ronald Reagan

Reagan was one of the eight presidents during my lifetime who served for two terms. As a professional entertainer, he was at home in the White House. The distance between the image he projected and the nuts and bolts of his politics finally did him in. Reagan lost touch with everyone but the rich of his generation, and the illusions produced by his screen career were not good for morale when social problems bore in on those students who passed through my classroom.

George H. W. Bush (1989-1993)

I will keep America moving forward, always forward,
for a better America, for an endless enduring dream
and a thousand Points of Light. This is my mission,
and I will complete it.

George H. W. Bush

George H. W. Bush was a dedicated public servant whose understanding of the American citizenry lagged his professional experience. He seemed like an honest professional and was a highly qualified candidate for the presidency.

433

William Jefferson Clinton (1993-2001)

> *If you live long enough, you'll make mistakes.*
> *But if you learn from them, you'll be a better person.*
> *It's how you handle adversity, not how it affects you.*
> *The main thing is never quit, never quit, never quit.*
>
> William Jefferson Clinton

William Jefferson Clinton was the first baby-boomer president, and he appeared to represent his generation as one might expect he would: the coordinator, the facilitator, the balancer of unreconciled adversaries. He seemed to excel at such skills which his generation has been forced to master.

He seemed to relish the necessities of the office: Going directly to the people, relating diverse elements of complex problems, and meeting with groups of different sides of various questions. He appeared to enjoy lively debate, even to relish taking part in conflict. I feared I might quickly tire of his southern, silky-glossy style, and his yuppie pulse, but his reflective, measured nature seemed to be quickly deepening and enriching his character, encouraging a presidential demeanor.

It was interesting to watch this product of the boomer generation settle into the most difficult job in the world. I saw his generational characteristics, which I associated with my classroom, assume the leadership of the country. I don't recall a president who took charge with such vigor and dispatch, not since FDR. But I was only five years old then. There are some things that simply do not connect over the years. Nonetheless I recognized something important to be happening.

I didn't think I would be interested in visiting Hope, Arkansas, Clinton's birthplace. But we did so, once on the way to San Antonio and on the way back. We saw his birthplace, the badly run-down house where his grandparents raised him, the elementary school where he attended first grade, and the empty lot where the hospital stood in which he was born.

Clinton had a great deal to prove as president. However, for the first time in over thirty years, a source of inspiration threatened to emanate from the White House. I couldn't help it. Even as I think about that inspiration during my retirement years, it makes me want to return to the classroom and help out.

George W. Bush (2001-2008)

> *I believe the most solemn duty of the American president is to protect the American people. If America shows uncertainty and weakness in this decade, the world will drift toward tragedy. This will not happen on my watch.*
>
> George W. Bush

As the 2000 presidential campaign headed into its final stages, we again had the possibility of a son following his father as president. Twenty-four years and three presidents separated John Adam's term (1797-1801) from his son's (1825-1829). John Adams was eighty-nine when his son was elected and died before his son's term was half served.

Only eight years and one president separated father George Herbert Walker Bush's term from the term of his son George Walker Bush.

For the first time, there was a direct connection, other than family, between father's presidency and son's possibility of a dynasty.

George W. Bush was not the only progeny in the Bush family. John E. "Jeb" Bush, banker, real estate developer and politician, was governor of Florida.

Third son Neil M. Bush, an oilman like his brother George W. and father George H. W., came under public scrutiny during the savings and loan scandals of the late-1980s.

The Bushes presented an interesting set of circumstances in the light of American history. The question that recurred regularly was, could George W. Bush be a presidential nominee were he not the son of his president father?

Although there is little danger in such family successions, one can appreciate the potential. Nominee Bush, his vice-presidential running mate, and his president father have all been corporate executives. All were in oil, which you have to admit is a sensitive subject. It may be well to point out that corporations pretty much run the world.

Barack Obama (2008-2016)

> *Change will not come if we wait for*
> *some other person or some other time.*
> *We are the ones we've been waiting for.*
> *We are the change that we seek.*
>
> Barack Obama

In view of the problems the country faces, it is easy to suggest that we clear the slate and start over. Current U.S. problems will not allow that to happen. However, we do need fresh new minds. In that sense clearing the slate is a good idea.

Senator Barack Obama passed critical tests during the debates in 2007. He stood even with John McCain on McCain's strength, foreign affairs. In that process, Obama was even-handed. He looked at his opponent and was clearly in control. Senator McCain never looked at Obama, never used his name, or grimaced, but he looked uncomfortable any number of times. Who would most likely be firm, friendly, direct, and civil with Russia's Vladimir Putin?

His choice of Senator Joe Biden as running mate was a sign that he is not afraid to have experienced people around him who have strengths and knowledge where he may be short of it. I thought of *Team of Rivals(2005)*, Doris Kearns Goodwin's book about President Lincoln and his cabinet. They all were potential enemies and had been in the 1860 campaign against him in one way or another.

Obama showed himself to be prepared where it was important to be prepared for the presidency. President Obama made youth, intelligence, and diplomacy look good again. He seemed to be cut of the right cloth. Inexperience isn't all bad. The key to the Oval office was being thoughtful and having good people around you.

Whence Presidential Campaigns

Since I came to the White House, I got two hearing aids,
a colon operation, skin cancer, a prostate operation and
I was shot. The damn thing is, I've never felt better in my life.
Ronald Reagan

American presidential campaigns are going on more than one out of every four years, that's over twenty-five percent of the time.

What may we learn about the current candidates that hasn't already been presented to us? If these presidential aspirants really discussed the nation's problems, all this might be worthwhile. But that's not what they do. Between attacking each other personally and carrying on woefully general rhetoric, there is not much of substance to be found.

Does this long and laborious routine guarantee effective presidents? Definitely not.

Who stands to gain from this long process? That is pretty obvious. The media, and particularly television, which will take in billions of dollars for each presidential campaign.

How much will we learn from endless thirty-second bites and their often bitter and negative content? Aren't there other ways to learn about candidates?

Reading is the safest bet, but though there are books by and about all the candidates, not too many Americans will be drawn to this strategy, at least that subject matter.

Another way of approaching each year's presidential politics may be to examine the experiences of the predecessors of the next president. Cable television's C-SPAN produced a long series, *American Presidents: Life Portraits*. Forty-one presidents examined in forty-one weeks, each presentation lasting several hours.

In conjunction with the series, a survey of fifty-eight presidential historians was conducted. That sounds like a substantial study, even more so when you consider that each historian was asked to rate each president on a ten-point scale for each of the following skills:

1. Public persuasion
2. Crisis leadership
3. Economic management
4. Moral authority
5. International relations

6. Administrative skills
7. Relations with Congress
8. Vision/agenda setting
9. "Pursuit of equal justice for all"
10. Performance within the context of his times

Four of the five top-rated presidents are always in the top five of such rankings: Presidents Lincoln, Franklin Roosevelt, Washington, and Theodore Roosevelt (in that order in this survey).

President Truman was the fifth. Though his popularity was low when he left office in 1953, regard for him has risen steadily since. It has become clear that many of Truman's decisions were farsighted and helped shape today's world.

Another key to presidential success is the ability to deliver during crises. The top-ranked presidents faced major crises in their presidential and personal lives: The Revolution, Civil war, emerging national power, World War I, the Depression, World War II, Europe's recovery and the Cold War, the social problems developing out of the post-WWII population explosion, Vietnam. It appears presidents must undergo tests that force their leadership.

Today's candidates try to appeal to everybody, which seems counterproductive. Surely our first U.S. president was right: "To please everybody is impossible; were I to undertake it, I should probably please nobody." This truth escapes most of today's seekers of public office.

In 1972, three years after he left office, and less than a year before his death, Lyndon Johnson told the *New York Times*. "The presidency has made every man who occupied it, no matter how small, bigger than he was; and no matter how big, not big enough for its demands."

We sometimes forget that the electorate is more important than the candidates. How seriously do we take presidential hopefuls, who of necessity must be serious? Are we merely the shadow of our presidents? Is President Clinton representative of the generation from which he comes? Will any of our presidential candidates represent what we *are* as a people, not only what we *expect*?

One way or another, we need presidents who will stick by their principles, and we had better recognize those qualifications in candidates. Former New York Governor Mario Cuomo, who was declined opportunities to run for president, told an eastern university audience the following (1985):

> The problem is that sticking by your principles requires that you explain your principles, and in this age of electronic advocacy this process can often be tedious and frustrating. This is especially so when you must get your message across in twenty-eight-second celluloid morsels, when images prove often more convincing than ideas.

As Harry Truman had many opportunities to recognize, "A President needs political understanding to *run* the government, but he may be elected without it." The crucial question, however, is: Do we citizens recognize these qualities and characteristics in candidates? Are we capable of "looking past the glitter, beyond the showmanship, to the reality, the hard substance of things?" (Mario Cuomo)

I guess what we are after is a president who can tell right from wrong, and then act on the knowledge. A president who ought to know, Lyndon Johnson, declared, "A President's hardest task is not to do what is right, but to know what is right."

Trust and Vision in Leaders

It is difficult to think that one person directing one-hundred other persons can establish a rapport which will yield shared experience and worthwhile objectives. In other words, a fair-minded arrangement is needed.

That arrangement is what high-school teachers have to work at, and those hundred students who come sit in our presence every day, relate to us in varying degrees. They respond in all the ways students can respond, but only to the extent that the nurturing of trust takes place.

It is more difficult to imagine the chief executives of corporations establishing reciprocity with one thousand or five thousand employees. The relationship of CEO to workers is different from that of teacher to students, though some general objectives may be the same. I didn't pay my students. All we exchanged was trust and the need to work together to

439

achieve course objectives. Is that a fair-minded arrangement?

CEOs cannot personally know all of their employees. What they can do is develop general operating principles that allow for the building of trust, with each understanding he/she owes something to the other. It is easy to recognize the gravity of the corporate leader's responsibility.

What CEOs need to know to carry out their responsibilities ranges far and wide. The decisions they make not only affect how profitable their business will be, but also how hundreds or thousands of employees will fare. Is that a fair-minded arrangement?

Carry this question one step further. To what extent can a president of the United States carry on a relationship with nearly 300 million people? As in the classroom, the only bond consists of trust, rapport, and mutual goals. The paycheck is not involved as it is in the corporate structure. It's all trust.

What does a president have to know to function effectively? It is hard to imagine. In an age of technology with its miracles of communication, with instant this and instant that, it is hard to imagine any one person comprehending enough to function in the role.

The main feature of a president's experience must be his ability to cultivate relationships with those he has to trust to carry out his executive function. He cannot possibly know two hundred eighty million people. He can't even know everyone in the executive branch of his government. Is this a fair-minded arrangement?

The president's chief responsibility is the development of goals. This responsibility involves broad overviews. Presidents must be able to communicate. Vision requires elucidation. Presidents need to understand history, and not only American history.

A president who understood these qualities was Abraham Lincoln. The common circumstances of his background enhanced his effectiveness. As president, he regularly employed stories and anecdotes from his frontier upbringing. The fact that he was self-educated didn't hurt Lincoln one bit, anymore that it hurt Mark Twain, Will Rogers, or Harry Truman.

Vision and trust are not necessarily mutually exclusive. If vision calls for understanding, then the necessity for trust seem implicit. When one thinks of vision and presidents, Jefferson, Lincoln, both Roosevelts, and Wilson come to mind. Both Kennedy and Reagan had broader goals, but

440

Kennedy died before his could develop, and Reagan's had limiting elements that his age and experience could have affected.

No matter what other experience one has, it is education that supplies the broad underpinning. Not that experience isn't education, but there is so much to learn that an effective education system is almost mandatory.

Who would question Lincoln's education? He never experienced more than a rudimentary minimum of formal education, probably no more than a year. He learned to read at home. He devoured all the books he could get his hands on. Later, he read his way into the practice of law. His dedication to learning was intense, even though hardship is the only way to describe his formative years.

It seemed that wherever he went, he gained the confidence of others. Whether running a country store, serving in the state legislature of Illinois, practicing law, or riding the judicial circuits of the countryside, he gradually gained the trust of the people he encountered.

Of course, all of these experiences yielded dividends when he became president. Vision and trust: the key ingredients to leadership in the four years of the Civil War.

Somehow presidents in our time do not come equipped with these characteristics. We live in a much more complex age; yet the complexities have made communication easier. There is no reason our leaders cannot develop trust and convey their visions, since they have almost instant access to the American people. But technology itself does not nurture trust or provide vision. Contemporary presidents were not fortunate enough to have had backgrounds that worked for them the way Lincoln's did for him. You don't have to be born in a log cabin to develop skills and wherewithal to succeed as president.

Considering the dangerous circumstances in which the nation finds itself, the November election shapes up as important as any in memory. If ever we needed a president and a Congress we can trust, if ever we needed vision from our leaders, it is now.

Though it doesn't always seem so, public opinion is still the primary power of a democracy. Though polls take snapshots at different moments, only the ballot box can take the measure of the public. This is the ultimate fair-minded arrangement.

Voting Makes a Democracy

I voted in all presidential elections since I was able to vote. How much good it did, I don't know. It's those numbers. In a country of three hundred million people, *one* is not a very impressive number. I have trouble thinking of one vote having much significance among sixty-seven, let alone one thousand or one million. Three hundred million is beyond comprehension.

But somehow, over the almost seventy-plus years since I first voted, I have come to understand that if it weren't for me, the system would not work. If it weren't for you and me, the democratic process could not function. Our neighbors, the people in the town down the road, Walworth County, the state of Wisconsin, all fifty united states of America – we all have to think that way for the system to work. Although it does work badly at times, it does work.

When only sixty-one percent of eligible citizens vote, one cannot help thinking something is wrong. That is the fragile nature of a democracy. Everyone must participate, or there will be erosion of liberty. Maybe this erosion doesn't show all that much yet, but one day it will take on more serious proportions.

That brings me to the people who run for public office. How much good does it do to vote when I do not have confidence in candidates? Probably as much good as it would if candidates were qualified. This is democratic process, after all.

Why can't candidates convince us of the directions they would take us? No doubt some have been visionaries with strong and good ideas about where they would lead us, but most could not communicate them. Others had the ability to convey ideas but did not have strong objectives.

For some, their trust has been questionable. Still others could not encourage confidence in their fellow citizens. I am sure our presidential candidates have been fundamentally good men. I cannot think of a single candidate in these seventy-plus years who has not wanted and needed the trust and confidence of the public.

But that is not enough. They have to gather people around them who are as worthy as they are. They have to be able to assess qualifications and character. They must persuade others to follow their lead and learn the fine art of compromise. The president's reasonable relationship with

Congress is, for example, fundamental.

Candidates have to be able to convey their sense of purpose to the people. President Franklin Roosevelt's radio fireside chats during the depth of the Depression left the feeling that someone was not only in charge, but also looking out for us.

We don't get that from presidents anymore. The changes in communication, the increased population, the overwhelming technological advances, a pronounced decline in education—maybe these discourage the development of sound personal qualifications in potential candidates.

Of all the president's functions, his dialogue with the people is primary. I recall President Kennedy's informal, informative, and often humorous press conferences. He was at ease talking to people. You got the feeling someone was in charge, that there was direction and momentum.

JFK said early in the 1960s that we were going to put a man on the moon before the decade ran out. If you are old enough to remember how things were in the early 1960s, that must have seemed like a pipedream.

Our nation expended a great deal of effort in the 1960s: civil rights, Vietnam, campus protest, and a man on the moon. Leadership must turn needs into action. That is what presidents in a democracy have to be able to do, but they can't do it without all 300 million of us.

Presidents, Press Conferences and Public Opinion

> *I am the people—the mob—the crowd—the mass.*
> *Do you know that all the great work of the world*
> *is done through me?*
>
> Carl Sandburg

"Public opinion in this country is everything." That is what he said, that is what Abraham Lincoln said.

The sixteenth president understood the importance of being able to read the public mind. Lincoln achieved a high degree of success mainly because he got along with reporters.

Lincoln enjoyed having reporters around him and answering their questions. He also asked them questions, which would have alarmed modern journalists. John W. Starr, Jr., author of *Lincoln's Last Day (1922)*,

443

wrote, "How he would have relished the ready give-and-take, bringing his quick wit into play and larding his answers with anecdotes! And how the newsmen would have loved it!"

The criticism Lincoln underwent during his Civil War presidency would have been unbearable to us, but he took it in good humor. The reason became apparent later. The president learned more from reporters than they were learning from him. He gained a feel for the public pulse.

As one of Lincoln's secretaries, William Stoddard, pointed out, "Probably they (the reporters) have no idea how much they tell him. As if through so many magnetic wires, he receives message after message from the current thought and purpose of popular masses whom he understands so much better than they do."

Lincoln understood that the president's power rests with the people, and that it was mandatory to keep in touch. Modern presidents with as widely varying temperaments as Franklin Roosevelt, Harry Truman, Dwight Eisenhower, and John Kennedy all spent many hours in conferences with reporters. Somehow this useful relationship of president, reporters, and the people has fallen on hard times.

Some recent presidents have given few prime-time news conferences. That is not democracy in action. Presidents may not want reporters to have too much preparation time.

After all, "Why should there not be a patient confidence in the ultimate justice of the people? Is there any better or equal hope in the world?"

And that is what he said. That is what Abraham Lincoln said.

Liberals, Conservatives and Change

Not all Democrats are liberal. Not all Republicans are conservative. President Carter was a Democrat, but one would think twice before calling him a liberal. President Lincoln was called a Republican, but we would be hard pressed to define him as a conservative. Everyone has some liberal tendencies, and everyone has some conservative habits.

It probably would be a good idea to define the terms. We'll have to admit the current political climate requires that we think about them. President Franklin Roosevelt defined "liberal" during his 1932 presidential campaign:

444

Lincoln Memorial, National Park Service, Washington, D.C.

...say that civilization is a tree which, as it grows, continually produces rot and dead wood. The radical says: 'Cut it down.' The conservative says: 'Don't touch it.' The liberal compromises: 'Let's prune, so that we lose neither the old trunk nor the new branches.'

445

Not bad. That is one way to look at the differences.

William Safire, who was as close to being national lexicographer as we have, produced a political dictionary some years ago. As the latest of its editions state, it's "the definitive guide to the new language of politics."

Safire defined "liberal" as "one who believes in more government action to most individual needs; originally, one who resisted government encroachment on individual liberties."

He defined a "conservative" as "a defender of the status quo who, when change becomes necessary in tested institutions or practices, prefers that it come slowly, or in moderation."

One cannot ignore these terms and the ideas they project if change is to be understood. The current and continuing controversy involving what constitutes liberal and conservative seems to revolve around the idea of change.

In a world that has known hardly anything but change, defending the status quo has become more problematic. It is not only a liberal world we live in, but the perpetual and profound changes call for reasonable and regular responses, that is, new ideas, different ways of solving problems, all of which require enterprise, experiment, re-examining the status quo. If the world changes, we have little choice but to change with it.

But a thinking people have some control over how the world changes. Over the long haul we are a liberal people. As those incorrigible, smarty French folk, whose ideas fed our "liberal" American Revolution, say, "Only that which is provisional endures."

Maybe that is why the French have survived common borders with so many neighbors as well as they have. They tend to think and go their way.

After all, next to bugging the rest of the world, the French are best at political sagacity. You don't suppose there's a connection, do you?

On Sports

My love for sports began in high school when I played football. I also played first base for a while, and lefties were always hitting line drives my way.

As an undergraduate at the University of Wisconsin-Madison, I tried out for the football team for three weeks. To be honest, the long practices each day left me exhausted. I could see that I would not have time to play football and to study.

During my first tour of duty in the United States Navy (McAlester Naval Ammunition Depot, Oklahoma, 1945-46), I did not play sports. When I served in the United States Army (Kobe, Japan), my station baseball team lacked a catcher. I was persuaded to take on the job. Despite the demanding physical exertion, I was fascinated by what a catcher does. It is baseball's toughest job, and I swore I'd never do it again. Also, on-the-job training is not a good idea for catchers.

However, my interests in sports remained strong, especially for the teams in Chicago, Milwaukee and Green Bay. The following essays contain my observations about some of the ways sports has changed.

CONTENTS

Baseball: Rhythms, Loyalties and Nuances

Baseball is the national pastime, little doubt about it. Its rhythms, loyalties, and nuances are parts of the fabric of society. They are also parts of a majority of Americans, and I might add a pretty fair hunk of the minority, too, even though they pretend baseball is not part of their lives.

We love to think that life could be lived at the pace baseball is played, with short spurts of action and plenty of time to think about them. Those whose strong and long-lasting loyalty to a particular baseball team are in possession of faith that is rare in other institutions anymore.

Baseball is entertainment, but its meaning stretches beyond score cards and headlines. Sometimes when I think of the game, it seems awkward and unnatural. One man throwing a very hard ball toward another who attempts to hit it with a long piece of wood about three inches in diameter at one end tapering to handy-gripping size at the other. Since the ball has seams, which aid gripping, and the bat has smooth, curving surfaces, which can deflect the ball in all kinds of crazy directions, the game clearly belongs to the man who throws the ball.

It is a dangerous game, especially for hitters, pitchers, and catchers. Despite its slow pace, it requires attention. But most of the time, the game seems graceful, thoughtful, humbling. I remember seeing Joe DiMaggio and Willie Mays effortlessly shag fly balls in center field. I can still see Ted Williams and Stan Musial and their wondrously smooth and fluid swings. Rick Sutcliffe pitched the ball in the same way Lou Brock stole second base – instantly, easily, effortlessly.

This team game, as do others, requires intense concentration and thinking. Mistakes in thinking lead to personal embarrassment and lost games. Outwitting an opponent is as important as outplaying him. A special kind of honesty is involved.

Baseball is the kind of game that can bear lessons to children, parents, and generations. So, even though the Chicago Cubs haven't gone to a World Series since the year I was graduated from high school, that one summer day every year when a group of men who respect each other took sons, daughters, and friends to Wrigley Field, was the kind of ritual which revived and renewed us.

Yes, baseball is entertainment, a diversion. Yet it is engaging, all the while mirroring society. It is a personal game. What sport other brings out the personalities of its participants, the character of its fans? What other sport contributes as massively to the English language? The game is part of the fabric of America. If baseball is so important, maybe we can learn something from its greatest players. What is the nature of the game's heroism? One may also ask: What are life's most important values?

I can remember the proposition that used to come up periodically in conversation. If you could put together the perfect team, who would you want on it? My first choice was always Pete Rose. Not only did he have talent, but perpetual desire. No matter what day, what game, what moment, he could provoke action. He was action.

When a pitcher walked him, he ran to first base as though someone were trying to throw him out. His kind of half-crouch batting stance sent a message to pitchers and fielders that he could put the bat on the ball and hit it where no one could field it three times out of ten, but especially when it was important.

Rose stole bases with the same abandon that he did everything else, head first and in a cloud of dust. 'Charlie Hustle' spearheaded the game, kept it in an attack mode. He was good-natured firebrand.

How many times it crossed my mind that only two teams in baseball wear that much red, St. Louis' Cardinals and Cincinnati's Reds, two teams that keep coming at you year in and year out. Pete Rose is the first guy I want on my team. Now that is all changed. It turns out that Pete Rose was a gambler, bet on baseball, and bet on his team. What a humbling experience, my hero cheated the game which made him great. He hurt this boy's faith in the game. He may be damaging one of the only institutions left in which people have faith.

The rhythms, loyalties, and nuances of baseball will continue, but as a game of choices and deception, we want a very clear line between the game and life. We expect a lot of our heroes. We know they are overpaid, that their careers are short, and that their bodies are their tickets to success. But if the boys of summer are not morally tough, what more can we expect of the boys of next summer?

The Homerun Outbreak

It's getting to me. I mean the frequency of major league homeruns these days. One player has hit forty already (as of mid-July). Seven have thirty or more. Seventeen have twenty through twenty-nine. Get this, eight major league hitters have stroked from ten to nineteen homers. This mid-season. The average number of games played by the thirty American and National League teams at this point is ninety-three, or fifty-seven percent of the season.

The year Babe Ruth hit sixty (1927), sixteen major league teams hit a total of 922 homers. So far in the 1998 season, thirty teams have hit 2857 homeruns (almost one hundred per team). At that rate, five thousand for the season are inevitable.

Forces are at work changing the game of baseball. The year Ruth hit sixty, teammates Lou Gehrig and Tony Lazzeri hit forty-seven and eighteen respectively. These three Yankees accounted for one hundred twenty-five of the team's one hundred fifty-eight homers (eighty percent of the team's output). That's right, the World Series champion New York Yankees of 1927 hit only one hundred fifty-eight homers.

In 1930, which has been called a hitter's season, baseball produced 1565 homeruns. Sixteen teams did that. So far in 1998, in only sixty percent as many games, 2857 have been hit, almost twice as many.

1961, when Roger Maris hit sixty-one, the eighteen major league teams managed 2730. That's 127 less than were hit by July 15 this year.

My source, *The Baseball Encyclopedia*, carried records through 1989. Twenty-six major league teams hit 3083 homers that year. 1998 will surpass that by at least sixty percent.

What is causing the torrent of round trippers? In the seventy-plus years I've followed baseball, there has been talk at times about the composition of the baseball itself. That is, the "live" ball, which naturally "hits out" easier than a "dead" ball.

In the 1960s, pitchers dominated the game, when multiple shutouts were common. The names of Bob Gibson and Juan Marichal come to mind. When pitchers dominate, it is easy to call the game unexciting.

In more recent times, troubles have plagued major league baseball. Owners tried to put more action in the game. They needed to restore bodies to empty stadium seats. Presto. 1998. Almost three thousand homers.

Another factor was players' salaries which were at a level unhealthy for the game's long-term survival. Owners appeared to have placed dollars over the integrity of the game. Fans lost interest, partly because a lot of the game's appeal has been eliminated. Strategy gave way to hell-bent hitting because overpaid, under-motivated players do not know the game and have not mastered its skills and subtleties. The most talented young players never see the minor leagues, and they are given large contracts before they produce and do not have the urge or necessity to be motivated consistently. Imagine how the real pitchers and the real hitters, even homerun hitters, thrive on that.

Owners resorted to tricks. Covered stadiums, for example, were built. That tactic began to ruin the game. The owners of the first domed stadium, the Houston Astrodome, learned that grass will not grow without the sun. So that led to artificial turf, which made the baseball bounce bafflingly. The people who sold artificial turf to owners of stadiums must have been descendants of the salesmen who sold refrigerators to Eskimos.

Another mistake was the DH, the designated hitter. Why should pitchers not hit? They could pick up tips from other pitchers. Hitting also keeps pitchers honest. Throwing a hard ball toward a batter only sixty feet away at ninety miles per hour should not be a one-way proposition.

The pitcher was not the main reason for the DH. It was for older hitters who could still swing a bat, but who could not get around the field as well as they once did. Their abilities were not quite major-league caliber anymore. But they could hit homeruns.

The major reason for the torrent of homers, however, was the decline of pitching. It made sense that thirty teams of twenty-five players (seven hundred fifty) were going to have less talent than sixteen teams of twenty-five players (five hundred), which was the way it was forty years ago. The talent ran thin, and this fact was especially noticeable in pitchers. Forty percent of a team's roster were pitchers. We had only so many competent major leaguers, and it was not seven hundred fifty.

We could have more if there were still a training ground for them. That is, a minor league system, which today is but a shadow of what it once was. When you go to a major league ballpark, you expect to see major league baseball.

Still, homeruns are excitement. Forty homers by the middle of July is

451

an amazing total. But if Mark McGwire hits seventy-five in this hitting environment, it will be akin to a fifteen-foot-high corn stalk in a field of fourteen-footers, not all that impressive.

If McGwire, or Ken Griffey, Jr., or Sammy Sosa, or all three, are going to hit over sixty homers, let them hit enough over sixty to erase the dubious distinction of claiming sixty-two homers in a 162-game schedule, remembering Ruth hit his sixty homeruns in a 154-game season.

Eight games is five percent of a season. Imagine McGwire hitting sixty homers by the end of 154 games. To have established a record, he would have to hit four in those last eight games to say he had broken Ruth's record.

Baseball is still the most interesting game, even if it is not the most popular. It has demonstrated its flexibility and durability during the last fifty years. Plenty has happened which could have destroyed it.

The most exciting single baseball event is the homerun. The fact that it is exaggerating itself probably is a warning sign. Watching TV sportscasts endlessly panning toward outfield stands trying to follow the flight of a baseball, is a bewildering, counterproductive activity.

I am not worried about baseball's survival, only its quality.

Harry Carey

As a lifetime resident of Wisconsin, I am sometimes asked, why are you a Cub fan? They find out I'm a Bear fan and, for the last fifteen years or so, a Bulls fan, CWJ (commencing with Jordan). Recent events have presented the opportunity to explain why I am a Cub fan, indeed, a Chicago fan.

A little over sixty years ago, my father and mother took my brother, sister, and me to see the St. Louis Cardinals play the Cubs in Wrigley Field. In the 1960s, I began taking my son to see the Cubs play. Now more often than not, he takes me.

If you've never been to Wrigley Field, you have little idea how friendly, green, and cozy a place can be while holding thirty-eight thousand people.

I remember how curious we were about the broadcast booths. Well, after all, that was the place of origin of the games we listened to and watched at home. Jack Brickhouse was an institution, and Lou Boudreau was a Hall-of-Fame player and manager. They were our connection to this pleasing place in the summer sun. When Brickhouse retired, I thought something was leaving that could not be replaced, and I believe many other fans agreed.

But from across town came Harry Carey. Sixty years ago, out in Grant County (Wisconsin), I remember dialing the radio late at night and picking up Harry Carey on KMOX doing Cardinal games. He was in St. Louis for twenty-five years, then with the White Sox for eleven, and finally he came to the Cubs.

It took a little getting used to, but Harry had something special. He showed that you didn't need to have a mellifluous voice and fast talk-radio style. His spontaneous repartee brought excitement and surprises to a game which has natural gaps and boundless opportunities for commentary.

Harry Carey's passing recalls numerous occasions of other Cub tragedies. In the best-of-five series in the 1984 National League playoff with San Diego, for example, the Cubs won the first two games handily, one with double-digit runs – but then lost three in a row.

That year of mighty Cub frustration established Harry Carey's reputation.

Being at Wrigley Field was marvelously relaxing, especially when the guy in the booth talks to you as though he knows you. It's a human place. This letter to the *Chicago Tribune* (2/20/98) covers the Harry mystique:

> I was lucky to meet Harry Carey, for only a minute, but I'll always remember it. I was a news photographer and often worked next to many of the media 'superstars,' most of whom wouldn't give you the time of day.
>
> Once, while covering a Cubs game, I was walking toward the press box and saw Harry coming my way. Most other media stars would look at the floor and walk right by, but not Harry. He looked me right in the eye and said, 'Hi there, youngster!' I said, 'Hiya, Harry,' and we both moved on.
>
> It was only a moment, but I remember walking with a smile on my face. It still makes me smile. Thanks, Harry –you were really one of the nice guys." (Bill Oakes, Libertyville, IL)

Harry Carey's influence was therapeutic. His keep-the-faith approach overrode the reality of a losing franchise. You can't do better than the ambience of Wrigley Field and the cheerleading of Harry Carey. Despite his many hundreds of gaffs, mispronunciations, and excitedly garbled prose, he caused fans to conclude that he was one of them, a man of the fans.

Easily the most visible sign of this intimacy was the seventh inning "Take Me Out to the Ball Game" tradition. Bill Veeck, the colorful White Sox entrepreneur, was responsible for the idea which began in old Comiskey Park in the late-1970s.

Musically, Harry had no business singing with a microphone in his hand before twenty-five thousand people and who knows how many more out in media land. But I think the typical non-singing fan may have thought, if Harry can do it, so can I. I am a non-singer myself, and I believe I did it a couple of times.

Harry was popular because he cared. He cared about the game, the fans, and the laid-back, rustic glory that is the game of baseball.

What will happen at the end of six and half innings at Wrigley a month from now? "Take Me Out to the Ball Game," that silly but ecumenical little tune, will seem out of place now that the most effective, if not melodic, implementer is gone. But they will sing it. It won't be the same, but they will sing it. That's because Harry Carey, number-one Cub fan, will, as one Cub fan put it, "be an angel in the outfield."

All of this tradition may inspire Mark Grace and his fellow Cubbies to win the division. No, we're Cubs fans. Let's not lose our perspective.

How can you keep such an upbeat, positive attitude when your team hasn't gone to a World Series in fifty-two years and hasn't won a Series in ninety years? The Cubs drew over two million fans in 1997 (over twenty-five thousand per game), while losing ninety-four games. How can you keep coming back with unabashed enthusiasm after heart-breaking setbacks?

But we do know this: We have lost "the ultimate fan and all-around good guy." Another fan said, Harry is "something real in a pre-packaged age," just as Wrigley Field is an oasis in an urban clutter. Though he lacked diplomacy, Harry told the truth, no matter whom he made uneasy.

As R. Bruce Dold of the *Chicago Tribune* wrote, "… you can talk of Harry Carey in the same sentence as (Mike) Royko and (Studs) Terkel …

like them, he connected with, and valued the importance of, people who otherwise were ignored." An orphan, Harry Carcy learned how to give and was paid back a hundred-fold.

Here are some of Harry's most memorable quotations;

Ah, you can't beat fun at the old ballpark.

I've always worked the same way, really ... I try to make it fun for the fan, to remember it's just a ballgame.

It might be, it could be, it is! A homerun.

Listen, my dear. I love the White Sox. I love the ballpark. I love the fans. I just don't like those (#*$/@!!) owners. (To a female fan who criticized him for leaving the White Sox for the Cubs)

Holy cow!

Don't take yourself too seriously but take your responsibilities very seriously.

That wouldn't be a homerun in a phone booth.

Cubs win! Cubs win! Cubs win!

So long, everybody.

The Wrigley Experience

Those stories about the relaxed atmosphere and union of spirits prevailing at Chicago's Wrigley Field are true enough. We Cub fans have always followed the team in hopes that one year, or decade, or ... did you know that the one-hundredth anniversary of the last year the Cubs won a World Series is only five years away, or that the sixtieth anniversary of the last time the team made it to the Series is only two years off?

Since such lofty aspirations have escaped us Cub fans, we have settled for the neighborhood ambience, the cordial environs, and the green of ivy. It's as though winning had been replaced by the fact that this event is after all major league baseball and not everyone can go to the World Series. Only one team in fifteen can do that in any one year.

But we could see real major league teams at Wrigley Field, and we always knew that some real champions would show up. Giants, Dodgers, Cardinals, Braves… they all have won championships, and they all show up regularly at Wrigley Field. The Atlanta Braves, for example, have appeared in eleven out of the last twelve National League playoffs and have won five pennants and one World Series. If the Cubs can't win it all, we can at least go see teams that do.

Yet, Wrigley Field means so much more than baseball. It's a social phenomenon. It is community. It cuts across age groups. It includes grandfathers who recall lean years and have stuck with it. It includes boomers who remember the grand 1969 opportunity going bust but continue as believers. It also includes young people who pick up on such loyalties quickly.

And what is extraordinary about these traditions is we all do it together. There's a kind of fraternity, a fellowship. We celebrate together. Now that the team is becoming successful, it is even more rewarding.

Miller Park
Wrigley Field it is not. Were the local folks happy to see Cub fans flock north to help attendance reach forty thousand for four straight games? You bet!

We're talking about Miller Park where beer and brats are the winningest combination, and where my daughter, son, son-in-law, daughter-in-law, grandson, and I watched Brewers win one out of a four-game series in their new stadium.

Stadium is not really the right word. What this structure turned out to be is a twenty-first century steel coliseum digitally programed to entertain the eyes and to drive noise into the brain.

I couldn't decide whether we were inside or outside, until a lake breeze gently shifted the air, and the waxing blue moon drifted into the darkening space above.

"We're in heaven," I said as we took our seats. Well, not quite. But it certainly was nose-bleed territory.

Conversation is one of the pleasant amenities at a baseball game. But not at Miller Park. Every moment that is not baseball is filled with digital babble and amplified rock racket. We're talking loudly. You'll never hear Andres Segovia or Joe Pass at Miller Park.

We were fifteen rows up the fourth terrace, just under one of two huge walls which support an odd-looking roof structure which opens and closes. On a hot summer day, the southwest breezes would be completely blocked off. I suppose then the odd-looking roof structure closes and we have air conditioning.

But this outing was a pleasant late July evening. Even the parking was easy. The walk to the stadium itself a considerable distance. I registered about one mile to, from, and at Miller Park.

This outing was also my first experience with tailgating. You can't do that at Wrigley Field, though the neighborhood bars and eateries make up for it. As we trekked toward the "Park" (somehow "Park" is the wrong word), we came upon a charter bus outside of which was a coterie of folks celebrating the occasion. Brats, burgers, potato salad – oh, and beer.

As we made our way through the crowd, they invited us to join the party when they discovered we were Cub fans.

Many more tee-shirts proudly displaying "It's All About 'U'" on the front and a "U-Jeans" logo on the back. They were Antioch (Illinois) fans, and "U-Jeans" is a bar on route 83 on the city's south side.

One of the two owners, David Kioseff, third generation American of Bulgarian descent, said he purchased forty tickets, hired the bus, covered all the other expenses, and then sold the tickets to customers to cover his costs. Here they were in the Brewers parking lot inviting us to join them, which we did. They made us feel right at home.

Since the Cubs seriously thrashed their division rivals the two previous nights, expectations were that Kerry Wood and his buddies would make the evening a complete success. They didn't, but we'll remember the Antioch connection for a long while. Go Cubbies!

When in enemy territory, it is tempting to make the most of every opportunity. As the ticket-taker performed his function, he said, "Have a good night." I could not help myself: "Only if the Cubs win" and was rewarded with a non-smile.

No sooner are you inside Miller Park than a major impression is revealed: this is a game land. So much activity going on that has nothing to do with baseball. My son called it an arcade.

We boarded the escalator that took us up to "heaven."

I kept a scorecard, which is a must for me at a major-league game. No one else was doing it. In fact, concentration on the game was not the general mode. Keeping the mind on the game is hard when so much is going on. That is true in any major-league park. It's one reason I keep a scorecard.

Our seats were just far enough removed from the action to miss the game's finer points. I don't remember a seat at Wrigley Field that made concentration that difficult.

One spends a lot of time just looking around. When all 41,588 customers were in place, it was hard to ignore all that Cubbie blue. Cub fans everywhere. When catcher Mike Barrett hit his second inning homerun, you'd swear we were in Wrigley Field. It was one of the few deafening crowd roars of the night, even though the Brewers were winning handily.

For what they are worth, here are some more Miller Park impressions:

- The nuances of the game itself were difficult to follow. The digital screen above the scoreboard in centerfield really helps. So, the big screen helped. Let's hear it for volume controls.
- The scoreboard was full of easy-to-use information.
- Commercialism dominated to the point of crassness. Example: "This pitching change is brought to you by Chevy." Then a Chevrolet drove along the track beyond the outfield. I wondered how the new relief pitcher felt about that.
- They don't use real chalk for the chalk lines.
- I don't understand the "Bernie's Dugout" thing. Or the sausage race silliness.
- The lights from the top of the outfield wall are hard on my eyes, at least for those of us in "heaven."
- You can't see into the bullpens. Wrigley Field's bullpen is down the left-field line between the line and the seats. The teams must put someone to watch for errant foul balls as relievers warm up. At Miller Park, I saw the Chevy before I saw the new pitcher trudging toward the mound.

- I didn't realize *Take Me Out to the Ball Game* was sung at Brewer games. It seemed a hurried, impersonal gesture, considering what this ritual is at Wrigley Field.

I'm glad my daughter and son took me to see the game. The ninety-year-old Wrigley Field sold out for the year early on. That's the main reason this outing was planned. It was the only way we could see our team play this season. It is handy to have a home away from home.

I feel about sports the way I feel about jazz, music, and photography. Each is a kind of perpetual excitement, a lot like adolescence. I guess in that sense I could say I never grew up. No one should ever grow up.

Conversations for Our Nation's Future

I advocate for wide reading and effective writing as essential practices of informed citizens. Mark Twain said, "The man who does not read good books has no advantage over the man who can't read them." The same could be said about citizens who do not write.

In *And Gladly Would He Learn*, I used my first avocation of writing to report what I learned from several cultural icons about living creatively, productively, and courageously in a democracy. To become active citizens, I encourage ongoing discussions, not just walk-by conversations, using such questions as these:

- **What can our cultural icons teach us about living in a democracy?**

- **How can we ensure the balance of powers our democracy needs?**

- **What leadership does our country need for the future?**

- **What conversations do we need to have about media in our lives?**

- **How do presidents affect our personal lives and national character?**

Epilogue

If you are planning for a year, sow rice;
If you are planning for a decade, plant trees;
If you're planning for a lifetime, educate people.
                                        Chinese proverb

My teaching career, first hour through eighth hour, Monday through Friday, September 1957 through June 1986, was almost a minute-by-minute experience of not knowing for sure that I had a stake in that process. No more than Shakespeare could have known his legacy, or Beethoven, or my father. I never thought of rice and trees; I thought only of my eighteen-year-old students who were about to enter their world.

As an English teacher, I felt that I needed to develop interests that promote making the language a realistic, useful tool. I had better be able to use the language and then live for promoting its intelligent use. I developed more than a passing interest in Shakespeare, journalism, grammar, biography, photography, American presidents, music, genealogy, Charlie Brown, and the singular and persistent desire to understand the members of the baby-boomer generation.

These ingredients, in their seasons, generated connections with my students. During my teaching career, I discovered everything had a season:

> A time to teach, and a time to learn;
> And time to read, and a time to write;
> A time to nurture perspective;
> A time to consider the past;
> A time to act on the present;
> A time to relate the local to what is national;
> A time to recognize the universal;
> A time to study Shakespeare in the minds of the young;
> A time to comprehend humanity through the minds of the young.

Measured in time, my adventure began with a year of student teaching, a year and a half of teaching in Osseo and twenty-eight years in Lake

461

Geneva, each with its one-hundred-eighty classroom days, and each of those days with its five hours of instruction. We teachers can do a lot of things with 27,450 hours for over three thousand young minds.

Measured by financial matters, I must admit I wasn't paying attention, because teachers are not remunerated by their effectiveness. As long as bills were paid and the bank balance ran in the black, my wife Beverly and I grew accustomed to financial flatness. Besides, money was not where the action was.

Measured in rewards, I would hope what I wrote serves as proof enough. This collection of essays selected from 1487 essays should, hopefully, stimulate thinking, discussions and actions on ways to improve schools for our nation's youth.

What better legacy could a person leave than to have influenced the education of young people for their future? It is my hope you will catch a glimpse, feel a vibe, sense the theme that characterizes the adventure that is teaching. Whatever your age, consider teaching. It lies at the heart of America's future.

And Gladly Would He Teach and Learn

Index

National Council of Teachers of English – 95, 144
Nixon, Richard Milhous – 348, 417, 430-32
Numbers – xiii, xvii, 25, 384-85, 392-94, 442

Obama, Barack – 418, 436
Osseo (WI), Teaching in – vi, x, 13, 22-23, 328, 461

Pavlik, Robert – 244
Petranek, Robert – 236, 242
Photography – xiii, xiv, xvii. 23, 192, 199-201, 256, 360-61, 395-402, 412-17, 459, 461
Pienkos, Mark – 205
Pollock, Vernon – 23, 197, 203, 236, 237-39, 240, 242, 245
Presidential campaigns – 418, 437-39
Presidents and Presidency – xiii, 418, 419-46
Presidents Information Center – 418-21
Presley, Elvis – 94, 289, 347, 350
Prologue to the Canterbury Tales – xvi, 4, 106, 110-11, 200, 280
Proverbs – 134, 174-76
Public Opinion – 418, 441, 443-44
Pyle, Ernie – 296, 310-11

Rauhut, Paul – 236, 241-42
Reagan, Ronald – 300, 418, 420, 433, 437, 440, 441
Reeve, Christopher – 296, 311-15
References, Student – 50, 209, 233-35
Reinke, Karl – 181, 205, 236, 238-39
Reunions, Class – xiv, 192, 208, 260, 269
Ripken, Jr., Cal – 296, 316-18
Rockwell, Norman – 296, 318-19
Rogers, Fred – 296, 319
Rogers, Will – 283, 296, 319-20, 355, 357, 440
Roosevelt, Franklin Delano – 285, 293, 382, 418, 421-25, 438, 440, 443-44
Rothe, Thelma – vi, 1, 2-3, 8
Royko, Mike – 296, 320-23, 453

Made in the USA
Monee, IL
04 April 2021

63565269R00272